# EASY
# WOMEN

# EASY WOMEN

## Sex and Gender in Modern Mexican Fiction

DEBRA A. CASTILLO

University of Minnesota Press

Minneapolis

London

The University of Minnesota Press gratefully acknowledges permission to reprint the following: a shorter version of chapter 2 appeared as "Meat Shop Memories: Federico Gamboa's Santa," in *Inti* 40–41 (1994–95): 175–92; a shorter version of chapter 4 appeared as "Borderliners: Federico Campbell and Ana Castillo," in *Reconfigured Spheres: Feminist Explorations of Literary Space,* edited by Margaret R. Higonnet and Joan Templeton (Amherst: University of Massachusetts Press, 1994), copyright 1994 by the University of Massachusetts Press; several pages of the section on Mora in chapter 6 appeared as "Reading Loose Women Reading," in *Modern Language Quarterly* 57, no. 2 (1995): 289–303.

Published by the University of Minnesota Press
111 Third Avenue South, Suite 290
Minneapolis, MN 55401-2520

http://www.upress.umn.edu

Printed in the United States of America on acid-free paper

The University of Minnesota is an equal-opportunity educator and employer.

**Library of Congress Cataloging-in-Publication Data**
Castillo, Debra A.
  Easy women: sex and gender in modern Mexican fiction / Debra A.
Castillo.
    p.    cm.
  Includes bibliographical references and index.
  ISBN 0-8166-3112-3 (hc : alk. paper). – ISBN 0-8166-3113-1 (pbk.
: alk. paper)
    1. Mexican fiction – 20th century – History and criticism.    2. Women
in literature.    3. Sex role in literature.    I. Title.
PQ7207.W6C37   1998
863 – dc21                                                    97–40102

10  09  08  07  06  05  04  03  02  01  00  99  98        10  9  8  7  6  5  4  3  2  1

¡No era mujer, no; era una...!

— FEDERICO GAMBOA, *Santa* 15

Vende caro tu amor, aventurera,
da el precio del dolor a tu pasado,
y aquel que de tu boca la miel quiera,
que pague con brillantes tu pecado.

— AGUSTÍN LARA, "Aventurera"

A writer — by which I mean... the subject of a praxis — must have the persistence of the watcher who stands at the crossroads of all other discourses, in a position that is *trivial* in respect to the purity of doctrine (*trivialis* is the etymological attribute of the prostitute who waits at the intersection of three roads).

— ROLAND BARTHES quoted in S. Felman,
*Literary Speech Act*

# Contents

Acknowledgments     ix

1. Ellipses and Intersections     1

2. Meat Shop Memories: Gamboa     37

3. Desire in the Streets: Rulfo, Garro     63

4. Deterritorializing Women's Bodies: Castillo, Campbell     100

5. Reading Women: Sefchovich     135

6. Signifyin', Testifyin': Mora, Bandida, Serrano     160

7. No Conclusions     215

Appendix: Transcripts     243

Notes     253

Works Cited     261

Index     271

# Acknowledgments

I owe a debt, first of all, to my husband, Carlos Castillo-Chavez, a biomathematician working on social dynamics and models for infectious diseases, who told me that finally I was writing something he could collaborate on and who provided me with access to reports from the Mexican Ministry of Health and other internally circulated materials. I also thank my colleagues Rosemary Feal, Amy Kaminsky, and Cynthia Steele for their careful readings and thoughtful suggestions for improvement. This book owes an enormous amount to María Gudelia Rangel Gómez and to Armando Rosas Solís, without whose insights it could never have been finished. Gudelia and Armando's sociological and public health research has taken them to all parts of Mexico, where they have conducted surveys among hundreds of prostitutes and held taped, in-depth interviews with many of them. They have generously shared this primary material with me, along with oral and written commentary and many, many hours of intellectual exchange.

# Chapter 1

# Ellipses and
# Intersections

I begin with two anecdotes about Mexican women who have transgressed unwritten gender boundaries. The first comes from anthropologist Oscar Lewis's reports on his twenty-year interactions with the family of Pedro Martínez, a campesino from a small town Lewis called Azteca (Tepoztlán), located in the state of Morelos. At one point in the narration, Martínez talks about his youth and mentions that "lots and lots of women went into the fields in those days to help their families. The men would send the women into the fields and would even play around with them there." Martínez immediately goes on to comment on the precariousness of these women's lives:

> My grandmother used to say that people here were more cruel in the past. For example, the way they treated their mistresses, the loose women who went with many men. According to the old people, these same men would get together and say, "Well, how is it that she is going with me and with you and with him? She is just causing trouble. Why should we fight and kill each other while she has a good time? So, now let's do something to her."
>
> One of them would take her out and then they would all get together and carry her off into the fields. And the things they would do to her! They drove a sharpened stake in the ground and greased it with a lot of lard. Then they all made use of her and had fun with her. They didn't kill her first but stuck her onto the point and there she sat until she died. Then they would undo her braids and put a *sombrero* on her head and a red kerchief around her neck, like a man. They would put a cigar in her mouth and cross her shawl on her chest the way a vagabond does, to show that she tried to revel and make merry like a man. (Lewis 1964, 56, 59)

1

For Pedro Martínez, loose women — women who work in the fields, women who have sex with many men, women who assume a man's right to have fun — represent dangerously deviant forces in society, and yet that danger can be controlled because violence against such women could, at least in the cruel old days, be committed with impunity. In the anecdote, Martínez emphasizes that women's assistance in the fields was necessary to help support the families in those chaotic times and even that men were responsible for initiating this shift in tasks by "sending" women into the fields. From the men's point of view, women doing fieldwork offered a double gain: the extra hands in the fields better responded to family needs, and the female dislocation from the homes proved convenient for pursuing illicit affairs. Nevertheless, the anecdote does not concern itself with a man's right to order his woman to take on whatever task, including ones perceived as nonfeminine in nature; rather it stigmatizes those women who began to show up in places deemed inappropriate to their sex. For whatever reason — whether through personal initiative or obedience to their men — women in the fields represented a disruption of and a threat to a male-dominated social order. In reversing accepted gender roles and taking on the man's prerogative of working the fields and of having multiple sexual partners, the loose woman became marked as abnormal. Scapegoating one of them helped restore the proper social hierarchies. Adorning her murdered body with the outward signs of masculine identity (cigar, sombrero, crossed shawl) stressed that her punishment was for her unnatural unwomanliness, while it warned other women against such transgressions. Her torture suggested the ubiquity of male-on-female violence in this society. Furthermore, this rape and violent murder of a loose woman exorcised the brooding violence threatening between men, who could displace it onto a female who was at the same time unprotected and defeminized, and thus through killing her they reinforced male bonds. Finally, while Pedro Martínez specifically marks this anecdote as his *grandmother's* story in his retelling of it to Oscar Lewis, and frames it as a tale of the bad old days, nevertheless, the anecdote — and others like it — serves to reinforce specific cultural stereotypes about the proper social roles of men and women; in Martínez's terms, contemporary loose women are no less deviant or defeminized; they are just less subject to extreme punishment for their transgressions.[1]

The second anecdote comes from a series of interviews conducted a few years ago in Tijuana by public health worker María Gudelia Rangel Gómez. One of the women, when asked how she came to be involved in prostitution, describes a complex situation of continual workplace harassment that forces her into paid sex work:

What did I work at? The first time I worked in a shoe store in Acapulco. Then in a furniture store, then I went and worked in a tobacco shop, then in the Hyatt Hotel in Acapulco. That was where I began this. Well, I had already been widowed for several years and I had a lot of problems in my jobs...because they see you a widow and because they see you divorced, and they see you young and with a child....Because it is not for nothing, but often influences you that men do not respect you at work. When one is working, one wants to have a calm life, but you have to be constantly changing jobs every little while because otherwise you have to sleep with the boss, not to mention that they only pay you the going rate for a salary. All sorts of things. And you find yourself becoming his mistress and his personal prostitute. The thing is, I always analyzed that and how it was possible that I fought it so much. And the long and short of it is that I was offended....In those days when one was alone with a small child, and a widow, the guys were harassing you sexually all the time. And you say to yourself, why?, you're offending me. And then it turns out that after all you have to do it because besides the fact that you need the money, in any case you are doing it after all. And you don't even have the liberty to do it or not. Because they turn it into another situation. And it is really hard, in fact, when one is young, and single, and has a child. It was a tough situation. (See appendix, under "Aurora")

The Tijuana prostitute's dilemma is an all too common one, repeated over and over again in the Rangel Gómez interviews. A young woman, particularly a young woman with a child, continues to be typecast according to a model indicating that Martínez's provincial Mexico of two generations past remains pertinent for the modern cosmopolis. A young woman who works (in the fields, in the factories) is stepping outside of a stereotypically proper role; if she has no husband to protect her, then she is by definition a loose woman. Corralled and pressured by continual harassment, she has the choice of acceding to the boss's sexual advances or changing jobs, and if she does the latter, the constant changing of jobs gradually wears down her resistance. In the case of this informant, rebelling against sexual harassment on the job took the form of becoming in fact the prostitute that the bosses pretended to believe she already was.

Both these anecdotes describe a national culture in which presumed gender boundaries for women *and the transgression of these boundaries* are deeply imbedded features of the social fabric. It is precisely this area of slippage between boundaries and their transgression that concerns me in this book, where women — through the force of circumstance or personal choice — step outside such dominant culture codings of female behavior and thus enter into a sliding category: loose women, easy women, public women, "locas," prostitutes. Women who infringe upon the public space remain scandalous, and this continuing scandal, I believe, resides initially in the impact of a female-gendered human being in an unexpected public space, quite apart from assumptions about her sexual availability. This book, then, outlines the literary traces and contemporary permutations of a continuing Mexican obsession with the figure of the loose woman. Paradoxically, while women are punished for transgressive behavior, this slippage also undergirds a particularly potent dominant social construct. It marks an important realm of male entitlement and defines an uneven relationship involving social pressure and the demands of male privilege. This entitlement is, curiously enough, ambiguously encoded in the federal constitution, which, for example, leaves prostitution in a nebulous no-man's-land of semilegality while formally creating legal penalties against *lenocinio* [procuring]. The effect, as Patricia Barrón Salido acutely observes, is that known houses of prostitution in legal *zonas de tolerancia* [red-light districts] cover up their main activity, calling themselves "bars," "clubs," and so on, with the result that all employees in such establishments are assumed to be prostitutes (Barrón Salido 1995, 39). Whole professions — waitresses, for example — thus become stigmatized by extension: a clear example of the operations of this slipperiness of the presumably transgressive woman.

Furthermore, these anecdotes, which suggest an extreme confinement of women's sexuality and women's physical bodies to strictly delimited domestic spaces, need to be put into the context of an underdiscussed history of what was arguably the most important social upheaval of this century. Some scholars estimate that during the Mexican Revolution of 1910–20 more than half of the women in Mexico were forced to turn to prostitution in order to survive (see, e.g., Macías 1982, 44). For the last few years, I have obsessively asked all Mexicans I have met what they think about this figure. Some agree; some find it high and guess that the real figure might be closer to a third or a fourth of the women in the country. It partly depends on definitions. That bloody and protracted civil war was notable for the participation of *soldaderas* — generally perceived as sexually free women, if not actual prostitutes — in the ranks of all the conflicting armies, and there were also well-known women soldiers, such as La Coronela, who dressed and behaved like men, commanding forces and demonstrating stereotypically male heroic qualities.[2] Whatever the exact numbers of female soldiers, *soldaderas*, and actual prostitutes (given the confusions of war, any estimates can only be more or less speculative), there is general agreement that, in that period of tremendous social upset, women were largely on the loose and on their own in Mexico.

One half of all Mexican women: What happened to them? A student who makes a cursory study of the Mexican Revolution could be pardoned for concluding that, with the exception of a few heroic *soldaderas* and a few evil whores, the vast majority of Mexican women remained in their homes, grinding corn for the next day's tortillas and caring for their children. The war's multiple traumas have been discussed obsessively in Mexican literature since 1920, but seldom have women of any sort appeared in more than a token role; the two obvious exceptions — Nellie Campobello's slim volumes of memoirs, *Cartucho* and *Manos de Mamá* [Cartridge and My mother's hands] and Elena Poniatowska's *Hasta no verte, Jesús mío* [Until we meet again, Dear Jesus] — tend to be consistently signaled by critics as exactly that: exceptions to the great bulk of fiction about the Mexican Revolution. The role of the Mexican woman in the revolution, and specifically the role of the vast numbers of Mexican women who took an active role as women and as warriors, has been largely suppressed, and popular images of the revolutionary woman in still-popular *corridos* [ballads] stress the figure of the devoted woman who accompanies her valiant man. Yet, here too, in the revolutionary songs and legends, an attentive reader/listener will find hints of how the cultural emergencies provoked slippages in gender conventions. As Steve Stern notes, "This impact, which men resisted and which they had every reason either to hide or to trivialize in joking banter among men, was at best a half-acknowledged secret. . . . The impact of women's will on the dynamics of patriarchal rule was the ultimate secret within a secret history of gender" (Stern 1995, 319). Up to one-half of all Mexican women had shaken loose from their traditional roles. The enormity of this phenomenon marks modern Mexican society and literature with a deeply felt, if largely unwritten, catachresis.

This historical ellipsis conditions modern and contemporary Mexican literature, in which the loose woman is remembered and put under erasure in the same gesture — displaced, as Octavio Paz would have it in his seminal *El laberinto de la soledad* [Labyrinth of solitude], onto the single, vilified figure of Spanish conqueror Hernán Cortés's indigenous lover/translator, Malinche, safely distanced more than four hundred years in the past. Stern rereads this trope with reference to Roger Bartra's clever portmanteau description of the archetype as "Chingadalupe." Says Stern: "Chingadalupe prevails precisely because women cannot live up to the ideal prescribed for them and are prone to immoral treachery. The Malinche/Chingada archetype encodes what men ought to expect if they fail to control their women; the Virgen/*soldadera* archetype encodes an idealized womanhood of devoted suffering that few real women can match" (Stern 1995, 343). In the revolution's aftermath, contemporary loose women were exiled once again to the margins of dominant discourse, though they continue to exercise a powerful, focal pull on twentieth-century cultural productions.

This simultaneous remembering/forgetting of a loose woman/foremother (buried in the distant past or, problematically, repressed under the image of one's own mother or grandmother) contributes a peculiarly ironic twist to the Mexican cult of the saintly mother. Most strikingly, in typical middle-class parlance, the category of "womanhood" is decoupled from the adjectives "loose" or "decent" to hover unambiguously over only a certain type of female behavior, pushing other female persons into a discursive abyss. Note, for example, the following comments recorded in a book by Roberto Martínez Baños, Patricia Trejo de Zepeda, and Edilberto Soto Angli, comments in which freedom of sexual expression is immediately translated by the middle-class women interviewed into a de facto definition of prostitution, one that presupposes that sexual freedom is incompatible with womanhood itself. The interviewees further describe the essential characteristic of prostitution not as the exchange of sex for money but as an immoral and degenerate enjoyment of sexual relations:

> Corazón: Yo conozco a muchas muchachas que salen con uno tres días y al cuarto, a la cama. Y esto pienso que es negativo porque esa mujer ya no es mujer; ya es otra cosa, ya es una mujer que se vende: para mí es una prostituta, es una mujer de la calle.
> Patricia: Si por puro placer, sin sentir amor, se acuestan con el primero que se encuentren, pues, realmente sí, son prostitutas.
> Corazón: Y está peor, porque ni le pagan. (Martínez Baños, Trejo de Zepeda, and Soto Angli 1973, 91)

> [Corazón: I know a lot of girls who go out with a guy for three days and on the fourth, to bed. And I think this is negative because that woman is no longer a woman; she becomes something else, she becomes a woman who sells herself: for me she's a prostitute, a streetwalker.
> Patricia: If they go to bed with the first guy they meet just for pure pleasure, without love, then, well, yes, they really are prostitutes.
> Corazón: And it's worse, because they aren't even getting paid.]

This exchange not only manifests an internalization of the traditional double standard by which women are divided into two camps — decent and evil — but also reveals that those female human beings who refuse to fit easily into either category are stripped of womanhood itself. For Patricia and Corazón, as for Federico Gamboa and Octavio Paz, "woman" is defined not only in opposition to "man" but also in contradistinction to that other-gendered being, the sexually transgressive female. In their conversation about such women, Corazón and Patricia echo the famously elliptical phrase of Gamboa referring to his prostitute-protagonist, Santa, "¡No era mujer, no; era una...!" [She was not a woman, no; she was a...] (Gamboa 1903, 15). Curiously, the interviewed women find their sexually liberated counterparts even more morally reprehensible if they do not participate in the single most traditional act of the prostitute — the exchange of sex for money. The loose woman poses a particular threat to society if she has sex for pleasure because she thus violates both of the stereotypical categories for women: that of the decent woman indifferent to sex and that of the prostitute who accepts money for an unpleasant service.

Historically, as well as in terms of contemporary popular culture, where her figure permeates folk songs and popular movies, this elided being, this dislocated and transgressive woman, stands at the crossroads of modern Mexican literary culture. In each of the works I will be discussing in this book, this figure marked by an active sexuality serves as a crucial narrative intersection that conditions narratives about women, whether or not the novel's ostensible central focus is on prostitution/sexual freedom. Her role, even when nonprotagonic, forces a narrative realignment. I will be looking at the discursive construction of these women in modern Mexican fiction since the turn of the century, frequently but not exclusively focusing on the figure of the prostitute or the woman perceived as such in order to ask why this character exerts such a compelling influence as a rhetorical trope, to explore how socially biased stereotypes and preconceptions structure both authors and readers, and finally, to try to understand the transgressive woman's own response to society's fascination with the myth and marginalization of real women. Thus, while I ground my readings in the most reliable surveys and socioethnographic studies available, I am inevitably less directly concerned with what is objectively true about the loose woman than with how Mexican writers have positioned her in their works.

I worked for over five years on this project, and despite my enthusiasm, nothing I have ever written took me so long or caused me so many doubts. I have come to understand that these doubts arose largely because I have no personal, experiential knowledge upon which to base my analysis in this work, for which position is so important. To supplement this lack of an organic relationship to the women whose lives underwrite this project, I thought about starting this book with a survey of historical and professional studies on prostitution in Mexico from Aztec times to the present. Such studies, in fact, have been undertaken by other writers, and little purpose would be served by repeating them here, where I suspect they would merely tend to highlight a personal insecurity — as if an extensive bibliography could paper over such difficulties. Furthermore, the deeper I read, the less confident I felt. Current professional studies on women who work in *el ambiente* [the life] in Mexico tend to one of three types: sociological, medical, and legal.[3] But neither those studies nor the historical studies seemed to provide the grounding I needed to answer the fundamental questions I wanted to ask about the relationship between women and reading. Even worse, the material is spotty and incomplete, plagued with evidence of the researchers' preexisting stereotypes and the women's distrust.

Much of what has been written about these women who exist on the margins and in the ellipses of dominant discourse in Mexico is derivative, overgeneralized, and untheorized, a problem recognized even in the context of existing studies themselves. This lack of serious study is true even of the most clearly defined category in this sliding scale of women marked by their sexual activity: the ordinary streetwalker or brothel prostitute. As Rangel Gómez writes, "Todas estas investigaciones han sido tan generales y en ocasiones tan particulares que los resultados de los mismos no pueden ser usados de manera apropiada.... [A]lgunos de los resultados...reflejan un gran vacío de conocimiento respecto...de la prostitución en México" [All this research has been so general and on occasion so narrow that the results cannot be used in an appropriate manner.... Some of the results reflect a great vacuum in knowledge related to...prostitution in Mexico] (Rangel Gómez, n.d., 1). Rangel's point is well taken; the most important conclusion to be drawn from existing studies is the recognition of their inadequacy. Likewise, in calling for scientifically valid studies of prostitution by fellow sociologists, Lourdes Pacheco Ladrón de Guevara writes, "No obstante el hecho de que la prostitución es reconocida como un problema de la estructura social, no se encontró ningún planteamiento serio sobre esto" [Despite the fact that prostitution is recognized as a problem of the social structure, no serious proposals on this topic could be found] (Pacheco Ladrón de Guevara 1988, 138). Further, F. Gomezjara et al., in their standard sociological treatment, *La sociología de la prostitución* [The sociology of prostitution], complain specifically about the lack of information other than semiautobiographical fictions related to the analogous problem of male prostitution: "Su estudio y sistematización en Europa y Norteamérica lleva varios años dentro de las ciencias sociales, lo que en México ni siquiera a nivel de planteamiento teórico existe" [Its study and systematization in Europe and North America took place several years ago in the social sciences, while in Mexico not even the theoretical question exists] (Gomezjara et al. 1978, 80). Mexican scholars have frequently tended to fill these theoretical and empirical gaps in knowledge with historical surveys and large chunks of paraphrased material from authors as diverse as Carlos Fuentes, Susan Sontag, and Simone de Beauvoir (see, e.g., Careaga 1990, 98, 108–11), supplementing them with postscripts indicating the relevance of such discussions to a Mexican social model.

It is not unusual, thus, to see citations from Fuentes's description of prostitution in his novel *La región más transparente* [Where the air is clear] used as sociological source material, or equally questionable references to the same author's mannered autobiographical reference to an adolescence spent in Mexico City brothels in a single paragraph of *Myself with Others* (e.g., "We would go to a whorehouse oddly called El Buen Tono, choose a Mexican girl who usually said her name was Gladys and she came from Guadalajara, and go to our respective rooms" [Fuentes 1981, 21]). Another common point of reference is Jorge Ibargüengoitia's semidocumental novel, *Las muertas* [The dead women], based on a notorious case of white slave trade and mass murder in Guadalajara in 1964. The real-life case of the Poquianchis, as María González reminds us in her study of the novel, first made headlines in the sensationalist tabloids like *Alarma,* and while resonance of the scandal still remains in the public imagination to this day, Ibargüengoitia reminds us that his novel is based on the least reliable of documentary sources of evidence: "[L]a historia era horrible, la reacción de la gente era estúpida, lo que dijeron los periódicos era sublime de tan idiota" [The story was horrible; the reaction of the people was stupid; what the newspapers said was so idiotic it was sublime] (quoted in González 1996, 124). The resulting studies, then, often recur to a somewhat vague and unfocused essay style that depends for its effect on dubious analogies, on shock value and self-analysis, as well as on the empirical evidence of a database constructed from a very few, often ambiguous, questions asked of an inadequate sample of the population. I want to emphasize, nevertheless, that such studies, however inadequate as descriptions of the circumstances and perceptions of the women themselves, do clarify the parameters of the process by which these women are constructed as intellectual objects of study. In reading them, we learn as much about sociological presuppositions and culturally biased observational methods as we do about the women themselves.

Furthermore, the social order, which erases the sexually transgressive woman, also protects her client. As in many other cultures, in Mexico the act of paying for sexual favors is not perceived with any particular censure, as long as the person doing the paying is male, and he pays to perform the active role in the couple. The man, as Clara Coria bitterly complains, has power, but there is no name for him by which to denounce his behavior: "¿Cómo se le dice a este hombre [que paga por el intercambio sexual]? Por mucho que busquemos resulta difícil encontrar la palabra que lo identifique. . . . No es casual que el idioma no disponga de una palabra que enuncie (¿denuncie?) este aspecto de la realidad" [What does one call a man who pays for a sexual exchange? No matter how hard we look it is very difficult to find a word that identifies him. . . . It is not by chance that language does not possess a word to enunciate (denounce?) this aspect of reality] (Coria 1986, 34–35).

One turn-of-the-century study, Luis Lara y Prado's 1908 book, *La prostitución en México* [Prostitution in Mexico], is still widely cited in current sociological texts, despite its very obvious biases. Lara y Prado's work is based largely upon statistics about prostitutes gathered by the health inspector in the process of maintaining registration records for a specific class of women working in Mexico City in the sex industry (i.e., legally registered prostitutes) at the turn of the century. He concludes in this study that despite their greater opportunities for gainful employment and their minimal material needs, lower-class women overwhelmingly fill the ranks of the prostitutes, thus proving the innate moral and cultural degeneracy of this social class (Lara y Prado 1908, 25–26, 39, 57–58). He further argues that "science" has proven that these women are psychologically inferior to decent women, lack the ability to reason, and are subject to nervous system perversions (88–90, 108). Surprisingly, Xorge del Campo's 1974 volume with the same title (*La prostitución en México*) differs not a bit from Lara y Prado's turn-of-the-century tome, including a shared reliance on "scientific" proof such as that derived from Cesare Lombroso and Guillaume Ferrero's 1893 book, *The Prostitute and the Normal Woman,* which claimed to show that prostitution, like other pathologies, is a consequence of an inherited psychological predisposition and tends to manifest itself in categorizable physiological deformations as well. Like Lara y Prado, del Campo finds that most of the women working as prostitutes come from the lower class, people who suffer naturally from a lesser mental capacity and subsequent moral instability: "[S]e explica, por tanto, que, en determinada época, al no corresponder el cociente intelectual al nivel mental, se origine un desequilibrio" [It explains, thus, that in a certain period, when the IQ does not correspond to the mental level, a disequilibrium is created] (del Campo 1974, 117). Del Campo explains that while the native inabilities and inherited propensities of the lower-class women are largely responsible for their falling into this way of life, insufficient maternal affection (107) and chronic laziness (99) can also be contributing factors. One "myth" that del Campo forcefully wants to dispel is the one most often promulgated by the women themselves, the frequently mentioned motivation of economic need: "[A]lgunas meretrices propenden particularmente a 'escucharse a sí mismas' y por eso confían fácilmente al filántropo que las interroga que ellas han adoptado este oficio empujadas por el hambre, por el desempleo, por la insuficiencia de salarios, etcétera. Nada puede estar más sujeto a duda que este género de testimonios" [Some prostitutes have a tendency to "listen to themselves" and for that reason easily confide in the philanthropist who questions them that they have adopted this job propelled by hunger, by unemployment, by inadequate salaries, etc. Nothing could be more subject to doubt than this genre of testimonials] (100). Interestingly, Lara y Prado and del Campo both explicitly reject the stories told them by the women in favor of their own preconstructed hypotheses about their nature, behavior, and motivations. These preconceived notions are understood to be more valid and scientific, since they derive from the investigator rather than from an untrustworthy witness — prostitutes, after all, are known for making up stories to fit their clients' fantasies. The women in most of these sociological accounts are implicitly or explicitly excluded from testifying to their own condition.

Although the Lara y Prado and del Campo books seem shockingly out of date, the social structure they so clearly lay bare is evident in other discussions of Mexican sexual mores. For his *Informe especial: El comportamiento sexual en México* [Special report: Sexual behavior in Mexico (1977)], a study roughly contemporary with the period during which several of the novels examined in this book were written, Osvaldo Quijada conducted both a sample survey and in-depth interviews. Among his findings: the great majority of Mexican men "know" that women are inferior (Quijada 1977, 79; this statistic could be related to a later question in which the majority of the men questioned indicate that they do not like intelligent women [147]). Sixty percent of all men questioned, and 70 percent of those married for more than five years, use prostitutes on an average of once a month (230–31). According to rather dubious self-reporting, 80 percent of the men also indicate that they have initiated at least a couple of virgins; as Quijada notes, "[P]or cierto, estas cifras deben analizarse con reservas toda vez que la sobrevaluación de la virginidad por parte del varón hace que el desvirgamiento constituya una de las obsesiones de la masculinidad" [Of course, these figures ought to be analyzed with a grain of salt since the overvaluation of virginity on the part of the male makes sex with virgins one of the constant obsessions of masculinity] (227). The interviews further clarify these men's sense of a proper and moral organization of society:

Encontré a mi hijo masturbándose. . . . Le dije que era una tontería
desperdiciar el tiempo de ese modo y que, si ganas tenía, se buscara
una amiguita. El tiene 15 años y creo que me entendió (burócrata,
38 años) (92)

Cuando éramos jóvenes, soñabamos con ser amigos de las prostitutas. . . . De todos modos, la prostitución es como un servicio
social. Sirve a los solteros y evita la masturbación. (profesionista,
39 años) (322)

¿Por qué se casa uno realmente? ¿Para tener orgasmos? No, señor.
Uno se casa para formar una familia, para que su mujer sea la
madre y formadora de los hijos. Una madre no tiene como misión
el orgasmo. . . . [C]on los hijos ya no puede ser. Hay respeto. Tiene
que haber respeto. (empleado, 44 años) (289)

[I found my son masturbating. . . . I told him that it was foolish to
waste time that way and that if he felt like he wanted it, he should
go out and find a girlfriend. He's fifteen years old and I believe he
understood me. (bureaucrat, thirty-eight years old)

When we were young we dreamed about making friends with
the prostitutes. . . . In any case, prostitution is like a social service. It serves bachelors and prevents masturbation. (professional,
thirty-nine years old)

Why does one get married, really? To have orgasms? No, sir. One
marries to have a family, so that one's wife can be the mother and
shaper of children. A mother has no business with orgasm. . . . With
children, it is no longer possible. There is respect. There must be
respect. (worker, forty-four years old)]

In this conception of society, decent women — *la mujer, la madre* — must
be rigidly controlled in both body and mind. The other females, the *ami-
guitas* and the prostitutes, seen typically in the plural, are both completely
objectified as well as virtually indistinguishable. At the same time, their
elliptical presence at the heart of a decent home serves as a cusp for the
smooth functioning of a moral social order. Men need these other women
as outlets for their own stronger sexuality and as protective buffers to
save decent women from the corrupting knowledge of their own potential sexual desires. Still further, if decent men worry that their wives not
be too intelligent, one of the most frequent accusations against prostitutes
is the contradictory assertion that they are both intellectually inferior and
far too able at making up stories to fool their clients into paying them

better. The latter conclusion is consistent with Del Campo's and Lara y Prado's analysis of the prostitute as an untrustworthy fictionalizer whose canny, but unintelligent, tales can be easily disproved by the experienced eye of the neutral and scientifically objective observer who is able to sift through the fictions to access the real truth about these women and their motivations.

Isn't there something suspicious about the rhetoric of these sociological texts, as well as about the language used by the men interviewed, with its combination of the terminology of fastidious hygiene and that of moral censure? What is there about the sexually transgressive woman that provokes such bizarre and conflicting comments? Is it repressed historical memory? Is it the public spectacle she offers? Is it the potential for contamination of decent women, who, once fallen from grace, are no longer either decent or women but some other slippery and unfathomable being? The prostitute in particular is suspect because, perhaps, underlying the falseness of her appearance and her propensity to tell tales the client wants to hear, she is presumed to maintain a fundamental honesty in her dealings with men; she sells her labor openly, whereas "decent" women call what they sell "love" and so implicitly prostitute themselves. Likewise, in asserting the need to protect the decent woman from the knowledge of her sexuality — since such knowledge would make her unfit as a mother — the husband also implicitly recognizes the potential fluidity of these categories; a single, thoughtless slip on the husband's part and the decent woman could be irremediably undone.

Psychoanalyst Clara Coria suggests that the real trauma for middle-class thinkers is not so much a sexual but an economic loosening on the part of the female half of the population. What happens, she asks, when women leave the domestic for the public sphere? What do we call women like Indira Gandhi and Margaret Thatcher? On analogy with men who dedicate their efforts to governmental and public-service functions (*hombres públicos*), logically, such women would be *mujeres públicas*. The impossibility of such an appellation points to the historical problem that Coria summarizes in a sarcastic equation:

la mujer + dinero + ámbito público = prostitución
woman + money + public space = prostitution (Coria 1986, 37)

This equation points to a problem that Coria calls *el fantasma de la prostitución* [the phantom of prostitution], a dilemma that hovers over women who wish to define themselves in any realm other than the domestic (leaving aside, for the moment, the fact that the prostitute's most notorious function is, precisely, a domestic one). Coria writes: "[C]uando se

unen los términos mujer, sexualidad, dinero y ámbito público, ello evoca y
remite — consciente o inconscientemente — a la idea-vivencia-creencia de
prostitución" [When the terms "woman," "sexuality," "money," and "public space" come together, they evoke and remind one of — consciously or
unconsciously — the idea-life-belief of prostitution] (36); and they do so
to such a degree that even when the sexuality factor is left out of the
equation, the phantom still arises:

> El fantasma de la prostitución está presente de manera encubierta
> en la *vergüenza* y la *culpa* que muchas mujeres sienten en sus prác-
> ticas con el dinero....Es sorprente la abundancia de referencias
> que es posible encontrar en relación a la *vergüenza* que sienten
> cuando descubren a sí mismas gozosas por ganar dinero y con deseos
> de ambición económica. La vivencia de *culpa*....la encontramos
> preferentemente asociada con el hecho de trabajar fuera del hogar
> utilizando sus energías en el lugar público en detrimento de la tarea
> hogareña. (40)

> [The phantom of prostitution is present in a covert manner in the
> shame and guilt that many women feel in their monetary practices.
> ...It is surpassing how abundant are the references that can be
> found with relation to the shame that they feel when they discover
> themselves pleased by earning money and with desires for economic
> ambitions. The existence of guilt...is discovered as generally asso-
> ciated with the fact of working outside the home and using one's
> energies in the public space to the detriment of household tasks.]

Coria's language in this text cannily makes use of the sexualized language of desire, pleasure, and so on, to evoke the specter she is defining
as a particular quality of middle-class women's guilt. The phantom, then,
takes shape as an intolerable significance, impossible but real. Money, for
these women, is tainted by an unrecognized association with a guilty sexual pleasure. Still further, Coria's perceptive juxtaposition of *el hombre
público* with *la mujer pública* suggestively points to what is a disjunction
on one level and a strikingly pertinent connection on another; quite apart
from the monetary aspect, the displacement of women into the public
space carries implications for the body politic.

One factor contributing to the confusions about the status of sexually
transgressive women in Mexico is that while prostitution is decried as an
inescapable social evil, and prostitutes are considered both immoral and
pathological, the act of selling one's body for money falls into a legislative
gray area: not quite illegal and more or less regulated depending on local

policies and statutes. In the section of the Mexican penal code dealing with *los delitos contra la moral pública* [crimes against public morality], the following are identified as criminal acts: "utrajes a la moral pública o a las buenas costumbres, corrupción de menores, lenocinio, provocación de un delito y apología de éste o de algún vicio" [contempt of public morality or good customs, corruption of minors, procuring, inciting crime, and defense of this or another vice] (González de la Vega 1968, 304; Moreno 1968, 239). Thus, prostitution is technically legal, while houses of prostitution are outlawed under the prohibition against procuring. Despite this federal regulation, individual states have sometimes opted to legalize and regulate houses of prostitution in so-called *zonas de tolerancia* [red-light districts]. As Salazar González notes, these functioning state laws are in conflict with the federal code and thus seem to be unconstitutional (Salazar González 1986, 99, 122). Because of the ambiguous legal status of prostitution, the continuing harassment of streetwalkers in most of the country is technically based not on the act of exchanging sex for money but on the prostitute's personal appearance, for which she can legally be charged with *un atentado contra las buenas costumbres* [assault on good customs] and can be held for thirty-six hours (Lamas 1993, 111). The prostitute, then, embodies an immoral but legal vice, a crime more against taste than against the social order. As Barrón Salido acutely comments, even in respected studies of marginal figures, "parecería que la prostitución queda entre puntos suspensivos" [it seems that prostitution remains in the ellipsis] (Barrón Salido 1995, 9).[4]

The problem of addressing these questions is exacerbated for me by an additional dilemma. As a non-Mexican feminist literary scholar necessarily coming to this hedged cultural phenomenon with foreign eyes and foreign expectations, where do I find the language to enable me to enter and address a powerful tradition so multiply fortified against women's (re)appropriation? The progress made by feminist thought in Mexico seems at times restricted solely to the upper-class women and barely manifested in literary rebelliousness.[5] To apply such a theory uncritically to working-class, marginalized women is to incur the same error of observer-bias that I decry in facile sociological treatises on prostitution and that I analyze in modern novels where a woman who steps outside dominant-culture expectations for female behavior plays a crucial, if stereotyped, role.

Furthermore, even among women who work as prostitutes, the internalized double standard of decent and sinful women often applies in a way that empowers them in some contexts at the same time as it stigmatizes them in others. Barrón Salido's conversations with certain street prostitutes in Tijuana, for example, revealed that for many of them "la maternidad es el aspecto más importante de su vida, aún las que no tienen hijos es su mayor aspiración, simbólicamente es lo que le da sentido a su actividad lo ven como 'purificar sus pecados'" [maternity is the most important aspect of their lives. Even for those who do not have children, it is their greatest dream; symbolically it is what gives meaning to their activities. They see it as a way of "purifying their sins"] (55). Here, ironically, the street prostitutes create for themselves a double persona — the sinful sex worker and the decent mother — in which the sins of the first become the honorable sacrifices of the second.

In Ecuador, I've heard, prostitutes and political prisoners are housed together as equally dangerous to the civil order. Whether or not this hearsay is true, it points toward an imbrication of gender and politics, of national and sexual identities, that seems to me pertinent to the discursive construction of the nation in Mexico as well. Certainly, gender must be theorized as an analytic category with political implications and cultural-literary repercussions. Jean Franco reminds us that in Latin America, the position of the intelligentsia and the discourse of nationalism are "indivisible from the sexual division of labor" and that "this discourse is only interrupted when the differentiation between male authorship and female reproduction is exposed as a socially constructed position" (Franco 1988, 505–6). In a parallel vein, Doris Sommer has analyzed the persistent compulsion in Latin America to frame novels of national foundation as historical romances that end in marriage. She finds that "unproductive eroticism is not only immoral; it is unpatriotic and often related to the barbarous prehistory of the American mission and can be represented by 'unnatural' women for whom sensuality is power" (Sommer 1990, 87). There is a continuity between the historical fictions described by Sommer and those street prostitutes interviewed by Barrón Salido, a common nostalgia for uncomplicated maternity. Maternity, patriotism, and morality are lined up on one side of the scale; eroticism, social antipathy, and sexual desire stand on the other as the necessary counterpoint. Yet if traditional historical fiction is a family romance, then revolution complicates and changes the plots available for narrative use, allowing for new ways of conceiving the nation, of imagining social change, of contemplating political interests, of representing human relationships. The loose woman set in the midst of narrative and social change also loosens up the narrative; she stands precisely in that spot where the social and narrative order is disrupted, and she calls old verities into question. The national identity that in foundational fictions is metaphorically imagined as a maternal presence gives way, in fiction that uses a transgressive woman as a pivot figure, to an ideologically demonized and highly problematic elliptical space. Once a character is identified as a loose woman/prostitute either by euphemistic ellipsis or direct definition, the whole of the narration in effect shifts in focus to become reformulated as either the confirmation of or the counternarrative to the story of the whore.

Popular Mexican culture after the 1910 revolution is notorious for highlighting a sanitized version of the overtly sexually active woman, most famously captured in Agustín Lara's sensual boleros of the 1920s and 1930s and in the *rumbera* and *cabaretera* films of the 1940s and 1950s. Carlos Monsiváis precisely identifies the attraction that brings together the mythologized loose woman and the ideologically charged postrevolutionary atmosphere in a series of curiously persistent mass-culture stereotypes:

[C]antarle a la prostituta equivale — con los cortinajes y disfraces explícitos — a vocear las recompensas del sexo en una sociedad cuyas metas declaradas han sido la amnesia (no venimos de una lucha armada sino de la legitimidad eterna), el afianzamiento de vínculos con la pudibundez (programa de gobierno familiar) y la negación dramatizada de la frase de Luis G. Urbina: "Los generales y los ministros terminaron con las mujeres románticas, con las mujeres desinteresadas."

Los sueños de la hipocresía engendran prostitutas ideales y desvanecen la sordidez de la explotación abyecta de miles de mujeres en cuartuchos insalubres. Por gracia de esta mitología la prostituta... no vende orgasmos sino súplicas de amor para yacer como privilegio exclusivo de la conversación entre varones. (Monsiváis 1977, 73)

[Singing to the prostitute is equivalent — with all the explicit veiling and masking — to speaking of the recompenses of sex in a society in which the declared goals are amnesia (we did not come from an armed fight but from an eternal legitimacy), strengthening the ties of chastity (family planning program), and the dramatized negation of Luis G. Urbina's phrase: "The generals and the ministers ended up with romantic, disinterested women."

The dreams of hypocrisy engender ideal prostitutes and dissolve the sordidness of the abject exploitation of thousands of women in unhealthy rooms. Thanks to this mythology, the prostitute... does not sell orgasms but rather amorous yearning so as to lie flat as an exclusive privilege in the conversation between males.]

Lara's music, like the peculiarly Mexican films that often use his boleros in their musical scores, characterizes prostitutes less as moral exempla of the wages of sin than as markers of the tensions and anxieties inherent in a society in flux. A strong current of social and political dissatisfaction underlies even the most frivolous comedies and melodramatic tragedies of young women flocking to, or forced to become part of, the cabaret scene. As disillusionment with the revolution grows, so too, I would argue, the transgressive woman comes to stand in for the mother in a bitterly acknowledged *and* refused association that is as pervasive as it is historically accurate and overtly repressed. Thus, for example, that staple of tear-jerker films, the prostitute with the heart of gold, is stereotypically domestic, passive, vulnerable, and abject (a displaced maternal image, in short), while her counterpart, the evil vamp, is a sensual, ruthless, amoral bitch-goddess, reinscribing the myth of national foundations and national identity onto a complex and ambiguous territory. As the sexless, or at least unfruitful, prostitutes of song and film demonstrate, female sexuality or moral degradation is less at issue than a conversation about the nature of the emerging national culture. At the same time, as Monsiváis implicitly notes, the quantity, popularity, and persistence of these images demonstrate that they have touched home in a more than superficial way, not only in terms of the conversation between men over a woman's supine body but also with respect to the daily reality lived by many women in the difficult postwar years.

Sexual availability is both presumed in these songs and films and delicately circumscribed. The sexualized woman's body is at the same time insistently present and disturbingly abstracted into a play of trope, which is also an unconscious social commentary. Beneath the myth of the glamorous, sensual, but sexless prostitute lies the reality of grinding poverty, of an underdeveloped country suffering through a series of economic crises and political changes. In the postrevolutionary state, by dressing up the image of the prostitute with Hollywood glamour, the Mexican film industry avoids (while at the same time implicitly recognizing) the realities of hunger and misery that force many women who head households into prostitution as their only hope of feeding themselves and their children. At the same time, the good prostitute, who (filmically at least) does not fully expose her body or engage in overt sexual acts, assures her audience that the purity of the nation is preserved even in the brothel setting; she does this by displacing all the degrading and repugnant stereotypes onto a scapegoated evil prostitute figure (who seems to enjoy her job a tad too much, though film conventions of the immediate postwar period disallowed evil women's nudity as well). I am not interested in trying to determine whether the "mother" or the "vamp" image is more realistic or more representative of actual women's lives in modern Mexico. What I do find interesting is that the mythologized images, and the shifting between two extremes of a degendered representation, are consistent with the opinions both of the middle-class women interviewed by Martínez, Trejo, and Soto and of the Tijuana prostitutes interviewed by Barrón Salido. Both see motherhood and prostitution as separate identities, the former highly valued, the latter valueless.

Ironically, what is valued in the mother is her absence or lack — she is the negation that defines maleness to itself and makes it signify — and in this respect she perversely and essentially resembles the mythic and despised figure of the sexualized woman, that female person denied positive womanhood and vulgarly characterized as a hole into which men ejaculate: a nonreproductive but infinitely reproducible verifier of masculinity. Rhetorical usage confirms this understated perception. Octavio Paz has famously analyzed the uses of the vulgar verb *chingar* [to fuck], which always carries a charge of sexual violence. *El chingón* is a strong, active, masculine figure; *la chingada* is weak, imposed upon, feminine or feminized. As Paz notes, *la chingada*, above all, represents the mother, and the cry "¡Viva México, hijos de la chingada!" [Long live Mexico, children of the raped one!] recognizes the implicit, underlying connection between the raped woman and the nation, between the children born of violence and the Mexican male-force. It reflects as well an aggressively denied fear of future violence against the motherland, a penetration by, say, the United States, that Mexican men would be powerless to prevent. And yet, as Paz says, in these paranoid constructions of gender and sexual norms, while *la chingada* is ineluctably associated with the mother, her very passivity leaches her identity and her name; she is nothing and no one: "[E]s la Nada" [She is Nothingness] (Paz [1959] 1980, 68, 72). Ultimately, the mother in this masculinist system is "nothing" precisely to the degree in which she is conceived of as pure and unprofaned. At the same time, the profaned female is also "nothing," not even a woman, and certainly not *la mujer*. The ultimate insult — *chinga tu madre* [motherfucker] — substitutes one nothing for another, and is directed not at the woman but at what is supposedly a man's most vulnerable spot, the institutionalized myth of motherhood, a myth in which the saintly mother exists only as the function by which the son takes cognizance of himself.

In their feminist analysis of linguistic patterns, Eli Bartra and her collaborators pick up where Paz left off. "En el concepto de la 'chingada,'" they write, "se resume atrozmente la condición femenina de una sociedad sexista" [The concept of *la chingada* summarizes the atrocity of the female condition in a sexist society]. Similarly, other gender-marked exclamations and insults reflect traditional ideas of male and female roles: "La identificación de la mujer-madre, '¡a toda madre!,' '¡tan venerada!,' con la nada es obvia en expresiones como '¡vale madre!' o '¡esto es una madre!,' que equivale a no vale nada. En cambio, decimos '¡qué

padre!' cuando algo nos gusta. El padre en el lenguaje connota hermosura, belleza, agrado" [The identification of the woman-mother, "¡a toda
madre!," "¡tan venerada!," with nothingness is obvious in expressions such
as "¡vale madre!" or "¡esto es una madre!," which is to say, she is worthless.
On the other hand, we say "¡qué padre!" when we like something. The
father in our language connotes handsomeness, beauty, agreeableness]
(Bartra et al. 1983, 101–2).

   If, in the complexities of national myth, the nation is both mother
and whore, then national pride and perceived deficiencies in the national
character derive from a common cause. Moreover, if sexualized women
are to blame — literally or metaphorically — for society's problems, tacitly national pride is also bound up in the admission that nothing can
be done to improve the situation since the beautiful, yearned-for father
is always already gone. Mexican men, metaphorically born to the good
prostitute (*la chingada*), wake up to find themselves victims of the evil
vamp prostitute and so have no recourse but to commit violence, including sexual violence, against women and against their fellow man so as to
shore up a sagging and threatened identity as the possessor of a powerful
and inviolable male body. Paz, from his masculinist point of view, and
Eli Bartra and her collaborators, from their counterpoint feminist stance,
all come to the inevitable intersections of male fantasy, national mythology, and sexual exchange. Male desires serve as the basis to define what
is supposed to be a female character. Gender, class, and sex are linked
in contradictory and highly political ways, conceptualized in a complex
symbolic order marked and refined by the overwhelmingly male or male-
identified intelligentsia of the country and applied indiscriminately to the
population at large. If one problem in understanding the transgressive
woman's role in literature and society is related to an insufficiency of serious and well-conceived scientific studies, another stumbling block is the
polarization of middle-class, male-identified, and, yes, feminist scholars
around and against the abstracted image of *la chingada* or la Malinche as
a figure for national identity and historical presence.

   Yet, I insist, the persistence of such images in popular as well as
high art forms suggests that something is going on beyond a simplistic
misidentification of reality with semiotics. In both cases, the loose woman
serves (services) as she places into question ingrained sexual inequalities.
There is, as Coria might say, a phantom presence that infects middle-
class constructions of social interaction with a recognition of a gendered
relation to desire upon which being, meaning, language, and historical
memory are all founded. I want to make this somewhat abstract overview
more specific through a brief exploration of the issues involved in the literary construction of sexualized women, and I will do so by reference to

two controversial modern plays that make prominent use of the figure of a prostitute: Rodolfo Usigli's *Jano es una muchacha* [Janus is a girl] and Rosario Castellanos's *El eterno femenino* [The eternal feminine].

Usigli's 1952 social critique/comedy tells the story of a young woman of good family who moonlights as a prostitute and of her father, Víctor, ostensibly a respected "notario de provincia, gordo, importante" [fat, important country lawyer] (Usigli [1952] 1966, 406), who is uncovered in the course of the play as a corrupt ex-revolutionary and (the inevitable sideline occupation) owner of the brothel. The play ends happily; the evil Víctor receives his just deserts in the form of a bullet to the head, and his daughter goes off to marry Felipe, the famous writer and her would-be client. The play, thus, both exposes the absurdity of the sexual double standard operative in Mexico and registers a metaphorical protest against the hypocrisy and corruption of the postrevolutionary society in general. However, despite its high moral thrust, the play predictably gave rise to a firestorm of protest, including the playwright's depiction as *enemigo número uno* [public enemy number one] on Liga de Decencia [Decency League] posters — the league objected to the work as an offense to chastity and decent behavior (González Rodríguez 1993, 41). According to the Decency League, Usigli's play sets a bad moral example, apparently not only because it tricks decent people into viewing immorality but because it suggests the possibility of confusion between a decent woman and a prostitute. As one of Usigli's characters says in the play, "[U]na muchacha como usted la describe, no puede existir más que en uno de dos sitios: en un colegio de monjas o en una casa mala" [A girl like the one you describe can only exist in one of two places: a religious school or a house of sin] (417). The play raises the nasty suspicion that loose women, rather than representing unnatural violations of the proper social order, might indeed unmask the secret of well-trained Catholic femininity itself. Georges Bataille defines this position straightforwardly:

Not every woman is a potential prostitute, but prostitution is the logical consequence of the feminine attitude. In so far as she is attractive, a woman is prey to men's desire. Unless she refused completely because she is determined to remain chaste, the question is at what price and under what circumstances will she yield. But if the conditions are fulfilled she always offers herself as an object. Prostitution proper only brings in a commercial element. (Bataille 1986, 131)

Bataille's comment effectively describes the situation critiqued in Usigli's play, by which the beautiful woman becomes a trophy bartered between men for their exclusive (marriage) or shared (prostitute) pleasure. Felipe, the great writer and Usigli's point-of-view character in the play, comments that all attractive women are two-faced Januses who project modesty and sensuality in equal and alternating proportions, and he insinuates that men confine them in brothels and convents so as to restrict their powers. In either case, the woman is an object, even to herself, and her only options relate to the conditions under which she hands herself over to the man. This is her fascination. Both Bataille and Felipe leave out of this equation of "beautiful woman = object" the woman who refuses to submit or who, because of her unattractiveness, is not offered the choice. Usigli, however, does not. He casts the shadowy figure of the maiden aunt in a crucial role as the administrator of the fatal justice against her brother-in-law, who is also her sister's abuser and the man she has always silently loved.

Even more troubling about the play for upper-class members of the Decency League was the suspicion of class confusion. If all that distinguishes (lower-class) prostitutes and (upper-class) decent women is the clothes they wear, then decent women who dress to make themselves attractive to men and prostitutes who use their ill-gotten gains to indulge in expensive clothes blur class lines as well as boundaries of decency. As Clara Coria would say, the possession of money combined with mobility in the public sphere makes these women transgressive; the loose woman hints at an imbrication of social and sexual liberation. Likewise, attractive, decently married, upper-class women suffer from a certain intranquility deriving from the corrupting influence of money and its association with prohibited freedoms.

The "Janus" of Usigli's play has the evocative name of Marina in her schoolgirl guise and Mariana in her role as a come-hither temptress ("Marina, Mariana," muses Felipe, "una letra de diferencia. Es extraordinario lo que una letra de diferencia puede hacer" [Marina, Mariana: one letter different. It is extraordinary what one letter of difference can do] [412]). The young woman's name resonates both with the name of the Blessed Virgin (María) and with that of the young indigenous woman who translated for conqueror Hernán Cortés (Malinche, baptized Marina). For Usigli's more literary audience, the name of the protagonist echoes as well the title of one of the most notorious plays of the nineteenth century, Victor Hugo's tale of a prostitute and her doomed lover, Marion de Lorme. In striking parallel with Usigli's later work, after a severe conflict with the censors in 1829, Hugo's play became the sensation of 1830–31, when it was understood not only as a titillating tale of immorality but also as a concomitant act to the July 1830 revolution. Jann Matlock says that contemporary critics of Hugo's play, and of other related challenges to the social order, were scandalized as much by the revolutionary implications as by the play's debauchery of decent moral standards: "[T]he critics' fears of *Marion de Lorme* generated anxieties about what liberties might be demanded — and taken — in a moment of revolution.... Hugo's drama... helped to generate a counterdiscourse that worked corrosively upon the containing discourses of the nineteenth century" (Matlock 1994, 84–85).[6]

Much the same analysis could be applied to Usigli's play, where the sexual double standard and a hypocritical morality are tied specifically to the figure of an opportunist who misuses the turmoil of the Mexican Revolution for personal gain. It is his daughter Marina/Mariana who embodies the corrosive counterdiscourse to the pious hypocrisies of men like her father. Felipe calls her "Janus" not only for her double face but also because the Roman original was the god of doorways — standing in the threshold between past and present, between the world that has ended and the one that has not yet come to be. For Felipe, this threshold also suggests political conflict and social unrest: "[S]u templo en Roma se cerraba solamente cuando la República estaba en paz. Es decir, nueve veces en mil años" [His temple in Rome was closed only when the Republic was at peace. That is, nine times in a thousand years] (415). Marina/Mariana, then, like Hugo's Marion, focalizes the fear and reality of revolutionary change. The present moment is condensed in the single and ambiguous figure of the rebellious seventeen-year-old girl.

Mexico itself, like the young woman, is two-faced. When Felipe asks one of the prostitutes in the prologue to the play how Mexico is doing, she replies: "Según por donde usted lo mire. Por un lado, podrido en millones; por el otro, pudriéndose de hambre" [Depends on where you look. On the one hand, rotten with riches; on the other, rotting of hunger] (393). What the two conflicting views have in common, of course, is the sense of something unhealthy, of some unburied corpse-like corruption. Rotten or rotting, the people are suspended as passive victims in the threshold of the client/writer's and the prostitute/storyteller's gaze. Likewise, the two spaces that define the play are characterized by a kind of suspended threshold quality in Usigli's poetic stage directions. Of the brothel he says, "El todo comunica el sentimiento de una especie de *no man's land,* de tierra neutral del tiempo, en la que el tiempo no se mueve, no actúa, no opera, exactamente como si no existiera más que en la forma de una película de polvo húmedo apenas perceptible, apenas palpable. Es una impresión análoga... a la que producen las iglesias pobres, las cárceles y los manicomios o los cementerios de la provincia inmóvil" [Everything communicates the sense of a type of no-man's-land, of a neutral temporal space, in which time does not move, does not act, does not function, precisely as if it did not exist except in the form of a barely perceptible, barely palpable skin of damp dust. It is an impression analogous to that produced by poor churches, jails, and madhouses or cemeteries of immobile provinces] (389). Thus, Usigli's stage directions require the audience to receive a double impression of deathly immobility (the provincial timelessness) and indefinitely suspended hostilities (the no-man's-land). The other face of the stage is Víctor and Marina's upper-class residence: "Se siente una limpieza fresca en el aire mismo — esa 'frescura de rebozo y de tinaja' de que habla López Velarde; — y la presencia imponderable de las manos amorosas de mujer que bruñen cada detalle de la casa. Sin embargo de la luminosidad, la frescura y la limpieza del ambiente, falta algo definible" [One feels a fresh cleanness in the air itself — that "freshness of shawl and basin" that López Velarde speaks of, . . . and the imponderable presence of the loving hands of a woman brushing over every detail of the house. Despite the luminosity, the freshness, and the cleanness of the atmosphere, something indefinable is missing] (403). Here again, the view is doubled: of freshness and yet of indefinable lack.

The play's conflict comes to a head when Marina/Mariana's father, the self-righteous lawyer, goes to the brothel at the end of the second act of the play and demands his rights as brothel owner to go to bed with the *maravillita* Felipe had been telling him about, only to come face-to-face with his own daughter:

> Víctor: . . . ¿Mi hija una mujer de éstas? ¡Qué inmundicia! ¡Qué vergüenza! Vete de aquí en seguida, miserable, estúpida niña, vete a tu casa, basura. No te reconozco. . . .
> Marina: ¿Podría reconocer a mi padre en este animal? . . .
> Víctor: ¡Mi hija en un burdel!
> Marina: Y mi padre . . . Vete tú. (440)

> [Víctor: My daughter, one of these women? What filth! What shame! Get out of here right now you miserable, stupid child; go home, you piece of garbage. I don't recognize you. . . .
> Marina: Could I recognize my father in this animal? . . .
> Víctor: My daughter in a brothel!
> Marina: And my father . . . You get out.]

The confrontation between father and daughter uncovers all the ugly hypocrisies by which provincial men like Víctor maintain their social standing. In order for the system of trickery and self-delusion to work, the men who come to the brothel need to locate themselves in an elliptical intersection of reality and fiction-making in which the ugly reality they perceive changes places with the sordid illusion they create to mask their own Janus faces. It is, in fact, precisely this play of representation and illusion that is valorized in the commercialized sex act. As the madam tells Felipe in one of his indignant moments: "¿Se cree usted héroe de novela que levanta el ángel caído? . . . Aquí se vende ilusión, no realidad. . . . Y déjeme usted decirle la verdad: los hombres llegan aquí llenos de lodo hasta el alma, pero con la idea de que es en mi casa donde se enlodan. Eso les permite hacerse la . . . bueno, las ilusiones. . . . Y para convencerse, tratan de enlodarnos y nos llaman . . . " [Do you think you're the hero of some novel that raises up the fallen angel? We sell illusions here, not reality. And let me tell you the truth: men come here full of dirt to the very soul, but with the idea that they are dirtied in my house. That permits them to do . . . well, illusions. And to convince themselves, they try to throw dirt on us and call us . . . ] (429–30).[7] Dora's plain-speaking with the client/writer is marked by two significant ellipses: the first leaving unstated what men do under the cover of illusion, and the second eliding the name they give the women they do it with. These ellipses leave their marks not only on the women but also on the men. As Usigli says in the stage direction describing Felipe, "[T]iene aire de 'haber vivido,' es decir, de haber hecho muchas porquerías elegantes" [He has the air of "having lived," that is, of having done a lot of elegant vileness] (391).

In Felipe's case, the vileness is as much of the mind as of the body. Usigli's play points up a traditional association of the writer and the prostitute as parallel professions in that both put themselves on the market for sale to anonymous clients, and both deal in illusion rather than reality. Throughout the play, there is a continual interplay between these two fiction-making careers. When Felipe introduces himself as a writer, the brothel madam informs him that she too writes poems. When he tries to clarify that, although he has come incognito to the brothel, "[S]i le dijera yo mi nombre, aullaría usted de gusto" [If I told you my name you would howl with pleasure], she responds dryly: "Gracias, pero todavía no hago alianza con los perros" [Thanks, but I still haven't allied myself with the dogs] (394). When Marina challenges his reasons for coming to the brothel, Felipe accuses her of having read too many French novels about prostitutes and says, "Mira, chiquita, no hagamos literatura, que ésa puedo hacerla yo solo, y de mejor gusto" [Look, little girl, let's not make literature. I can do that on my own, and in better taste] (401). When he explains why he no longer writes, he complains: "Me da asco escribir, me parece una de las profesiones más prostituidas del mundo" [Writing makes me nauseous, it seems to me one of the most prostituted professions in the world] (400).

While the lawyer's hypocrisies eventually do him in, the poet's truth-telling becomes his salvation. He finds love and a new source of inspiration in the impertinent young Marina/Mariana. At the same time, he is not quite picking up the fallen angel from the filth when he goes off with her at the end of the play. Although the girl behaves like a prostitute, Usigli is careful to avoid confirming what the audience would naturally infer from her setting. There is no evidence that she has actually exchanged sex for money although she, or the brothel madam, does accept Felipe's payment; rather, the suggestion (and later, her repeated assertion) is that she has been playing at prostitution without ever having taken the final step of giving her body to a client. She is, then, that perfect threshold contradiction: the virgin whore.

Finally, Usigli's moral tale does more to confirm than to disrupt conventional moral schemes. Despite its clear-minded polemic against the dung heap of postrevolutionary Mexican politics and its critique of the sexual double standard, Usigli reinscribes a conventional moral standard (albeit with more open communications between the sexes) as a model for social and political change. Felipe admits to a far-too-excessive experience with life's cesspools; he calls himself a whore and worse at one point, when he tells the brothel madam that when a man uses prostitutes too much "el hombre se emputece. Esas mujeres que no saben mucho de lenguaje, dicen que el hombre que las toma demasiado se hace puto" [the man prostitutes himself. Those women who don't know much language say that the man who uses them too much becomes a whore], and he even suggests there is another name for men like him, one that is used for men who like to sleep with boys (431). Nevertheless, he is, at a well-used forty-three, considered a viable and even desirable candidate for the hand of a seventeen-year-old convent-bred virgin. When he accepts the young woman despite her transgressive behavior and language, the audience is meant to see his action as an unusual concession, albeit one that propels the lucky couple into the never-never land of the happily ever after.

Marina/Mariana, in contrast, despite her attraction to the brothel, has maintained her bodily purity and will go to Felipe a virgin: the only way a happy ending of domestic bliss can possibly be ensured in this 1952 drama. It is, in fact, an index of Felipe's worth as a husband that he is mature enough and broadminded enough to understand that his future wife may indeed have sensual needs and desires (theoretically, at least, since during the final act the play insistently reminds us that Marina has never acted upon her desires and, in fact, is hewing to convention by saving herself for the right man). Felipe is dissolute, but he's no hypocrite, and the reminder that he is a great writer for whom Marina will serve as a convenient muse only increases his value in the audience's eyes.

Marina/Mariana is Janus-faced, but so are all women, Usigli hints, and conventional society functions by repressing one side of women's nature. This conclusion is consistent with the observation, coming from the feminine side of the equation, made by contemporary Algerian feminist Marie-Aimee Helie-Lucas about women in her country:

> Being the guardian is so central to the threatened identity that it is also identified as the weakest point, the most vulnerable to be protected from alien influences.... Laws should be codified which... bind women to their role as guardians and prevent them from any possibility to... show the other profile of their Janus face, prevent them from betrayal and destruction of the community. (Helie-Lucas 1994, 494)

The play, then, shocks its audience with a confirmation of men's suspicion that decent women might indeed have an interest in sexuality, while it confirms the dominant double standard that the only fit match for a man is an untried woman and that the only fit man for such a woman is one made glamorous by his libertine propensities. Furthermore, as Usigli's brothel owner suggests, and Helie-Lucas confirms, there is a political stake involved in keeping women's sexuality tightly under control as the filthy illusions of a certain contained group of loose women. "Woman" is produced, in the brothel and in society at large, as the result of a continuing social imperative that is both interminably renegotiated and structurally anachronous. Usigli succeeds, then, in matching the critique of the national project to the figure of the transgressive woman, but his critique of the social institutions are, to use his own language, Janus-faced.

In contrast to Usigli's work, Rosario Castellanos's broad-stroke drama, *El eterno femenino* [The eternal feminine], does not propose a critique of the national project as such but focuses more directly on gender-inflected social institutions as the target of her satire. She leaves individual material bodies out of her play as much as possible, and rather than focusing on sexuality, she concentrates on exploring the constructedness of gender relations that necessarily leads to inequality and repression. In this respect, Carl Good is quite correct in his characterization of the play as "una instancia particular del umbral afectivo de la enunciación" [a particular instance of the affective threshold of enunciation] that confronts the twinned limits of linguistic expression and silence (Good 1995, 62, 71). Castellanos describes her work as a farce, and in her stage directions she indicates that "se trata de un texto no de caracteres sino de situaciones" [it deals with a text not of characters but rather of situations] (Castellanos

[1975] 1992, 21). Among these "situations" she includes such prominent and mythologized historical figures as La Malinche, Sor Juana Inés de la Cruz, Empress Carlota, Josefa Ortiz de Domínguez, and Adelita alongside stereotypical images of the housewife, the hairdresser, the prostitute, and the maid. Each of these images is deployed to enter into dialogue with "Lupita" and, in the series of vignettes that make up the play, to further her process of coming to a political and social consciousness about women's status in Mexican society.

For the purposes of this book, the episodes that most interest us are Castellanos's description of Lupita's transformation into a prostitute by way of a wig named "Flor de Fango" [Flower of the Mire] (145) and her depiction of Lupita's encounter with the life of an ordinary streetwalker. Castellanos strips the tattered illusions from stories like Usigli's and describes her stereotyped street prostitute as shaped by the hard realities of violence and territorialism and as disguising her fear with a bravura performance covering fear and an impulse to flee. And yet, at each point in the discussion, the menacing reality is described with a slightly different metaphor, each drawn from and ultimately pointing toward an elite worldview. This is true irrespective of whether the language used is drawn from warfare, from business, or from descriptions of stereotypical male-female relations.

The neophyte prostitute of Castellanos's vignette is immediately exposed to the dangers of the streets. The first person who approaches her is a pimp, whose unsubtle threat reminds her that there is no more independence on the streets than there is in the homes of decent society:

> Cinturita: ¿Cómo se le ocurren tamañas imprudencias? Andar a deshoras de la noche y por estos rumbos...Cualquiera puede equivocarse y tomarla por lo que usted no es.
> Lupita: Pero *sí* soy. Tengo mi licencia de Salubridad y todo....
> Cinturita: Las mujeres, como usted sabe por experiencia, no deben de andar solas, sino siempre bajo mano de un hombre. Y usted ¿para qué se va a meter entre las patas de los caballos cuando aquí tiene a su mero mero papachón? (146–47)

> [Cinturita: How can you be so imprudent? Wandering around late at night and in this neighborhood...Anyone could make a mistake and take you for someone you're not.
> Lupita: But I *am*. I have my permit from the Health Bureau and everything....
> Cinturita: Women, as you know by experience, should not wander around alone, but should always be under a man's hand. And

you, why are you going to throw yourself under the horses' hooves when right here in front of you is your very own big daddy?]

Violence, then — implicit or actual, his or the client's or that of the police — becomes the foundation for the contract between the pimp and the prostitute and is inherent in the conventional paradigm described by Castellanos. As soon as the man projects his fantasy onto the woman ("She looks like a whore . . ."), that fantasy (whorishness) is presumed to define her character, and she becomes a violable object: the "mistake" that Cinturita menacingly talks about. When Lupita identifies herself as a woman of the streets, Cinturita changes tactics, appealing to the dominant class's unwritten law that all women belong under the command of a man; again, however, Cinturita threatens violence if she insists upon loosing herself from this natural order.

The second street encounter is also defined by violence. Another prostitute, hidden in the shadows during the exchange with Cinturita, comes forward to defend her territory. To Lupita's challenge, "La calle es de todos" [The street belongs to everyone], the more experienced prostitute rejoins, "Te equivocas, chiquita. La calle es de quien la trabaja" [You're wrong, little girl. The street belongs to the person who works it], and she attacks the neophyte in defense of her turf (148). The experienced prostitute in this exchange lays out a complicated unseen geography of opaque territoriality and invisible influences — what Cinturita defines in terms appropriate to a battlefield:

Fíjese bien: la calle está dividida por áreas de influencia. En cada área hay un grupo de trabajadoras. . . . Se trata, desde luego, de unidades móviles; pueden avanzar, retroceder, inclinarse hacia un flanco o hacia el otro, de acuerdo con las necesidades tácticas. Por lo que no pueden hacer nunca, bajo ninguna circunstancia, es invadir el área de influencia ajena. (150)

[Listen carefully: the street is divided into zones of influence. In each area there is a group of workers. . . . They are, of course, mobile entities; they can advance, retreat, lean toward one flank or another according to tactical necessity. But what they can never do, under any circumstances, is to invade a neighboring zone of influence.]

Superimposed on the city is an invisible grid of a marginal territoriality, dividing the city first of all into decent and marginalized zones; in this grid, the "zones of tolerance" represent the space where all repressed and prohibited desires are separated from the body politic and cast out.

These zones of tolerance are then reterritorialized, reclassified, and controlled from within. Using Cold War terminology, Castellanos configures the shifting zones of influence and fluid relationships among marginal peoples.

Besides the language of warfare, and the language of masculinist assumptions about women's place, Castellanos also evokes a third rhetorical structure to define this marginalized geography: that of a "business" (a word that she sometimes leaves in English and sometimes uses in Spanish) complete with its manual and its regulations for the smooth working of the company. In the play the exchange using the vocabulary of warfare is followed by another in which the pimp evokes terminology drawn from the marketplace: "the product," "the competition," "the boss" (152–53). Selling oneself, says the older prostitute, is a better job than some because "se cobra por adelantado" [you get paid in advance] (156). Lupita, too, participates in this discussion, defining herself slyly — with reference to Mexico's stereotypical inferiority complex about its industrial products when compared to those of the United States and Europe — as "no estoy tan mal para ser del país" [not too bad considering I'm a national product] (152).

Finally, Castellanos's Lupita, like Usigli's Janus-faced women, learns that to succeed in her new business she needs to become a fictionalizer. When, after a negotiated resolution to their initial conflict, the more experienced prostitute takes on the role of mentor to Lupita, she asks the younger woman why she became involved in this type of work. Lupita answers carelessly that she enjoys having sex, so why not get paid for it? The older woman immediately advises her: "¡shhh, cállate! eso no se dice...porque desanimas a la clientela. El cliente...es un enemigo. Y lo que le gusta es pensar que te está chingando. Que eres una infeliz, tan infeliz que ni siquiera te das cuenta de si él es muy macho o no. Tan desdichada que, aunque sea un desdichado cabrón, seas tú la que provoque lástima, no él" [Shh, shut up! you don't say such things...because they discourage the clientele. The client...is an enemy. And what he likes is to think he's screwing you over. That you are wretched, so wretched that you don't even realize if he's a real macho or not. So miserable that, even though he is a miserable son of a bitch, you're the pitiful one, not him] (155). Castellanos's prostitute is consistent with Usigli's madam in that both characters describe their primary function in the client-prostitute exchange as that of masking themselves as the physical manifestation of male needs and fantasies, fantasies that then are used by dominant society to define both what the prostitute *is* and how she behaves: that is, whorishly, duplicitously. Castellanos's sarcastic lesson from the experienced prostitute to the neophyte is consistent with Amy Kaminsky's

observation based on her reading of Argentine texts about literary prostitutes: "[P]rostitution is more about humiliation and submission than it
is about sex" (Kaminsky 1984, 130). The prostitute invents a pathetic
front to exploit men, while at the same time she uses her client-tailored
performance to underline and — because it is based on a recognized fiction — implicitly to undercut machista [hypermasculinist] representations
of male sexual superiority. Still further: this bolstering of men's fantasies
about themselves can only function in a state of sexual inequality and
implicit violence. While both the inequality and the violence are real, the
valued result slips away since the prostitute's body, no matter how objectively real, disappears behind the illusion that creates her as a symbolic
object. The man pays to abject another; the woman performs abjection.
Each pole of the transaction is loosely defined by a dynamic of needs
and desires fueled with fiction-effects at the heart of the commercial and
sexual exchange.

This aspect of Castellanos's and Usigli's plays epitomizes an ill-defined
area of literature that I call, borrowing the term from Mexican *cronista*
José Joaquín Blanco, *la novela de la transa*.[8] The *transa* [sting or con
operation] is, as Blanco notes, also a *trenza* [a weaving together] of disparate elements of society, with the common ground of a *supervivencia
ilusionada* [an illusionary survival] based on the con-artist's confidence in
his own cleverness. Unlike the U.S. model of the confidence game, the
Mexican *transa* is less focused on the individual doing the manipulating,
more on the action as transaction between two individuals, each of whom
knows that a *transa* is taking place, each of whom thinks he (it is usually
a "he") has the advantage. *Transa,* then, eventually involves *autotransa.* It
is a quintessentially urban phenomenon powered by an awareness of desires ignored/disguised by the bourgeoisie. If Usigli emphasizes the social
quality of the transaction in the encounter between the libertine and the
virgin-whore, Castellanos focuses more specifically on the nature of the
sexual transaction.

Deeply problematized in the rereading of the sexually transgressive
woman's poetic topography is the role of the reader or viewing public. The audience's gaze upon these public/private literary spectacles is
hypothetically voyeuristic, but the issue becomes more complicated because the circuit of exchange involves a recognition of the audience as
voyeur looking upon a primal scene of narcissistic self-contemplation
that is, nevertheless, a staged scene, meant to be overlooked. In the
archetypal economy, the man (lover, writer, critic) reads (seduces/is seduced by, writes, interprets) woman (the prostitute, the work of art,
the text). But what happens when the audience is a female reader? Is
the text unreadable? Does the reader automatically reposition herself as

a transvestite? Is the female reader a "she" posing as a "he" posing as a "she"?

While the figure of the prostitute offers a particularly powerful and coherent example of the workings of this image of the transgressive woman, it is not — as I noted above — the only available figure of a powerfully sexualized woman, and attention limited to the figure of the fictional prostitute would oversimplify the slippery and sliding scale of Mexican cultural confrontations with problematic female transgression of dominant-culture boundaries. This book discusses the figure of the sexualized woman in texts that to my mind demonstrate some of the most significant and dramatic instances of the myth as well as some of the most cogent challenges to it. In this respect, this book offers itself as a modest contribution to a historical/sociological debate as well as to the literary-critical exploration of an important discursive trope that has served as an elided intersection of much social and literary commentary. Chapter 2 studies Federico Gamboa's turn-of-the-century novel about a Mexico City brothel and that brothel's star resident, the eponymously named Santa. This novel calls attention to a rhetorical structure in which an abstractly imaged female sexuality serves as a distorting lens on so-cial interaction and in which these social codes have a specific impact on aesthetic practices. The novel is filled with representations of mod-ern mechanized production. Of these images, the meat shop becomes the most persistently repeated metaphor for the brothel, and the butchered animal foreshadows Santa's fate at the novel's end. The brothel is the central metaphor of female consumption, but since other industrial-age institutions also function in a similar manner, Gamboa's social critique is extended to a critique of modern dehumanized industrial practices. It is, furthermore, in Gamboa's repeated evocation of the meat shop that his aesthetic aims begin to merge with the novel's implicit and explicit ideological agendas.

Both of the authors studied in the third chapter, Juan Rulfo and Elena Garro, cede narrative point of view to a sexually transgressive woman. By this technique, the prostitute becomes not only the object of narrative but the agent for narrative self-reflexivity. Thus, in these two fictions, the fallen woman creates herself in what she tells, and in what she withholds, of the story of herself, and the narratives likewise demonstrate or call into question the social and political conditions of textual production in the interstices of her story or her silence. They are, then, in some sense textual heirs to the novel examined in chapter 2 and can be adequately read only in relation to a literary history involving Gamboa's appropria-tion and construction of the loose female. At the same time, they insert themselves into a literary social context that is at least contextually aware of previously existing first-person accounts and sociological studies that give voice to the prostitute, albeit in greatly mediated or textually over-determined forms. Both Rulfo and Garro, in shifting the narrative from an implicitly masculine to an explicitly feminine voice, also look at the larger implications of universalizing a female point of view.

Chapter 4 explores the loose woman's fictional representation in the bitterly conflicted cultural space of the Mexican-U.S. border. In Federico Campbell's novella set in Tijuana, *Todo lo de las focas* [Everything about seals], and Ana Castillo's novel of two border-crossing Latinas, *The Mixquiahuala Letters*, what seemed to be knowledge reveals itself as a cultural practice open to question and interpretation. In both books, the encounter between two cultures and two people opens a site of exchange and also of cultural contestation. One of the most ambiguously negotiated sites in both novels is that of female identity. In both books, the borderlands seem to bring to consciousness the most extreme variants of each culture's stereotypes about itself and about the other culture. Likewise, in both books these stereotypes are focused in and through the feminine, and specifically, through the conflicted reaction to female sexuality. In the encounter between two versions of male and female stereotypes about each other meaning is not so much lost, as subject to negotiation, as are the other products of cultural conditioning, and in such renegotiations of identity cultural constructs are both eroded and reinforced.

Chapter 5 looks at another way in which national cultural constructs are being renegotiated in its reading of contemporary best-selling author Sara Sefchovich. According to this successful writer and critic, her own success and that of other contemporary Mexican women writers point to a very important change in the audience for narrative. Whereas earlier Mexican best-sellers (including the century's first major best-seller, *Santa*) tended to be not only male-authored but also implicitly aimed at a male audience, modern Mexican best-sellers are more likely to be woman-authored and aimed at an audience of women, especially those leisured middle-class women who are now assumed to make up the bulk of book buyers in the country. Sales figures indicate not only that these women read prodigiously but that they overwhelmingly read works by other middle-class women in which women have positive protagonic roles. Even more interestingly, works like Sefchovich's and those of her colleagues who make it to Mexican best-sellerdom tend to highlight images of women who freely express their sexuality and who are not castigated for their adventurous love lives. National allegory, it seems, is giving way in these best-sellers to meditations on sexual politics, at least in what sells to the eager Mexican audience. And yet in my reading of Sefchovich's work, I conclude that in rejecting certain aspects of the dominant male tradition, both female readers and writers find themselves ambiguously still formed within the structures of thought inherited from these rejected models.

All of these works have established the tradition within which or against which recent first-person memoirs/*testimonios* by those women defined by their transgressive sexuality have been published, including the works that I study in chapter 6: Antonia Mora's *Del oficio* [The life]; Irma Serrano's *A calzón amarrado* [Knotted panties], *Sin pelos en la lengua* [Telling it straight], and *Una loca en la polaca* [Spoke in the wheel]; and Eduardo Muñuzuri's *Memorias de "La Bandida"* [Memoirs of La Bandida]. The two stories — that of the loose woman and that about her — fit together like jigsaw puzzle pieces. These first-person works suggest further the degree to which the middle- to upper-class bias of the narrative voice in traditional works needs to be rethought and reconfigured in the context of an urban, increasingly industrialized society, one disaffected by and disillusioned with the Mexican Revolution.

Indeed, the very concept of a *testimonio* by such a woman is theoretically fraught with contradiction. The linchpin of testimonial narrative for Western readers is its absolute reliability. By definition, the sexualized woman, and particularly the prostitute, cannot testify. The loose woman who writes is in the same double bind as the prostitute who speaks of her past. She points toward her life but without license to discuss it, without the reader having to openly acknowledge her or accept her testimony as part of the socially real. She is, by convention, an unacceptable witness to her own reality, since she cannot be counted upon to see the difference between truth and falsehood. Nevertheless, the women in these books have discovered another method of trading on their own use-value; when the loose woman/writer brings her textual goods to market, she literalizes the established metaphor about her and eliminates the middleman. There is, then, at the level of publication and book sales, an overlapping of projects at the same time as the mechanism of exchange is exploited and reversed to allow a formerly silent non-subject to speak.

In each of these chapters, in each of these texts, the loose woman is the textual fulcrum; whether as agent or object, she organizes the scene of narrative. What makes her a particularly interesting narrative force is that in the social as well as the literary imaginary, the transgressive woman is always already characterized disjunctively as both a social and a literary threat. Whatever attenuated or real autonomy she possesses, she owes to her abilities as a storyteller, thus creating in the literary text or the *testimonio* a paradoxical effect of hyperdetermined falseness matched to a gritty verisimilitude.

While portrayals of prostitutes are prevalent in every literary tradition with which I am familiar, in the Mexican context there seems to be a particular valence given to the presence of the sexually transgressive woman in a text and an especially charged discussion around this literarily constructed figure. In addition, as women writers become ever-more popular in Mexico, a specific politics of containment and a moralizing theoretical structure are subtly and discreetly mobilized to resist the slippage from a male to a female readership, from male to female popular writers, from serious to frivolous literary topics, from *mujeres fáciles de leer* [easy women to read] to *mujeres fáciles* [easy women]. The well-publicized 1992 debate between the journals *Macropolis* (special issue: *Por una literatura fácil* [Toward an easy literature]) and *Vuelta* (special issue: *Defensa de la literatura difícil* [Defense of difficult literature]) was staged to a large extent upon precisely such moralizing grounds. Oddly enough, the literary debates about easy women (to read) tend to be couched in terms that recall strictures against sexually easy women; and yet literary metaphors and social practice diverge considerably. Easy women writers and literarily constructed easy women participate in a debate that alludes to what could presumably be imagined as real women active in prostitution, but the literary debates do so without taking cognizance of those women's actual situations, in some sense reifying the typical response to prostitutes so often noted in the literature — that is, a bourgeois disgust that manifests itself in a simultaneous reaction of temptation and terror.

These maneuverings for position in a shifting literary market seem to me to reproduce extremely stereotyped gender positions in only slightly disguised terms. To point up this correspondence, it helps to step outside the literary debates briefly in order to look at them from another angle. Here, for instance, is Oscar Lewis summarizing his research from the 1950s in the highland village of Azteca (Tepoztlán) in the state of Morelos:

> It is believed that women have less *naturaleza* — that is, that they are sexually weaker than men. Husbands do not expect their wives to be sexually demanding or passionate, nor do they consider these traits desirable in a wife. Women who "need" men are referred to as *loca* [crazy] and are thought to be in an abnormal condition which may have been brought about by black magic....
>
> Aztecans believe that wives who suffered beatings or other harsh treatment may take revenge through sorcery....The most feared type of sorcery is a potion made from a well-known herb called *toloache*, secretly dropped into a man's coffee or other drink....In Azteca it is...believed that it will make a man *tonto*....The most

important symptom to Aztecans is that the drugged man can no longer control his wife but is dominated by her. The man's mother or sister may attempt to cure him by secretly putting a counterpotion into his coffee. (Lewis 1964, 499–500)

While Lewis's field research materials now seem dated, and have been subjected to extreme pressure by the anthropological establishment, I find the text itself exceptionally interesting. I have the sense in reading some of the attacks on popular women writers in Mexico that their male counterparts implicitly appeal to a shared sense of proper literary/gender roles involving, on the one hand, an understanding of a man's *naturaleza* similar to that depicted in Lewis and, on the other hand, a similar repugnance toward evidence of abnormal or crazy women's needs. Perhaps they fear the effects of a collective metaphorical dose of *toloache*, turning the readers and reviewers and writers into *tontos*, dominated by *locas*, with no counterpotion in sight.

One of the frustrations for me in writing this book is that I as a critic am inevitably returned to what I can now only see as a consolidation of stereotypes. Alternative constructions of femininity — whether authored by women or men of whatever class background — resolve into verbal evocations projected against this preexisting backdrop. Resistance is as marketable as adherence to the norm, and it remains to be seen if Mexican easy women writers' contestations of dominant imagery will translate into meaningful oppositional politics or, more radically, into more than a symbolic resource in the reconfiguration of knowledge structures and gender identities. In my hopeful moods, I like to believe that — to give an example — Serrano's slippery testifyin' practice suggests the potential for a way out of this impasse, for the conversion of theater into politics and into such reconfigurations of identity.

# Chapter 2

# Meat Shop Memories

## GAMBOA

Gritty verisimilitude evoked and elided is at the heart of Federico Gamboa's perennially popular novel, *Santa*. Critics and historians coincide in pointing out the importance of loose women to Mexico's developing sense of a national identity. Brothels were an important gathering place for the Mexican elite during the presidency of Porfirio Díaz at the beginning of the century, and the concept of *la venta del placer* [selling pleasure] remains, as Carlos Monsiváis notes, one of the central tenets of a sophisticated Mexican erotic system, a tenet that clearly applies exclusively to the male half of the population: "[L]a noción *placer*... no puede provenir del Hogar Sólido donde aguarda la Mujer Legítima, lo establecido no genera *placer*. . . . La noción *placer* ha implicado comercio, ilegitimidad, abandono temporal de los sentidos y aventura" [The idea of *pleasure*... does not derive from a Happy Home where the Legitimate Wife awaits; the establishment does not generate *pleasure*. . . . The idea of *pleasure* has implied commerce, illegitimacy, the temporary abandonment of the senses, and adventure] (Monsiváis 1977, 303). Monsiváis reminds us that in 1904, Mexico City had 368,000 inhabitants and 10,937 *registered* prostitutes — common sense and the testimonials of the period remind us that in addition to the women officially registered with the Ministry of Health, there were many unregistered prostitutes as well as unfortunate women such as servants who were often forced into occasional prostitution (Lara y Prado 1908, 19–29). At the same time, and as a point of comparison, Paris, with a population five times greater than that of Mexico City, had a population of about 4,000 registered prostitutes (Monsiváis 1977, 66; Macías 1982, 13). A minimal control over this vast population was instituted through the Ministry of Health registry and through the establishment of "red zones" where prostitution could be legally practiced in a reclusive setting that would not offend decent society. A turn-of-the-century legal code required that

37

[n]o se establecerá burdel alguno en casa de vecindad, ni a distancia menor de cincuenta metros de los establecimientos de instrucción o beneficencia y templos de cualquier culto. No tendrán los burdeles señal alguna exterior que indique lo que son.

Los balcones o ventanas de dichas casas, tendrán apagados los cristales, y habrá, además, cortinas exteriores. Tendrán también un cancel en el cubo del zaguán, dispuesto de modo que no se vea desde la calle el interior del burdel.

En los burdeles sólo habrá mujeres de la clase a que pertenezcan aquéllos, quedando terminantemente prohibido admitir las de clase diversa. (quoted in Monsiváis 1977, 67)

[No brothel may be established in a communal dwelling, nor at a distance less than fifty meters from educational or charitable establishments, nor churches of any sect.

The balconies and windows of such houses will have closed windows and exterior curtains. They will have an entrance from the front yard, placed so that one cannot see the interior of the brothel from the street.

In the brothels there will only be women of the class to which they (the clients) belong, and it remains totally prohibited to admit women of other classes.]

Echoes of the Porfirian code remain in current state law (as distinct from the federal constitution), for although brothels are illegal in modern Mexico, prostitution per se is not, and several states and communities have elaborate codes to establish legal "red zones."

Unsurprisingly, in this context Federico Gamboa's 1903 novel, *Santa,* about a turn-of-the-century brothel and its star resident, is Mexico's perennial best-seller. Permanently in print both in cheap paperback and in expensive leather-bound editions, it was the first novel chosen for mass-market promotion in supermarkets. It spawned a host of imitations, created a minor tourist industry of readers avid to visit Santa's "birthplace" and her "tomb," inspired popular songs (most famously, Agustín Lara's "Aventurera," "Santa," and "Mujer"), and served as the basis for dramatical skits, burlesques, parodies, and several feature films, including Mexico's first talking picture — a movie that one critic considers so bad that it is "mysteriously lacking in the poetry that time tends to attach to even the worst of films" (Emilio García Riera, quoted in C. J. Mora 1989, 35). Salvador Elizondo attributes *Santa*'s phenomenal success to the "peculiar condition" of Mexican psyches that divides Mexican women into good mothers and bad whores and drives men in terror from their mothers into the arms of the prostitute (quoted in C. J. Mora 1989, 35–36). For José Joaquín Blanco, Gamboa's novel is emblematic of many other similar cultural products: "La sociedad y la cultura mexicanas le deben mucho a la prostitución. No sólo la canción, el cine y la novela están hechos en gran medida, explícita y veladamente, a partir de las prostitutas y en trato con ellas" [Mexican society and culture owe a great deal to prostitution. Our music, cinema, and fiction derive to a large extent, either explicitly or covertly, from prostitutes and dealings with them] (Blanco 1988, 68).[1] In another of his books, Blanco discusses more fully the demonization, eroticization, and appropriation of such *apetecibles cuerpos de la miseria* [delectable bodies of misery]: "Entre más desamparada, más erótica. . . . Así, dentro de una jerarquía social de grados de victimización, la esposa asume los honorables (abnegaciones, docilidades, renunciaciones, etcétera), y las otras víctimas sexuales los deshonrosos" [The more helpless she is, the more erotic she becomes. . . . Thus, within the social hierarchy of degrees of victimization, the wife assumes the honorable aspects (abnegation, docility, renunciation, etc.), while the other sexual victims take on the dishonorable aspects] (Blanco 1981, 72).

Finally, Carlos Monsiváis argues that while women have generally remained absent from any analysis of Mexican culture, "Woman" exists powerfully as an abstraction; that is to say, only the abstract Woman is powerful, and Woman is powerful only insofar as she remains abstract. One of the few exceptions Monsiváis finds to this conjugation of femininity with power, absence, and abstraction is the prostitute, and she is exceptional only by displacement. Monsiváis writes: "[L]a puta le recuerda a quien no lo es que a ella también se la define por su sexualidad: mujer, solterona, lesbiana, quedada, y le recuerda que la mayoría de las mujeres dependen de los hombres para la sobrevivencia social y que la mayoría, de un modo u otro, aseguran su sobrevivencia a cambio de la comodidad demandada por los hombres" [The whore reminds the woman who is not one that she too is defined by her sexuality: woman, old maid, lesbian, leftover, and reminds her as well that the majority of women depend upon men for social survival and that the majority, in one way or another, assure their survival in exchange for a commodity men demand] (Monsiváis 1980, 108–9). But if the unmarried nonprostitute represents a purity in excess (in excess since not in demand), it does not follow that the prostitute refers to or represents an excessive sexuality. Representations of the prostitute specifically elide her sexuality, making it abstractly present by displacement onto her body, but all the more hyperdetermined and false because of this displacement: "[E]n la literatura o en el cine o en la canción popular la figura de la prostituta significó la posibilidad de referencias implícitas al sexo sin necesidad de representarlo, discutirlo o aceptarlo. Del porfiriato a la década de los cincuenta, la prostituta no es la presencia sino a alusión indirecta al sexo" [In literature or film or popular song the figure of the prostitute signified the possibility of implicit references to sex without the necessity of representing it, discussing it, or accepting it. From the time of Porfirio Díaz to the 1950s the prostitute is not the presence but the indirect allusion to sex] (Monsiváis 1980, 110). Monsiváis concludes: "En suma, la prostituta será aquella que se comporta como si fuera prostituta y que, por lo mismo, delata con gestos" [To sum up: the prostitute is whoever acts as if she were a prostitute, and thus gives herself away with gestures] (111). At issue, then, is not the woman's sexuality, or her participation in sexual activity, but a gestural economy potentially making any woman available for male interpretation under the sign of prostitution.

All three of these authors — Elizondo, Blanco, and Monsiváis — hint at a complicity between the fascination with prostitution and the victimization of women in general. They all signal the doubling of women into virtuous mothers and wicked whores, and all point to the ineluctable and ineradicable link between the two fantasized images of women, although Monsiváis also adds reference to the unmarried woman who is neither wife nor whore. For Elizondo, curiously, it is the victimized woman who paradoxically victimizes her victimizer. Prostitutes reaffirm a masculinity placed into doubt by the monumentally powerful passivity of the self-sacrificing mother-saint. The logic of the argument follows that of the famously developed discussion of Mexican character in Paz's classic *El laberinto de la soledad* [Labyrinth of solitude]; the woman that can be possessed lays herself open to degradation and in practice ought to be defiled by any self-respecting machista. Thus, the sainted mother by definition — so goes the theory — must remain exempt from possession, and yet for that very reason she poses a threat to her son's (or her husband's) sexuality. The prostitute, then, serves as a defensive countersite or as a socially approved outlet for surplus male repression.

Blanco's text additionally suggests that Mexican men tend to eroticize weakness and victimization in a general sense, intimating that at some level a mother's presumed abnegation and a prostitute's imagined sexual ferment are equivalent, or at least parallel, erotic structures and that, furthermore, these erotic structures are perpetuated through literary and cultural markets that find them valuable aesthetic currency for maintaining social hierarchies. What Blanco calls attention to, thus, is not an inadvertently revealed truth about Mexican character but a rhetorical structure in which an abstractly imaged female sexuality serves as a distorting lens on social interaction. Finally, Monsiváis moves this discussion specifically into the realm of the intersection between social codes and aesthetic practices.

The pages that follow will explore the aesthetic exploitation of the image of the prostitute in Gamboa's *Santa* and will investigate the concept of female sexuality operative in that book in relation to a rhetorical/ideological construction of the loose/lost woman. Certainly, the ubiquity of the prostitute in modern Mexican letters and culture, as well as the continuing fascination exercised by works like *Santa*, suggests a fantasmic investment far in excess of the admittedly extensive social phenomenon. Primarily, though, I want to argue that Gamboa's novel, while clearly and unmistakably the cultural product of a late nineteenth-century/early twentieth-century masculinist aesthetic, can also be read against the grain in order (1) to be made to reveal how the workings of the Porfirian gestural economy define and displace sexuality onto an aesthetic representation that later takes on its own increasingly solid afterlife, and (2) to help to uncover and to begin a discussion about the deeply disturbing links between poverty and the fantasized erotic object.

Like many European novels with which it has often been compared (Zola's *Nana*, Flaubert's *Madame Bovary*, Tolstoy's *Anna Karenina*) and the literary representations of prostitutes the author himself evokes in his prologue (Manon Lescaut, Marguerite Gauthier), *Santa*/Santa provides an irresistible combination of vaguely illicit titillation and upstanding moral values, ending with a shocking dramatization of the wages of sin. This novel is — no matter how influenced by European, and particularly French, models — clearly a cultural product of the Mexico that came into being in the twentieth century with the increasing urbanization following upon Porfirio Díaz's rise to power. Santa is not a prostitute with a heart of gold (as is Marguerite Gauthier), nor a vicious schemer who drags men down into her degenerate depths (Nana), nor a self-deceived dreamer (Emma Bovary). Trapped between bad luck and her own vile nature, she more closely represents the potential for perversion in any attractive natural order. In this world, people and landscapes mirror and reflect each other. The values and morals espoused in *Santa*'s idealized countryside stand in strict contradiction to those common among urban peoples.

Gamboa describes the rural setting that gives birth to Santa as a paradise populated with poor but honest folk who work the idyllic Mother Earth that gives freely of her fruits to her pure and loving children. The eponymous heroine's story, writes Gamboa, is "la historia vulgar de las muchachas pobres que nacen en el campo y en el campo se crían, entre brisas y flores; ignorantes, castas y fuertes; al cuidado de la tierra, nuestra eterna madre cariñosa; con amistades aladas, de pájaros libres de verdad, y con ilusiones tan puras, dentro de sus duros pechos de zagalas" [a com-

mon story of poor girls who are born in the countryside and who are
brought up ignorant, chaste, and strong in the countryside among breezes
and flowers, in the care of the earth, our eternal loving mother, with the
winged friendships of truly free birds and with pure illusions in their
hard maidenly breasts] (Gamboa [1903] 1989, 35). This idealized landscape contains no lecherous landowners/masters to take advantage of the
innocent young women. All the corruption comes from outside this pastoral setting, first in the form of the factory that brings industrialization
and vice to the farming community and then with the military barracks
that contributes lustful young men. Santa's downfall comes at the hands
of one of these outsiders, a soldier who seduces her, gets her pregnant,
and abandons her to her fate. Upon Santa's fall from grace, her link with
the innocent countryside is irremediably severed. She is forced into the
perils of the metropolis, where she serves as an emblematic reminder of
the fundamentally alienating forces of urban life and where, stripped of
illusions, she struggles to adapt to an increasingly experienced, unchaste,
and weak life among corrupted teachers and false friends.

At the same time that Gamboa sets up an opposition of rural versus urban, pure versus corrupted, and innocence versus vile education, he
also expounds upon the fatal flaw in Santa's nature that inevitably leads
her to the brothel. Santa is the weed that must be extirpated from the
carefully tended garden of her Mother Earth. Once her seduction by the
young army officer is accomplished and Santa's family ejects her from
her childhood home, her fall into prostitution is precipitous. Gamboa
concludes piously, "[P]or lo pronto que se connaturalizó con su nuevo
y degradante estado, es de presumir que en la sangre llevara gérmenes de
muy vieja lascivia de algún tatarabuelo que en ella resucitaba con vicios
y todo. Rápida fué su aclimatación, con lo que á claras se prueba que la
chica no era nacida para lo honrado y derecho" [By the ease with which
she came to accept her new and degrading state, it must be presumed
that she carried in her blood the ancient germs of lasciviousness from
some great-grandfather that she resuscitated in herself with all his vices.
Her acclimation was so fast that it clearly proved that the young woman
was not born to be honorable or correct] (75).[2] Santa's fall, thus, is both
tragic and inevitable; it is a story of seduction and of natural propensities. Gamboa wants his readers to see that she belongs to the city, to
the French-style brothel with its macabre mother-substitute, Elvira, and
not to the innocent home of her self-sacrificing mother and responsible
brothers in the countryside.

Yet, as Blanco so acutely notes, at least to some degree the eroticizing
of the *cuerpos de miseria* [bodies of misery] operates across the board —
Gamboa's evident seduction by his own prose descriptions of the lushly

ripe feminine countryside is a case in point — and not just in the depraved sections of the wicked city. There is no story in innocence, only an unwritten pre-text. Beautiful flowers and spiritually uplifting birds remind the author naturally (if oh so subtly) of the attractions of hard, young breasts. Santa's physical beauty, combined with the challenge of her untouched chastity and her inborn sensuality, makes her an obvious target for the depraved lust of the young soldier as well as the presumably compassionate fascination of the voyeur-reader. The reader can either see or ignore this erotic landscape and its youthful embodiment, but his own virtuous nature goes unquestioned in the coy peekaboo of the text. Because Santa's fall from chastity involves an inborn genetic flaw, the reader, like the soldier, has a perfect alibi: the woman got what she was looking for; if not at the soldier's hands now, then at another's soon. And so the reader/soldier is absolved of guilt, and the erotic responsibility shifts back solely to the culpable young woman.

Not the least of this novel's titillations is the manner in which Gamboa cannily does not quite make the eroticized identification among all the key images of femininity. The juxtaposition — and near overlap — of virtue and vice is one of this titillating novel's more slyly seductive features. Santa shares her humble home in Chimalistac with her saintly mother and her two hardworking, virtuous brothers, and Gamboa tells us that Santa shares a bed with her mother in a simple room with two pictures for decoration: la Virgen de la Soledad and la Virgen de Guadalupe, doubled portraits of the chaste and pure mother-queen of the heavens, to inspire the prayers of the saintly mother and her innocent daughter. Gamboa juxtaposes these holy images with other, more worldly ones. Brothers Esteban and Fabián also have their walls decorated — with "una infinidad de pequeñas estampas de celebridades: bailarinas, cirqueras, bellezas de profesión, toda la galería de retratos con que obsequia á sus compradores la fábrica de cigarrillos" [an infinity of small images of celebrities: dancers, circus performers, professional beauties, a whole gallery of the portraits that the cigarette factory gives to the buyers of its products] (38). It hardly needs mentioning that such early twentieth-century tobacco-product beauties were not celebrated for their beautiful souls or blameless lives and that the brothers' unforgiving outrage at Santa's fall may have some connection to their own less-than-chaste contemplation of their interior decorations. Santa, of course, lives out the promise of these juxtaposed walls; she slips from *reina de la casa* [queen of the house] (49) to *reina de la entera ciudad corrompida* [queen of the entire corrupt city] (123), from aspirant to holy maternity to celebrated professional beauty, until she becomes a fabricated product, a cipher of displaced erotic longings: her clients', first of all, but also those of her author-sculptor and those of the reading public. Still further: while Gamboa does not comment explicitly on this feature, the fierce Catholicism of many prostitutes has been much noted by other culture critics, as has many prostitutes' tendency to feature reproductions of la Virgen de Guadalupe in their rooms and to set up altars honoring her (see Monsiváis 1980, 111).

In this juxtaposition of paintings, and in the brothers' wholly typical reaction to Santa's fall, Gamboa offers a concise representation of the double standard that operates in Mexico's patriarchal heterosexist model. This model says, briefly: (1) all women are objects, either of veneration or of erotic imagination; (2) all women are potential prostitutes except the Virgin Mary and one's own mother; and (3) in an unstable gestural economy focusing on representations of one sort and another, any man can be excused for any mistaken attribution, and any woman is responsible for the consequences. Of course, in order for this model to work, one's own mother, like the Virgin Mary, must retain a forever inviolate virginity in thought and action; the sexualized mother is erotic fair game. Unsurprisingly, Gamboa makes Santa's mother a widow, thus deflecting any potential conflict or unease.

The import of Santa's transformation from an object of innocent aesthetic appreciation to a vulgarly usable body moves in two distinct directions. She is reinvented, first, as an aesthetic object, eroticized in the traditional sense as the seductive work of art that becomes *Santa;* second, she is re-created as a deaestheticized commodity, a common whore, a member of the perversely eroticized underclass described by Blanco:

> La civilización burguesa se excita precisamente con lo que reprime legalmente; sueña con lo que ella misma prohibe y alimenta su erotismo con los hechos, las imágenes y los actos que previamente demoniza y persigue institucionalmente....Y es toda una posesión, un acto de apropiación, hacer a, o dejarse hacer por un jodido; nunca hacer *con él*...El burgués nunca copula con nadie, más que consigo mismo. (Blanco 1981, 71, 73)

> [The bourgeois civilization finds exciting precisely what it legally represses: it dreams about what it itself prohibits and feeds its eroticism with the stories, the images, and the acts that it has previously demonized and that it persecutes institutionally....And it is entirely an act of possession, an act of appropriation; (the bourgeois gentleman does) it to (someone else) or lets a poor shit do it to him; (he) never makes it *with* (another)....The bourgeois gentleman never copulates with anyone but himself.]

Blanco's point is well taken. Whether as an aesthetic object or as a commodity, Santa becomes precisely that demonized and alienated figure of repression that allows her client, her author, and her (male) reader an intimate relationship with himself. She is, first of all and above all, an object, even to herself. Santa is that made-over (fucked-up) body described by Blanco. She is a beautiful female object and therefore guilty of attracting the attention of weak and vicious men. The men use her and display their possession of her in an ongoing distasteful game of one-upmanship with one another; her value to them is her perceived value to other men. This aestheto-erotic bias reveals not only the heterosexist bias of fantasized/real underworld interactions but also the extremely limited repertoire of political positionings that define ethics, erotics, and subjectivity as implicitly masculine traits.

*Santa* begins with a dedication to Jesús F. Contreras, *escultor* [sculptor], and a prologue in the supposed voice of the heroine in which she proposes an exchange with the artist: her "clay" — her story — for his molding ability: "Barro fuí y barro soy.... Me cuelo en tu taller, con la esperanza de que compadecido de mí me palpes y registres.... Acógeme tú y resucítame ¿qué te cuesta?...¿No has acogido tanto barro y en él infundido no has alcanzado que lo aplaudan y lo admiren?" [I was clay and I am clay.... I hang around in your workshop in the hope that, taking pity on me, you feel me and notice me.... Pick me up and bring me back to life. What does it cost you?... Haven't you picked up so much clay already, and with the products haven't you achieved admiration and applause?] (n.p.). Santa, at the pinnacle of her success as Mexico City's premier sexual object, was applauded and admired; the prologue anticipates the further transformation of the sexual object into an aesthetic one, so that she (or her creator) can continue to enjoy a success now measured in aesthetic rather than economic terms. One of the aspects that I find extremely interesting in this fictional exchange between the artist and his model is that both "Santa" and "F. G." share an understanding of the woman's role — in life, as in art — as that of commodified spectacle. Thus, while Santa may make a plea for the artist to uncover her human heart, she uses the same language as that employed by the customers and the police who abused her body (*palpar* and *registrar*) — she is in effect asking him to "feel her up" and "shake her down." Likewise, the uncovering of her heart takes the form of shaping and covering the artist's mold with her substance, the "barro pestilente y miserable que ensucia, rueda, lo pisotean y se deshace" [miserable, stinking clay that dirties you, rolls under foot, gets stepped on, and falls apart] (128). Thus, on the one hand, Santa's plea resonates with pathos while, on the other, it reminds us of the vocabulary of oppression. Her savior is her present client and ultimate pimp, shaping her now-disembodied clay for the equally displaced and disembodied delectation of her new public. Furthermore, while the author/artist, "F. G.," can separate himself from his aesthetic property — the sculpture that wins him applause, the best-selling novel — Santa, the woman and the artist's clay, has no recourse but to bring herself to market. She is the commodity, not the producer of a separable eroto-artistic object.

The artist's response to the prostitute is, finally, as Blanco intimates, to appropriate her for a self-conscious manipulation of aesthetic categories, whereas the woman's capacity extends no further than the attenuated agency that permits her to say, "Take me, I'm yours." And yet while Santa's voice fades into the background except for rare conversational exchanges in the body of the novel, it is her voice opening the text that grants authority to the writer and, in traditional narrative fashion, establishes the spurious authenticity of the pseudobiography. The novel, *Santa,* then offers a bipartite body: the prostitute's posthumous last testament and the biographer/artist's creative resuscitation. She speaks to him; he speaks of her. As Amanda Anderson says in another context, "The distortions involved in depicted encounters with prostitutes, and in the rhetoric of fallenness more broadly conceived, derive precisely from the abstraction out of any potentially dialogical relation to the other" (A. Anderson 1991, 116–17). It is an observation very much in accord with Blanco's recognition of the preeminence of the bourgeois subject. She is; he imagines. Her immoral ugliness becomes his moral tale; her falseness, his aesthetic truth. Her filth is transmogrified in his art. There is, however, no dialogue with her, but only the displacement of her into the continuity between the artist and his created object.

Yet there is another sort of implicit dialogue established by the novel. *Santa*/Santa is the conduit by which "F. G." establishes a dialogue, not with the prostitute, but with his readers/himself, in what José Joaquín Blanco, following Gore Vidal, would call an onanist relation to society that brings together the polity with property, propriety, power, politics, and aesthetic norms (see Blanco 1981, 73). The appropriation of Santa as an artistic property and the reshaping of her tale in accord with F. G.'s sense of aesthetic requirements and the demands of propriety force the author to choose a path of discreet titillation that reads in a definitely dated manner to a contemporary audience. That tightly constructed dialogue is based on a shared understanding of social norms and a shared delight in transgressing them delicately. For instance, Gamboa never allowed the vile word for Santa's profession to pass onto his pristine pages. A contemporary dialogue with this complicitous author/reader tends to give such tactful considerations short shrift and uncovers the appropriative gesture the delicate transgression carefully eludes. I quote Margo Glantz:

> Esta popularidad [de la novela] es tan ambigua, como la caracteri- zación de Santa, de quien dice su autor: "Santa no era mujer, no; era una..." Y con estos puntos suspensivos calla la palabra "nefanda," haciendo de la prostituta un ser equívoco; ni mujer ni palabra pronunciada, la puta como animal marginado, aunque público; fe- menino, aunque negado a la feminidad, terreste apenas: un cuerpo solamente. (Glantz 1983, 42)

> [This popularity (of the novel) is as ambiguous as the characteriza- tion of Santa, of whom the author says: "Santa was not a woman, no; she was a..." And with this ellipsis he conceals the "nefarious" word, turning the prostitute into an equivocal being, neither woman nor pronounced word; the whore as a marginal, although public, animal; as feminine, although denied femininity; barely terrestrial, solely body.]

Curiously, the most insistent quality of this uniquely corporeal non- woman, this immoral animal, her physicality, is the most elusive as well. For while Santa "comercia con sus partes 'pudendas,'...esas partes pudendas permanecen intocadas por el lenguaje narrativo" [conducts busi- ness with her "immodest" bodily parts,...those immodest organs remain untouched by narrative language] (Glantz 1983, 43). Gamboa fragments his sentences and fragments the body of Santa in one and the same equiv- ocal gesture; the author's and the character's assumption of im/modesty occupy the same narrative space. The peekaboo flirtations of this well- understood im/proper dialogue both generate and mediate the text's repressed eroticism.

At the same time, for the modern feminist reader, Gamboa's teasing el- lipses, his punctilious equivocations, and his turning away from dialogue with the other keep the space open for what we might call the feminine "equivoice" (the word comes from Cixous 1980, 252) that counters the oppressive "equivocations" of patriarchal discourse. Certainly Glantz's in- telligent and sometimes sarcastic voice stands in dialogue with another kind of reader entirely different from that sculpted in Gamboa's appeal. For while the artistic agency of the novel belongs to the male, the objects created in the novel, both male and female, exhibit similar characteristics of being overpowered and made passive by a system over which they have lost control. The commodification of women through prostitution pro- vides the opening into the text, but it is, as we shall see later, only one of the forms of modern human commodification, to which the other great social institutions — notably schools and factories — contribute equally. In reaction to such a perversely repressive society, the aesthetic impulse itself is reconstituted as a feminine "equivoice." Rita Felski writes: "[I]n the social imaginary, the aesthetic became increasingly feminized in relation to the 'objectivity' and 'rationality' of a scientific worldview. Both art and women could be seen as decorative, functionless, linked to the world of appearance and illusion and divorced from the work ethic and the reality principle" (Felski 1991, 1098). Thus, while one reading of *Santa* would see the novel as an example of the working out of a worldview shaped by commodity aesthetics, another reading would argue for the insurgence of the equivoice in the interstices and ellipses of the text, an equivoice that blurs accepted valences of authenticity and value. Gamboa does not speak for, but against, the bourgeois appropriation he describes and solicits.

In this respect, then, Gamboa operates out of a carefully defined and circumscribed marginality that decries the moral emptiness of the scientific worldview and propounds the superiority of an aesthetic reshaping of reality. And, in fact, he works against the grain of his own dominant discourse in order to establish the artistic equivoice. Gamboa chooses as his protagonist one of the most equivocal figures in society, a frequent symbol of inauthenticity and moral corruption, and plays even more with the interstices of truth and falsity by having the prostitute, an official nonbeing, give her authenticating imprimatur to the still nonexistent work posthumously. It is partly this equivocally represented concern with the play of authenticity and inauthenticity that distances the modern writer from his Victorian counterpart, that distinguishes Gamboa from the nineteenth-century European novelists with whom he is often compared. The Victorian era, Lionel Trilling reminds us, was filled to bursting with such moralizing speeches as that which opens Gamboa's novel — discourses on Beauty, Truth, Immortality, and so on. Trilling, like Glantz, would find such effusions excessive but rather ironically touching, and the more so "because we will not fail to perceive the inauthenticity in which it issues: the very hollowness of the affirmation attests to the need it was intended to satisfy." Trilling concludes:

> We of our time do not share that need of the Victorians. We are not under the necessity of discovering in the order of the universe, in the ineluctable duty it silently lays upon us, the validation of such personal coherence and purposiveness as we claim for ourselves. We do not ask those questions which would suggest that the validation is indeed there, needing only to be discovered; to us they seem merely factitious. (Trilling 1971, 118)

Gamboa's equivoice stands in tentative agreement — for he puts the moralizing discourse into the mouth of an unacceptable speaker: not an eminent scholar or priest or artist (despite the framing of the text with the reference to the sculptor), but a lowly prostitute, the woman given (albeit penitently) the first voice in the text.

The result of this modernizing gesture, as Trilling would tell us, is a kind of moral appeal for an authentic stance, which stance varies positionally, as it is created through a cultural assent that does not necessarily involve either credence or commitment on the part of the authenticating body. What moral weight, then, and what social responsibility accrue to the validation of the authentic and the usable as criteria over the purely (purely?) aesthetic? And what is the cost? Here Trilling is instructive once again. He reminds us of the violence explicit in the etymology of the word "authentic": "*Authenteo:* to have full power over; also to commit a murder. *Authentes:* not only a master and a doer, but also a perpetrator, a murderer, even a self-murderer, a suicide" (131). Authenticity, individual or communal, carries with it a certain tainted charge of an inherent, if repressed, violence.

Thus Santa, in her very inauthenticity, in the elliptic unreadability of her profession, in the violence done her, serves as a marker for other reprehensible social practices that deny representability and authenticity to other social subjects/objects. Alongside the image of a loving earth, bringing forth her gifts to her grateful children, Gamboa offers the counterimage of a violent rape. "¿Queríais América?" [You're looking for America?], asks one of his characters, "pues ¡hala! a los campos, ahí en la tierra que há menester de fatigas y sudores, de hombres que la violen y la fecunden; preñadla de trabajo y ella os parirá cosechas y cosechas que carezcan de fin" [well, it's there in the countryside, there in the earth that demands fatigue and sweat from men who will violate and fecundate her, who will impregnate her with their work, and she will give birth to harvest and more harvests without end] (191). The dialogue fragment characterizes the speaker's brutality, but it also echoes and contrasts with the narrator's more aestheticized perception. The violence of this second, later description of the relationship of human beings and the land effectively deauthenticates the narrator's earlier idealistic version of a pastoral Mexican landscape and the people who work in the countryside. It is a point graphically underlined with reference to the central, authenticating image in the novel.

Only a few pages after this misanthropic exchange about man and the earth, the narrator describes Santa, found under the covers in the early morning, as the embodiment of just such a sensual, rapable landscape, implicitly linking the corrupted young woman with the demythified al-

legorical figure of a violated America: "[S]u anca soberbia señalándose
á modo de montaña principal,... las negras crenchas rebeldes, cayendo
por sábanas y espaldas, como encrespada catarata; en seguida, un hombro,
redondo, como montaña menos alta; luego la anca, enhiesta y convexa,
formando grutas enanas con los pliegues... por final, la cordillera humana
y deliciosa" [Her regal rear showed itself as the highest mountain,... the
rebellious black curls, falling over sheets and her back, like a curvy water-
fall; next, a round shoulder, like a smaller mountain; then the upstanding,
convex buttocks, forming miniature grottos in their folds,... and finally,
the delicious human mountain range] (208). The interchangeability of
women and landscape as metaphors for each other suggests not only an
aesthetic project but also an economic and social dynamic based on the
passivity of women/land and their accessibility to domination and exploitation. And while there is a disjunction between the two versions
of the Virgin Land/Violated America, the novel universalizes the gaze,
implicitly male, as the exploiting agent and value-constructing subject
with reference to both objects of sensual and economic appropriation.
Importantly, however, in universalizing the male gaze, Gamboa also
disembodies the male, leaving in the text only empty landscapes, un-
populated by men. Once again, in the conversation between men, the
disagreement opens the way for another voice.

A parallel fragmentation of aesthetics and ethics occurs in Gamboa's description of the neighborhood school. Gamboa suggestively (and,
in terms of the Porfirian code, illegally) places the school next to the
brothel — "también tiene, frente por frente del jardín que oculta los
prostíbulos, una escuela municipal, para niños" [exactly on the other side
of the park that hides the brothels (there is) a government school for
children] (4) — and while he ostensibly sets up a contrast between them,
the very juxtaposition of the two hints that the courses of study followed
in the two institutions are less dissimilar than they may appear at first
glance.[3] Thus, the madam of the brothel in which Santa finds refuge
begins the new woman's orientation to the life of a prostitute with "un
catecismo completo; un manual perfeccionado y truhanesco de la prostituta moderna y de casa elegante" [a complete catechism; a perfect, roguish
manual about the modern prostitute and the elegant brothel]. The narrator underlines the similarity of this orientation to a class lecture: "Sus
recomendaciones, mandatos y consejos, casi no resultaban inmorales de
puro desnudos; antes los envolvía en una llaneza y una naturalidad tales
que, al escucharla, tomaríasela más bien por austera institutriz inglesa"
[Her recommendations, demands, and advice almost did not seem immoral they were so naked. She wrapped them up in such a natural
straightforwardness that, in listening to her, one would take her more eas-

ily for an austere English governess] (18). Gamboa is, of course, playing upon the popular tradition that employs the word *pupilas* for the inmates of a brothel, but the specific comparison of the horrible Elvira to an English governess underlines the connection already established by the proximity of the elementary school and the brothel in the opening pages of the novel.

In the larger context of the neighborhood, the school and the brothel are two of a series of similarly described buildings, all of which have the goal of fragmenting and mechanizing human beings. Santa's arrival at the door of the brothel is accompanied by a rhythmic sequence of dehumanizing sounds, abstracted from their human producers:

> Del taller de los monumentos sepulcrales, de las cobrerías italianas y de "La Giralda" salían, alternados, los golpes de cincel contra mármol y contra el granito; los martillazos acompasados en el cobre de cazos y peroles; y el eco del hacha de los carniceros que unas veces caía encima de animales muertos, y encima de la piedra de tajo, otras.... Los transeuentes... cerníanse fragmentos errabundos de voces infantiles, repasando el silabario con monótono sonsonete:
> — B-a, ba; b-e, be; b-i, bi; b-o, bo... (5)

> [From the tombstone workshop, from the Italian copper-working shops, and from the "Giralda" factory alternated the sounds of the chisel against marble and against granite, the rhythmic hammerings in copper pots and bowls, the echoes of the butchers' axes that sometimes fell on dead animals, and on the sharpening stone, and other times... The passersby... could distinguish wandering fragments of children's voices, repeating syllables in a singsong monotone:
> — B-a, ba; b-e, be; b-i, bi; b-o, bo...]

The chisels, hammers, axes, and monotone voices mark off the time of industrialized production. Santa's arrival at the brothel door coincides exactly with the noon bell, releasing children and factory workers into the streets, sending her into her new profession. Once inside the brothel, her own minimal instruction complete, she too will become integrated into the mechanized rhythms of the neighborhood, into the dehumanization already evident in the fragmentation of bodies into implements of work, of voices into isolated nonsense syllables. Their monotonous repetition of exactly duplicable actions will become for her the monotonous repetition of confusingly equivalent bodies. The brothel, then, is an emblematic presence, but not an isolated one, and the perversion reigning there extends to other institutions and other levels of society traditionally considered remote from its contamination. Gamboa explores the interplay between the ceaseless functioning of such mechanical forces and the concrete solidity of the institutions that house them. Such attention to the machine requires as well examination of the individual inextricably bound into the infernal functioning; in Foucault's words, "it is not that the beautiful totality of the individual is amputated, repressed, altered by our social order, it is rather that the individual is carefully fabricated in it, according to a whole technique of forces as bodies" (Foucault 1977, 217). Santa, the schoolchildren, and the factory workers are, perforce, carefully fabricated in and by their respective institutional compulsions as the endless hammerings, chiselings, disembodied syllables, and pseudoerotic couplings fabricate the society in which they are compelled to live.

Gamboa reinforces this analogy throughout the text, and many of the most successful passages of the novel capture in the repetition of the prose a sense of the dulling repetition operative in the lives of these city-dwellers. The laundry's noon steam-whistle punctuates the text, signaling moments in which all the school and factory rhythms will be interrupted and the bodies will spill out onto the streets; some of the bodies will also find their way to Elvira's brothel, where the bawdy house pupils take over the shift work. "Los serios, y los viciosos, de bracero, enderezaban sus pasos . . . á las vinaterías y cantinas baratas, á los figones; los serios, á sus distantes hogares humildes: serios y viciosos, lentos, fatigados, fatigados del día, de la semana y del mes, fatigados de los años y fatigados de su vida" [The serious men and the vice-ridden ones, the day laborers, straightened out their steps . . . on their way to the wine shops and the cheap bars, on their way to the chophouses; the serious ones went to their far-away humble homes. The serious men and the vice-ridden ones, slow, tired, tired of the day, of the week, of the month, tired of the years, and tired of their lives] (153).[4] The cumulative effect of this passage lies in the narrator's repetition of "serios y viciosos," the insistence upon their state of fatigue, the ticking off of their lives in exhausting, and exhaustingly similar, days, nights, and years. It is lulling, monotonous, terrifying. In another section of the novel, Gamboa uses a more graphic, but analogous, metaphor of industrialization's effect on human beings when he says of the tobacco factory that it lulls the workers to sleep "á modo de gigantesco vampiro, les chupa la libertad y la salud" [like a gigantic vampire who sucks their freedom and their health] (51). The workers are not only lulled into monotony; they are lulled into death.

Of all the various representations of modern mechanized production, however, it is the meat shop that becomes the most persistently repeated metaphor for the brothel, the butchered animal foreshadowing Santa's fate. It is, furthermore, in Gamboa's repeated evocation of the meat shop that his aesthetic aims begin to merge with the novel's implicit and explicit ideological agendas. The brothel is the central metaphor of the consumption of the female, but other industrial-age institutions also function in a similar manner. The workers devolve into *bestias humanas* [human beasts] consumed by the factory, which becomes the *monstruo insaciable y cruel, devoradora de obreros* [insatiable and cruel monster, the devourer of workers] (52). The equation established between human beings and meat for consumption is the most insistent metaphor in the book, and the self is not only commodified but commodified for cannibalistic consumption in very specific ways. In her seminal article on Gamboa's novel, Margo Glantz analyzes this juxtaposition with admirable clarity and concision:

> El pudor con que Gamboa destaza el cuerpo de Santa para venderlo en el prostíbulo por donde desfila toda la ciudad concupiscente, acaba por convertirse en la esencia del libro y definir una mecánica del poder. Sólo cortándola en pedazos la carne de reses puede ser vendida, aunque antes se la exhiba en grandes garfios que se ostentan por su belleza y sanidad. Cuando la carne se corta, el cuerpo se fragmenta y el de Santa deja de ser cuerpo humano desde el momento mismo en que a Santa la ha reducido a una negación, a un epíteto sugerido por puntos suspendidos a una frase que elude la "palabra nefanda" o a una fragmentación de descripción que destaza el discurso. Santa no es mujer, es un cuerpo destazado. (Glantz 1983, 45)

> [The decorum with which Gamboa parcels out Santa's body to sell it in the brothel through which the whole concupiscent city parades, ends up becoming the essence of the book and the defining feature of its mechanics of power. Only by cutting cattle into hunks of beef can meat be sold, although prior to chopping it up it is displayed on great hooks to show off its health and beauty. When the meat is cut up, the body fragments. Santa's body has lost its humanity from the very moment in which Santa has been reduced to a negation, to an epithet suggested in the ellipses of a phrase that avoids the "nefarious word," or to the descriptive fragmentation that chops up the discourse. Santa is not a woman; she is a parceled-out body.]

Santa is stripped bare and stripped apart by the author's originating negation. This negativity, then, generates the meat metaphor operative in the rest of the text. She becomes the piece of meat, stripped to the bone by her hungry predators. To this admirable analysis, I would add only that the dissection of Santa begins not with the negation of her womanly essence ("no era mujer, no; era una . . . ") but much earlier in the text, in the prologue to the novel proper, with Santa's plea to the artist to take up and reshape her clay. The identification, then, is at least triple: body/meat/work of art. Gamboa in this manner merges the aesthetic aims of the artist with the mundane task of a butcher and with the exploitative efforts of the madam, the work of art with a hunk of trimmed meat or a trained prostitute, the artist's workshop with the butcher's meat market or the elegant brothel, the reading public with the hungry consumer or the prostitute's client. At each step, the overlaying images comment upon each other, suggesting pointed critiques of aesthetic criteria, social forms, ideological positions, and economic realities. Once again, the blurring of these categories forms part of the larger critique of those contemporary authenticating structures that have been increasingly reformulated (as the artist might say) by the devouring (as the butcher might say) logic of commodity aesthetics.

The progressive dehumanization of the workers puts the prostitute ever more in demand. Because she becomes for them nothing more than a fragmented body, a piece of meat, she restores the bodies to her clients in the same way that the artist restores her body to its imminent textuality. The workers dream of freedom and humanity that have been sucked away by factory life; they carry this emptiness into the brothel, where they pay to impose their freedom against another's body. As Blanco says in another context, the sexual encounter can be read as the expansion of an attenuated body over another body that is symbolically, at least, more fully endowed with flesh. Furthermore, sexual violence can be interpreted as an *asalto a la* propiedad *del cuerpo ajeno* [assault against the *propriety* (property) of the alien body] (Blanco 1988, 125), where the double meaning of *propiedad* as "property" and as "propriety" is very much to the point. The author/audience as well partakes in this carnal festival on another level; disembodied by the text, the reader/artist/author takes on reality in the act of devouring the body/flesh/text of *Santa*/Santa. Blanco continues, "La tradicional fascinación de los burgueses (que son 'menos cuerpo,' pues realizan su personalidad sobre todo en extensiones materiales o simbólicas de propiedad, familia, capital, Estado, comercio, religión, etcétera) por los cuerpos de miseria, reside en que, en efecto, estos cuerpos son la Gran Interpretación Carnal sin mediaciones" [The traditional fascination of the bourgeoisie (who are "less body" because they fulfill their personalities above all in the material or symbolic extensions of property, family, capital, State, commerce, religion, etc.) with the bodies of misery rests in that, in effect, these bodies are the unmediated Great Carnal Interpretation]

(126). What Blanco does not say, but which is perhaps implied in his text, is that any disembodied gaze, any construction of the prostitute as devourable object of consumption, will complete the unmediated carnal interpretation only in an illusory sense. The fetishization of the *cuerpo de miseria* and its consumption as pure object only and ultimately reinforce the consumer's abstraction. The objectification, after all, occurs in metaphor and in an observing subject's interpretation and not in a mutually constructed compact about reality, or even representation.

In *Santa*, abstract/aestheticized hunger is sidetracked in the ellipses of the text; the carnal interpretation — the unmediated encounter of body with body — increasingly metamorphoses itself in the meat shop metaphor. Hunger, then, is never satiated and in the novel leads only to greater and more perverse hungers. The male population of the city "se precipitaba sobre la carne sana de las rameras de refresco, que, igual á manadas de reses, vienen de todas partes á abastecer los prostíbulos, los mataderos insaciables" [throws itself upon the healthy meat of the replacement whores who, like herds of cattle, come from everywhere to fill up the brothels, those insatiable slaughterhouses] (350–51); the women are *ganado sumiso* [submissive cattle] (280). Elvira uses a version of the metaphor when she reminds her new pupil that the clients demand that "hemos de quererlos como apetecen" [we have to love them according to their tastes]. At the same time, she adds, the prostitutes "sabemos muy distinto, picamos, en ocasiones hasta envenenamos, y ellas [las esposas] no, ellas saben igual todos los días" [taste very different; we're spicy, sometimes poisonous, and the wives aren't. They taste the same every day] (19). Santa, like her fellow prostitutes, is consumed by this metaphorically cannibalistic passion: "[U]n enfermero que la miraba, la miraba como con ganas de comérsela" [A nurse that stared at her, stared as if he wanted to eat her] (14); another client "ardía en deseos de morder aquella fruta tan en sazón" [burned with the desire to bite that lushly ripe fruit] (54); still another says, "[S]i . . . no te como á muchos bocados para saborearte á mis anchas . . . [mañana] te voy á devorar" [If . . . I don't chew you up in many little bites so as to fully savor your taste, . . . tomorrow I'll devour you] (207). A young man "mostraba afilados colmillos y un apetito insaciable. Cómo mordía ¡canijo! cómo mordía y cómo devoraba . . . a lo natural, con glotonería de diez y seis años, deliciosamente!" [showed his sharp eyeteeth and his insatiable appetite. How he bit! The little runt! How he bit me and how he devoured me . . . naturally, with his sixteen-year-old gluttony, how deliciously!] (310). Hipolito, the blind lover, kisses Santa "con glotonería de can hambreado que hurta carne exquisita" [with the gluttony of a starving dog that steals an exquisite piece of meat] (347).

Santa's predisposition to prostitution impels her to participate in her own self-consumption: "[M]ás que sensual apetito, parecía una ansia de estrujar, destruir y enfermar esa carne sabrosa y picante que no se rehusaba ni defendía" [more than a sensual appetite, it seemed to her a need to tear apart, to destroy, and to sicken that tasty and spicy meat that neither defended itself nor rejected them] (73). As Elvira knows well, time "en cortísimo tiempo devoraría aquella hermosura y aquella carne joven" [will shortly devour that beauty and that young meat] (6), and as she begins her fall, Santa is no longer "manjar de dioses" [dish for the gods] (147). Thus, Gamboa establishes the relation between food and sex at key moments throughout his text and hints that this cultural equation derives from the encroachment of Porfirian industrialization and consumer capitalism, which sucks life from factory workers, which fragments the voices of children in schools, and which turns human relationships into metaphorically cannibalistic carnal exchanges. In this manner, as carnal desires become identified with food pornography, so too the production of meatstuffs and the consumption of food become fraught with hints of taboo. Not only is the brothel a butcher shop, where the madam dresses the meat for her clients' tastes, where nothing is left too long on the hook, and where spoiled meat is thrown out, but at the same time, the meat shop becomes sexually charged, so that the joints hanging in the back rooms of the slaughterhouse, buzzing with flies, offer a comment on the neighboring establishment. This reciprocity of concupiscence reproduces itself at every level.

The murder trial that Gamboa reproduces in this novel provides the reader specific food for thought on his/her own role as cannibal-voyeur in relation to this text. Gamboa first describes the circumstances surrounding the murder in the brothel, and the murder itself, in precise and minute detail (252–59) for the delectation of his readers. He then follows with a repetition of the story, this time for the consumption of judge, jurors, and a deliciously scandalized public. As the narrator tells us, "[E]l delito era de los que por derecho propio despiertan en las hipocresías sociales afán inmoderado de conocerlos aun en sus detalles más repugnantes y asquerosos" [The crime was one that by its very nature awakens in the social hypocrites an immoderate desire to find out about all its most repugnant and repulsive details] (262), displacing in this manner concupiscent desires onto the hypocritical members of the listening audience within the text and discreetly bypassing reference to identical passions aroused in the reading public, which has savored this twice-told tale directly first and then mediated by the reaction of the jury. The narrator clarifies the connection between the story and meat, food and sex, hypocrisy and perverse consumption, when Santa takes the stand: "Habituada Santa á despertar apetitos, y aun á provocarlos, nada hizo en esta vez, ni siquiera realzar sus encantos, que más de uno de los que la devoraban tenía saboreados" [Although Santa was accustomed to waking up appetites, and even provoking them, she did nothing on this occasion, not even primping to bring out her enchantments, which more than one of those who devoured her with their eyes had already tasted] (277). In repeating the story of the murder in the brothel, Gamboa emphasizes that this episode, more than any other, represents an overdetermined moment in the novel. With this incident, both aesthetic and erotic realms involve specular excess, for not only is there an implicit parallel between the butcher shop and the brothel, but with the murder and its reenactment literal as well as metaphorical butchery takes place.

By his own hand, the murderer becomes the agent of making (of a corpse) and unmaking (of a human being); the prostitute in court stands in the privileged position of the knower (of the truth) and the knower of the bodies (both men were regulars in the brothel). Importantly, the acts that create both these figures — murder, prostitution — tremble on the edge of the unspeakable, and the perpetrators become inseparable from the act that identifies them. The nonsignifyingness of the two transgressors of the accepted moral code increases their fascination; they are what they do, and their knowledge is acquired through violence. And in Gamboa's book, where unspeakable acts are often cut out of the text in a kind of literary butchery, these figures' most crucial signifying gesture, despite the dramatic telling and retelling of events, is made unreadable (or at least illegible) as well. Unsurprisingly in this context, Santa's testimony has no legal weight. The court disregards her words and focuses only on the gestures she makes and declines to make, on the scandal of her transgressive bodily presence in a legal setting.

Standing behind these two treacherous figures, both overdetermined and insignificant, is the equally overdetermined and insignificant figure of the author/sculptor. Like the murderer and the prostitute, the artist is also a figure of knowing and making, of unknowing (not telling) and unmaking (at least insofar as he ends the novel with the butchery of his protagonist). Like them, his making and knowing involve the manipulation of bodies — the narrator figures himself as a sculptor who shapes clay into a living artistic creation — rather than the manipulation of abstract thoughts. This authorial handiwork, the physical product of reading and writing, dominates in the trial scene, with its superimposed layers of oral and written testimony, recorded response, and hypocritical underpinnings. The author and the reader share a privileged knowledge over the trial scene, a complicity resting on their shared recall of the previous telling of the story, a tale that is, in turn, marked by pregnant ellipses and deco-

rous silences all too easily filled in the reader's imagination. The author/
reader pairing knows more than it tells; during the trial the prostitutes
tell what they know, but the story that is heard is not the story of the
men's conflict but the tale of what is known or assumed to be known
about the women — their other story, though told in the text, becomes
a legal ellipsis.

The written word-sculptor's clay impinges upon the novel in other important moments as well, frequently associated with other ellipses — the
author's text-butchery. His ellipses, of course, are filled with meaning, albeit a meaning that the "proper" reader will pretend not to know. Santa's
knowledge, however, spills out of her in the presence of the unspoken,
magic word defining her role, and that knowledge becomes meaningless,
an extratextual ellipsis. At times, that ellipsis serves as a commentary on
the shadowy and infrequently evoked figure of Santa's virtuous counterpart, the wife. Thus, for example, Santa's degenerate lover, Rubio, "vació
en su querida las hieles que su esposa le vertía" [emptied into his mistress the acid that his wife spilled into him] (296), and these insalubrious
ejaculations are both oral and physical.

At the same time, Rubio confirms the established perception of the
insignificance of Santa's court testimony. He is safe confiding his degen-
eracies to her because in her hands the weapon of his secrets dissolves
into nothingness. She has no legal status, no credibility, no substantiality in the eyes of the state: "No te envanezcas por los secretos que te he
confiado, porque te he dicho lo que á nadie debe decirse; no creas que
armada de ellos podrías causarme daño...tú no eres peligrosa...¡quién
ha de hacerte caso siendo una...?" [Don't start getting vain about the
secrets I have confided in you, although I have told you things that
should not be said to anyone. Don't think that armed with them you
can cause me harm.... You're not dangerous.... Who would pay any attention to a...?]. Implicitly, what he tells Santa is equivalent to being
untold, unless it is overheard by the author/reader and charged with
meaning through his agency. She is no one at all, a walking ellipsis. At
the same time, Santa's body accepts his poison, and his unspoken word
takes on substance as a weapon to wound her: "La palabra horrible, la
afrenta, revolteaba por los aires. En los muebles, en las paredes, en las
lámparas, en la comida, en todas partes Santa veíala escrita y sin tarta-
mudeos la leía: la maldición, las cuatro letras implacables" [The terrible
word, the affront, twisted in the air. Santa saw it written everywhere —
on the furniture, on the walls, on the lamps, in the food, in everything —
she saw it and without stuttering she read it: the curse, the four implacable letters] (296). Written and unwritten at the same time, the four
implacable letters take on an almost physical presence — and yet they re-

main unspoken, unwritten, in the body of the novel. Likewise, and at the same time, Santa is nothing but her body and no-body at all. She is a creation of words, but no words touch the most crucial aspect of her being.

Similar uses of elliptic word-weapons abound in *Santa*. In the first pages of the novel, Santa meets an aging prostitute, Pepa, whose grotesque body signals to the young "semivirgin" the inevitable decay of her own beauty. Pepa listens to Santa's story of violation and abandonment and, "ocupada en pasarse una esponja por el cuello y las mejillas, Pepa asentía sin formular palabra" [busy passing a sponge over her neck and cheeks, Pepa agreed without saying a word] (10). She watches dispassionately as Santa breaks down into tears: "Pepa conocía esa historia, habíala leído y releído" [Pepa knew that story; she had read and reread it]; it has been her own story, written in her own body, in the "muertos encantos" [dead enchantments] that no longer serve to attract any but the most undiscriminating clients. She knows the story as well in the coins that pay for her services, coins that she has earned "peso á peso y á costa de . . . una porción de cosas" [peso by peso and at the cost of . . . some portion of something] (11). Pepa's ellipsis is the narrator's as well, cutting short the reading/rereading of the story of her life, so similar to the story we are reading. The story Pepa reads, the story we read, and the story Santa tells and no one hears — these all contain a significant omission, or the omission of signification.

Santa's story involves other butchered tales as well. At one point in the novel, the unhappy young woman meditates: "Mi patria, hoy por hoy, es la casa de Elvira, mañana será otra ¿quién lo sabe? . . . Y yo . . . yo seré siempre una . . ." [My motherland, today, is Elvira's house. Tomorrow it will be another. Who knows? . . . And I . . . I will always be a . . . ]. At this point the narrator interrupts: "Y la palabra horrenda, el estigma, la deletreó en la ventanilla de la calandria, hacia afuera, como si escupiese algo que le hiciera daño" [And she spelled out the terrible word, the stigma, on the window of the lark's cage, aiming outside, as if to spit out something that injured her] (103). The word is not spoken, but written, and Santa's writing is not reproduced in the text. As is the case with Rubio, it is, furthermore, a nonwriting that is accompanied by a physical reaction; the writing is a spitting up, or spitting out, of a poisonous substance. And the lark, the caged bird, cannot but evoke the winged freedom of Santa's youthful, innocent life in the country; it serves as a gesture toward that lost innocence. Santa is nounless, and therefore insubstantial, but associated metaphorically with a caged bird, with a poisonous word, with unshaped clay. Fallen, false, and unreadable, she yet defines a specific kind of industrialization of violence and dismemberment.

*Santa* is a disembodied body, a purely abstract evocation of a purely corporeal presence, who exists only in the insubstantial evocation of non-words between the printed words on a page. The prostitute in this novel galvanizes and defines the category "woman," if only as a countersite, in a similar manner as the brothel, the butcher shop of the soul, defines and categorizes a contested view of culture. Says Michel Foucault, "I am interested in certain [sites] that have the curious property of being in relation with all the other sites, but in such a way as to suspect, neutralize, or invert the set of relations that they happen to designate, mirror, or reflect. These spaces, as it were, which are linked with all the others, which however contradict all the other sites, are of two main types": utopias, which have no real place, and heterotopias, among which Foucault includes brothels, which are both specific sites and nonplaces and which are "capable of juxtaposing in a single real place several spaces, several sites that are in themselves incompatible" (1986, 24–25). The brothel, then, is not just another space among the various institutionalized spaces of instruction and production; it is also a compendium of the others. Meat shop and school, factory and cemetery, the brothel is a microcosm of society and an index of all that is wrong with the other sites. Schools robotize students, factories consume laborers, farm production rapes the earth, and in the real or figurative cemetery, finally, the meat of human illusions putrefies under a stone epitaph-self.[5]

The prostitute in Gamboa's world is a slippery creature. She is a commodity posing as a person, a fungible body reimagining itself as intangible word, the execrated definition of sex unaccompanied by any account of her sexuality, the locus of an erotic wish that continually unsites itself. She produces no children and yet continually evokes the erased sign of the saintly mother. "What multiplies through her," says Catherine Gallagher in an article on *Daniel Deronda*, "is not a substance but a sign: money. Prostitution, then, like usury, is a metaphor for one of the ancient models of linguistic production: the unnatural multiplication of interchangeable signs." Furthermore, Gamboa's novel associates itself with a form of linguistic procreation that Gallagher would identify with the feminine metaphor: "According to the father metaphor, the author generates real things in the world through language; according to the whore metaphor, language proliferates itself in a process of exchange through the author" (Gallagher 1986, 41). It is a silent and unequal exchange — whore's substance for authorial voice — that provides the generating metaphor of the sculptor's task; it is another silent exchange — meat to the butcher's knife — that enables the bulk of the text. *Santa*'s author was prone to comment, in later years, that he lived off of Santa,[6] humorously playing with the metaphor of author-pimp but at the same time implicitly commenting on the superseding of a moral by a commercial economy — of writing, at least.

Gallagher's study of the British nineteenth-century novel focuses on the striking parallels between the images of the prostitute and that of the usurer. Gamboa's novel, deriving from an only partially overlapping cultural context, foretells what I call, following Blanco, *la novela de la transa*. Fiction based on a model of such marginalized and criminal transactions is of necessity acutely aware of a sphere of exchange that traces the limits between moral and commercial economies, while playing on the expectations of both.

Gamboa takes as his charge that of defining those characters most traditionally associated with the underworld side of these negotiations, but he does so from an equivocally chosen position on the bourgeois side of the social divide. Deeply problematized in the rereading of the body's poetic topography is the role of the reader or viewing public. The audience's gaze upon these public/private spectacles is hypothetically voyeuristic, but the issue becomes more complicated because the circuit of exchange involves a recognition of the audience as voyeur looking upon a primal scene of narcissistic self-contemplation that is, nevertheless, a staged scene, meant to be overlooked. Santa, after all, from the very first words of the novel, offers herself to the author and to the author's audience as a public object of display. In this archetypal economy, the man (lover, writer, critic, sculptor) reads (seduces/is seduced by, writes, interprets, molds) woman (the mistress, the work of art, the text, the statue).

Finally, as Gamboa admits, "la mujer es por sí sola la naturaleza toda, es la matriz de la vida, y por ello, la matriz de la muerte" [the woman is herself all of nature; she is the womb of life, and for that reason, the womb of death] (232). In Santa's case, the unnatural and unproductive overuse of her *matriz* leads to a "characteristic" illness — uterine cancer (348–49). Her only slight hope of survival involves another butchery, the extirpation of the uterus by hysterectomy. Implicitly, such an operation will slice out as well the hysterical proliferation of solidified poisonous words, both those spoken and those repressed under ellipses. Santa dies on the operating table, and her faithful friend, Hipolito, takes her mutilated body back to her childhood town of Chimalistac for burial. The text of the novel, likewise deprived of its *matriz*, dissolves as well. The end result, as Jann Matlock reminds us in her study of another famous novelistic prostitute, is that this woman of the lower classes, reinvented through the trappings of the bourgeoisie, reinscribes precisely those commodity values in which she is so ambiguously masked. Matlock concludes: "[S]he rallies support for bourgeois values.... Her pitiful death transforms her into a commodity to preserve family values, property values, promised wage values for men, and most of all, men's liberties" (Matlock 1994, 11). What is left after the woman has been killed off and dismembered into the novel is this tombstone, this statue, this written epitaph.

But what happens when the reader is female? However much we may read Gamboa's novel against the grain, exploring the delicate apertures to the equivocal female equivoice, theorizing about the feminization of the text, discussing the social critique that imbues the novel, *Santa* still to some degree *nos transa* [cons us]. The female body, existence, voice are all vicarious; her urges in this Great Carnal Interpretation come to us mediated by the shaping hands/voice of the sculptor/storyteller. What most clearly drops out of this discussion of the extremely sexually active female is any understanding of her sexuality. What Gamboa does in his novel is to chart the possibilities of an authority that is not entirely patriarchal nor fully authenticable and to explore the slippages in an economic system that, while ostensibly grounded in a common moral contract, nevertheless foregrounds another, superseding economic structure. Furthermore, while Gamboa's novel does not approach an understanding of female sexuality, it offers the first step toward such a discussion in that it raises the issue in a form impossible to marginalize. *Santa,* then, provides an opening for other discussions, gestures toward other conceptualizations in which the question of women's sexuality can be raised in a different way, and serves as the forerunner for other texts in which later authors can rethink and revise the manner in which female sexuality will be understood in Mexican culture and represented in Mexican fiction.

# Chapter 3

# Desire in the Streets

## RULFO, GARRO

The scandal of novels like *Santa* lies partly in their inversion of inherited narrative conventions that maintain that the proper subject for narrative involving male-female relationships is one involving honor on his side and virtue on hers. From Golden Age plays like Calderón's *El médico de su honra* to popular romances like Isaacs's *María,* feminine virtue is correlated not only with identity and inner value but also with conditions of readability and narratability themselves. Gamboa's focus on the fallen woman, though aestheticized and patronizingly distanced, still opens up new narrative possibilities. In contrast with traditional tales focusing on feminine virtue, Gamboa focuses on vice; in Peter Brooks's words, "The prostitute... stands out as the key figure and term of access to that eminently storied subworld, realm of power, magic, and danger; she exemplifies the modern narratable" (Brooks 1984, 162).

Both Juan Rulfo, in his 1940 novel fragment "Un pedazo de noche" [A piece of night], and Elena Garro, in her 1963 novel *Los recuerdos del porvenir* [Recollections of things to come], cede narrative point of view to a loose woman. By this technique, the prostitute becomes not only the object of narrative but the agent for narrative self-reflexivity. Thus, in these two fictions, the fallen woman creates herself in what she tells, and in what she withholds, of the story of herself, and the narratives likewise demonstrate or call into question the social and political conditions of textual production in the interstices of her story or her silence. They are, then, in some sense textual heirs to the novel examined in the previous chapter and can only be adequately read in relation to a literary history involving Gamboa's appropriation and construction of the transgressive woman. At the same time, they insert themselves into a literary social context that is at least contextually aware of previously existing first-person accounts and sociological studies that give voice to the sexualized female figure, albeit in greatly mediated or textually overdetermined forms.

Both Rulfo and Garro, in shifting the narrative from an implicitly masculine to an explicitly feminine voice, also look at the larger implications of universalizing a female point of view. Women, as Carlos Monsiváis reminds us polemically, do not exist in Mexican culture, and womanhood exists powerfully only as an abstraction (Monsiváis 1980, 102). Judith Butler would seem to support a similar generalization in the U.S.-European context of her work and asks, as if in response to Monsiváis's statement, what happens "when the lost and improper referent speaks":

> If "women" within political discourse can never fully describe that which it names, that is neither because the category simply refers without describing nor because "women" are the lost referent, that which "does not exist," but because the term marks a dense intersection of social relations that cannot be summarized through the terms of identity. . . . To call into question women as the privileged figure for "the lost referent," however, is precisely to recast that description as a possible signification, and to open the term as a site for a more expansive rearticulation. (Butler 1993, 218)

In Monsiváis as in Butler, to open the space for articulating "women" is also to open a space for the necessarily radical retheorizing of social relations and historical presuppositions in which social norms and gender norms are complexly interwoven. To speak "woman" is also to mark a resistant site to traditional symbolic and political orderings. We can turn to Mexican literature as one place where this ongoing process of theorization is taking place.

Rulfo's story, told from the point of view of a first-person female narrator, begins with a brief allusion to an initiation ritual, and the first two sentences of the text, in establishing the interplay of what can be told and what will be withheld from the story, set the tone for the rest of the tale. In a prefatory paragraph the narrator refers briefly and obliquely to her personal prehistory before taking up a life of prostitution and mentions obscurely the episode that ensured her rights to her bit of territory as a streetwalker: "Alguien me avisó que en el callejón de Valerio Trujano había un campo libre, pero que antes de conseguirlo tenía que dejarme 'tronar la nuez.' No quiero decir en qué consistía aquello" [Someone told me that in Valerio Trujano Street there was an open spot, but that in order to claim it I had to let them "crack my nut." I don't want to talk about what that involves] (Rulfo 1977, 143). This initiatory experience is intentionally left unexplained, apparently not out of shame, as she hastens to explain that she has no shame left, but because of a certain reticence that even the shameless need to preserve: "[H]ay algo dentro de mí que busca desbaratar los malos recuerdos" [There's something in me that wants to take apart the bad memories] (143). The experience, narratively unexplored, marks and defines the streetwalker, her sense of herself, and her relation to the two communities with which she interacts: that of her clients and that of her fellow prostitutes in the zone, who have always undergone this ritual with their common pimp, who is always referred to as "el que 'tronaba las nueces'" [the "nutcracker"] (e.g., 144).

The prostitute, says Blanco, "llega a volverse una conducta límite, casi una viñeta selvática, a veces grotesca y otras feroz, pero siempre *límite*" [becomes a limit behavior, almost a savage vignette, sometimes grotesque, sometimes fierce, but always a *limit*] (Blanco 1988, 67). She defines the limit-realities of the city, the place where life (or death) disturbs and challenges the margins of discourse. Rulfo would add that such limit-characters are also defined by limits — the limits of her territory, beyond which she must not stray without chancing retribution, the limits imposed by her pimp's requirements, the limits she imposes upon herself in both her physical and her narrative openness. These limits must condition as well our attempt to read in and about the unknowable, because unwritten (unwriteable?), spaces of her territory, both urban and narrative.

Garro's novel, even more fully than Rulfo's novel fragment, is saturated with the "scriptural" of an overtly feminized narrative,[1] and like Rulfo's short story, *Los recuerdos del porvenir* insists upon a sharply demarcated territory, a space that is both physical and linguistic, and one with clearly drawn limits. Within these narrative boundaries, the town of Ixtepec is selectively omniscient; outside the town limits is unknown territory, supplemented only by vague references to mountains, to guerrillas, to a train that arrives seemingly from nowhere bringing war and firing squads, and to the indistinguishable and indeterminate number of hanged Indians who serve as reminders of the town's borders.

Words take plastic form and range themselves against ephemeral bodies. In Ixtepec (the name means "obsidian mountain" [see R. Anderson 1980–81, 27]), language solidifies in the streets, becomes weighty, angular, cuts like a stone knife. Thus, the narrator-town, the bedrock of the real, strips away the sedimented processes of historical accretion and social custom to reveal a territory that needs to be defended. Both the narrator-town-rock and the aggression mounted against its existence frame themselves as concrete bodies. Only Juan Cariño, tellingly the only male inhabitant of the town brothel and generally dismissed as the local madman by everyone except the prostitutes (who call him "Mr. President" with real respect and recognize his brilliant potential), has the prescience to recognize this literalization of the power of language. Early in the novel, the narrator defines Cariño's self-imposed task:

> Su misión secreta era pasearse por mis calles y levantar las palabras malignas pronunciadas en el día.... Al volver a su casa se encerraba en su cuarto para reducir las palabras a letras y guardarlas otra vez en el diccionario, del cual no deberían haber salido nunca.... Todos los días buscaba las palabras ahorcar y torturar y cuando se le escapaban volvía derrotado, no cenaba y pasaba la noche en vela. Sabía que en la mañana habría colgados en las trancas de Cocula y se sentía el responsable. (Garro [1963] 1977, 59–60)

> [His secret mission was to wander through my streets and pick up the evil words spoken during the day.... Returning home, he went to his room to reduce the words to letters and preserve them once again in the dictionary, which they never should have left in the first place.... He searched every day for the words "to hang" and "to torture," and when they got away from him he arrived home in despair, did not eat, and stayed awake all night long. He knew that in the morning there would be more bodies hanging by the road to Cocula, and he felt that he was responsible. (Garro 1969, 55)]

Juan Cariño's daily search for evil words graphically reminds Garro's war-weary audience how even the most graphic language can become as abstract as the anonymous bodies on unseen trees and reminds us as well how these words, reconcretized, take on a force that motivates a rethinking of the relationship of language and being. He exposes language as a repressive surface and cuts through to the real, to that which upsets and exposes conventional, abstract arrangements of text and social relations. Furthermore, this disruption forces awareness of the imbrication of social convention, racial discrimination, and sexual inequality. Juan Cariño recognizes that at the level of the bedrock real, phrases like "Woman does not exist" (Lacan), "Society does not exist" (Zizek), and "Indians do not exist" are nothing more than legalistic fictions imposed to ward off the threatening consequences of the resistance inscribed in the concrete recognition of their existence.

At the end of the novel, Juan Cariño, defeated by the military forces that rule Ixtepec, returns to the whorehouse only to discover that he has been forgotten, given up for dead. The weighty evil words he collected optimistically in the early part of the narrative find their echo in the inscription that marks/tortures the fallen Isabel-stone at the end of the novel. The two sets of words frame the novel, marking its crucial moments of self-reflexivity, words that should never have escaped the dictionary and that now, ineradicably, shape the real.

Like Rulfo, Garro not only signals the strange shape of an embodied language but also continually foregrounds its gendered quality. In Spanish, of course, unlike English, gender marks all nouns; it is a grammatical feature that always startles new Anglophone students of the language but that remains philosophically unquestioned in their accounts of grammar. For Garro, however, the implications of gendered language are far from neutral, and the aggressive nonuniversality of her narrative voice is one of its distinguishing characteristics. The novel begins: "Aquí estoy, sentado sobre esta piedra aparente. Sólo mi memoria sabe lo que encierra. La veo y me recuerdo... vengo a encontrarme en su imagen.... Yo sólo soy memoria y la memoria que de mí se tenga" (9) [Here I sit on what looks like a stone. Only my memory knows what it holds. I see it and I remember... (and) come to find myself in its image.... I am only memory and the memory that one has of me (3)]. The embodied town, anthropomorphized and given a first-person voice, loses its masculine universality in association with its foundational stone (which, we later learn, is the metamorphosed Isabel, thus intensifying the implications of its gendered femininity). Thus, the universal and the inhuman — *el pueblo* [the people], *la piedra* [the rock] — become humanized and particular; and the gender assignations, marked and remarked, leap boundaries. The Nahuatl root of the town's name, Ixtepec, is also a rock name — obsidian, femininely gendered in Spanish: *obsidiana*. Ixtepec, the masculine "I" seated on the feminine rock, speaks of finding itself/himself in its/her image [*la imagen*] and also refers to itself/himself as *la memoria*, another femininely gendered noun. In this way Garro disturbs the transparent gendering of language and she anticipates philosophers like Monique Wittig or Jean-François Lyotard whose recent meditations on the ontology of gender have helped me to understand Garro's practice.

In his collection *The Inhuman*, Lyotard divides the first essay, "Can Thought Go On without a Body?" into two sections, one entitled "He" and the other "She," set in implicit dialogue with each other about the foundations of philosophical discourse and the possibility of philosophy beyond the end of humanity. At the end of the first section, "He" concludes: "What makes thought and body inseparable isn't just that the latter is the indispensable hardware for the former, a material prerequisite to its existence. It's that each of them is analogous to the other in its relationship with its respective (sensible, symbolic) environment: the relationship being analogical in both cases" (Lyotard 1992, 16). "She" adds to the discussion a reminder about the essential role of gender: "Sexual difference isn't just related to a body as it feels its incompleteness, but to an unconscious body or to the unconscious as body. That is, as separated from thought — even analogical thought" (21). Lyotard's dialogue is instructive, if somewhat artificial, in its assumption of a gendered philosophical dialectic. However, the debate seems incomplete; both voices are abstract simulacra of a single, "inhuman," technologically inflected stance that tends to re-reify language as a universalizing "He" supplemented with a gendered footnote.

Monique Wittig, writing before Lyotard, already provides a complementary response to the "inhuman" voice of Lyotard's "He." In her 1984 essay "The Mark of Gender," Wittig reminds us that in French (as in Spanish, and unlike English),

> Sex, under the name of gender, permeates the whole body of language and forces every locutor, if she belongs to the oppressed sex, to proclaim it in her speech, that is, to appear in language under her proper physical form and not under the abstract form, which every male locutor has unquestioned right to use. The abstract form, the general, the universal, this is what the so-called masculine gender means. (Wittig 1985, 6)

What Garro does in her novel, as Rulfo in his fragment, is to disturb this assumed universality of the masculine gender by foregrounding gender itself as a problematic social and ontological category.

Ultimately, both of these Mexican writers carefully circumscribe a specific bit of territory, a gendered space, in which to ask large questions about the nature of humanity and the implications of representation. In each work, the prostitute, or the transgressive woman, embodies the self-reflexive qualities of this textual territory; she is in this way a linguistic or symbolic construct. At the same time, in a very concrete manner she inserts her physical presence into the mediation of thought and body. Finally, both these works involve spaces that might best be defined using Foucault's term "heterotopia" — that is, they are spaces, real or imagined, that serve as what Foucault calls a "reserve of the imagination" (1986, 27) and "that have the curious property of being in relation with all other sites, but in such a way as to suspect, neutralize, or invert the set of relations that they happen to designate, mirror or reflect" (25). Not surprisingly, Foucault concludes that brothels and colonies, along with cemeteries, libraries, and ships, are illustrative types of heterotopias. My reading of these two pieces of fiction, thus, will center on an analysis of these circumscribed, heterotopic spaces and on what these extremely formal rhetorical structures have to say about the production of social selves and literary texts.

# I

For Peter Brooks, "Narratives both tell of desire — typically present some story of desire — and arouse and make use of desire as a dynamic of signification" (Brooks 1984, 37). Juan Rulfo's early text "Un pedazo de noche" [A piece of night] reflects the motivating force of this textual and extratextual desire in a particularly effective manner. The brief work is a double fragment: piece of a night and excerpt from a lost/unfinished/ destroyed novel, it begins *in medias res* and ends with an ellipsis, arousing and frustrating the reader's narrative desire for a closed and complete form. And yet in the first paragraphs, the narrator suggests that the story she is about to tell is a familiar fable of sin and redemption, framed from the distanced perspective of a reformed prostitute's wedded bliss. The intercalated story of the woman's first encounter with her future husband deals with frustrated desire of a more literal sort; a man with a child approaches a prostitute, and in a strikingly grotesque reenactment of the travails of the Holy Family, the unlikely threesome wanders through the city looking for a place to make love only to find that for them there is no room at the inn.

"Un pedazo de noche" has received very little critical attention; Juan Rulfo considered the text *muy malo* [very bad] (Rulfo 1976, 316), and critical discussions of it seem restricted to a token acknowledgment in the interest of bibliographical completeness. Such is the case, for example, in Felipe Garrido's study of *Pedro Páramo,* which mentions the fragment in the context of a critical-biographical introduction to the novel (Garrido 1982, 15). Donald K. Gordon, who speaks of the fragment at some length in his study of Rulfo's stories, apparently assumes his reader's unfamiliarity with the text and gives over a significant portion of his study to plot summary. He too damns with faint praise: "[L]e falta la maestría que demuestra en años subsecuentes; empero, posee algún mérito artístico" [While it lacks the mastery that he will demonstrate in later years, it does possess some artistic merit] (Gordon 1976, 51), and later, in his concluding paragraph, he mentions "una o dos fallas" [one or two mistakes], suggesting that "Rulfo no peca de ninguna de estas debilidades desde 1945 en adelante" [Rulfo will not commit any of these weaknesses from 1945 on] (58). Yet, despite the impression left by such generally dismissive evaluations, "Un pedazo de noche" is a disturbing and powerful narrative and deserves greater recognition than it has received.

The narrative is structured around a series of needs and demands and of unsatisfied and unsatisfiable desires that mediate "between the implacable mechanism of need and the dizzy solitude of demand" (Serge Leclaire, quoted in Wilden 1968, 143). The story opens with a narrative frame-tale, evoking "un pedazo de pared" [a piece of wall] that is a counterweight to "un pedazo de noche" [a piece of night]. The wall represents the prostitute's territory, the minimally solid backing that provides an infinitesimal degree of protection from even worse conditions: "[E]ra mucho mejor estar aquí, trabajando en chorcha, que andar derramada por las calles" [It was much better to be here, working with a group, than just spilling myself out on the streets] (143). The general meditations on her situation follow a natural, if ominous, and logical succession: she recalls her initiation into a specific prostitution ring, evokes her cruel and terrifyingly cadaverous pimp, speaks of becoming accustomed to the constant presence of fear, and mentions in this context the man she is to marry. The impressions are brief, lapidary, elliptical, and are interrupted by an appallingly commonplace event that launches the anecdote that is to dominate the text: "Una noche se me acercó un hombre. Esto no tenía importancia, pues para eso estaba yo allí. . . . Pero el que se me arrimó esa noche se distinguía de los demás en que traía un niño en brazos" [One night a man came up to me. That was not important in itself, since I was there for that reason. . . . But the guy who made a move on me that night was different from the rest in that he brought along a little kid] (144).

It is the child, that perverse Christ child, whose unexpected presence in the negotiations between the prostitute and her prospective customer provides the nexus for a preliminary examination of the multiple, frustrated structural and contextual desires. In terms of the plot strategy, the child serves as the blocking force that prevents erotic union between the prostitute (Virgin Mary) and the grave digger (Saint Joseph). "Ya ves que no se puede" [Now you see that we just can't], says the woman on being refused at the first hotel, a "no se puede" that is repeated in various forms in the story. They are rejected at the second hotel by "una voz chillona que nos gritaba que allí no era casa de cuna" [a shrill voice yelling at us that they weren't running a nursery] (145), and later, on wandering too far from her territory, a policeman warns her, "[N]o te desparrames" [Don't get out of line] (146) — effectively voicing another form of the dominant "no se puede" motif. Even the indefatigable grave digger echoes this imperative at the end of the long and unprofitable search, as in the motif of deferral "can't" becomes "couldn't": in dreams "hago de ti lo que quiero. No como ahora que, como tú ves, no hemos podido hacer nada" [I do whatever I want with you. Not like now when, as you see, we couldn't do anything] (150). Present tense becomes past, signaling a kind of frustrated closure to this narrative of unfulfilled desire. The reader is understandably relieved by this sequence of frustrations culminating in a recognition of failure; tradition requires greater decorousness in dealing with the transactions of adult desire than the grave digger is prepared to allow, and even the prematurely jaded prostitute recognizes the presence of a child as an abomination in the sordid hotels where her business is transacted.

Yet this child is no innocent — "[T]enía los ojos como de gente grande, llenos de malicia o de malas intenciones" [He had eyes like a grownup, full of malice or evil intentions] — and over the prostitute's objections to his blighting presence on a sexual encounter, the grave digger suggests that "no estaría por demás que ya se fuera instruyendo [en estas cosas]" [it wouldn't be a bad idea for him to start learning about these things] (144–45). The child, then, represents an extraordinarily disturbing and problematic force in the narrative. This much-mistreated newborn of spectacularly indifferent drunken parents fleetingly resuscitates human, maternal instincts in the young prostitute: " — Oiga — le dije, poniéndome seria — , este niño debía estar dormido en su cama. Haría bien en llevárselo. Y si la madre no le da de mamar, pues hágalo usted, aunque sea nada más por consideración" [ — Listen — I told him, getting serious — , this kid ought to be in his bed, sleeping. It would be a good idea to take him there. And if his mother doesn't nurse him, you ought do something, if only out of kindness] (147). The unattended requirements of a small child contribute a textual force that must be recognized and accounted for in the economy of this narrative field comprised of conflicting needs and desires. The portrayal of the child, provided, importantly, from the point of view of the prostitute's tale, skirts the edges of a naturalistic depiction, arousing sympathy in the reader but at the same time prohibiting sentimentalization or pity. Indeed, from the point of view of the frame given through the prostitute's present, more experienced, reflections, it is by no means certain that her momentary sympathy is well placed. Neither is it certain that the woman would still be capable of or even interested in making the effort to show this fleeting concern for another. She is, after all, very new to the streetwalker's life at the time of this encounter, and her sympathy for the child parallels her equally misplaced sympathy for the shabby grave digger, which prompts her to mistake the customer for a beggar and instinctively reach for "unos centavos" [a few cents] to offer him.

The infant is metaphorically a thing ("eso que llevas encima...envuelto como tamal" [that thing you've carried around...wrapped up like a tamale]) or an animal ("se revolvía como gusano" [he wiggled like a worm] [144–45]). As he turns and thrusts, thrusting against reality, turning toward pleasure, his incomprehensibly repulsive, wormlike, little body figures a condensation of all the story's temporal and spatial displacements into a single, restricted movement. A metonymic representation rolled and packed, "como un tamal," into a metaphorical package, this too-experienced newborn also reaches for the prostitute to satisfy his needs/demands/desires. His absent mother does not give him her breast, so when the baby is literally and symbolically handed to the prostitute, immediately "aquel niño...buscaba con su boca allí donde sabía que estaba la comida. A rasguño y rasguño fue abriéndome la blusa hasta que sus manos se agarraron a mis senos" [that kid...searched with his mouth down there where he knew food was. Scratching and scratching, he pulled my blouse open until he grabbed my breasts with his hands] (145). Shockingly, we readers tend to confuse the grasping hands of this malicious-eyed infant with those of the mature customer. The baby is guilty, born guilty, stained with the impacted canker of the original sin of a misplaced desire already charged with destructive rage.

"Un pedazo de noche" does not, however, highlight the child's story, despite the importance of the child as a metaphoric presence combining innocence and malevolence in the tale's burlesque re-creation of the iconic scene of the Bethlehem Christmas eve, for the text is presented from the point of view of the impossible mother, the Virgin Mary cum prostitute who is the mutual client of the grave digger and the infant. As a prostitute's tale of her senseless (and unprofitable!) wanderings one night, the narrative form most closely approximates that of the picaresque novel, a form strikingly, if sacrilegiously, appropriate for the demystified retelling of the Christmas tale. For if the desire of the male characters is focused on *her*, the prostitute's desire is more clearly articulated in the act of telling her story and in the parallel solicitation of the reader as her accomplice in pleasure or pain.

Significantly, the narration is both a retelling of a single paradigmatic encounter between a prostitute (narrator) and her customer (reader) and a rehearsal of thousands of other such encounters vaguely hinted at in the anterior past of the narrative substratum and projected into the unstated future life of the woman, whose grave digger husband apparently substitutes himself for the unsavory and cadaverous former pimp. Despite the self-consciously fragmentary structure of the tale, the narrator of "Un pedazo de noche" is able to provide a certain narrative completeness in this selection of one typical episode out of an autobiographical recitation that would naturally present itself as a ceaseless repetition of the same encounter, endured many times over. This impression of narrative completeness is enhanced through her use of the preterit tense, with its suggested temporal closure, a strategy borne out in her tactical decision to open her life story with a version of the picaresque hero's classic remittance to the beginning of life. "Yo estaba entonces en mis comienzos" [I was just starting out] (143), she writes in the opening paragraphs, and she ends with the tired picaresque hero's yearning to rest even if, chillingly, that rest can be achieved only in the unrepresentable final rest pursuing both her and her grave digger husband, the desired death that words cannot broach, the end of the narration and the end of the picaresque life: "[Q]uiero dormir . . . de otra manera [el esposo] acabaría por perderse entre los agujeros de una mujer desbaratada por el desgaste de los hombres" [I want to sleep . . . otherwise he'll end up losing himself in the holes of a woman torn apart by men's waste] (151). The "holes" in the woman are tellingly reproduced in the holes in her narrative. The closing ellipsis recalls the one following her interrupted prologue, and the anecdote that makes up the bulk of the story is also and only "un pedazo de noche" itself interrupted by another grammatical ellipsis. The prostitute's tragedy is concisely signaled by the ellipsis, by her inability to put a period to her narrative.

Maurice Blanchot carries the implications of the narrative yearning for closure to their extreme logical consequences when he says that "the writer [or narrator], then, is one who writes in order to be able to die [peacefully], and he is one whose power to write comes from an anticipated relationship with death" (Blanchot 1982, 93). Paz locates a sentiment akin to Blanchot's in the particularly Mexican love of form, and he suggests that this formalistic impulse can also be translated into a *nostalgia de la muerte* [nostalgia for death] (Paz 1959, 56). It is at the moment of the peaceful or nostalgically anticipated death that life ceases to be fragmentary or merely repetitive and becomes transmissible in a continuous past tense with a cleverly delimited beginning and end to the picaresque wanderings: the prostitute's tale foreshadows a nostalgia for Pedro Páramo's Comala.

Nevertheless, while the story takes as its trajectory the narrativization of a prostitute's desire, the narrator/central character is of all human beings the one most impervious to the ordinary expressions of human sexual need. Her narratable life effectively begins with the death of desire. The prostitute is a woman fragmented, *desbaratada*, whose felt need to *desbaratar* memory is coupled with an equally compelling drive to find an image from which to construct a metaphorical whole out of her meaningless wanderings and her sexual encounters void of desire. Otherwise, she realizes that she too will be irremediably lost *entre los agujeros*. It is the holes, then, the fragmentation, that describe the workings of her subjectivity, marked off in a gendered identity that becomes increasingly tenuous. Likewise, her text both offers itself to the reader-client's de-

sire and resists his reading (it is too full of holes). At the same time
the narrator-prostitute recognizes that her client is feeding on that resistance, opening new holes in signification, increasing her corporeal/
linguistic fragmentation until her unending rounds within her territory,
her limit-condition, become confused with an imminent nonexistence.

The unimaginable prefatory experience, like the equally unimaginable
anticipated closure, clearly marks the transformation of the woman into
the prostitute, into a sexual mechanism exchanged between men. The
pimp quite callously plays on this social commonplace, rigorously imposing on the women of his stable a daily quota "así una estuviera vomitando
sangre" [even if they're vomiting blood] (148), misusing the prostitute
until her feminine nature is used up, "desbaratada por el desgaste de los
hombres" [torn apart by men's waste]. Reduced to a pair of breasts at
which the infant fruitlessly pulls, a hidden sex the·grave digger cannot
rent, a largely silent physical presence that serves as a reflective mirror for
her customer's monologue, the prostitute, despite her central role as the
point-of-view character of the autobiographical tale, is an indistinct figure. Her condition is not unusual. As Paz writes, concisely formulating a
definition for the social text that underlies much of Mexican literary culture: "[L]a feminidad nunca es un fin en sí mismo, como lo es la hombría"
[Femininity is never an end in itself, unlike masculinity] (Paz 1959, 32);
thrust in the role of protagonist, the woman restricts herself to a subor-
dinate function in her own tale, creating a curious narrative aporia at the
focal point of the converging lines of desire.                    doubt

Even her name, that quintessential indicator of selfhood, remains unknown. She refers to herself marginally and reluctantly as both Olga and
Pilar and shows no preference for one name over another: "Da lo mismo
un nombre que otro. Para lo que sirve" [One name is the same as another.
For what it's worth] (146). There is in this insistent indifference a tanta-
lizing suggestion that the woman intentionally hides behind her generic
function, perversely emphasizing her lack of specific qualities, her derivative and deviant nature as a reflection of man's desire, as an image created
by and for man. It is as if she stresses her nature as a deindividualized
form without ability to reflect upon herself. Certainly, she cannot be seen
by the reader/customer except insofar as she identifies herself with the
created object she has become, turning her function into her secret meaning, imaging her prostitute's mask as her private essence. In this manner,
as Luce Irigaray says so poetically, "she may be taken, or left, unnamed,
forgotten without having been identified, 'i' — who? — will remain un-
capitalized" (Irigaray 1985, 22). She is no one, nothing, displaced desire,
an undifferentiable, indifferent intimacy.

In her nature as a penetrable object of desire who remains impenetrable to desire's need/demand for complete possession, the prostitute represents a monstrous fusion of Eros and Thanatos, of love and death, in the sexualization of mortality. Not only does she write in an anticipatory past tense, figuring her most important relationship as that she shares with death, but she is first initiated into prostitution by a pimp whose "cara seca y sus ojos sin zumo y sin pestañas y su carcaje huesudo" [dry face and eyes without moisture and without eyelashes and his bony carcass] (143) unmistakably suggest his nature as ambulatory death. Even more tellingly, in the story proper, she chooses (or is chosen by) another customer-pimp-husband who also metaphorically embodies death's very figure, the grave digger Claudio Marcos. Instinctively, then, she is drawn to death, the death that is her destiny, the death that represents her only hope of peace and rest from the demands of the innumerable men who accost her night after night. Her own needs, as defined by her narrative, are limited to "un pedazo de noche" in which desire might be checked; Eros, for her, is merely a disturber of sleep.

The issue becomes somewhat more complex with the addition of the third figure of this grotesque family grouping. It is already paradoxical that the silent female body gives voice in this narration, a voice focused through a mutilated figure of Eros; the story becomes more paradoxical when the role of the grave digger is factored into the tale. If a feminized Eros, for some inexplicable reason, is able to recount the trajectory of her encounter with a masculine representative of Thanatos, himself a perversion of the linguistically grounded Spanish figure of a feminine death (*la muerte*), so too, through his dialogic intromissions, does Thanatos suggest his intimate relationship with desire. The prostitute is for him the attractive death, the closure he can never quite achieve for himself. Typically, he is most attracted to the qualities in her that he imagines as specular reflections on his own nature. "[T]e conozco de vista desde hace mucho tiempo, pero me gustas más cuando te sueño" [I have known you by sight for a long time, but I like you better when I dream about you], he tells her and hints that they will never truly find each other until "te asegure bajo tierra el día que me toque enterrarte" [I make sure of you underground the day I have to bury you] (150–51). By his continual, almost uninterrupted, speech, which informs the narrative background and which limits the woman's rest, Claudio Marcos brings the prostitute closer to this anticipated moment in which her silence will be assured, her rest eternal, her specular identity with him stabilized in the final encounter.

The grave digger's speculative/specular assumption is that the two of them represent in a parallel manner the overriding force of the death instinct; in his dream vision of her he sees not only the forbidden object of desire, the factor that resists death, but also and more importantly the figure of his own need to reveal death's meaning to himself. His beloved aunt "se murió de repente...y lo único que conseguí con todo eso fue que el corazón se me llenara de agujeros" [died suddenly...and all I got out of it was that my heart filled up with holes] (149). In his dream version of this "pedazo de noche" the grave digger hopes to explore the "agujeros" of a prostitute in his search for the subtle relationships between death and love he was unable to preserve in his memory of his aunt. His speech fills her holes, until there is more of him and progressively less of her. In his final, dreamed goal, her speech becomes subsumed in his, and her body can finally be interred in that other heterotopic site, the graveyard.

The prostitute's narrative, then, is complemented in a very specific manner by her largely unspoken dialogue with the grave digger's speech, and the two characters reflect precisely opposing theories of narrative. She speaks (or writes) out of her desire for silence, and the result is this fragment of a life, or this neatly closed tale of a paradigmatic episode in that life. His garrulousness derives from his insight that speech is antithetical to death and that somehow, through his linguistic overpowering of the prostitute, she, the silent teller of the tale, will become his death; he will bury her and bury his death with her rather than the reverse. Thus, if she (Eros) writes to die, he (Thanatos) speaks to become immortal. His calm assumption that she will predecease him remains unchallenged at the end of the story as death's problematic conviction of its own immortality. Her instinctive rejection, "Salgamos fuera.... Me siento sofocada" [Let's go outside.... I feel asphyxiated] (149), is life's protective response to the seductive death wish.

The infant, of course, does not speak, and I would like to return, in trying to effect a closure to this fragment of an analysis, to the child, that abominable newborn life and grasping premature death. The infant is in equal parts fascinating and repellent. His presence in close association with the two figures of an urban underworld lifts the narrative fragment from banal naturalism or social commentary, provoking the undefinable shudder of a reader who witnesses an inhuman, uniquely unforgettable vision. In his justly famous article on Rulfo's only novel, Carlos Fuentes asks, "Infancia y muerte: ¿serán éstos los dos temas verdaderos de *Pedro Páramo*? ¿Se resuelven en esta cercanía las oposiciones entre mito y epopeya, el pasado idílico...y las pesadas palabras que matan a Juan Preciado?" [Infancy and death: Are these the two real themes of *Pedro Páramo*? Can this approximation resolve the oppositions between myth and epic, the idyllic past...and the weighty words that kill Juan Preciado?] (Fuentes 1981, 21). Neither past nor future offers an idyll in "Un pedazo de noche," but the perverse mixing of myth and social history obtains here as in the later work. Infancy and/or death? Carlos Fuentes

wisely left the question open, intuiting that a too strenuous attempt at
closure would be at the very least tantamount to violation of a dearly held
cultural taboo and, perhaps more radically, could be rejected as incredible,
unnatural, inhuman. A child with maliciously adult eyes, wrapped like
a tamale, wriggling like a worm, is our closest approximation to what
must be left unsaid, open, fragmented. Desire, and the human needs and
demands that motivate an encounter under the streetlights, may be the
dynamic of signification, but Rulfo clearly demonstrates that it is no
panacea.

*space · reserved · the imagination (Foucault)*

## II

Garro's heterotopia, like Rulfo's, is an extremely formal structure, a world
powered by illicit desire and alternately constituted and dissolved in the
play of memory and forgetfulness. The opening lines of the novel establish that the town and its founding stone are monumental spaces that
speak through memory's inscription and whose identity is coterminous
with that memory. Yet it is equally well established that memory is itself
defined and circumscribed by the loss of memory and by the desire to
forget. As in Rulfo's novel fragment, in Garro's novel the holes are more
relevant than the increasingly fungible narratives that they interrupt: "Yo
sólo soy memoria...," says Ixtepec; "Quisiera no tener memoria" (9) [I
am only memory....I wish I had no memory (3)]. Ixtepec's narration, its
recall of Isabel's funeral inscription, comes to us from beyond the end
of history. The town's monumentally embodied narration recalls the moments leading up to Isabel's double fall — into sin and into death —
and occurs in the space of that other memory intuited by Isabel's father,
Martín, who ritually stops time by stopping the clocks: "[É]l sabía que
el porvenir era un retroceder veloz hacia la muerte y la muerte el estado
perfecto, el momento precioso en que el hombre recupera plenamente su
otra memoria. Por eso olvidaba la memoria de 'el lunes haré tal cosa'"
(33) [He knew that the future was a swift retrogression toward death,
and death the perfect state, the precious moment in which man fully re-
cuperates his other memory. And so he forgot the memory of "Monday I
will do such-and-such a thing" (28–29)]. In life, Martín intuits, only the
moment of death carries any weight or consequence. Yet Martín gains
no special privileges by his insight; his swift retrogression toward death,
the jostling competition among memories of things he has never heard
or never seen, leaves him effectively paralyzed in life.

At the same time, death exists. It is the only final, absolute fact of
the narrative. And death defines the relation of town and memory, of

narration and the holes in narration. People disappear under ominous circumstances; in the morning, hanged men appear on the trees outside of town, sometimes continuous with the disappearances, sometimes not. And it is the presence of death, rather than mere corpses, that defines that other time frame; they exist, as Martín would say, in that other time, that other memory, in the perfection of death that Ixtepec remembers, that defines the town's nature as memory, and that also describes the cycle of violence it most wishes to forget. The hanged men are images, perfect in themselves, yet they do not speak. They are the victims of the evil words Juan Cariño struggles to contain, the embodied, petrified words that precipitate their brief and truncated fall into death. They are willfully forgotten, even in the town's obsessive memory of their loss:

> Pasaron unos días y la figura de Ignacio tal como la veo ahora, colgada de la rama alta de un árbol, rompiendo la luz de la mañana como un rayo de sol estrella la luz adentro de un espejo, se separó de nosotros poco a poco. No volvimos a mentarlo. Después de todo, sólo era un indio menos. De sus cuatros amigos ni siquiera recordábamos los nombres. Sabíamos que dentro de poco otros indios anónimos ocuparían sus lugares en las ramas. (91)

> [Several days passed and the figure of Ignacio as I see it now, suspended from the uppermost branch of a tree, breaking the morning light as a ray of sunshine shatters the light in a mirror, gradually departed from us. We never spoke of him again. After all, his death only meant that there was one less Indian. We did not even remember the names of his four friends. We knew that before long other anonymous Indians would occupy their places in the trees. (86)]

Individuals are infinitely forgettable because of death's infinite reproducibility. Furthermore, this reproduction of death mediates between knowledge and narration, between what is seen and what is said, between what is remembered and what is actively, intentionally, forgotten.

Death, then, is the precondition for this narration, yet it is a force that cannot be remembered, spoken, or understood constructively. Ixtepec's memory and the narration itself belong to the perfect order that Georges Bataille calls "deleterious toxic time" and that Allan Stoekl describes as follows: "[T]ime is not the progressive, constructive phenomenon in which and through which we do a job; instead it is the fall, the irrevocable expenditure of God's control of power, control by the head, of control by God's proxy, man" (Stoekl 1985, 106). It is the fall that most interests Garro in this novel — the fall of Isabel from decent woman into political betrayal and sexual license with the general of the occupying army, the fall of the anonymous Indians and disappeared townsfolk into death by hanging, the fall of Isabel at the end of the novel from the mountain and her conversion into an inscribed stone marking and reconstituting all the falls and all the deaths of the novel. *Recuerdos del porvenir* [Recollections of things to come], as its title indicates, stands suspended in the fall, between two times, at the end of one history and in anticipation of the return of that, or an analogous, toxic historicity. Bataille projected a time at the end of history in which war would be done away with; Garro is not so optimistic, and Stoekl in his critique of Bataille could be describing Ixtepec: "[W]e would argue that this realm itself, however, was liable to be betrayed, to forget itself and become unknowable, to mutilate itself and its embodiment, the victim-writer" (108). Time and history, like language and desire, turn on their own impossibility in this toxic time of falling.

Ixtepec documents the fall, the multiple falls, but it is General Rosas who serves in the text of the novel as God's proxy, the controller of power. He represents the rule of military law in this town, and he also figures the transgression of the limits of lawfulness. In his presence, the people forget their knowledge of the hanged bodies even as they live the estrangement between that knowledge and their knowledge of the law. Rosas dominates all aspects of life and death in the town: "El tiempo era la sombra de Francisco Rosas. No quedaban sino 'colgados' en todo el país" (32) [Time was the shadow of Francisco Rosas. There was nothing but disillusionment (hanged bodies) in the whole country (28)]. Rosas's power is real; it is he who causes the disappearances of townsfolk, and he who orders the executions by hanging or by firing squad. At the same time, the general's power is magnified because it is more than real. Rosas knows that in order to keep his actual power, he must to some degree hide the workings of that power, keeping its extent and ramifications an unfathomable mystery. In this manner, he also possesses the power of dominating people's minds. He exercises this influence through the town's imperfect knowledge of the shadowy mysteries of his own incompletely understood persona and through the gossip surrounding his relationship with "la querida de Ixtepec" (26) [the love object of Ixtepec (22)], Julia Andrade, the mysterious and beautiful fallen woman who dominates the first half of Garro's novel. In the second half of the novel, after Julia's disappearance/flight, her place is taken by the local beauty, Isabel Moncada.

Up to this point, my description of the novel, and its narration, bears the outlines of a mythic representation, focused on the universalized male power figure. Such appearances, however, would be deceptive. If

the Indians, for example, seem as anonymous in death as in life, the very
insistence of their anonymous bodies impinges upon the reality of Ixtepec, forcing at the very least a conscious effort of active forgetting to
ignore their silent bodies. And further, as Garro notes, in their anonymity
lies a counterposing power to that of the individualized, if unknowable,
Rosas: "Todos los indios tienen la misma cara," says one of Ixtepec's smiling racists, "por eso son peligrosos" (25) [Indians all look alike — that's
why they're dangerous (21)]. Here Rosas directly articulates a common
racial injunction. The Indians' sameness, their unintelligibility, excludes
them from discourse, while at the same time that unintelligibility, that
absolute otherness, is a product of the ideology that excludes them. Their
bodies must be present, but their existence is excluded from the town's
memory; in Rosas's political system, their unintelligibility regulates and
stabilizes his ideological system. Their reality is needed as an impossible
"outside" to narration. They are peripheral, uncounted, and unaccounted
for; nevertheless, they are required specifically so as not to count. The
Indian is an obligatory specter/spectator who must be both evoked and
destroyed so as to avoid a destabilizing contamination of territorial and
discursive boundaries.

The larger question raised by this tactic is similar to one asked by Judith Butler: "How and where is social content attributed to the site of
the 'real,' and then positioned as the unspeakable?" For Butler, "[T]he
production of the *un*symbolizable, the unspeakable, the illegible is also
always a strategy of social abjection" (Butler 1993, 189–90). The issue
is, of course, directly political, since the production of intelligible meaning depends on the exclusion of the culturally unintelligible and on the
nonrecognition of that excluded element haunting the textual/territorial
periphery. In this book, as Garro astutely observes, such unintelligible,
unsymbolizable disruptive formations include those of politicized Indians
and sexualized women. At the same time, the insistent return of the Indians' hanged bodies to the outskirts of town and the women's sexualized
bodies to the town's center creates a crisis in legibility at the very site of
ideological reality formulation.

In an analogous manner, this story of a forgotten war (the Cristero
rebellion has been consistently underrepresented in official Mexican history until the aborted effort to rewrite history textbooks for use in the
public school system during the Salinas de Gortari administration, thirty
years after the writing of Garro's novel and some fifty or sixty years after
the events she chronicles) comes to us from an unexpected source — not
through the universalizing, implicitly male narrator of most war fiction
but as filtered through an insistently gendered perspective dominated by
the perceptions of the town's fallen women. Garro's project, then, offers

a point of view similar to that espoused by Monique Wittig in her novel *Les Guérillères.* Wittig writes:

> [T]here is a personal pronoun used very little in French, not existing in English — the collective plural *elles* [*they* in English] — while at the same time *ils* [*they*] often stands for the general with the sense of *one: they say,* meaning *people say.* This general *ils* does not include *elles,* any more than *he* includes *she,* no more, I suspect, than *they* includes any *she* in its assumption. . . . At least when it is used, the rare times it is, *elles* never stands for a general and is never bearer of a universal point of view. . . . In *Les Guérillères,* I try to universalize the point of view of the *elles.* (Wittig 1985, 10)

Garro, too, privileges the point of view of the feminine "they," the collective *ellas* who provide the basic grounding of the town's knowledge of itself and whose gossip, dismissed in traditional circles as irrelevant narrative, serves as the backbone of this novel. In Spanish, as in French, and unlike English, there exists a distinguishing third-person pronoun to express this collective feminine voice; in Spanish, unlike French, the pronoun is not required and is seldom used in standard grammatical constructions. The sign-pointing of the *ellas,* then, even from a grammatical standpoint, must be far more subtly conveyed. In Garro's novel there is no attempt to counterpose *ellas* to *ellos* overtly in a universalizing gesture, but rather an attempt to open up the discourse to a multiplicity of distinctly positioned *ellas* whose streams of voice combine to create the narrative point of view.

Thus, while the concrete social and political conflict defining the novelistic territory involves the military repression of the Cristero revolution — personified here in the opposing figures of, on the one hand, General Rosas and his military troop and, on the other, the Moncada brothers, backed by the shadowy forces of Abacuc and his Indian allies — the narrative terrain is distinctly dominated by the female protagonists of the novel. In the first half, the town is less obsessed with the actions of General Rosas than with the daily comings and goings of the general's mistress, the mysterious Julia. Julia disappears from the novel at its midpoint, and her preeminent role is taken over by Isabel Moncada, who also succeeds her in the general's bed. Julia and Isabel, then, form on the first level the narrative *ellas* through which the narrative point of view is filtered.

Their feminine "they" is supported at another level by at least four other subgroupings of narrative voices, all and also exclusively limited to *ellas.* Corresponding to the worlds on which Julia and Isabel depend are two correlated sets of voices: those of the other women from the Hotel Jardín, also mistresses of military officers and far more garrulous than the silent, secretive Julia; and those of the "decent" women of Ixtepec, the mestiza women of Isabel's own leisured social class. The voices from these two worlds have in turn their correlating and counterpointing voices: those of the frankly (and, from the point of view of the military, unimaginably) politically committed Luchi and her band of whores in the town brothel and those of the almost unseen and unheard Indian women whose very invisibility allows them to move from house to house within the town and from the town to the surrounding mountains where the rebels hide. The chorus of these voices, then, becomes the voice of memory, the voice of Ixtepec. It is a voice, or chorus of voices, distinguished by a particular narrative reticence analogous to the "holes" in Rulfo's prostitute's tale and marked as well by the continual awareness of the displacement of physical bodies in space.

Traditional accounts of war not only universalize the male voice but insist upon the construction of a gendered divide between war and women. War stories, almost by definition, are stories about men going off to fight other men. In such texts, the woman's place is either firmly in the family home where she is her man's inspiration or his grieving mother or in that other, pseudohome, the brothel, where she provides erotic distraction. The man leaves these spaces of respite to do the fighting and then returns (or not, as the case may be) to the woman's arms. She is not the subject of war narrative and does not take part in the actual fighting, although, like Helen of Troy, she may be war's ostensible object or the symbolic cause of the hostilities.

Part of the accomplishment of the female perspective dominant in Garro's novel is to provide us with the complementary other half of the experience of war; *Recuerdos del porvenir* helps negotiate the gender divide, representing women as subjects of the discourse about war. At the same time, the nature of that discourse itself changes as Garro cedes ground before the dreadful literalness of war's devastation. The disembodied voices of the women, past memory, and future memorial stone always find their counterpart in the unrepresentable, incommensurable bodies of the Indians. Implicitly, this communal voice asks herself hard questions about the narrator's role in representing these deaths; the loss of each incomparable, unrepeatable individual (e.g., the shock of seeing Ignacio hanging from one of the trees) heralds the collapse of memory and of language (the four friends whose names are forgotten, the countless other unidentified and unidentifiable Indians hanging from the same trees). Women and corpses, the two highly allegorized elements of traditional war fiction, here pass from the background of meditations on war to the foreground that no amount of military-strategy talk can disperse.

Near the end of the novel, one of the fallen women, the mistress of one of the military officers, comes to the realization that her time in this town is nearly over: "'[E]l placer se acaba...' ¿Adónde irían ahora?... Serían las queridas de alguien. Rafaela quiso adivinar la cara que ocultaba la palabra alguien. La esperaban otros pueblos y otros uniformes sin cuerpo y sin prestigio. Los militares se habían vuelto absurdos desde que se dedicaban a ahorcar campesinos y a lustrarse las botas" (235) ["The pleasure is ending...." Where would they go now? They would be the mistresses of someone. Rafaela tried to see the face concealed in the word "someone." Other towns and other uniforms, disembodied and without prestige, awaited her. The officers had become absurd since they had been spending their time hanging peasants and polishing their boots (228–29)]. Rafaela's role and that of the military officer are complementarily futile games; she sees to his pleasure, he kills Indians. In both cases the actions devolve into empty rituals, endlessly repeated in nameless towns and meaninglessly absurd. And just as the towns blur, so do the bodies. Pleasure fades into boredom; someone becomes no one: an empty uniform and a pair of polished boots.

Luchi, the madam of the local brothel, sees the functioning of this system of relationships as established over and through the body of another woman: "Damián Álvarez, como todos los hombres que se acostaban con ella, buscaba el cuerpo de otra y la miraban con rencor por haberlo engañado...y los hombres desnudos se convertían en el mismo hombre, su propio cuerpo, la habitación y las palabras desaparecían" (99) [Damián Álvarez, like all the men who slept with her, searched for another woman's body, and they eyed her with rancor for having deceived them.... and the naked men turned into the same man, while her own body, the room, and the words disappeared (95)]. Luchi's many men steal her words and her identity, leaving her silent in the void. Or nearly so.

For Luchi, if not precisely the prostitute with a heart of gold, nevertheless reserves a hidden heart. She and the other women in her brothel are secret revolutionaries, below suspicion because of their perceived insignificance. When Captain Flores is sent to the brothel to spy on the women, he fully expects nothing more than a comfortable night on the town: "¿Y por qué la Luchi? ¿Qué podía saber una pobre mujer como ella, aislada del mundo, encerrada en una casa mala? ¡Nada! La certeza de que la mujer estaba al margen de la desaparición del cuerpo del sacristán lo tranquilizó" (188) [And why Luchi? What could a poor woman like her know, cut off from the world, cooped up in an evil house? Nothing! The certainty that the woman was in no way connected with the disappear-

ance of the sacristan's body reassured him (183)]. The two narratives —
Luchi's and Flores's — intermesh. Luchi's observation about her reduction to silence and nothingness in relation to the men who use her in
the illusion of seeking someone or something else echoes with the similar realization of Rulfo's prostitute in "Pedazo de noche." From the man's
point of view the prostitute is in both narratives a nothing, a hole into
which he pours his desire. Flores adds that this poor soul, this marginalized and isolated woman, not only is, but knows, nothing. One narrative
slips into the other, and yet there is a difference. While in Rulfo's narrative, and in Flores's, the fallen woman falls further into nothing but a
sexualized hole, in Garro's narrative Luchi is able to use her relative invisibility, even to herself, as a source of empowerment. Nearly reduced to a
disappeared body herself, she is eminently qualified to disappear another
body, and the brothel becomes the staging ground for that disappearance. Her brothel, far from an isolated or marginalized place, is actually a
crossroads of the town, where men of all backgrounds and political views
share the bodies of the prostitutes. Thus Luchi, because she is nothing to
the men who use her body, actually comes to know more.

The woman who dominates the town by her presence in the first half
of this novel is, of course, Julia Andrade, and while Julia rarely speaks,
or rarely makes any comment beyond the commonplace, her fascinating
young body attracting all eyes at the center of town evokes the changes
wrought by war to an even greater extent than the silent, forgotten bodies
hung outside the town. As Sandra Messinger Cypess writes in her article
on Garro, Julia "is the one who all women, old or young, secretly would
like to be" (Cypess 1990, 122) and whom all men, old and young, would
secretly or not so secretly like to have. Always dressed in her trademark
pink, Julia tantalizes women and men alike with her erotically loosened
hair and exotic, sleepy-eyed indifference to her surroundings. That very
indifference makes her all the more seductive and all the more secretly
powerful since she chooses not to wield the influence that everyone assumes she possesses: "[P]ara todo Ixtepec, Julia era la imagen del amor.
Muchas veces, antes de dormir, [Nicolás] pensó con rencor en el general que poseía a aquella mujer tan lejana de las otras, tan irreal" (95–96)
[For . . . all Ixtepec, Julia was the personification of love. Before he went to
sleep [Nicholas] often thought indignantly of the general who possessed
that woman so unlike other women, so unreal (90)]. Julia is a mystery
who comes to Ixtepec with the military train and disappears at the end of
the first part of the novel with Felipe Hurtado under circumstances even
more mysterious. Her unknowability, her unreality, feed her attraction.
Julia seems to exist in the town without context and without past; she is
for everyone a beautiful object who belongs to whomever has the strength

to take and hold her. Her origin is impenetrable even to the inventions of rumor, but gossip says the general stole her and that she had previously been loved by many men before falling into the general's hands. Curiously, her theorized past as a whore makes her even more attractive.

Beautiful, unreal Julia is a measure of the general's status. He takes her out in the evenings, dressed in gorgeous gowns, dripping in jewels, to take a turn around the plaza, the cynosure of all eyes. And the general, having achieved his object upon displaying his lovely possession to the town, whips the men who stare at her and beats Julia when she stares back. She is for the town as for the general an alluring toy. Julia is all body — desire animated — and the general yearns to penetrate that beautiful shell with more than his physical self, to possess the memories he imagines behind her eyes. But Julia, always open, always available to the general's desire, never gives her interior self along with her freely given body. Strikingly, in Ixtepec's retelling of this tangled relationship, it remains unclear whether or not there is any self to discover other than her compliant body. Her poised indifference may just as easily suggest a strategy of minimalist resistance to further abuse or hint at a human self lost in the multiple victimizations of a war in which an attractive woman is repeatedly kidnapped and raped by soldiers from one band or another.

Still, Julia's body is inextricably linked to those other bodies, the ones hanging outside town. She is equally recalcitrant, even more unreal. If her beauty represents the secret dream of Ixtepec's women and the hidden desire of its men, that beauty and that indifference weigh heavily against her. Doña Elvira expresses the conviction of many of her townsfolk when she complains, as she does repeatedly, of Julia's heavy responsibility in the sufferings of Ixtepec: "¡Es Julia!... Ella tiene la culpa de todo lo que nos pasa...¿Hasta cuándo se saciará esta mujer?" (81) [It's Julia! She's to blame for everything that happens to us. How long will this go on? (76)]. The town also signals Julia as the focus of the town's anger, but, in addition, it indicates her role as scapegoat: "Julia tenía que ser la criatura preciosa que absorbiera nuestras culpas" (90) [Julia had to be the precious creature who would absorb our guilt (85)]. The general's bloodthirsty assistant, Rodolfo Goríbar, the man immediately responsible for the deaths of suspected revolutionaries, waits patiently for the general's frustration with Julia to reach the point of explosion: "[C]uando se enojaba con Julia era el momento en que concedía todas las muertes" (77) [He would concede all deaths when he was angry with Julia (72)].

Julia, the love object, the town's scapegoat, is also the general's scapegoat, and, as Delia Galván notes, his focus for victimization is the fascinating face that makes her so unforgettable in the town (Galván

1990, 149). He beats her when other men look at her or try to talk to her; he beats her when he believes she is ignoring his needs; he beats her more fiercely when he imagines she is thinking of other men; he beats her because he remembers imagining the other men and imagines that she does not forget them. In one of his most revealing moments, the general describes the relationship between them as one of a wartime siege in which Julia represents the self of the town under attack: "Se encontró frente a ella como un guerrero solitario frente a una ciudad sitiada con sus habitantes invisibles comiendo, fornicando, pensando, recordando, a afuera de los muros que guardaban al mundo que vivía adentro de Julia estaba él. Sus iras, sus asaltos y sus lágrimas eran vanas, la ciudad seguía intacta" (78) [When he was with her he felt like a lonely warrior in the presence of a besieged city with its invisible inhabitants eating, fornicating, thinking, remembering, and he was outside of the walls that guarded Julia's inner world. His rages, his fits, and his tears were to no avail: the city remained intact (73)]. Julia, then, the seductive woman from an Other place, becomes in his imagination the town itself, and her passive resistance to his pressures becomes the town's resistance. The deaths he orders have a direct connection to his abuse of her, and the silent testimony of her bruises serves to mark within the town her function not only as scapegoat (for the general, for the town) but also as witness to those atrocities.

Rosas suffers constantly in his obsession with Julia. He wants her to be fully his and remains intrigued by her because she somehow manages to escape his complete possession. What he loves about her is her resistance to him. If she were the zombie she sometimes seems, her value to Rosas would be lost. He craves her will and her desires, not only her body. At the same time, she is and must remain for him as distant as the star he imagines when he first sees her: "El día de su encuentro con Julia tuvo la impresión de tocar una estrella del cielo de la Sierra" (78) [When he met Julia he had the impression of touching a star from the sierra sky (73)]. If that particular star were to come to earth, if the besieged city were to surrender, Julia would lose her value. She is, therefore, the embodiment of an unintelligible desire; his possession of her is riddled with knowledge he must reject; her flight is an unspeakable loss. At the same time, Rosas's story — and the town's story — about her displaces Julia from her own existence. As the concrete embodiment of an unspeakable real invading the heart of town, Julia cannot *be* Julia; she is required to be the unintelligible erotic object. Likewise, in the second half of the novel, Isabel cannot be Julia either; but she is that erotic object's displaced representation. This triangulation (town-woman-Rosas) and the discursive gaps that envelop it serve as the point of departure for rethinking the novel's entire ideological frame, with its sexualized vectors of race and political arrangements.

Julia's motivation in relation to Rosas, or even the question of whether or not she is self-motivated, remains much less clear. In one reading of the novel we would see her as a severely damaged woman with nothing left to help her survive further abuse but her passivity and her indifference to her self and her body. In this first reading, her eyes hide nothing; they are empty screens where Rosas projects his own anxieties and fear of inadequacy. In another reading, we can imagine Julia as more self-aware. In the second reading, the victim consciously turns on her victimizer and dominates him by refusing to disclose her innermost identity, that posited identity upon which Rosas props his own shaky sense of self. Her revenge on him, we might theorize, is to remain merely a thing, to maintain her perfect composure, her distanced unreality. She refuses to allow herself any reaction to his outbursts, thus forbidding him any access to that reality dependent upon her recognition of him as well. In either case, however, Julia's body remains inextricably linked to the town's consciousness. She is in this respect the objective correlative of that passive — if not entirely pacified — town of the first half of the novel, the town divided between an inwardly focused attention on the details of daily life and a distanced recognition of the atrocities taking place outside its besieged walls.

The dilemma that Julia presents to the town of Ixtepec and its communal narrator is never resolved. We have no way of knowing whether the patterns Julia traces on Rosas's skin with her fingers are ones she traced on other bodies, in other circumstances, or whether any of these theoretical men who enjoyed sex with her were also, in the true sense of the word, her lovers. We have no way of knowing whether Rosas's need to remember/reinvent her story, and his concomitant need to make her forget everything but him, derives from anything at all in her. What is clear is that Rosas, both in relation to Ixtepec and in relation to Julia, is engaged in a violent process of alteration and reinscription as he struggles to impose not only his presence but his narration on a town and on a woman who, passively or actively, resists his story. In the intertanglements of need and desire, there is no space to trace any of these stories back to their obscure origin.

Neither can the stories be concluded. Julia's escape from Ixtepec with Felipe Hurtado occurs in obscure circumstances, under the cover of fog and an endlessly prolonged night, her pink dress blending in with the pink dawn sky. The story of that disappearance is neither realistic nor even persuasive. It is, however, exemplary. Julia escapes in the night, into the horizon, into the sky, like the fugitive star that Rosas once imagined he captured when he stole her. She is the object of his desire that holds him firmly attached to a military reality, but she slips from the world — of reality or of appearances — back into the sky, or, alternatively, she falls into the unrecoverable objectivity of death. (But in this novel, death too has its tie to the fluidity of appearances.) When memory of her returns, it is tied to the nameless dead in the trees: "Así le habían arrebatado a Julia... enseñándole imágenes reflejadas en otros mundos. Ahora se la mostraban en los muertos equivocados de los árboles" (182) [That was how they had taken Julia away from him... showing him images reflected in other worlds. Now they showed her to him in the mistaken dead in the trees (176)]. Even in this phrase, it is unclear whether Rosas sees the deaths as wrongful or whether he is wrong about the men in the trees being dead. The delicate warning that such wrongs, whatever their nature, could somehow be put right helps spell out once again the shifting code of Julia's danger to the town and to the soldiers.

Like Julia, Isabel Moncada hints of danger by her very existence. Like Julia, she is also compared to a star, and in that comparison Ixtepec foretells her eventual fate: "Isabel podía convertirse en una estrella fugaz, huir y caer en el espacio sin dejar huellas visibles de ella misma, en este mundo donde sólo la grosería de los objetos toma forma" (30) [Isabel was capable of changing into a shooting star, of running away and falling into space without leaving a visible trace, in this world where only the grossness of objects takes shape (26)]. There are differences, however. Julia is doubly imagined as the beautiful lost soul or the beautiful unreadable star — in either case the simulacrum of a mythic presence, differentiated and sharply distanced from the human beings of Ixtepec. Isabel is equally unreadable, but hers is not the cool shining of the mountain star. Rather she is a fierce, swiftly burning comet, fleeing and falling through space. And when she falls to earth like a meteor, and burns up, she leaves behind the smallest reminder of herself in the monumental stone whose presence opens and closes Garro's novel. Her scandal is not double, but multiple.

The essential quality that both Isabel and Julia share is their suspension between unreality and an objective presence that is purely corporeal. Nicholas, like the other inhabitants of Ixtepec, is drawn to Julia by her air of unreality. The same quality attaches itself to his sister, Isabel:

> Había dos Isabeles, una que deambulaba por los patios y las habitaciones y la otra que vivía en una esfera lejana, fija en el espacio. Supersticiosa tocaba los objetos para comunicarse con el mundo aparente y cogía un libro o un salero como punto de apoyo para no caer en el vacío. Así establecía un fluido mágico entre la Isabel real y la Isabel irreal y se sentía consolada. (29)

[There were two Isabels, one who wandered through the rooms and the patios, and the other who lived in a distant sphere, fixed in space. Superstitiously she touched objects to communicate with the apparent world and picked up a book or a saltcellar to keep from falling into the void. Thus she established a magical flux between the real Isabel and the unreal one, and felt consoled. (25)]

Both Isabel and Ixtepec fluctuate among conflicting versions of the relationship between the young woman and her world. That world is both solid and real, and only apparently so. People become ghosts, walls turn transparent, time demonstrates an amazing flexibility. And, at the same time, words solidify and fall to the street as objectively real and sharp-edged fragments, and a young woman falls from the mountainside and is converted into stone. As Rosas realizes in a later passage, "Nada tenía cuerpo en Ixtepec.... El pueblo entero era de humo y se le escapaba de entre las manos" (181) [Nothing in Ixtepec had a body.... The whole town was made of smoke and it was slipping through his fingers (175)]. Isabel walks these apparently solid paths of her town but also maintains a distant, starry existence quite separate from the town's reality or unreality. Which Isabel is real, and which unreal? The novel is less concerned with such determinations than with establishing the magical flux between them that allows the two Isabels to exist simultaneously in both realms and to stave off the ever-present threat of falling.

This indeterminacy between substantiality and unreality is an essential component of the aggressively feminized voice in this text. Recent feminist studies have discussed with great precision and force how the traditional metaphysics of substance operates to reflect the experiences of a stereotypically masculinist, Western European ideal. Simplified, the argument goes like this: women bear children, and men bear ideas; women are beautiful, and men create beauty; women are the objects and men the subjects of discourse.[2] Women, in this schema, must represent the realm of the purely bodily processes, leaving men free for the higher functions of mental work. Thus, the Enlightenment conception of the self involves a distinction between the body and the mind, and feminist philosophers have explored the implications of this division of self as it represses women. The results are far-reaching. In particular, the division of the self creates an unresolvable linguistic dilemma for the speaking woman.

In his 1959 classic, *El laberinto de la soledad,* Garro's then-husband Octavio Paz writes: "[W]oman is an incarnation of the life force, which is essentially impersonal. Thus it is impossible for her to have a personal, private life, for if she were to be herself — if she were to be mistress of her own desires, passions, or whims — she would be unfaithful to herself"

(Paz 1961, 36–37). Paz, like the Enlightenment philosophers he often
resembles, insists upon seeing woman as a symbolic function. She represents, in terms of the masculinist universal, the embodiment of sexuality
and desire, but she can exercise no control over her own desire, since such
control would contradict what that phallogocentric schema defines as her
very nature. Moreover, Paz suggests that if women were able to express
themselves freely, authentically, the entire fabric of society would be at
risk and would naturally militate against it: "How can we agree to let her
express herself when our whole way of life is a mask designed to hide
our intimate feelings?" (38). The "our" here requires careful attention. It
seems clear that the expansively inclusive phrase omits one half of the
species and suggests an applicability limited only to a community of men
in which the function of women is not only to lose themselves in myth
but also to provide a comfortable, silent, malleable mask for their men
as well, so that their privacy can be protected. Men, in this model, have
the choice of either speech or silence, a choice contingent in either case
upon the continued silence of women. It is this widespread perception of
women as the silent witnesses to male speech that underlies and informs
the backdrop of Garro's novel.

Monique Wittig addresses the additional problems that arise when a
woman does take voice. She writes, "[N]o woman can say *I* without being herself a total subject — that is, ungendered, universal. . . . But gender,
an element of language, works upon this ontological fact to annul it as far
as women are concerned and corresponds to a constant attempt to strip
them of the most precious thing for a human being — subjectivity." If
the female self is restricted to the body and the male marks itself off as
universal (and thus, implicitly incorporeal), then the woman's voice poses
a particularly difficult conundrum. Wittig concludes: "So what is this divided being introduced into language through gender? It is an impossible
being, it is a being that does not exist, an ontological joke, a concep-
tual maneuver" (Wittig 1985, 7). Both linguistic gender and gender as
an attribute of a person denote something similar to the phenomenon
that Garro describes as a magical flux between two apparent and unreal worlds: not the conflict between female materiality and masculine
thought or even the conflict between substance and unreality. Garro's poetic depiction of Isabel describes, rather, a point of convergence among
numerous culturally coded sets of behaviors and ways of imagining the
relationship between self and the world.

Garro goes further, however, in this deconstruction of masculinist
discourse. She not only questions the Enlightenment heritage of a mind-
body split but also outlines the far more radical question about the nature
of representation itself. As Butler says of Irigaray, in words equally appli-

cable to the Mexican writer: "Irigaray would maintain, however, that the feminine 'sex' is a point of linguistic *absence,* the impossibility of a grammatically denoted substance, and, hence the point of view that exposes that substance as an abiding and foundational illusion of a masculinist discourse" (Butler 1990, 10). If, following Butler's argument, we agree that "the female sex eludes the very requirements of representation," then it also follows that "the feminine could not be theorized in terms of a determinate *relation* between the masculine and the feminine within any given discourse, for discourse is not a relevant notion here. Even in their variety, discourses constitute so many modalities of phallogocentric language. The female sex is thus also the *subject* that is not one" (10–11). Isabel, the perfect exemplum of the speaking voice in this novel, is the subject that is not one — that is, she is not a singular subject but multiple in her indeterminacy. She is also the subject that is not one in that she is not the grammatical subject of the narrative sentence (that voice belongs to Ixtepec) but rather that sentence's conundrum, its narrative object. And she is, for Garro's text, that "point of linguistic *absence,* the impossibility of a grammatically denoted substance," that makes her both the object of desire (the illusory woman in red in her amateur theatricals and in her sexual relationship with Rosas) and the unreadable hole in signification that absorbs both desire and the hope of substantiality. In her wake, the town without illusions becomes, as Rosas realizes, illusory, a ghost town populated by phantoms, the first and foremost among them, himself.

Once again, as is the case with Julia, Garro poses the unreadability of a key figure as the central problem in this text. We readers (impossible objects) are asked to explore this unreadability and to respond to the experience, not by decoding the text, but by finding ourselves in its shifting formations. The project is unthinkable by Enlightenment standards and for that very reason has a precise ideological value. Furthermore, in so doing, Garro does not ignore the world, nor the world of inscriptions, that exists in twentieth-century Mexican society.

Julia's defining quality is her distance, her real or apparent indifference to her surroundings and to the man (men?) who use her body. Isabel burns more hotly; her defining characteristic is her anger. Isabel defies, first of all, a system of values that divides women along the axis of wife and whore. Garro is well aware of the repressive nature of matrimony in provincial Mexican society, and her words, with a strikingly different charge, echo against and counterpoint those of Paz. In a few concise sentences, her narrator describes the lived experience of marriage for one typical woman, Elvira Montúfar, now happily a widow: "Cuando se casó, Justino acaparó las palabras y los espejos y ella atravesó unos años silenciosos y borrados en los que se movía como una ciega. . . . La única memoria que tenía de esos años era que no tenía ninguna" (27–28) [When she married, Justino monopolized the words and the mirrors and she endured some silent obliterated years in which she moved about like a blind woman. . . . The only memory she had of those years was that she had no memory (23)]. Elvira Montúfar does not gain a new identity from her position as wife and mother; instead, she loses herself during all the years of her marriage, her words and her face subsumed under those of her husband. The only advantage, as Paz noted, is her husband's, since he defines himself against her absence and her silence. The young woman, whose identity is circumscribed by her reduction to a prenuptial female, becomes even less herself under the pressures of male requirements. As Judith Butler writes, "[T]he woman in marriage qualifies not as an identity, but only as a relational term." Furthermore, "she *reflects* masculine identity precisely through being the site of its absence" (Butler 1990, 39).

Isabel is infuriated not only by the absenting of self and identity she sees in the abnegation of married women to their husbands' whims but also by the nature of the presence allowed to women. She knows very well that men and women come to marriage with different expectations. She is perfectly aware of a woman's role in marriage as an article exchanged between men, and she also knows that no decent alternative exists for a sexually mature female: "A Isabel le disgustaba que establecieran diferencias entre ella y sus hermanos. Le humillaba la idea de que el único futuro para las mujeres fuera el matrimonio. Hablar del matrimonio como de una solución la dejaba reducida a una mercancía a la que había que dar salida a cualquier precio" (22) [Isabel disliked having differences made between her and her brothers. The idea that a woman's only future was matrimony she found humiliating. For them to speak of marriage as a solution made her feel like a commodity that had to be sold at any price (17)]. Isabel decides never to marry and in so doing establishes her reputation for that obstinacy that is to define her. Moreover, her impasse describes the impossibility of a free expression of a woman's sexuality.

Prostitution is a false alternative to marriage, since it involves nothing more than a multiplication of the men for whom the absent presence of the woman serves as a relational term. The woman is still a commodity, although the price is different. The women in the Hotel Jardín, with their privileged status as mistresses to the military rulers of Ixtepec, realize this fact very clearly, as do Luchi and the other prostitutes in the town brothel. Their bodies serve as the conduit for a performative enactment of sexuality, but not of a woman's expression of herself. Furthermore, they are as tied to their houses as the married women of town, and like

Elvira Montúfar, though in a less socially approved manner, they too fall prey to the dissolution of the self in the porosities of desire and death.

Isabel wants some other alternative, some escape. She chooses, in all her stubborn obstinacy, to go to bed with the enemy, to become the mistress of General Rosas, even in the full knowledge that the general was responsible for the death of her brother Juan and the imprisonment of her other brother, Nicolás. In her article on Garro, Cypess notes that "by giving herself, Isabel is not merchandise controlled by another but an agent in her own right who makes deals for what she wants.... Isabel's behavior, then, deconstructs the dominant social practices, and she is far from the passive and submissive female creature of tradition." Cypess concludes: "[H]er attempt at liberation fails because she too is still male-oriented" (Cypess 1990, 127). With Isabel's admittance to the Hotel Jardín, says Ixtepec, the dark days return to the town: "Isabel había entrado al corazón del enigma. Estaba allí para vencer a los extranjeros, tan vulnerables como cualquiera de nosotros, o bien para decidir nuestra derrota. Su nombre borró al recuerdo de Julia.... La invisible presencia de Isabel empequeñecía a las demás y las convertía en comparsas de un drama en el que no querían participar" (250) [Isabel had entered the heart of the enigma. She was there to conquer the strangers, as vulnerable as any one of us, or to decide our downfall. Her name erased the memory of Julia.... Isabel's presence made the others seem insignificant, changed them into supernumeraries in a drama they did not want to take part in (243)]. In her fall, in taking the place of Julia, the bright lost star, Isabel precipitates the fall of Ixtepec as well.

And yet Isabel, like Julia, like Ixtepec, is not only obstinate but enigmatic. Her story, like Julia's, refuses a straightforward conclusion and tends toward the ambiguous slippages of a multiply staged and voiced unreadability. She is not just a bright young thing on the way to a happy-ever-after ending; her shooting star blazes light and dark in equal proportions. The two key words in the passage I just cited are "memory" and "drama"; Isabel's enigma is inextricably tied to both concepts. She is, as the town reminds us in the first and last pages of the novel, the apparent stone, the embodied memory. Within the pages of the novel, it is Isabel who brings drama back to the town that admits "habíamos renunciado a la ilusión" (116) [we had renounced illusion (111)]. She restores illusion to Ixtepec with her enthusiasm for the play that precipitates the crisis in the first half of the novel and for the play-acting in the party that serves the same function in the second half. At the same time, Isabel's role in the play that so delights Ixtepec and pulls it from its self-contemplation is a dark role, one that speaks of tragedies that are to come:

Conchita iría de blanco; Isabel de rojo.

— Es la luna, la misma luna la que sale en este minuto en escena — les repitió Hurtado, mitad en serio, mitad en broma.

Ellas asentían convencidas y repetían los versos una y otra vez. (117–18)

[Conchita would wear white; Isabel red.

"It is the moon, the selfsame moon which rises on stage at this moment," Hurtado recited, half seriously, half joking.

They agreed enthusiastically and rehearsed the verses over and over again. (112; translation modified)]

Conchita, unequivocally, is the moon's bright, virginal aspect — the idealized moon goddess, Diana of Greco-Roman tradition. Isabel represents bloody madness. It is, perhaps, not coincidental that in Aztec mythology, the moon goddess, Coyolxauhqui, is the sister of Huitzilopochtli, the god of war. According to myth, Coyolxauhqui attempts to kill her mother, Coatlicue, and is in turn killed by Huitzilopochtli and thrown down the Coatepec mountain. Her dismembered body, captured in stone, lies at the foot of Huitzilopochtli's side of the great pyramid, the manmade mountain.

The Greco-Roman tale, of course, is one of the founding myths in the Western repertoire, and while it is only delicately recalled in Garro's allusive text, the underlying structure of this chapter's discourse, and the assumptions I can naturally make about the audience for it, make it unnecessary for me to repeat that story here. I cannot make the same assumptions about the story of Coyolxauhqui. And yet the Nahuatl place-names and the frequent allusions to native belief systems make such an identification as inevitable as the former. Furthermore, the potential and actuality of violence associated with Coyolxauhqui infect the text far more fully than most critics have noted in their readings of this difficult and enigmatic work. Those Aztec gods are, to Western eyes, imposing, terrifying, unknowable, and strangely fascinating. Benedict Anderson reminds us that national genealogies are frequently constructed on the basis of reminding us of tragedies that we must forget and that stories of national identity must be narrated precisely to insist upon these "forgotten" memories (B. Anderson 1991, 201). One of those repressed memories is precisely the memory of Coyolxauhqui and Huitzilopochtli, and behind that memory is still another that Garro likewise evokes in her drama within the novel: the vague memory of a fiercely suppressed matriarchal order superseded by the rule of Huitzilopochtli. The climax of the drama brings all these allusions together forcefully:

Felipe Hurtado calló y todos volvieron del mundo ilusorio.... "¡Mírame, Julia!" decían que le pedía. Y Julia se asomaba a sus ojos almendrados y le regalaba una mirada ciega. Isabel rompió el silencio....

Vuelvo al pabellón y escucho todavía flotantes las palabras dichas por Isabel y que provocaron su interrupción: "¡Mírame antes de quedar convertida en piedra!" (119)

[Felipe Hurtado stopped talking and they all came out of the world of illusion.... "Look at me, Julia," people said he begged. And Julia peered out of her almond eyes and gave him an expressionless stare.

Isabel broke the silence.... I hear Isabel's words, which caused her to stop short, still floating on the air: "Look at me before turning to stone!" (113–14; translation modified)]

Isabel's words mirror Felipe's words, ending the criss-crossing exchanges of the gaze that goes from the townsfolk to the stage, from Felipe to Julia, from Julia and Rosas and Isabel to Felipe, from Isabel to Nicolás and Juan and Conchita, to Ixtepec and back to Isabel. "Look at me," says Felipe, and Isabel echoes his words, "Look at me." Julia, Isabel, and Conchita are reflected and refracted in each others' eyes and in the eyes of the brothers, Juan and Nicolás, and of the strangers, Francisco Rosas and Felipe Hurtado. "¡Mírame antes de quedar convertida en piedra!" says Isabel: before she (Isabel? Julia?) is turned to stone (a prediction of her fate as Coyolxauhqui) or (with the slight slippage of a single letter that marks the feminine gender) before s/he is (or they are) turned to stone, echoing another Greco-Roman tale, of Medusa's victims.

Julia is an enigma of a sort familiar to Western-trained readers; Isabel is nothing of the kind; she is an enigma from an Other reality, and it is no wonder, then, that despite their superficial parallelism, Francisco Rosas realizes that Isabel's presence, far from exorcising the memory of Julia, makes the absence of the beloved woman all the more intolerable (Span.: 251; Eng.: 244). The fallen woman, says José Joaquín Blanco, becomes a limit-condition (Blanco 1988, 67). Lyotard's "He" writes: "You explain: it's impossible to think an end, pure and simple, of anything at all, since the end's a limit and to think it you have to be on both sides of that limit. So what's finished or finite has to be perpetuated in our thought if it's to be thought of as finished" (Lyotard 1992, 9). Garro's Isabel knows what and who she is but remembers nothing of herself and so gropes forward until self and suffering overtake each other, reach a monumental limit, and hold writing in abeyance. Only the drama allows for a provisional escape from the tyranny of appearances, since only art contains, as it represents, a fullness of unreality.

The scene of the drama, with its tightly interwoven circuit of over-determined gazes, is repeated at the end of the novel in the staging of Doña Carmen B. Arrieta's party. In this episode, the drama unfolds simultaneously in three enclosed/forbidden spaces, corresponding to three discrete chapter breaks in the second half of the novel, where the shifting counterpoint of the women's voice(s) imposes the limits to what can be imagined, thought, or said. Each of these realities is linked to the others, but only in a certain reshuffling of characters involving an exchange of men among the various nonintersecting spaces.

In the prehistory of the event, Doña Carmen offers to give a party to honor the general and to celebrate the newly established peace between townsfolk and the occupying military forces. Rosas quite rightly suspects that the party may be a trap and plans a surprise of his own to entrap the plotters. The party, however, takes on a reality of its own. Originally designed as a distraction to allow the Cristeros to smuggle the priest out of town, the party causes the people to forget that which the party was organized for them to remember: "Se diría que en un instante todos olvidaron la iglesia cerrada y a la Virgen convertida en llamas.... Todos querían olvidar a los colgados en las trancas de Cocula. Nadie nombraba a los muertos aparecidos en los caminos reales" (194) [It seemed that in an instant they all forgot about the closed church and the Virgin transmuted into flames.... Everyone wanted to forget the hangings along the road to Cocula. No one mentioned the dead who had been found on the highway (189–90)]. Ixtepec, of course, remembers what the townsfolk want to forget, and the readers of the novel are likewise reminded of the ongoing atrocities by the litany of what the people ignore. The party, then, begins as a political act and takes on its own dramatic presence as a celebration of life predicated by and dependent upon the exclusion of those atrocities that the people now want to forget. That willful forgetfulness creates the first limit on the party.

The second limit comes from General Rosas. Suspecting a trap, he uses the party as an opportunity to do a mopping up operation of his own. He orders the party to continue, the music to go on, and everyone to dance until he returns. And then he leaves, effectively locking the conspirators into Doña Carmen's house, while he is free to conduct his search of their empty houses during that endless night. Isabel, fearless in the midst of the frightened crowd, tells her father, " 'Siempre supe lo que está pasando.... También lo supo Nicolás.... Desde niños estamos bailando en este día...,' " as she sits tranquilly "en su traje rojo que pesaba y ardía como una piedra puesta al sol" (207) ["I always knew what was going on. Nicholas knew, too. Since we were children we have been dancing on this day.... I knew it," Isabel repeated in her red dress, which weighed and coruscated like a stone in the sunlight (201)]. As Isabel sits quietly in her stone dress in Doña Carmen's house she is also and has always been dancing with her brother, who is desperately trying to elude Rosas's forces outside.

On the night of Doña Carmen's party, the women from Luchi's brothel lock the doors as they disguise the priest so as to smuggle him out of town to the safety of the mountains where Abacuc and the Cristero forces lie in wait. None of the prostitutes are particularly optimistic about their chances; Taconcitos sits on the floor morosely repeating, "[Y]a se está amontonando la desdicha" (223) [I told you, I told you that misfortunes are piling up (217)], and even the normally strong madam recognizes the inevitability of her fate: "¿Qué vale la vida de una puta?... Siempre supe que me iban a asesinar" (224–25) [What is a whore's life worth?... I always knew they were going to kill me (218)]. At the same time as Rosas is telling the upper-class townsfolk to keep dancing, his soldiers are breaking into Luchi's house. As Doña Carmen's fireworks light the sky, that house, too, is surrounded with troops.

Finally, the military officers' mistresses also come to recognize their imprisonment on the fateful night of Doña Carmen's party. The sound of the fireworks reaches them, and each woman, for her own reasons, thinks of fleeing from her respective officer. Each, in turn, recognizes the futility of that dream: "Y miraron los muros del cuarto que las tenía prisioneras. No podían escapar a sus amantes.... Ixtepec estaba preso y aterrado como ellas" (237) [And they looked at the walls of the room where they were prisoners. They could not escape from their lovers.... Ixtepec was a prisoner and as terrified as they were (230)]. In each of these cases, it is the woman's body that focalizes — as the woman's voice expresses — the concrete reality of the revolutionary act.

In this juxtaposition of an upper-class home, a brothel, and a scandalous hotel, Garro makes explicit what might more comfortably remain implicit — that from the point of view of dominant social practice the three incommensurable spaces are more alike than not. It is not the women themselves who are at issue, nor their actions, but rather the nature of a masculinist worldview that defines women according to their containment in their proper space and always as accouterments to a male interchange: what Isabel recognizes as the dance that she has been dancing all her life. Butler explains: "[T]he relation of reciprocity established between men, however, is the condition of a relation of radical nonreciprocity between men and women and a relation, as it were, of nonrelation between women" (Butler 1990, 41). The women in these three different spaces are strangers to one another except insofar as their voices blend together in the overarching feminine voice of this text. The fighting men — both Cristeros and army — circulate in the streets of the town, deeply subsumed in a reciprocal relationship based on perfect understanding of one another and the others' motives, an understanding that excludes women. They will kill one another or be killed. They will fall in battle or hang from trees or fall into their prepared graves when brought before a firing squad.

Yet while the relations between men and women, and the spaces they occupy, can be described as fundamentally nonreciprocal, these spaces and voices exert a force that breaks through the narrative form describing and defining them. Michel Foucault, in a text I cited earlier, calls these imaginative reserves "heterotopias" (Foucault 1986, 25). Such is the case with the three exemplary spaces that reflect one another and the town on the night of Carmen B. Arrieta's fatal party. In each of these parallel spaces, furthermore, the attention centers on fallen women — unlucky Luchi and her band of prostitutes in the brothel, absent/remembered Julia and the other officers' mistresses from the Hotel Jardín, doomed Isabel in her stony lunar dress surrounded by the upper-class invitees at Doña Carmen's party. The problem from the masculinist point of view is not uncontrolled male violence but unconfined female bodies. In each space, the authority slips from the voices of the men to that of the women, from military distance to self-reflexivity, from control and readability to an unreadable loss of control.

Yet this tight concatenation of structures, this palimpsest of spaces and voices and forms, fails to account for the most puzzling and incongruous happening in this narrative — Isabel's decision to become the mistress of her brother's murderer. One of the town's readings of this decision sees her as a heroine who gives her body to the general in an attempt to bargain for her surviving brother's life; another sees her as motivated by her irresistible love for the general. Both readings, however, will strike the reader as partial and unsatisfactory; both seem narratively trite in terms of the economy of the novel and implausibly out of character for the strong-minded young woman.

Imagine, however, another motivation, one more likely to match the character of the fallen lunar goddess, Coyolxauhqui. Isabel's unreadable, and therefore unwritten, motivation could well involve the expression of that unresolved feminist determination that leads her to speak so strongly against marriage. Just as the Cristeros desire political and religious freedom, and fight to the death for their rights to practice their religion, so too Isabel's actions are fueled by a particular desire for freedom and for freedom to express her desire. If it is not love nor yet political conviction that motivates her to involve herself sexually with Rosas, it could very well be an emotion that Coyolxauhqui would share: lust. And that is a motivation that even Garro's narration finds hard to accept, to articulate, or to theorize. As Donna Guy says in another context, "[B]oth revolution and carnal union...were too dangerous to consummate" since a procreative union in such a context would also imply consummating the revolution (Guy 1991, 168). The whole of the novel, then, with its intensely circular structure of repetition upon repetition, enacts an intense circumnavigation of a fantasy of lust so great and so obsessive that it hollows out selves and identities: lust for power, lust for freedom, lust for the body of another person, lust for death. And "lust" is a word that Juan Cariño would not have to go out into the street to capture; it has solidified all around him in the actions of the men who come to his brothel-home to have sex with Luchi and the other women. That brothel heterotopia lays bare the emotions that military and townsfolk alike prefer to hide under other names with their ongoing theater in the more public streets of Ixtepec. In learning the forbidden word, the unnamable shape of a woman's lust for a man, Isabel also learns, as indeed all Ixtepec learns, that while some fantasies are more powerful than others, all have to be paid for. Lust carries a heavy price in Ixtepec — the loss of a world.

Garro's novel joins Rulfo's text in describing a textual economy that yearns toward closure but that recognizes in the demand for closure a moral drama counterbalanced by the drama of the heterotopia and its counterpart, the fallen woman-traitor-witness hollowed out by the world and still witnessing to the tendency of the world to betray itself, to forget itself, to fall into the unknowable. Ixtepec's tale and Isabel's memories end with Isabel's death on the mountain, her fall into stone, and Gregoria's inscription on that stone. Rulfo's fragmentary, allegorical tale of the grave digger and the streetwalker falls off into the void left by the woman's too porous body. In each case, however, the narrative of falling does not quite reach closure. The woman falls, but death does not cut her off. She falls and continues to fall in the textual figure of the recurrence of falling that goes on and on, opening out the world as she falls, hollowing that world out into memory, which is another word for the void. There is no buried truth to be found in such texts, only the broken, hesitant rhythms of a speech that reminds us of the recurrences of death, and of desire, on unquiet streets.

# Chapter 4

# *Deterritorializing Women's Bodies*

## CASTILLO, CAMPBELL

The broken rhythms and textual hesitancies explored in the previous chapters are differently nuanced and more strongly colored in texts like those of Federico Campbell and Ana Castillo that explicitly play the expectations of two cultural realities against each other. Lust and the porosities of a desire turned unspeakable give shape to Rulfo's story and to Garro's novel. In Campbell and Castillo, too, carnal desire is the framing image of their narratives, and in the case of these latter two authors the writing of that need is inflected by a consciousness of complications arising from a specifically borderized sense of identity. Even more potently than in the previous works studied in this book, the novels of Campbell and Castillo explore the imbrication of territory and women's physical bodies. Furthermore, these novels focus attention on the shifting definition of transgression — always a slippery slope in describing female sexuality — as it is doubly inflected by the grating of two sets of cultural mores against each other. In this manner, an already problematic category of womanhood becomes even more unstable, at the same time as the clash of cultural expectations highlights and sharpens the limits of each country's perception of itself and of the other.

Late in Campbell's novella *Todo lo de las focas* [Everything about seals], the voices of the two main characters alternate in a dialogue fragment, picked up as one of the many vignette-like exchanges between them. One of the characters (Beverly) has given the other (the first-person narrator?) a copy of Leo Lionni's children's book, *Little Blue and Little Yellow*. Campbell's characters summarize the plot of the story: two spots, one blue and one yellow, hug each other until they are green, go out to play, and return home to be rejected by both sets of parents until they decompose themselves back from a single green entity into a blue spot and a yellow spot once again. In their conversation about Lionni's book, significantly, the two speaking voices of the characters also merge; neither voice is marked or inflected in any way so as to readily identify the speaker as the Mexican man or the U.S. woman, and the conversation begins with a rejoinder to an unrecorded question about the book. The giver of Lionni's book has prefaced it for the other interlocutor with a dedication — "para que aprenda a desobedecer" [so that you can learn to disobey] — and the recipient assures the giver that the book was read in that spirit and will be treasured forever. The same speaker ends the brief conversation with the elliptical remark, "Una historia para niños..." (Campbell 1989b, 102, 103) [A children's story... (Campbell 1995, 110, 111)].

Lionni's book, so prominently cited in Campbell's novella, clearly suggests itself as something other than just another children's story. It is, as both characters agree, one of the formative texts of their border-reality, an unforgettable book that taught them the virtues of disobeying restrictive parents in the name of friendship and that showed them graphically how other limits and borders, including the borders of the body, could be dissolved. Campbell's work can, then, be seen as a retelling of that simple story of the borderlands between one shape and another, of the interactions of "blues" and "yellows" in that border space, of the insights achieved by the intermittently emergent "green" friendships, and of the shocks created in the inevitable and repeated crashing of one reality against another.

The crashing of one reality against another is also a central theme in Ana Castillo's novel *The Mixquiahuala Letters*. Castillo's narrator, a Mexican-American woman named Teresa, recalls for her semiwhite friend Alicia a long-ago summer-school weekend spent in the pre-Columbian village named Mixquiahuala. Says Teresa, with apparent approbation: "[F]or years afterward you enjoyed telling people that i was from Mixquiahuala" (A. Castillo 1986, 20), and, as the title of the book suggests, that once-seen and now mythic town represents less an actual place than the state of mind that pervades these letters. It marks the unease of someone who, in Lionni and Campbell's terms, would be a "green" patch in a world that is sometimes "blue" and sometimes "yellow." In many ways, Mixquiahuala is an earlier version of the country that Castillo identifies in her second, and later, novel as "Sapogonia," which she describes as "a distinct place in the Americas where all mestizos reside, regardless of nationality, individual racial composition, or legal residential status — or perhaps, because of all these" (A. Castillo 1990, 5). Castillo goes on: "Sapogonia (like the Sapogón/a) is not identified by modern boundaries" (6); it is, then, a place both spiritual and physical that recognizes and celebrates the overlapping of two realities, two myths, two cultures, two ways of living and dreaming, two different political and economic modes of perceiving the world. The border between them is colored by hope and fear and faith. Thus, for both the Mexican male writer and the Mexican-American female writer, the two-thousand-mile political boundary drawn between the United States and Mexico identifies a notional truth, a reality that is also, like all things that merge blue and yellow, a fiction.

What is not at question in these books is whether that notional truth about Mixquiahuala or about Tijuana matches a geographer's or a politician's truth. More interesting to these writers is the task of delimiting the soul in the borderlands of these invented truths. And in both books that spiritual element is sought in the other country, the other sex, the other race, the exotic and abstracted Other who merges with the narrative self. This encounter, however, is far from the friendly embrace of two children who disobey their parents' unfair strictures in order to play together; in both books, narrative reality is painfully drawn against the norms of daily truth and even common sense. What seemed to be knowledge reveals itself as a cultural practice open to question and interpretation. In both books, the encounter between two cultures and two people opens a site not only of exchange but also of often bitter cultural contestation.

One of the most ambiguously negotiated sites in both novels is that of female identity. In both books, the borderlands seem to bring to consciousness the most extreme variants of each culture's stereotypes about itself and about the other culture. In both books, these stereotypes are focused in and through the feminine and, specifically, through the conflicted reaction to female sexuality. Homi Bhabha writes, "[C]ultural difference is to be found where 'loss' of meaning enters, as a cutting edge, into the representation of the fullness of the demands of culture" (Bhabha 1990, 313), and in these novels the "cutting edge" invariably takes the form of the encounter between two versions of male and female stereotypes about each other. Meaning is not so much lost as subject to negotiation, as are the other products of cultural conditioning, and in such renegotiations of identity cultural constructs are both eroded and reinforced.

For Castillo's Teresa, the cultural conflict is particularly intense, as the Mexican-American woman straddles the razor edge between two cultures, neither of which satisfies her spirit. The barely remembered, poetically reinvented pre-Columbian town of Mixquiahuala represents for her a spiritual homeland. "There was a definite call to find a place to satisfy my yearning spirit," she writes to her friend Alicia; she adds: "i chose Mexico" (46). Nevertheless, Mexico functions as a spirit home only from the U.S. side of the border; once she actually begins to live in Mexico she discovers that it is antagonistic to her sense of self. She recalls to Alicia, "i'd enough of the country where relationships were never clear and straightforward, but a tangle of contradictions and hypocrisies," and she captures her frustration in a poem: "This was her last night / in the homeland / of spiritual devastation" (54–55).

In point of fact, what Teresa finds spiritually devastating is not that there are contradictions and hypocrisies in the relationships between men and women in Mexico but rather that the relationships are altogether too clear and straightforward. Teresa's relationship with Ponce, a Mexican engineer, is a case in point:

> He began, "I think you are a 'liberal woman.' Am I correct?" His expression meant to persuade me that it didn't matter what I replied. In the end he would win. He would systematically strip away all my pretexts, reservations and defenses, and end up in bed with me.
>
> In that country, the term "liberated woman" meant something other than what we had strived for in the United States. In this case it simply meant a woman who would sleep nondiscriminately with any man who came along....
>
> *Liberal: trash, whore, bitch.* (73)

In this brief exchange, Castillo establishes two sets of cultural norms with their attendant illusions. For the Mexican man, liberated and liberal fold into each other, and both words, when stripped of their decorative rhetoric, come down to the same thing when applied to a woman — they mean she is a willing prostitute who does not even require payment for her services. For the Mexican-American woman who has dedicated herself personally and politically to the struggle for women's equality, such narrow-mindedness is appalling. But what makes the exchange spiritually devastating for her is that she also sees Ponce's equation of liberated = whore to some degree as an accurate, if pitiless, reading of a personal reality she recognizes and strives to reject, whereas her own politically advanced positioning becomes infected with a hypocritical and highly selective attitude toward both dominant white culture in the United States and her own Mexican heritage. For both the Mexican man and the Mexican-American woman, the whore is the grounding signifier where cultural difference and loss of meaning come to rest. But that signifier, so shocking, so stripped of pretext, stubbornly resists interpretation. In this respect, Castillo's protagonist echoes the angry, politically aware poetry of fellow Chicana poet Gina Valdés, who writes in her poem "Working Women":

> ...y yo no sé que ando
> aquí cruising so low, mirujeando
> this working women's scene, thinking
> of what rucas and rucos do to pay
> their rent and eat, I, a poet hustling
> hot verbs, a teacher selling brainwaves
> in the S.D. red light school district,
> feeling only un poco mejor than these
> rucas of the night, a little luckier,
> just as worn, my ass grinded daily
> in this big cathouse U S A, que a
> todos nos USA, una puta más in this
> prostitution ring led by a heartless
> cowboy pimp. (Valdés 1986, 58)

Campbell, too, grounds signification in the feminine and in the liberated woman apparently open to any man's sexual advances. He says of Beverly, in announcing his intention to seek her throughout the entire world, "Siempre fuiste la misma con diferentes nombres, la niña del barrio, la compañera en la escuela secundaria, la señora joven recién casada, la prostituta del casino, o la misma, tú misma, cuando a cierta distancia te dejaste perseguir por los andenes del aeropuerto" (81) [You were always the same woman with different names — the neighborhood girl, the middle-school classmate, the recently married young woman, the casino prostitute — or the same woman, yourself, to be pursued at a certain distance through the airport sidewalks (91)]. Campbell's parallel series is subtly shocking. He molds his image of the beloved woman as a sequence of snapshots representing the different phases in her life — child, student, married woman, prostitute — where the final profession suggests not only a logical next step in the sequence of a woman's growth in the borderlands but also an identificatory culmination of sorts. The images of femininity come down to this image, before dispersing in Beverly's resistance to the narrator's reading — a resistance revealed in her obscurity in his photographs.

Certainly, the ambiguous and distanced "yourself" of the "airport sidewalks" has none of the stereotyped distinguishing qualities of the little child, the schoolgirl, the young wife, the casino whore. Nevertheless, it is telling that when the narrator once again returns to the image of the mysterious woman, he figures her in one of the most familiar Hispanic stereotypes of female ambiguity: the sexually available woman, the *maja*. Like Goya's *Maja desnuda*, the narrator's *maja* apparently opens herself unself-consciously to the artist's hands and eyes and artistic re-creation.

Still, Beverly, like the earlier *maja,* retains a secret amusement about her apparent offer of herself to the painter or to the photographer, and that secret negates her physical availability. In fact, in Campbell's novel, the woman instigates the play of appearances, and it is perhaps this self-conscious self-construction as the model of a male fantasy that prevents her appropriation as yet another catalogable image in the narrator's album. The narrator muses: "¿Y el sillón Recamier donde posaste como maja? Retrátame, me dijiste. Puertas cubiertas de seda y espejos de pared iban del suelo al filo de las lámparas de araña. Oprimí varias veces el disparador de la cámara y surgiste entre sombras, oscura y distorsionada como si no hubiera habido suficiente luz en aquel cuarto" (89) [And the Recamier chair where you posed like a maja? "Make a portrait of me," you said. Silk-covered doors and mirrors hanging on the walls stretched from the floor to the chandeliers. I pressed the camera's shutter a number of times and you emerged from the shadows, dark and distorted as if there had not been enough light in the room (98–99)]. Beverly, the twentieth-century U.S. woman, distorted, like Goya's women, by light and shadows and artistic will, nowhere escapes the narrator so fully as in giving herself up to the camera, in taking the role of a late eighteenth-century Spanish courtesan, in a French chair, in a Mexican studio, in the bordertown of Tijuana.

This chapter will explore the process whereby the liberated-woman-whore/casino-prostitute-*maja* comes to take on significance as the dominant trope of femininity but at the same time deconstructs, or self-destructs, under the pressures of an identity construction traversed by too many borderlines. In Campbell's novella, the mysterious pilot and beloved woman, Beverly, appears deterritorialized in the familiar-exotic surroundings of Tijuana, where she represents that Mexican border city without losing her primary identification with the unachievable and ambiguously desired other side, Beverly Hills, with all of its pop cultural products and material advantages. In Castillo's novel, two U.S. Hispanic women, one white, one Indian-featured, see themselves as exiles in their own country and make multiple trips to Mexico, and to affairs with Mexican men, in order to seek out a new territory for self-reconstruction.

In Campbell's novella, the obscure play of chiaroscuro around the figure of the mysterious gringa, Beverly, serves as a figure for the specular space in which the United States contemplates the strangeness of its own image. This image is then projected back in the excesses of a Mexican border town and at the same time cut off from view in the liminality of a borderline that ignores those strangenesses that derive from the unrecognized cultural space beyond its strictly drawn frontier. And the reverse. This novella offers the play of light and dark, of shadows that reform

as clarity, and light that distorts a captured image. It is not coincidental that the narrator of the novella identifies himself through his camera
and through photographic products. In this manner he not only evokes,
in a minor key, the profession for which Beverly Hills is best known but
also puts emphasis on the camera eye's view, an emphasis that reminds
us of the doubleness of the development process — from negative to
positive print, where shadow and light echo and reverse each other. For
the Mexican narrator, the United States is the specular space in which
he contemplates his other self. "Vivimos en mundos divididos, distintos"
(113) [We live in different, divided worlds (119)], the narrator says to
Beverly, and he is both right and wrong in saying so; his shadow is her
light; his light, her obscurity. In this agonistic play, the two cultures are
never quite double, never quite singular either.

This is the context of a border region in which, as Emily Hicks
acutely observes, "two or more referential codes operate simultaneously."
Hicks continues, "[I]n the U.S.-Mexico border region, there is no need
to 'become-other'; one is 'other' or 'marginal' by definition, by virtue of
living between two cultures and being 'other' in both" (Hicks 1988, 4–5).
Says Campbell in a short story, "Y uno se volvía la vista de un lado a otro,
de Los Angeles al DF y viceversa, como en un juego de ping pong. No se
decidía uno muy bien hacia cuál de los dos polos dejarse atraer; no que-
daba muy claro si las innovaciones en el caló o el buen vestir...procedían
de Tepito o del East Side" (Campbell 1989b, 170) [And you'd turn your
gaze from one side to another, from Los Angeles to the DF and vice
versa, like a ping pong game. You never could decide very easily which
of the two poles most attracted you; it wasn't ever very clear to you if
the latest innovations in speech or dress...came from Tepito or from the
East Side (Campbell 1995, 162)]. For the alienated narrator of *Todo lo
de las focas,* the constant to-and-fro from Los Angeles to the Distrito Federal (Mexico City), the continual play of light and dark, the increasing
slipperiness of people and places, leaves him oddly isolated.

The novella begins, "No siento diferencia alguna entre una ciudad y
otra....Todo me da igual....Soy el centro del mundo, el espejo: nada
importa, todo existe en función mía" (11) [I can't really tell much difference between one city and another....It's all the same to me....I am the
center of the world, the mirror. Nothing matters and everything exists as
an extension of my wishes (27–28)]. Difference, then, is coded in loss of
difference, loss of meaning, in which the ping-pong doubleness of view
comes to rest squarely in the viewing subject, who exercises control with a
closing of the eyes, a refusal of signification, or an artificially maintained
choice between the photograph and the photographic negative. Throughout the novella, in the precise moment when everything becomes strange,

the narrator pulls back upon himself with the tag phrase, "todo me da igual," repeated as a mantra to stave off both difference and undifferentiation. Late in the novella, for example, the narrator wakes up one morning to the panicked realization that the world has shifted ground overnight: "En un momento, de la noche a la mañana, cambia el mundo. Todo sale de su sitio y vuelve extraño. Todo me da igual. A veces lo único que me interesa realmente es comer y dormir, dormir mucho" (99) [In just one moment, from one day to the next, the world changes. Everything falls out of place and becomes strange. It's all the same to me. Sometimes the only things I'm really interested in are eating and sleeping — sleeping a lot (107)]. In such passages, Campbell's narrator falls back on the concreteness of the body and on the body's needs so as to deterritorialize his own sense of displacement and liminality. In so doing, however, he aggravates his own problem by reproducing a fiction of the illusion as an illusion of the truth. At the same time, the very juxtaposition of these two realms — abstract sensation versus bodily needs — fosters another illusion, the illusion that words on a page reproduce something other than syntactical structures, that the omnipresent photographs capture something other than a contingent and created reality. The narrator's ritual photography, ritual indifference, and ritual appeal to things of the body help maintain a slippery sense of identity, a minimal hold on a unified state of being, however attenuated.

Meanwhile, for the narrator, the political reality of the border cannot cease to impinge upon his self-imposed egoism. In the ping-pong view, central Mexican culture and the Spanish language exert a strong pull from one side, but Los Angeles's popular culture and the appeal of a secure income exert an equal and opposite attraction: "¿Dónde andabas, en Los Angeles?" [Where have you been, in Los Angeles?] asks a character in one of Campbell's stories, and the narrator muses, "La pregunta plantea un mito. Toda ausencia se relaciona con un destino de adulto en el East Side de Los Angeles" (Campbell 1989b, 152) [The question presupposes a myth. Every absence is related to an adult destiny on Los Angeles's East Side (Campbell 1995, 150)]. And yet, for the Mexican national, the ping-pong game has clear rules and a clearly marked net — the fence between Tijuana and San Diego. Campbell reminds us that illegal border-crossers in the Californian sister cities are not *mojados* [wetbacks] but *alambrados* [fence-climbers] or perhaps *alambristas* [high-wire walkers] who do not wade the river but instead confront the entanglements of the fence. In the unresolved exchange between LA and the DF, this fence rises up to divide his world and to divide himself — a steel fence in the soul dividing self from body, spirit from mind. Language, reality, truth, nationality: all are subject to the driving force of the divided being, transfixed by the steel fence of a borderline's liminality, allowing one culture to bleed into the other in the between-time, between-place of the borderland self. Campbell's narrator longs for safe limits — but not the limits imposed from outside, of a reality circumscribed by an all-too-real fence. He longs for an end to the dizzying ping-pong game — but that game defines his border-self. He wants to be firm and compact and self-sufficient — but the aching need for Beverly recalls to him that without her inscrutable presence to complete him and to complete his map of California, upper and lower, he is only, in Lionni's terms, a blue spot, not a green whole. He is only, in terms of the profession he has adopted, half of the photographic process.

The narrator, caught on the fence, suffers from indecision. Not so Beverly, who finds his inaction exasperating. Says the narrator about her, "Lo que importaba era su manera de estar, estar realmente y no plantearse demasiadas preguntas" (22) [What was essential was her style of *be-ing,* of really being, and not asking too many questions of herself (37)]. Campbell inaugurates here an untranslatable play between the two Spanish verbs of being, where "manera de *estar*" stands in for the more orthodox "manera de *ser.*" Beverly herself, with her limited Spanish, is not likely to capture such nuances, but the narrator delicately hints at two different ways of "being." Beverly's fluid *estar* stands in implicit contrast to the narrator's more intractable *ser,* and, moreover, her unrooted manner of being resonates with the tendency to embrace certainties rather than "plantearse demasiadas preguntas." Beverly aspires to "know" the city; for the narrator, such knowledge is fraught with danger: "Pero las calles eran interrogantes" (22) [But the streets were question marks (37)], he reminds us, his uncertainty and his surfeit of questions more than compensating for her confidence and her lack of them. Even at the level of the noun clause the narrator gives us nothing firm and resistant without also suggesting the irrational fault lines running through its confection, pairing abstract nouns to concrete modifiers to match his own diffuse and imprecise sense of self. The pattern is established as a young boy, during a nighttime bus ride with his mother: "[A] esa edad tuve una impresión, la primera, muy concreta de la inmensidad" (72) [At that moment I had an impression, my first, very concrete impression of immensity (82)]. This juxtaposition — a concrete impression of an incommensurable space — haunts the writer/photographer's later search for the concrete, which he locates in Beverly, and his love for the abstract, which, typically, he discovers in the same person.

For Beverly, the narrator's hesitation and propensity for concretized abstraction remain inexplicable. Whereas she seemingly can stand (the etymological root of *estar*) on her own, the narrator — despite his frequent and unconvincing declarations of independence — requires her reality upon which to prop his own indistinct sense of self. "Soy como puedo," he tells her, "Soy como tú crees que soy" [I am what I can be....I am whatever you believe me to be], to which she responds: "Vete a donde se están haciendo paises nuevos todos los días, haz algo, bueno o malo, pero haz algo. Sal de tu marasmo....Ve a la esquina y compra un cono de nieve" (33) [Go someplace where they are making new countries every day, do something, for good or ill, but do something. Wake up from your apathy....Go to the corner and buy an ice-cream cone (47–48)]. Typically, of the options for action that she gives him, he chooses the last, and they share the ice-cream cone: the abstract becomes concrete, an action and a noun, and consumption turns it ephemeral once again. Despite the fact that the reader sees Beverly only through his eyes and never independently of his construction of her, it is she, despite her mysterious fluidity, who anchors him to reality.

For Castillo's characters, too, self-identity and cultural identification rest on the borderlines of a loss of identity matched to an ambiguous surplus of stereotypical identities. As in Campbell's novella, with its Mexican male protagonist, Castillo's Mexican-American female defines herself against the other culture and other sex, only to discover that her own fragmented sense of self becomes forced into an unacceptably narrow mold or that her undecidability is uncomfortably confirmed. There are crucial differences, however. While Campbell's narrator focuses on a concrete border and a psychological profile of the border-self, Castillo, broadly speaking, emphasizes a spiritual borderlands and the interplay of race, culture, and economic position that defines what Anseleme Remy calls the "unholy trinity," a construct upon which Remy bases the concept of ethnoclass (Remy 1974).

Teresa looks to Mexico to cure the discomfort she feels with the markers of her U.S. ethnoclass — in the United States she is made to feel an outsider to her own country with the copper skin and fuller body type that mark her racial heritage, the slight accent that betrays her cultural background, the often angry reactions that betray her efforts to resist the traditions of her family's economic class. Teresa is attracted to Mixquiahuala largely because it satisfies in her a yearning for some concrete correlative of her own lightly marked Indian features: "[I]t explained the exotic tinge of yellow and red in my complexion, the hint of an accent in my baroque speech, and most of all, the indiscernible origin of my being" (20). Like Campbell's protagonist, Castillo's Teresa suffers the scars of a divided self that drives her to foreground those specific features she describes, but to do so in minimalizing terms: "the *tinge* of yellow and red," "the *hint* of an accent," "the *indiscernible* origin." Alienated from her ethnoclass by education and experience, but unable to find anonymity in the dominant society, she, like Campbell's protagonist, looks to the idealization of another culture for clues to her lost/fragmented identity. But with a difference. Where Campbell's narrator, a provincial Mexican man, performs a mental ping pong between two modern, and very cosmopolitan, centers, Teresa, a product of the large U.S. city, projects herself backward, toward an indiscernible, but determinably provincial, origin. That homeland, as she knows, functions best in dreams and is too fragile to stand up to waking reality:

> i too suffer from dreams.
>
> It was a provincial town, with cobblestone streets, shattered windows, and aged wooden doors and gates. In the scale of history: between the sixteenth century and the present...
>
> The people were of mixed blood, people of the sun and earth....
>
> i too was of that small corner of the world. i was of that mixed blood, of fire and stone, timber and vine, a history passed down from mouth to mouth since the beginning of time. (95–96)

Teresa knows that this terrain, while intimately hers in dreams, belongs to her only in dreams. Her own words distance her from Mixquiahuala when she is awake. Likewise, when she travels in Mexico, only one part of her divided self is coming home; the rest of her visits an exotic and unfamiliar land. She too, like the people in her fantasy town, is of mixed blood, but she has not grown up in the out-of-the-way provincial village of her dreams where copper-colored skin is the norm. Her skin color is racialized and defined by her U.S. reality in a way alien to that half-imagined utopic town. Her color is, as she says, "exotic," her origin, even to herself, "indiscernible."

Teresa's motivation for her trips to Mexico is likewise divided. On the one hand, she goes to Mexico to find people like herself, to understand her roots, to reaffirm the value of the ethnoclass from which she has sprung. On the other hand, like any gringa tourist, she finds herself most attracted to those aspects of Mexico that are, in terms of the dominant U.S. culture, exotic, foreign, and for that very reason, seductive. During one trip, in a visit to a "quaint Mexican town," Teresa describes a seduction scene in which a man named Alvaro appears in her bedroom from a balcony: "From behind his back he produced a mango the size of which i hadn't seen before. Isn't this what you said you craved back in Califas? i smiled. As he peeled back the skin, releasing the exotic juice, he entertained me with another of his fantastic stories" (50). On another trip Alicia stays behind in Acapulco because, says Teresa, she was "enchanted by the haunting beauty of the deserted hacienda, the virile lover of skin like polished wood, the hypnotic sea" (26). In both cases, the wording and imagery are similar; the exotic and the virile merge in episodes that are half-real, half-fantasy, and attractive because exotic and strange. As in fairy tales, enchantment and passion intertwine. Yearning for so much, it is no wonder that both Teresa and Alicia find Mexican men strangely recalcitrant; such men have their own dreams of seducing "liberated" gringa tourists, after all. For them, the definition of the exotic is inverted, but their reality, Mexican reality, exists in Castillo's novel only as distanced and rejected distopic moments of unpleasantness.

Neither Alicia nor Teresa finds in Mexico any alternative to the conflicts deriving from their ethnoclass situation in the United States, although distance and exoticism provide them with a space to imagine an idealized other world. From the U.S. side of the border, Mexico seduces as the tabula rasa upon which they might rewrite their pasts, and that familiar-but-alien other provides a more malleable form for this self-imagining than the resistant molds of their own country. Thus, to the degree that Mexico confirms her fictional image, including her dream of a seductive exoticism, Teresa loves it and its people; to the degree that it insists on deviating from her dream, on confirming a stubborn incomprehensibility (or worse, a matter-of-fact counterstereotype), she rejects it utterly. Again and again, in each visit to Mexico, Teresa's dream of finding a simple, exotic homeland fragments against the staged exoticism of a pragmatic seduction attempt. Each encounter is wounding, and each wound reconfirms her divided self. Castillo's epistolary novel does not attempt to resolve the tension of this double vision. Instead, the strained theatricality remains highlighted in the text, pointing directly at the heart of Teresa's confused longing, her double and distanced misreadings of two cultures' typical tropes.

Campbell too is concerned with tropes and with the imagined cities that inflect and corrupt border-reality. Los Angeles (LA) and Mexico City (the DF) are two such imagined, imaginary cities. Likewise illusory are the novella's Hollywood (seen through the eyes of a Tijuana native who has watched Rita Hayworth dance and Charlie Chaplin get drunk) and the tourist's exotic and tacky "T.J." Campbell's Tijuana graphically, geographically, illustrates the confluence of many types of borders, some of which negate the others, and all of which are presided over by a modern totem. One border is, of course, the political border between the United States and Mexico, physically impressed upon the consciousness of border-dwellers in the form of the fence that slices through the San Diego-Tijuana metropolitan area. Some roads, suggests the narrator of the novella, lead up to the fence and then abruptly cease to exist.

Others, a few, break off at a border-post presided over by an immigration officer and then resume mysteriously, discontinuously, on the other side. Anyone who drives a car in the border region is always aware of those possibilities opened by the paved surface and of those possibilities foreclosed. A second border is created in the encounter between land and sea, and Campbell recurs frequently to the metaphor of that border as well. Humankind follows the surfaces of the land or the traceries of its roads; fish swim the sea roads, and only those strange, ambiguous creatures, the seals, slip back and forth easily across the borders between them. Land and sea answer to each other in this borderland, just as the United States and Mexico must: the two borders, seashore and man-made fence, run perpendicularly to each other. This perfect conversation, these competing and cacophonous monologues — of land and sea, United States and Mexico, fence and shoreline, English-speaking woman and Spanish-speaking man — pervade both Californias. And in each case, the perfect conversation, the answering of negative to print, the to-and-fro movement of the ping-pong ball, also reminds the reader of all the untranslatable, unspoken abysses that mark the uncrossable limits of two disparate realities.

It is Campbell's task to disrupt the borders and shift the axes. He does so first of all by taking to the air.[1] The narrator as a child haunts the airport and is an avid constructor of model airplanes. In one memorable scene the young boy alternates his attention between the plane he is constructing and his neighbor's preparations to have sex with her lover. As the Spitfire slowly takes shape under the boy's hands, the woman seen through the window undresses, takes her lover's hand, and disappears below the window frame (Campbell 1989b, 56–57; 1995, 68–69). The boy, at least mentally, rises with the airplanes while the woman sinks to her bed — as it turns out, never to rise from it again. In fact, her sinking to the bed is the last action anyone sees her take before the discovery of her lifeless body in the same bed. The woman is landbound, never more so than with her death. The boy, in contrast, soars. Roads and fences fall away, allowing for a new awareness of space and surface. Other remembered episodes confirm both the obsession with flying and the fear of falling (into femininity, into death). Typically, the narrator's gang of school friends chooses a name that reflects their yearning to soar as well. They call themselves "Pegasos" (Pegasus) and wear red jackets with winged horses copied after the famous Mobil Oil symbol, jackets they only remove in order to fly, downward this time, from the springboard into the water of a local swimming pool (1989b, 52–53; 1995, 64). In these boys obsessed with flight, and afraid of flying, we see the opening of a new conversation over other borders —

Greek myth and U.S. advertising, winged horse and amphibious seal, air and water.

The airplane's height, the water's depth, force the borderlands dwellers to rethink concepts based on roads and fences. Air and water take social and political distinctions out of their land-based element. The narrator, in fact, describes one in terms of the other: "Las pocas veces que viajé en un avión . . . experimentaba el sentimiento de ser atraído, de estar suspendido en el aire, a flote o inmerso dulcemente en una alberca tibia. . . . Apoyaba la frente contra la ventanilla y veía como mi cuerpo y el cuerpo del avión irrumpíamos en las nubes y nos deslizábamos sobre la inmensidad blanca" (14) [The few times I actually travelled in a plane . . . I experienced a feeling of attraction, of being suspended in the air, of floating on, or of being sweetly immersed in a warm pool. . . . I rested my forehead against the window and watched how my body and the airplane sliced through the clouds and slid along their white immensity (30)]. His body and the airplane's body merge in a fearful symbiosis of border seal and mythic horse. Seeing Beverly descend from an airplane irresistibly brings to mind seeing her emerge from the sea — in both cases evoking a kind of birth the narrator urgently needs to capture and preserve in his photographs (1989b, 91; 1995, 100). Significantly, Beverly is a pilot, and fearless. Yet Beverly, framed in the airplane's door, inevitably recalls that other woman, the ambiguously sexually active neighbor framed in her bedroom window, overseen by the young boy during her last hours of life as he glues together bits of his model airplane in the next apartment.

Even more pervasive in the novella than the airplane/Pegasus images, however, are the recurrent images of the seals, which in this work are associated with the feminine occupation of the entire (border)space of narrative. In his reflections on the genesis of *Todo lo de las focas*, Campbell muses:

> [L]a pequeña novela se fue conformando alrededor de algunas imágenes: el sueño de una foca humanizada en una noche de playa. Quería dar a entender . . . que aquel mundo en el que se movía el personaje narrador era un espacio habitado por animales hembras, en el que los hombres no tenían cabida. . . . Un mundo, pues, en el que la actividad masculina no tiene ningún valor. (Campbell 1989a, 39)

> [(T)he novella developed around several images: the dream of a humanized seal on an evening beach. I wanted to suggest . . . that the world in which the narrator moved was a space inhabited by

female animals with no space for men.... A world, therefore, in which masculine activity has no value.]

Like the airplanes, the seals inspire a fearful fascination. The seals, says the narrator, are "seres a medias: metamorfoseados, fronterizos, en medio del camino hacia la vida terrestre, habitantes risueños de las olas, muñecas flotadoras, somnolientas, mudas, seres andróginos" (66) [Halfway beings; metamorphosed borderliners; halfway toward life on the land; laughing inhabitants of the waves; floating dolls; sleepy, mute, androgynous, and seemingly asexual beings (77)]. Like their human counterparts who live on other borders, the seals are the denizens of an indeterminately inhospitable intermediate zone, in this case that ambiguous space between land and sea. There is a price, the narrator hints, for such border-crossing abilities — the seals tend to be evoked in a context of mutilation, or death. In a complex sequence of associations, the seals become linked with those other deformed beings, the human border-dwellers, who are also in some ways "halfway beings," who also seem pathetic and mutilated when they cross the line from one space into another. The *foca* also evokes the *foco* — the narrative focus and the ever-present focusing and framing lens of the narrator's camera. The *focas* frame this border-tale of sea barriers and land fences; they also recall the interlingual obscenity, *fóquin*, the graphic signifier of a violent attempt to break down physical boundaries and merge one self with another.

Beverly, the woman who descends from the airplane and who rises from the sea, almost always appears in the text in close association with references to the herd of seals floating offshore. She plunges into the narrator's world from her airplane; he is terrified of surfacing and creates a miniature world within the border world through airplane models (dreams of flying) and photographs (stolen snatches of life). Beverly and the narrator go to the beach to see the seals; they see as well a lifeguard rescue a woman from the sea. When they look down on the beach from their vantage point above it, the seals and the human beings lose their distinguishing physical characteristics and bleed into each other: "[L]os puntos negros...eran los espectadores o las focas.... Los bañistas aclamaban al salvavidas, aplaudían el héroe. Se aglomeraban en torno al espectáculo de las focas.... La foca mayor aleteaba como un ser mutilado" (111) [The black specks...were spectators or seals.... The swimmers acclaimed the lifeguard, applauded the hero. They gathered around the spectacle of the seals.... The oldest seal waved its flipper like a mutilated being (117)]. The association between mutilated or heroic humans and seals, who are also conceived of as mutilated, remains constant in the text. As the narrator drives a dying Beverly north toward San Diego after her bungled abortion, the seals also float northward, toward Alaska (1989b, 12; 1995, 28). In their parallel existences, the seals stand in contrast to the humans as examples of the optimally adapted border-dweller, and yet they too, on land, seem clumsy, laughable, mutilated. They are by nature what the narrator yearns for and fears in his obsession with Beverly. His is a paradoxical desire to sink into the other, to resolve the fragmented photos that circumscribe his life, to *be* without foundation or limits, and yet at the same time to reject fragmentation or division and to soar heavenward in splendid isolation.

The seals, silent witnesses between sea and land, also stand in mute memorial for the ruined potential of fish-children. "Me duele una grave sensación de desperdicio," says the narrator, "y todo lo que significa desecho, desperdicio yo mismo y las gotas que esparzo inútilmente cada noche sobre las sábanas" (98) [I am painfully aware of a grave sense of waste... and everything that signifies waste. I squander myself and the drops that I sprinkle uselessly on the sheets (106)]. The waste of vital fluids, of the potential for life, causes nightmares: "[R]ompo la cuenta de los espermatozoides antes de que se acumulen y luego me sueño en mi sueño.... Emerge aleteando la figura de un pez visto bocarriba. Lo miro debajo de mis piernas, es mío, ascendiendo en dirección mía, es mío, siguiendo la cuerda entre mis piernas, es mío, y luego el pez agoniza sobre la arena, es mío, aletea, es mío, queda tieso, es mío" (98) [I have lost count of the sperm before they accumulate, and later I dream.... A fish emerges flapping from the water face up. I look at it lying at my feet — it's mine, it's rising toward me, it's mine, it's following the line up between my legs, it's mine — and then the fish expires on the sand — it's mine, it flaps; it's mine, it falls still, it's mine (106–7)]. The nightmare sperm-fish-penis-child finds its echo in the photographically paralyzed scene of a child offering an orange to a seal: "Niño y foca son partes de una misma pieza. Prolongación del hombro de la foca, los dedos de la mano palmeados, el cuerpo en forma de pez.... Así el niño se contorsiona por dentro de la foca mayor, o la foca mueve su hombro derecho" (119) [The child and the seal are parts of the same sculpture. The child is a prolongation of the seal's shoulder, its webbed fingers, its fish-shaped body.... Thus the child contorts himself inside the oldest seal, or the seal moves its right shoulder (124)]. Again and again, the narrator hesitates between two borders, two sets of images, two semiotic systems until this hesitation, this non(re)productivity, becomes the distinguishing sign of his tortured border-psyche.

Finally, while this book proposes to tell us "everything about seals," it ultimately can speak only around those strange border-creatures who escape definition, who achieve the floating existence, the self without foundation to which the narrator aspires, and which he fears is his. They are, then, an ambiguous but powerful symbol, an image of social values that remain in a fluid state, uncertain and ill-defined. They come to land, as awkward, mutilated spectators on terrestrial life, and they move with an incomprehensible grace in that other, incommensurable world of the sea. Like the airplanes, they belong to two worlds and neither and are sublimely indifferent to borders; they cross fences and shorelines with impunity.

Beverly too is a border-crosser. She is a pilot and in one of her incarnations flies planes in the air taxi service between Hollywood and the Agua Caliente casino (1989b, 17; 1995, 33). The very fact of piloting a plane makes her, in the narrator's point of view, another order of being: "El hecho de que supiera manejar un avión hacía que yo viera en sus manos una potencia y una superioridad que la separaban de mí infranqueablemente, como si ella procediera de otro mundo" (16) [The fact that she knew how to fly a plane meant that I saw in her a power and a superiority that separated her from me irremediably, as if she came from another world (32)]. Beverly is different from ordinary women in other ways as well. She implies to the narrator that she is a woman with a past, "que era alguien a quien marcaron para siempre otras manos, que había algo en ella fatalmente irrecuperable" (34) [that she was someone who had been marked forever by other hands, that there was something fatally irrecoverable in her (48)]. This irrecuperable element, the unknown experiences from the other side of the border, continually interrupts the narrator's efforts to construct her and, through her, himself. He creates her with his tongue, his hands, his body, his camera, but there is always some element of her that escapes him, that remains on the other side. She is a woman with a past, but that past is unknown and unreconstructable. Even her name (But can we even know if it is her "real" name?) evokes nothing so much as a place marker in the border-man's incessant ping-pong vision of two unknowable wholes — DF, LA. She marks the Hollywood side of the transaction; her name reminds us of the flight of U.S. popular culture over the border, uninhibited by fences. She is Beverly Hills incarnate, raising in the narrator's heart all the conflictive emotions of rejection and attraction to her romantic dream vision and to an alien, culturally coded myth. Her past is nothing he can imagine, and there are no recognizable faces assigned to it. And still, he wants to appropriate her, all of her, as exclusively his.

Yet, at one moment, he glimpses what this other element, the unimaginable presence of her past, might be. He recalls the English-speaking man who sometimes accompanies her on her flights to Tijuana. That man too has a place in this story, but in all the confusions of time and place and circumstance, the narrator is unable to write him in: "El, el que te acompañaba frío y distante en la barra del Blue Fox, debe ser el tercer personaje. Tu esposo, tu amado fantasma. El piloto maestro. El capitán. El aviador devorado por el cielo" (93) [He, that cold and distant man who accompanies you at the Blue Fox, ought to be the third character. Your husband, your fantasy lover. The master pilot. The captain. The aviator devoured by the sky (102–3)]. The fantasized master pilot should have been the third character in this tale, the apex of the romantic triangle, but he is not. Instead, phantomlike, he suggests all the possibilities of Beverly's life on the other side of the border, without concretely defining any of them. That other man, the Hollywood counterpart to her glamorous and distanced self, is what keeps Beverly unclassifiable; he is what makes the narrator, land-bound and border-transfixed, almost too obviously defined. Like the seals, she escapes his obsession with her but becomes, at one and the same time, the absolutely alien other and the embodiment of his border-dream.

The narrator's construction/recollections of Beverly involve a mass of unresolved contradictions. He enters into her reality, shares her history, and deterritorializes her past to match his changing needs. She is associated, first of all and above all, with the airplanes that the narrator dreams about and the fantasy of flight that paralyzes him with fear and longing. In the first stage of their relationship, he says, "ella seguía siendo un ser anónimo, distante e inaccesible, al que me limitaba a contemplar" (27) [she remained an anonymous being, a distant and inaccessible person who I was limited only to contemplating (41)]. At this point, he wants nothing more or less than to be the absolute and unknown voyeur on the absent space of his construction of her: "No podía yo entrar en ningún sitio porque ya estaba allí el susto de verla intempestivamente, el terror de encontrármela una vez más, aunque ella no se percatara de mi cuerpo" (18) [I could no longer go anywhere because I always carried within me the fear of seeing her suddenly, the terror of finding her again, even if she remained unaware of my body (34)]. Instead, he invades her house in her absence, sleeps in her bed, eats her food at her table, reads her books, listens to her records, peruses her photograph albums, wears her clothes, meditates on the fragments of her life revealed in letters she has received from friends (1989b, 28–29; 1995, 42–43). It is important to him that her suggestive absence be dominated by his body, his physicality, so that later, when he pursues her with body and eyes and camera, she will become more fully his object. Finally, he loses interest in the objects that surround her, the things that have touched her life; those objects and photographs and letters, he says, "empobrecían la imagen que yo quería formarme del ella" (32) [impoverished the ideal image I wanted to have of her (46)].

In this disymmetry of body and language, of physical self and constructed image, the narrator lingers on another borderline, a borderline that his actions both create and attempt to erase. Each time the narrator approaches Beverly through his construction/dematerialization of her, his deterritorialization of her and his body from both her homeland and his, that construction excludes him, makes her even more untranslatable, more alien, more incomprehensible. In order to speak of her, he must cross the border he has erected between them and confront the fence that divides his soul. With her, it is he and not the English-speaking master pilot who becomes the distanced third character in this first-person narration. In her absence, he undergoes a mutilated self-metamorphosis, reinventing his land-bound self as airplane or seal. Abdelkebir Khatibi describes it well in his novel of an analogous bilingual, bicultural relationship: "There was no exact symmetry between them, no encounter both vertical and parallel; rather there was a kind of inversion, the permutation of an untranslatable love, that had to be translated without respite" (Khatibi 1990, 20). In Beverly's letters, Campbell's narrator constructs her body; in her body he finds only a sign or trace of the woman he loves, and that trace remains untranslatable.

In other inventions of her, Beverly shares his childhood, and their histories together recapitulate the histories of the shifting relationships between Mexico and the United States in their impact on their shared border-region. Together Beverly and the narrator recall the waves of U.S. tourists flooding the Tijuana casinos for the gambling and nightlife in the 1930s; together they attend the school set up in an ex-casino closed by Lázaro Cárdenas in the 1940s (1989b, 79–80; 1995, 89–90). When she is twelve years old, her bicycle rides give shape to the growing town; the suburbs seemingly sprout in the wake of her passage (1989b, 20–21; 1995, 36). At the time of the Korean War, or the Vietnam War, or the invasion of Normandy in World War II, Beverly shares with the narrator the secrets of her newly mature body: "Los suyos fueron los primeros pechos que vi. Beverly tenía catorce años; yo, más de catorce" (46) [hers were the first breasts I ever saw. Beverly was fourteen years old and I was more than fourteen (58)]. In each case, he designs a picture in which Beverly's body organizes the scene; in each scene, this evoked corporeal presence is counterpointed by evidence of her body's absence: shifts in time, space, nationality. She is a woman with a mysterious past, he seems to suggest, so he lets her past stand for all the pasts of the borderlands, so that she and he between them can become — at least in his dreams — that ideal creature of Leo Lionni's children's story: neither blue nor yellow, but some other color, some border-color:

Me adentraba en ella como recorriéndola toda, habitándola, no sin-
tiéndola como parte de mí mismo sino como un mundo que siempre
había estado en ella y con ella, con todo su pasado y su manera de entender las cosas e interpretar mis palabras, un mundo, el
suyo, que procedía desde su infancia, que súbitamente, a través
del tiempo, se me hacía presente e inescapable, sin que me im-
portara no haber conocido sus paisajes exactos.... Me reconocía
sin embargo en ella, en su composición transparente que nos con-
fundía o refundía nuestros rostros y cuerpos, haciéndolos uno y
contrastándolos. (39)

[I went into her as if I were exploring all of her, inhabiting her, not
feeling her as part of myself but rather as a world that had always
been in her and with her, with all of her past and her way of seeing
things and interpreting my words, a world, her world, that began
with infancy and slowly, through time, became present and inescapable to me. It didn't matter to me that I didn't know her exact
landscapes.... Separate from me, I nevertheless recognized myself
in her, in a transparent composition that confused or reforged our
bodies and faces, making us one and contrasting us. (53)]

The sexual relationship between them becomes a metaphor for some
other kind of fusing of bodies and selves, not a male penetration of
the female, with the violence implicit in such an act, but rather a merg-
ing in which the narrator enters into and becomes one with her, and,
implicitly, she with him as well, with neither partner dominant in the
exchange of lives and selves. Beverly gives shape and language to his
surroundings — he, in an earlier passage, gives her his tongue: "Cada
mañana que comienza restituye a Beverly a los objetos y a mis primeras
palabras.... Le enseñaba a leer en español: Susi, Ésa es Susi, Susi se asea.
Así es Susi" (20) [Each daybreak restores Beverly to the objects and to
my first words.... I taught her to read Spanish (35)]. It is a string of
words that border on nonsense, anchored in the repetition of a woman's
name, not Beverly's, and in the variations upon that name. The repetition of the word "Susi" figures the narrator's desire to name and to fix the
woman, a naming undone in the singsong of the word echoes themselves,
a singsong that tends to dissect the words into their component syllables,
mere alternations of vowels and sibilants. The song of her voice stays
with him, however; scanning their rhythm gives order to his thoughts
and imaginings. Much later perhaps, resting with his head on Beverly's
belly, he recalls these words and takes obscure comfort in them (1989b,

117; 1995, 122). They provide a background murmur to his meditations, much like the comforting sound of the sea washing against the shore.

And yet even his meticulous analysis of their almost prelinguistic verbal pact, his geographer's awareness of their bodies' living territorial compact, represents only one of the permutations of this relationship. Other narrative moments privilege the enforcement of bodily, cultural, and political boundaries. At these times he cannot find the manner to enter into her: "Una y dos veces intentamos unirnos, pero la penetración no prosperaba" [Once or twice we tried to come together, but the penetration didn't work]. Rather than presenting a portrait of a union of contrasting and complementary bodies and realities, the narrator describes an intent blocked by "un bebé que salía de su sexo, apuntándome" (63) [a baby that came out of her sex, aiming at me (75)]. This child, silently *aiming* at him like a corporeal weapon, or like a camera, serves as mute testimony to his own failed creative powers.

In these versions of their tale, Beverly is wholly strange to him, and in her strangeness she is profoundly unknown. One day, sitting in the beachhouse, eating nuts, they engage in desultory conversation. Beverly falls silent, and the narrator comes to a startling conclusion: "Pero en aquel instante de enmudecimiento repentino no tuve la sensación ni la vaga sospecha sino la absoluta certeza de que Beverly jamás había estado viviendo conmigo" (40–41) [But in that moment of sudden muteness I did not have the feeling, not even the vague suspicion, but rather the absolute certainty that Beverly had never lived with me (54)]. Remembering her, inventing her, it is Beverly — the unforgettable seal-woman — who serves as focus and impulse for narrative. Even as he tries to forget her, her silence or her absence surrounds him and gives him shape.

Intermittently, we intuit that the same constraint does not hold for her; for example, when she asks the narrator, "¿Pero por qué añorar algo que no conocimos?" [Why yearn after what we don't know?], she continues, answering the unheard question: "Me duele decírtelo, pero no puedes hacer nada por mí. . . .¿Por qué nunca coincidimos? Tú, finalmente, no has sido lo más importante de mi vida" (36) [It hurts me to tell you this, but you can't do anything for me. . . . Why do we never coincide? You, after all, have not been the most important thing in my life (50)]. Abyssally, abjectly, he discovers that her indifference, too, is precious to him. It is a relationship consonant with that described in the epigraph to the novel, from *Las sergas de Esplandián*, a chivalric novel published for the first time in the portentous year of 1492: "[A] la diestra mano de las Indias había una isla llamada California . . . toda poblada de mujeres, sin varón ninguno" (10) [On the right hand of the Indies there was an island called California . . . totally populated by women, without a single man (27)].

The women of that island, writes Garci-Ordóñez de Montalvo, although not in the passage Campbell cites, ride to war on griffins — great flying monsters that are half-lion and half-eagle — border-crossing animals contemporary with Pegasus but more fierce and terrifying. Ominously, the Californian women feed their mounts with the bodies of their male infants, supplemented with occasional male voyagers who happen onto that island.

Strikingly, Mexican California *is* essentially an island — almost surrounded by water on three sides, separated from the mainstream of the country by its border-character, separated from its northern continuation by the political boundary with the United States, a boundary policed by the modern griffins of INS helicopters to which the narrator's pathetic border-Pegasus offers no concomitant threat. Though the novel is narrated by a man, the city he describes is a woman's land, contained and defined by fences and water boundaries. And, as in Garci-Ordóñez de Montalvo's romance, this island-California, like the imagined California of Esplandián's adventures, is located precisely "a un costado del paraíso terrenal" (10) [to one side of earthly paradise (27)]; in modern terms, from the Mexican side, it is just down the coast from Beverly Hills and celluloid heaven; in modern terms, from the U.S. side, the Mexican island-California is the home of easy women and cheap nightlife, only a short air-taxi ride away.

What, then, of the men in this island-California? They, like the narrator of this story, are originary immigrants, foreigners whose anxious spinning out of tales and photographs only confirms their belatedness. They have no name, no country, and a language borrowed from and propped on a female whose presence defines and destroys them. Enrique Lihn's parody comes close: "We are nothing: imitations, copies, phantoms: repeaters of what we understand badly, that is, hardly at all:.... the animated fossils of a prehistory we have lived neither here nor there, consequently anywhere, for we are aboriginal foreigners, transplanted from birth in our respective countries of origin" (Lihn 1979, 82).

In the island-California, the narrator invents an island-self, carefully inventing borders that he must cross (cannot cross), defining picture frames to organize a fragmented existence, going out into the city to look for, to invent, to ignore that solitary other who defines him and frames his existence and his desire: "[N]o descarto que tú sigas siendo el cuerpo sigiloso y el rostro que de mí mismo contemplo en el espejo porque he vivido conmigo mismo desde que nací y aún ahora no he podido, de una manera total, salir de mí mismo" (81) [I don't discount that you still remain in this quiet body and in my very own face contemplated in the mirror, because I have lived with myself since I was born and even now

I have not been able to get outside myself completely (91)]. Photography gives him the illusion of control. The camera is the necessary adjunct to his existence: "[M]e tomé la foto correspondiente a ese día" (18–19) [I took that day's photograph of myself (18–19)]. It also gives him a purpose for going out into the street and a method for creating a reality outside himself. It permits him to break up the tight intertwining of self and self that makes *him* see *her* when he looks at his face in the mirror. "Trataría de buscarte por todo el mundo," he says once; and a bit later, he adds, "[E]n muchas palabras, te inventaría. Ya me las arreglaría para hacer de ti una enemiga irreconciliable y así tenerte afuera, mía" (81, 83) [I tried to search for you throughout the whole world...In other words, I would invent you. I would manage to make of you an irreconcilable enemy and in that way to keep you outside myself, more mine (91, 93)]. Only in making her, and making her other, can he make her his, discovering himself, finally, in the mirror, her in the photographs, both in framed and multiply appropriated realities.

As he lives only in eyesight and in mediated visual images (his, hers, the camera's), when he goes out without the camera he feels like an amputee: "[C]uando me separé de la cámara sentí que una parte de mí mismo se había desprendido" (60) [When I was separated from my camera I felt that a part of myself had fallen off (71)], or again, "[S]algo a la calle y al saber olvidada la cámara en el cuarto siento como si una parte de mi cuerpo se hubiese desmembrado" (97) [I go outside, and when I realize that I have forgotten my camera, I feel as if a part of my body has been cut off (105)]. The camera fixes the fleeting image momentarily, allowing the narrator a distanced participation in the personal and social fluidity he describes, but only at the cost of losing bits of himself in the artificially stayed onward rush of life.

A similar dislocation, or superlocation, affects his writing as well. Such writing is also framed and fragmented and suffers from amnesia when the borders of life and language fail to overlap. Juan Flores and George Yúdice say that in the borderlands, "even for the most monolingual of Latinos, the 'other' language looms constantly as a potential resource, and the option to vary according to different speech contexts is used far more often than not" (Flores and Yúdice 1990, 75). In Campbell's work, the other language, like the other culture and the other sex, looms more ominously. The narrator's resources are impoverished by the need to keep both options open. The necessary encounter he seeks will eventually deprive him of speech and turn him into what Abdelkebir Khatibi, in his novel *Love in Two Languages,* calls a "bilingual cripple." Khatibi's character writes, "A strange sickness contaminates each one of my words, and it's easy for me to forget the names of flowers and perfumes. Amnesia in two registers..." (Khatibi 1990, 55). Campbell's character demonstrates a similar linguistic perplexity. He tells Beverly, "[S]ólo quiero preservar los hilos de esto que provisionalmente llamamos...¿Cómo lo llamamos?" (113) [I only wanted to preserve the threads of what we provisionally call...What do we call it? (119)]. The narrator has no name for the writing of Beverly that is taking place around him and by his hand; nevertheless, he forces himself on, stutteringly, hesitantly, by indirect allusion. Beverly has warned him earlier in the text that "las cosas se diluyen" (97) [things dilute (106)], and in the absence of a camera to fix the images of "things" and of Beverly to fix the order of speech, language too becomes an uncertain tool. By the end of the novel, with Beverly's death, the threads of narrative break off entirely. It is a loss of language felt as the slippage of sounds from the tongue and performed in the text in the abrupt breaking off of the novella:

[M]is palabras no son mis palabras, empleo términos que para mí no significan nada, o bien cambian de sentido con los años o se diluyen en una dicción que ni a mí mismo sirve, se pierden guteralmente y me quedo sin más remedio que enmudecer como enmudeciste tú, aunque tu silencio perteneció siempre a otro orden de ideas...me acuso, me acuso de estar aquí frente al mundo...en cuanto pueda desapareceré, no faltaba más, a la hora que usted guste, estoy para servirle, es que yo creía, es que (124–25)

[My words are not my words. I use terminology that means nothing to me, or that changes meaning as the years pass, or that dilutes itself in a diction that no longer serves even me. Words lose themselves gutturally and I have no option left but to fall silent, as you fell silent, although your muteness always belonged to another, and equally insubstantial, order of ideas....I confess; I confess to being here, before the whole world...as soon as possible I will disappear, whatever you say, whenever is convenient for you, I'm here to serve you, it's just that I thought, it's just that (128–29)]

The narrator focuses on his own alienation from language before ending the novel with a sequence of nearly meaningless Spanish courtesy formulas. In his auto-silencing, he evokes the physical apparatus of sound production, and he evokes as well the body that remains behind, uselessly, when words stutter into silence.

One of the things that makes this novel so powerful is that the narrator does not just slide helplessly into silence with Beverly's death, although some of his self-positioning might lead us to accept his self-definition, "[H]e vivido a medias, hablo en tono menor" (123) [I live halfway; I speak in a minor key (128)]. The minor-key life is, after all, one of the archetypal roles of the Mexican border-male who must live within the soul-crushing awareness of his own impotency in the face of the twinned powers of Beverly Hills and the island-California. However, the narrator of Campbell's novel actively propels himself into this situation. Frequently, he uses violent images and metaphors to seek and capture his photographic and narrative prey. The camera, for example, is, as he says, "un instrumento de relación," and the narrator admits that his eyes would not suffice to see anyone, to see any *woman*. With the camera, he borrows both potency and power. The imagery is relatively straightforward, setting up a scene of a visual rape/murder: "El teleobjetivo de repuesto, cilíndrico y alargado... salía erguido hacia enfrente. En cuanto la niña cambió de curso y entró en el foco al separarse de mí, disparé. Disparé varias veces. Varias veces. Volví a disparar hasta quedarme sin película y sin aliento..." (75) [The replacement telephoto lens, when added to the camera, is long and cylindrical... and sticks out upright in front. As soon as the little girl changed direction and entered into focus as she distanced herself from me, I shot. I shot several times. Many times. I kept shooting until I ran out of film and out of breath (85–86)]. Clearly, the narrator is not just gazing at the young girl — he is possessing her sexually and using her, through the mediation of the phallic camera lens, as the recipient of his lust. At the same time, he takes something, if only a photograph, from the girl and keeps it for himself. Still further: in Spanish, as in English, what he does with the camera is to "shoot" a picture. What he takes are snapshots. As Cristina Peri Rossi says in a more general context, "No hay duda de que para la mayoría de los hombres la visión es el sentido más importante como disparador del deseo" [There is no doubt but that for the majority of men sight is the most important sense as the trigger of desire] (Peri Rossi 1991, 175–76). Campbell, like Peri Rossi, builds explicitly on the multiple valences of the "disparador" [trigger]. Thus, in order to see a woman, the narrator in his novel takes the woman (takes her picture), and he shoots her (a metaphorical rape-murder). Campbell makes this connection absolutely clear: "La cámara fotográfica dejó de funcionar. Volví a ponérmela sobre el pecho. Devolví el obturador al máximo como quien pone seguro a una pistola y guardé la cámara en su funda de cuero" (78) [The camera stopped working. I put it back against my chest. I returned the shutter to its resting position like someone who puts the safety on a gun and put the camera away in its leather holster (88)]. It is only through the woman's death by photographs that the narrator is brought into the picture, so to speak, as the creator of that image-death. It is only through her paralysis and violation that he can create this narrative. But he can only do it in the instant of raping/shooting/seeing. And thus, the narrative takes place in that violent, displaced action, in that metaphorical wounding.

Roland Barthes in another context suggests that the wound left behind, or that wound's scar, is the culture-creating trope par excellence, and his formulation helps uncover the implications of the novelistic re/de-construction of a border identity as the counterpoint to a unified mode of existence:

> Neither culture nor its destruction is erotic; it is the seam between them, the fault, the flaw, which becomes so. . . . Whence, perhaps, a means of evaluating the works of our modernity: . . . they always have two edges. The subversive edge may seem privileged because it is the edge of violence; but it is not violence which affects pleasure, nor is it destruction which interests it; what pleasure wants is the site of a loss, the seam, the cut, the deflation, the dissolve which seizes the subject in the midst of bliss. Culture thus recurs as an edge. (Barthes 1975, 7)

Barthes intuits that violence has value as that double and ambivalent edge: the cutting edge that defines two possibilities, the cut edge that comprises one-half of the seam. Metaphorical violence allows the writing of the novel. Nevertheless, in Campbell's work, violent death is the narrative crux that also causes novelistic breakdown.

The opening pages of *Todo lo de las focas* describe the island-California, located to one side of the U.S. earthly paradise, as a kind of "tierra de nadie en que tanto los visitantes como los nativos se sabían perdidos" (23) [no-man's-land in which both natives and visitors knew themselves to be lost (38)], a place of little cheer, and a commercial base dependent on the industrialization of abortion. The novella begins with Beverly and the narrator's final trip from Tijuana north to the border after what we later discover was Beverly's bungled abortion. In a scene that is repeated and amplified at various points throughout the novella, Beverly tells the narrator that she is cold, and he abjures her to sleep. Her last two words, "tengo frío" [I'm cold], echo throughout the novel, establishing the only verbal link with the silent, sleeping presence in the vehicle moving slowing toward the United States. Only upon arrival at the U.S. customs station, at end of the novella, do we discover that this is a sleep from which she will never awaken; during the trip to the border, Beverly has hemorrhaged and, sometime before she arrives at the political border, crosses the other border between life and death.

Beverly, then, maps and defines the boundaries of the island-California, while at the same time she is antithetical to it. The narrator, the Mexican man, is both what frames the geography of her body and what accounts for her (and his) paradoxical deterritorialization. In order to understand her life, and his city, he must account for her death and her nationality. In a larger sense, he can do neither. Thus, he falls back on the evocation of a chiasmic encounter that takes place between land and sea, earth and air, man and woman, life and death, voice and silence. In the variations on the story of his search for the elusive Beverly, he tells of a Beverly only marginal to his life and one who dominates every aspect of it; a Beverly who says "tengo frío" and "Susi se asea" before falling into silence and one who defines the possibilities of speech; a Beverly he barely knows and one who dies aborting his fetus; a Beverly who drowns in a beach accident and one who, seal-like, Pegasus-like, slips smoothly between two realms; a Beverly who defines a borderlands existence and one who refuses to let lines and divisions of any sort to enter into her logic.

Campbell's starkly poetic novella ends abruptly. The truncated potential of the aborted child, "un bebé que salía de su sexo, apuntándome" (63) [a baby that came out of her sex, aiming at me (75)], hints at the impossibility of recovering the lost text of any enabling ritual whatsoever. Their aborted child points him/herself toward the narrator in an accusing gesture, one evoking as well the narrator's own aggressive handling of the camera, and points as well toward an aporia, the deeply ambiguous ending of a ruined bond that is as much transhuman as transnational. Both child and camera signal the presence of a rhetorical tradition in which the imagination and reality are discrete spaces, susceptible to metaphorical bridging, whether it be theoretically construed by the upflinging of the Hegelian *Aufhebung*, the minimal slippages of the Derridian *différance*, or the bar between signifier and signified. The disjunctions in Campbell (and, as we shall see, in Castillo as well) respond to a recognition that the abysses of metaphor are artificial cultural products, with temporal and spatial limitations. The metaphorical border-site attempts to make concrete the underpinnings between two vaguely shifting forms — insubstantial memoir, insubstantial world — and is constructed or painted out of the double haunting of an experience and a language that is also dual. These delicate distinctions and subtle displacements cipher a particular repertoire of linguistic practice that responds and corresponds to the need of the bicultural-bilingual writers to encode, in a more than trivial, more than superficial manner, their shifting set of mutually exclusive, equally valid, alternate roles. Furthermore, the underlying scene is compacted and complicated by the need to represent not only the temporal and spatial disjunctions but also those imposed by a living awareness of multiple cultures, multiple languages, and multiple time frames that impose their own rules and offer their own separate opportunities for distanciation and irony.

Ana Castillo also uses the aborted child as a frame, as the image of something that is unresolved or irreconcilable, but at the same time both incomplete and unforgettable. Teresa and Alicia have both had abortions, and both still reside to some extent in the territory of that remembered pain. The narrator evokes Alicia's experience as a pitiless awakening to reality and to a kind of bodily ending that will nevertheless remain with her for the rest of her life:

> Even while i dreamed, you had stopped waiting for knights in shining armor. . . . You were seventeen and, at first, had wanted the child, romanticized motherhood. . . . When Rodney stopped coming around, you were afraid to be exiled alone.
>
> A friend of a friend lent you her welfare card. . . . The nurse . . . drew up forms that were not presented to you until you were on the table, sedated, feet in stirrups and exposed to the world the way you had never been exposed before in your life.
>
> You were sterilized. (A. Castillo 1986, 120)

Teresa too suffers an abortion, a decision she makes in hate and rage when, as she puts it, her "womb is attacked" and her body betrays her with a man she no longer loves:

> i'm much better now and will be up and around soon to gather the pieces of the woman who was my self. . . .
>
> i had sent our child away, i told him, to wait out its turn to take part in this miserable world, where once being born it would no longer be innocent, for being was to survive and to survive, one must hurt weaker beings. (108–9)

Alicia's forced sterilization allows her no way back into the redemptive potential of childbearing. For Teresa, however, the end of the novel and the sign of her newfound self-confidence is her decision to bring her son, Vittorio, to term when she once again finds herself with child by another faithless lover. These failed relationships and the abortions that violently mark their definitive dissolution also define these two women's lives. The way they see themselves and the way they imagine future relationships are both affected by the scars of past failures. Teresa describes both abortions

at considerable length because these difficult and painful experiences of
"having life sucked out from between [our] legs" (109–10) are strongly
defining elements of the context in which these women see themselves.
For the life that is sucked out is not just the life of the potential child
but the potential life of the not-yet-mother, who must work harder at re-
erecting a definition of herself once she too has been sucked dry of life.

The women in Castillo's novel seem doomed to being sucked dry, and
not only by abortions. Early in the novel, the narrator asks why "so many
of our ideals were stamped out like cigarette butts when we believed in
them so furiously" and answers her own question, "Perhaps we were not
furious enough" (16). Certainly the protagonists in this novel suffer for
their efforts to define themselves and their lives. Furiously, they declare
their independence and their right to a relationship of equality with the
men they choose as husbands and lovers. It is a fury worn down in the re-
lentlessness of everyday life. Like infants, the men in these women's lives
suck them dry. Teresa writes, "A woman takes care of the man she has
made her life with, . . . as if he were her only child, as if he had come from
her womb. . . . There isn't a woman who doesn't understand this deathtrap"
(112). And yet, of course, she repeatedly falls into it. Teresa reminds Alicia, who is grieving over the suicide of her lover: "Abdel was a weak man,
Alicia, and he had already sucked you dry of more than what a child can
demand of its mother," for unlike a child, a man remains dependent on
the woman-mother figure (129).

In a parallel manner, the adult female who fails to attract and keep
a man is considered unwomanly or, in Teresa's mother's application of
the traditional double standard, too experienced to be able to expect a
relationship with a desirable man (93–94). The cultural production of
standards of beauty and desirability is very much at issue here. Teresa is
bitterly aware of the triple bind of the beauty system: attractive, experienced women attract the wrong kind of men; attractive, inexperienced
women attract danger; and unattractive women are considered valueless
and are condemned for the lack of effort they put into attracting men.
One of Teresa's dream-poem narratives slices through the hypocrisy of
her society in describing a drag beauty pageant haunted by danger and
violence:

> and no scene such as this is complete without Eric the Rapist . . .
>             and i didn't understand, Alicia
> how you danced with such carefree abandon
> when an hour before you escaped violation at the point
> of a gun
> danced because he liked you whispered some falsehood

in your burning ear while his lover whispered in the other
he'd slit your vagina
and I didn't understand how dance made you forget

. . . . . . . . . . . . . . . . . . . . . . . . . . . . . . . . .

              Again the self-appointed
guardian, i follow
                    knowing there is little in the end i can do, i
have a vagina too. (77–78)

Alicia's almost blithe inattention to her own danger represents a basic
character trait that Teresa refers to frequently throughout the letters.
It is a tendency that alternately attracts and exasperates her friend, but
mostly Teresa suffers her helplessness to protect Alicia as an assault on
her own physical reality. In this metaphorical/real situation in which Alicia is sandwiched between two versions of masculinity — one whispering
sweet nothings in her ear and the other whispering death threats — it is
only Teresa who understands that both men are in effect appropriating
Alicia's dancing body through repetition of the same story that has been
used to entrance women for ages. Teresa's own whispers go unheeded, and
her words cannot compete with the force and power of the men's words
and weapons. For while Teresa does not dance, and constitutes herself the
unnoticed guardian, she recognizes that she is an ineffective bodyguard,
equally susceptible to men's voices and knives: "[T]here is little in the end
i can do, i have a vagina too."

Teresa and Alicia look elsewhere for their earthly paradise, going to
Mexico to reinvent themselves and recover their past, to seek an alternative present, to dream a Mixquiahualan future. There, in that utopian
realm, they achieve real self-sufficiency. Even in Teresa's nightmare of
revolution, when the peaceful town finds itself subjected to violent attack, she imagines herself as a powerful woman. She is armed, and she is
a resistance leader. When the government troops arrive in her dream town
to confront her, she is ready to die defending her people: "My weapon.
It was my own and i had used it before, fit into my hand like that of
a faithful lover" (97). In her dream of mestizo resistance to oppression,
Teresa vindicates herself and finally overcomes the self-imposed limitations of her hyperawareness of her woman's body. Significantly, Teresa
can contemplate such a step only when she is doubly deterritorialized:
in her nightmare and in Mixquiahuala. Even there her revolutionary potency has limits; she stops short of actually firing the weapon. She ends
the retelling of the dream with the moment of lifting the weapon and
preparing to fire.

When Teresa steps back from her dreams and into the contemporary reality of the Mexico she has visited on various occasions with her friend, she finds no real alternative to the dilemma posed by the parable of the woman dancing between twinned threats of seduction and death. Mexico rejects the young women even more firmly than the patriarchal United States. It is not even that they are seen as legitimate prey (although they are) but that they go through the country unacknowledged and unaccounted for. Despite their longing to belong to an alternative reality, Mexico refuses to recognize them and, as Teresa notes, snips them out of the societal pattern. They are anomalies. Insofar as they exist at all in Mexican consciousness, they exist as exotic creatures, outside normal laws: "We would have hoped for respect as human beings, but the only respect granted a woman is that which a gentleman bestows on a lady. Clearly we were no ladies. What was our greatest transgression? We travelled alone" (59).

Not only do they travel alone; they do so in what is practically the uniform of U.S. tourists. In one encounter, after accepting a ride with a trio of heavily armed men, the men ask Teresa and Alicia if they are from the United States. Teresa replies: "i tried to laugh, as if the suggestion was ludicrous. How could they possibly think that? Couldn't they see by our color that we weren't gringas? It's the blue jeans, one said, as if stating a statistical fact" (63). What I find fascinating about this scene is that two clichés about the United States are played off against each other. The U.S. women of color assume that they can "pass" as non-U.S. by virtue of their race; underlying their presumption is a hurtful and deeply inbred feeling that the "typical American" (ugly or not) is necessarily white. Under that assumption, they do not fit in the United States, and thus it is both shocking and distressing for them to be immediately identified by a rejecting and rejected nationality in the country to which they wish to escape. The Mexican soldiers recognize the women despite their native Spanish by clichéd cultural markers the women don't care to disguise: their independence (traveling together without a man for protection) and their clothes (the cliché that all and only U.S. women wear blue jeans).

It is a scene that is replayed again and again, and Teresa seems to have a hard time catching on, perhaps because she so badly wants reality to match her dreams and so refuses to accept the realities that present themselves to her. In another encounter with two men in a Veracruz restaurant, one asks her if they are gringas: "'What makes you think we're gringas?' i asked, trying not to give away defensiveness. 'Easy. Your blue jeans,' he replied smiling" (69). The jeans that are so ubiquitous as to seem an invisible and unmarked class-dissolving fact of life for young people in the

United States become, in their chosen dreamland, a marker of an exotic and vulnerable femininity for the Mexican men. Pointedly, Teresa and Alicia meet very few Mexican women, except in dreams, and in dreams those women are motherly mestizas who work the fields and care for their children in provincial homes. They are not blue-jean clad adventurers. In fact, they look and act uncomfortably like Teresa's own mother and aunts in unromantic Chicago.

What saves this novel, and makes it interesting, is that Teresa does not rest on the clichés of a romantic deterritorialization. While in Mixquiahuala she holds up a dream weapon, and that weapon eventually becomes the tool she applies to attacking her own prejudices: her hatred of middle-class Chicano "brothers" with their intermittent and hypocritical commitment to "barrio" causes, her resentment toward white women as the ultimate in desirable possessions, her intransigent romanticism about Mexico. It is, of course, the friendship with Alicia that provides the most important contributing factor to this reevaluation.

These women define themselves, first of all, in relation to their attractiveness to men. Alicia, plain and flat-chested, "bore no resemblance to the ideal of any man / you encountered anywhere" (44). She hates herself and "would not be *loved*," although she allows men to copulate with her frequently in a semblance of relationships. Of the two, it is brown-skinned Teresa that men want: "i never had problems attracting men. You pointed out the obvious, the big breasts, full hips and thighs, the kewpie doll mouth" (113), and yet, as Teresa notes, the attraction is clearly superficial. Their skins, like their blue jeans, shape the perceptions of what they are, but neither woman is that physical object. Nevertheless, the perceptions change them, at least partially, into persons matching their physical images. Taught to valorize themselves through their attractiveness to men, both women hate the tyranny of the physical. Alicia feels rejected because of her unattractive body; Teresa feels insulted by men's purely physical interest.

At the same time, their very differences — of race, temperament, and background — bring them together, make them mirrors for each other and mirrors for their own self-reflection. They deterritorialize themselves, first in Mexico, where they find a dream that fits them, and then in each other, where they discover opportunities for both support and battle. They reserve their sharpest weapons for each other, and their most thoughtful and loving exchanges: "Each time we parted it has been abruptly. We picked, picked, picked at each other's cerebrum and when we didn't elicit the desired behavior, the confirmation of allegiance, we reproached the other with threatening vengeance.... We begged for the other's visit and again the battle resumed. We needled, stabbed, manipulated, cut and through it all we loved, driven to see the other improved in her own reflection" (23). Teresa calls their intense relationship "a love affair" (39), although of a particular, nonsexualized kind: "[W]e were experts at exchanging empathy for heart-rending confusion known only to lovers, but you and I had never been lovers" (121). This love affair between the two women is different from any relationship they share with their various male lovers. The men are exclusively interested in the physical being, in the mechanics of conquest, the triumph of possession, the fierce joy of imposing themselves indelibly upon the women. The men use women's bodies as markers of status, they use their own bodies as weapons, and they use weapons to mark women's bodies. Or, in the ultimate instance, as in the case of Abdel, they self-indulgently turn the weapon on themselves so that the woman can never escape the memory of finding the violent suicide, and she remains indelibly scarred by his death.

With each other, the women's battles have more productive ends. They learn to cut through the racialized distinctions and look into each other's brains and souls. No longer merely objects, no longer smooth-surface beings for male reflection, they actively reflect, and reflect upon, each other, and while they see the mirror in the other, they also seek the depths.

In the early pages of this chapter, I referred to Homi Bhabha's observation that "cultural difference is to be found where 'loss' of meaning enters, as a cutting edge, into the representation of the fullness of the demands of culture" (Bhabha 1990, 313), and suggested that Bhabha's comment could help us to find a point of entry into these novels. Then too, Bhabha echoes Barthes, whom I also quoted earlier in this chapter and who adds to the theorization of the cutting edge of culture a recognition of the pleasure that cohabits strangely with violence. Together Barthes and Bhabha help us negotiate the terrain of Campbell and Castillo, to come to terms with those authors' conflicted understanding of female sexuality and their awareness of the shifting relation of that sexual understanding to an ambiguously negotiated sense of self in a border-reality. In both these fictions, however, the cutting edge of cultural loss finds a literal-literary representation in a violent act that cuts off further contemplation: the cutting out of potential life with an abortion, cutting off of the narration subsequent to recounting a lover's violent death. At this point in the analysis, therefore, it becomes necessary to interrogate more closely the borderlands between loss of meaning and the fullness of culture's demands and the implications of these violent woundings of identity in respect to the interpretive strategies that have served me thus far. Where is the edge of the cut? Or, to paraphrase the question asked in another context by Marcos Sánchez-Tranquilino and John Tagg, What is the arc of the knife?

Sánchez-Tranquilino and Tagg interrogate another cultural and social figure of the borderlands, the pachucos/as, who in their aggressive self-construction seem to shrink the limits of the heterotopia to the highly restricted space of their own bodies and the clothing they wear. These critics' reading of the multiple readings of the pachuco/a provides an essential clue to the reading of the cut in Campbell and Castillo. The pachuco/a culture, they find, "repudiated *sub*ordination in a hierarchy of national cultures," moving through and appropriating the cultural markers of both Mexican and U.S. Anglo culture. And if, as Paz suggested years ago, the pachuco represents a "scandal of civilized meaning," neither the scandal nor the civilization is quite what Paz imagines, and the question of meaning is likewise problematic. For Sánchez-Tranquilino and Tagg, the pachuco first of all needs to be put in the context of a fuller cultural and sexual spectrum: both pachuco and pachuca; and one of the scandals of Paz's analysis and much subsequent mythologizing about the pachuco occurs because his counterpart is cut off and made invisible. In respect to the pachuco and the pachuca's affront to civilization (which?), Sánchez-Tranquilino and Tagg focus on the strategic repudiation of both poles. For the pachuco/a, neither Mexico nor the United States — at least in their dominant cultural representations — is "inside" or "outside": being pachuco/a ruptures "their structures of Otherness, at least for a moment, at least for the best times of the week." And this momentary interruption of cultural structures and strategies is both a fugitive phenomenon and a visual confrontation: "The clothes made meanings with their bodies. They made them hateful and desirable. They made them visible. But, worse than that, they made them readable in a way that had to be denied" (Sánchez-Tranquilino and Tagg 1992, 559–60). The pachuco/a, then, like the other borderliners studied in this chapter, crosses the field of interpretation not as resistance to reading but as a discursive product that offers too many readings and that yet has been consistently underread, from both sides of the violent, divisive cultural cut.

"What is unraveling now," Sánchez-Tranquilino and Tagg conclude, "is the discursive formation of a discipline — the conjunctural effects of its practices, institutions, technologies, and strategies of explanation" (557). This unraveling is particularly noticeable in such borderline texts as those by Campbell and Castillo that take the multiply valenced identity of the border-dweller as their subject. Such texts cannot be easily accommodated to the cultural histories of either nation. To paraphrase Sánchez-Tranquilino and Tagg again: these novels not only mark but provoke a certain kind of internal cultural crisis in narrowly conceived imaginations of nation, just as they mark, but refuse to inhabit, the gender roles, subject positions, and nationalistic spaces limned out for them in the violent conflicts of cultural miscegenation.[2] These wounds, these transgressive cuts, characterize a practice in which the conjunctural describes only one side of the seam.

# Chapter 5

# Reading Women

## SEFCHOVICH

Another side of the seam, or another seam, can be explored in the conjunction of a gender-conscious woman author and her female reader. As Jean Franco recognizes, the problem of the writing—and the reading—woman is particularly acute in intensely gender-divided countries like Mexico. Following upon a discussion of Octavio Paz's appropriation of La Malinche for his poetical theorization of Mexicanness, she concludes:

> The problem of national identity was thus presented primarily as a problem of *male* identity, and it was male authors who debated its defects and psychoanalyzed the nation. In national allegories, women became the territory over which the quest for (male) national identity passed.... Under these circumstances, national identity could not but be a problematic terrain for women novelists.... How could they plot themselves into a narrative without becoming masculine or attempting to speak from the devalued position? (Franco 1989b, 131–32)

Franco is quite right in her astute observation, as is Doris Sommer in her seminal study of just such fictions of national identity as those referenced by Franco. As these critics clarify in their feminocentric readings of traditional texts, in such works the national identity and the nation's readership are assumed to be male, and the female half of the population exists as a marginalized or exotic other that serves to confirm the privileged identity-construct. According to this model, the reading woman—a perfidious oddity — is ignored when she is not decried for her inappropriate or unfeminine behavior. In his chronicle, *Amor perdido* [Lost love], Carlos Monsiváis recalls the dictates of Antonio Manuel Carreño's famous best-selling turn-of-the-century etiquette book (a work also cited several times for satiric effect in Laura Esquivel's international publishing and film phenomenon, *Como agua para chocolate* [Like water for chocolate]). Among Carreño's admonishments to young women of good family is the suggestion: "[E]vitemos leer en la ventana para que los que pasan no crean que hacemos ostentación de estudiosos o aficionados a las letras" [Let us avoid reading in the window so that passersby do not get the impression that we are trying to look studious or show off our love of books] (327). Monsiváis reminds his readers that Carreño's book reconfirmed a kind of "realpolitik" of rigidly hierarchized social behavior in dominant society, while at the same time, official morality was underwritten by "la abundancia de literatura pornográfica en cuarteles y colegios, el deporte nacional de representación de actos sexuales en las paredes, y el éxito comercial de figuras libidinosas de barro, hechas en Guadalajara" [the abundance of pornographic literature in barracks and schools, the national sport of drawing representations of sexual acts on the walls, and the commercial success of libidinous clay figures, made in Guadalajara] (328). In this way, both official and transgressive national identities were defined by reference to the masculine-dominated value system, and women were pressed to the margins as libidinous themes or objects of ritual veneration.

That, of course, was then. In the days of Porfirio Díaz and in the theorizing of Octavio Paz, women have no function except as the exotic other required to define masculinity. Since the time of national foundation referenced by Monsiváis, Sommer, and Franco, however, both the writing woman and the woman reader have come to puzzling preeminence in Mexican letters. Like Franco and Sommer, Mexican socio-critic and best-selling novelist Sara Sefchovich (her extensive body of work includes important critical studies like *México: País de ideas, país de novelas* [Mexico: Country of ideas, country of novels] and the two-volume anthology *Mujeres en espejo* [Women mirrored] as well as two best-selling novels: *Demasiado amor* [Too much love] [1990] and *La señora de los sueños* [The lady who dreamed] [1993]) addresses questions about national and personal identity politics, but she displaces them onto other grounds. According to this successful writer and critic, her own success and that of other best-selling women writers like Angeles Mastretta and Laura Esquivel point to a very clear answer to the question, "Who reads novels in Latin America today?" Women, especially leisured middle-class women, read, and they overwhelmingly read works by other middle-class women in which women have positive protagonic roles (personal conversation, June 1994). Even more interestingly, works like hers and those of her colleagues who make it to Mexican best-sellerdom tend to highlight images of women who freely express their sexuality and who are not castigated for their adventurous love lives. The repetition of this model of empowered femininity in modern Mexican novels by women is so pervasive as to create a regularized discursive locus, one that in turn enables further iterations. Old assumptions about authorship and readership become complicated and are made problematic by such a scenario. National allegory, it seems, is giving way in these best-sellers to meditations on sexual politics, at least in what sells to the eager Mexican audience.

If we remind ourselves that *Santa*, Mexico's first major best-seller in the twentieth century, was not only male-authored but implicitly aimed at a male audience, we can begin to gauge the magnitude of the shift that Sefchovich outlines. As Luce Irigaray says, regarding the traditional male-dominated social order, "Commodities, as we all know, do not take themselves to market.... So women have to remain an 'infrastructure' unrecognized as such by our society and our culture. The use, consumption, and circulation of their sexualized bodies underwrite the organization and the reproduction of the social order, in which they never take part as 'subjects'" (Irigaray 1985, 84). As Franco's and Sommer's models intimate, even in rejecting certain aspects of the dominant male tradition, both female readers and writers find themselves ambiguously still formed within the structures of thought inherited from these rejected models. Sefchovich, in contrast, somewhat ambitiously proposes a model that slides into the ellipsis in Irigaray's text, in which, counterintuitively, the commodity *does* take itself to market and becomes an active partner in the mechanism of social exchange. Her first novel, *Demasiado amor,* not only deals with an exchange between females but does so based, like *Santa,* on the metaphor of a successful prostitute. In its implicit reference to the earlier best-seller we see how a critique of the social order can be proposed through the literary model describing the circulation of a highly sexualized body-commodity.

Since large numbers of people with the money and the leisure to afford and read books are clearly enjoying best-selling works such as those by Sefchovich, the problem for the critic is how to read and think about them. Brigitte Frase succinctly gauges the dilemma common to reading women whose purchasing power turns such tales of adventurous lives and loves as Sefchovich's into best-sellers, expressing the perfect combination of a longing for and rejection of specifically masculine-marked structures that points to an underlying identity in the basic value system:

> A few months ago I listened to Phillip Lopate read his new essay, "The Literature of Walking Around." There is a rich subgenre of poetry and prose about the ways a city reveals itself to someone aimlessly walking its streets, usually at night, when the life is freer and bawdier. Lopate was drawn to this literature because

he's a city walker himself. I love many of the writers he discussed, from Baudelaire to Benjamin. I look at them from my window and wave fondly and enviously, before I draw the curtain and lock the door. . . . Try to imagine a woman walking the streets like that. There have been no female counterparts to the dandy, only male impersonators: aristocratic women in London and Paris dressed as men in order to move about freely. And the model of the woman who strolls aimlessly, who loiters, who looks freely around her and into people's eyes, who roams the streets day or night? That's no *flâneuse*, that's a prostitute. (Frase 1993, 5)

Frase notes that for women of her class, the longing for adventure cannot be satisfied in culturally approved ways; in envious contrast to her male counterpart, she is left with the impossible image of the *flâneuse*, who only stands in for the reality of the prostitute as a figure for the female adventurer in the city. It is striking, however, that in Frase's feminist text, the discussion is predisposed and enabled (disabled?) by the burden of gender-based narrative habits, so that her discourse about gender still offers little more than a mirror for the man of the leisure class. The division of women into *flâneuse* and prostitute implicitly repeats the traditional moral divide between decent woman and whore and implicitly and noxiously echoes a parallel class division into leisured and working-class women. It is precisely the titillating potential of slippage between the adventurous *flâneuse* and the horrifying prostitute, the uncomfortable possibility of a confusion between decent and degenerate women, that gives rise to the powerfully evocative two-sided protagonists of such male-authored texts as Usigli's *Jano es una muchacha* or Buñuel's famous film *Belle du jour*. Frase's comment, then, reminds us of the degree to which structural habits of labeling exert a controlling pressure on thought. Mere evocation of the word "prostitute" in her text is a sufficient warning to chastise those other women — women like Frase and me — who might yearn intellectually to stroll through the city streets in flamboyant imitation of Wilde or Gide, but instead stay home behind drawn curtains and locked doors.

In an analogous discussion, Rosario Castellanos admonishes her fellow countrywomen to challenge these dominant moral myths, to take personal responsibility for their own mature actions and decisions, and to avoid repeating the excuses that have held women back in the past: "Tengamos el valor de decir que somos vírgenes porque se nos da la real gana, porque nos conviene para fines ulteriores o porque no hemos encontrado la manera de dejar de serlo. O que no lo somos porque así decidimos" [Let us have the courage to say that we are virgins because we feel like it, because it coincides with our ulterior motives, or because we haven't found a way to get rid of it yet. Or that we are not virgins because we decided not to be] (Castellanos 1984, 39–40). Castellanos recognizes the social reality into which she was born but finds in nonjudgmental activism a model for changing it. She takes note of the prejudices that have colored women's understanding of one another in the past and urges fundamental shifts in attitudes. To Frase's complaint, I could well imagine Castellanos responding, "Yes, life is unfair. Get on with it." A similar impulse undergirds the female fantasy representation of a fulfilled and happy prostitute in Sefchovich's first novel, *Demasiado amor;* Sefchovich's readers have the advantage of imagining the *flâneuse*'s existence, paired to that of the prostitute, snubbing the old, male morality — at least in the space of the fiction. Intermittently, intersticially, Sefchovich proposes a theory of the reading woman that takes into account these changes in taste and style, this new collusion between a female author and her female reader.

In the absence of local studies on *how* Mexican women read,[1] one likely place to start an analysis of the reading woman would be through reference to book sales. With a readership of over twenty million women and more than two hundred million dollars in sales per year (Christian-Smith 1990, 12), the romance market both epitomizes "low" culture for women and is the biggest paperback sales sector in the world, coming close to epitomizing book reading in general. Miguel Russo states that 20 to 25 percent of Argentine book sales fall into the series romance genre, and the editor-in-chief of Spain's Vergara Press says that in his country 30 percent of book sales go to the romance market (Russo 1994, 2–3). Since the books referred to specifically in Russo's article are the relatively expensive trade paperback translations of popular international romance writers (rather than less expensive mass-market paperbacks or the inexpensive *fotonovelas* sold in kiosks), we can assume a relative affluence in the book-buying readers as well.

Corín Tellado, the undisputed queen of inexpensive series romance in the Hispanic world, has, according to a 1973 UNESCO report, long since become the most read Spaniard of all time, with sales of her romances far surpassing the sales of Cervantes's *Don Quijote* (Russo 1994, 2). Her formula fiction is based on a series of invariable features that Cuban writer Guillermo Cabrera Infante roguishly identifies as follows: "La víctima que termina por amar a su verdugo. El incesto. El fetichismo. El masoquismo como prueba de amor. El sadismo que engendra frigidez que engendra amor que engendra celos que engendra sadismo" [The victim who ends up falling in love with her executioner. Incest. Fetishism. Masochism as a proof of love. Sadism that begets frigidity that begets love that begets jealousy that begets sadism] (Cabrera Infante 1975, 45). Certainly, the narrative of the formula romance is not about happiness achieved but about happiness frustrated or deferred, and it would not be an exaggeration to say, paradoxically, that romance narrative is premised on lack (of happiness, of love, of the right man): in essence, a variation on a sadomasochistic theme. Once the woman receives acknowledgment of her man's love, the narrative ends, with what could be called "the death of love." As romance writer Linda Barlow says ironically, "[I]f the heroine were to continue to increase in her power and authority she would see that once the passage from virgin to mother is accomplished, men, in a way, are no longer essential" (Barlow 1992, 51). Cabrera Infante, who has recently taught a course on series romance at the Universidad Complutense in Madrid, is right in identifying these themes — or their toned-down versions — as constants in the formula romance, and many of them appear in Sefchovich's novels as well, although in her works the romantic happy ending is either ironized (*Señora de los sueños*) or projected onto an unlikely protagonist (*Demasiado amor*).

Like the romance novels they reference and ironize, though with a greater level of technical complexity and stylistic innovation, Sefchovich's novels update and play with the mixture of titillation and prudishness we have already seen in *Santa:* what Sylvia Molloy calls "soft-porn effects" (Molloy 1992, 192). Unlike romance novels, however, Sefchovich's novels include a subversive intent alongside their titillating effects. Unlike *Santa,* Sefchovich's books address a female audience, one that no longer accepts as natural a hard-porn mentality that, in Catherine MacKinnon's words, "makes inequality into sex, which makes it enjoyable, and into gender, which makes it seem natural" (MacKinnon 1987, 3). If these novels can be said to have an implicit social and political agenda, it would be found in their investigation of society's control mechanisms and of the nuances of male/female relationships in which the play of dominance and submission is naturalized and eroticized. *Demasiado amor* not only develops an engaging narrative of an empowered female sexuality but also suggests that readers think about the relationship between traditional literary heroines and a general cultural misogyny, and in *Señora de los sueños* Sefchovich addresses these issues specifically through the textualized image of the reading woman, a typical housewife whose escape from the deadening cycle of housework is reading popular narrative.

This popular formulaic novel geared toward a female audience serves as one of the major referents for Sefchovich's work both implicitly and overtly. In her two best-selling novels, Sefchovich has cannily tapped into an audience that reads widely but without high cultural pretensions: what she calls the nonacademic reader or *lectora común* [common reader], who does not enter into Mexican critical discourse: "[S]e les considera poca cosa" [(Critics) think of them as very unimportant] (personal conversation, June 1994). As Janice Radway notes, U.S. critics as well tend to dismiss the best-selling novels that attract nonacademic readers "as products of a fundamental insufficiency, therefore as the result of a certain incompetence." This conclusion, as Radway reminds us, is based on a presumed understanding of "a single set of criteria against which all works are measured, and thus [an insistence] that there is only one appropriate way to read" (Radway 1988, 518). In Radway's judgment, the critical dismissal of women's best-sellers has everything to do with the system of values against which these works are judged as failures. More appropriate, she argues, would be to examine these works "as ways of writing rather than Literature, ways of reading rather than texts," since, for middle-class readers, "books play a quite different role in their lives and serve other purposes than they do for people who make their living producing, analyzing, and distinguishing among cultural products" (519). While critics can and do write about almost anything these days, we seem to focus on the high and low ends of the cultural scale — precisely the two poles evoked and blurred in the best-seller. Like popular culture, Sefchovich's novels are a form of entertainment, but because of their relative technical complexity, they are entertainment for at least moderately educated people.

Feminist cultural critics have identified still another reason why the critical establishment is wary of best-sellers, a reason based on a long-standing and now much-discussed discomfort with a perceived feminization of literature that coincides with a feminization of reading.[2] When both the hierarchy of literary values and the privileged mode of critical discourse favor "masculine" referents, it is no surprise that critics evince acute discomfort with any feminizing features — qualities that have to be all the more carefully guarded against because of the age-old suspicion that reading books is an effeminate (or feminizing) activity. The battle of the books between classical, masculine works and vernacular, feminine fictions has been refought on differing intellectual planes for hundreds of years as, curiously, an obsession of a masculinist literary establishment. David Simpson's concise formulation makes the point on a theoretical level:

The feminization of literature was not, of course, uncontested. Wordsworth's famous outcries against popular novels and plays and high modernism's reaffirmation of sheer difficulty and massive intellectuality are just two instances of a masculinizing reaction. But the struggle has always occurred from within an already feminized general construction of the literary mode. Literary criticism, as an appendix or companion to literature, has experienced the same struggles. Its attempted diversions into theory have often been gestures of remasculinization, and have been resisted by an establishment whose lexicon is dominantly feminized: intuition, exceptionality, sympathy, empathy, lived experience, and so forth. (Simpson 1994, 62–63)

Simpson points to the complicated and invariably, if often unconsciously, gendered relation of the critic to the text, even in terms of the theoretical model he or she manipulates. Thus, the qualities of high art would include such masculinizing elements as a spare style and an intellectualizing or reflective mode of expression, while such feminizing counterparts as lushness and appeal to sensation are explicitly rejected. The woman's novel, in pointing in both directions at the same time, is particularly resistant to a remasculinizing intent and particularly threatening to the high-art value system. As Jennifer Wicke reminds us, "[O]n a methodological level, this is to suggest the intimate relationship between 'high art' and its conditions of production, and its shadow partner, the mass communication form that constitutes its matrix" (Wicke 1988, 1). Wicke is exactly right in this observation, the more so because her use of the term "matrix" hints at the shadowy feminized underpinnings of an overtly masculinizing structure. By playing off competing value systems in an intertextual, overdetermined, and theatricalized setting, the women's bestseller also reminds us of the masculinizing nature of the assumption that there is but a single system of values.

   In an interesting aside on the cheap, comic-book romance (*historieta* or *fotonovela*) market, Germán Mariño Soto notes that while soft-porn *fotonovelas rosas* tend to sell to the female market exclusively, the *fotonovela roja* [hard-core] tends to have a more diverse audience, attracting lower-class male as well as female readers. While the basic sadomasochistic romance elements are the same in both types, Mariño Soto defines the difference in content between them along basic class lines: *fotonovelas rosas* deal with upper- and middle-class life, while *fotonovelas rojas* use lower-class characters. He cites approvingly the conclusion of Cornelia Flora about the readership: "[E]l contenido de las fotonovelas rojas se vende porque está relacionado con lo que la gente ve en la vida real. La madre adúltera, la muchacha campesina engañada que se convierte en prostituta, el padre que descarga sus deseos sexuales en su hija ... son cosas con las que los lectores logran identificarse" [The content of hard-core *fotonovelas* sells because it is related to what people see in real life. The adulterous mother, the abandoned country girl who becomes a prostitute, the father who releases his sexual desires on his daughter...are things with which the readers are able to identify] (Mariño Soto 1990, 141). The ingrained classist assumptions about readers who are attracted to these texts because they are themselves lower-class criminals are too obvious to require comment. What I do find interesting is the hint that besides the class difference, the audience is tagged by a shift from "amorous" to "erotic" interest; women read "soft-porn" about love while men are targeted by "hard-core" erotic texts.[3]

It is precisely this slippage between love and eroticism that defines Sefchovich's first novel, *Demasiado amor,* as well. Since the protagonist is a highly successful prostitute, it is not hard to read the title's coy suggestion of "too much love" as "too much sex." While the coding in the title is transparent, it also clearly marks Sefchovich's novel as a women's book, and the softened title aids in marketing efforts as well. A similar tactic is consciously employed by Margo Glantz in her volume of essays, *De la amorosa inclinación a enredadarse en cabellos* [Of the loving inclination to be tangled up in hair (1984)], a title suggested by the publisher to substitute for the racier "De la *erótica* inclinación...," which Glantz nevertheless retained, no longer on the cover page, as the book's first and longest section title. With Sefchovich, as with Glantz, and quite apart from any marketing maneuvers, the book's title strikes me as precisely right. In dominant cultural discourse, "sex" and the erotic describe the site of objectification in which women become consumable things among a plethora of other consumer items. The word "erotic" too blatantly evokes the unaesthetic dimensions of obsession. It too literally concerns itself with the linkage between sex and power and would, moreover, implicitly associate the author with other Mexican writers like the notoriously conservative Juan García Ponce, the author of an infamous series of high-class erotic novels. *Demasiado amor,* in contrast, speaks to and within the debate on sexually liberated women, but from a markedly feminine viewpoint that puts a premium on love and pays relatively little attention to the mechanics of sex — a lesson learned from enormously successful mass-market and trade-paperback romances.

*Demasiado amor* has a bipartite structure that alternates chapters addressed to a male lover (*tú*) with letters sent to the narrator's sister in Italy. The letters to the sister are ostensibly concerned with the sisters' shared dream of a *casa de huéspedes* [bed and breakfast] by the sea and the overseas sister's progress toward reaching this goal. The chapters addressed to the lover detail the couple's weekend journeys through Mexico and what they find there. The two addressees are kept completely separate in the narrative; the protagonist tells her sister about her everyday life, about her work, about her dreams. She refuses to tell her sister anything about her mystery lover. At the same time, she tells her lover nothing about her personal life; her chapters addressed to him take the form of long enumerative series strangely blending the language of the travelogue with that of erotic obsession. Only at the end of the novel does the reader learn that the bifurcation of the reader into male and female, lover and sister, is false. The chapters ostensibly addressed to the lover are personal notebook entries, and this notebook, implicitly along with the set of letters sent to the sister and retained in her hands, becomes the heritage of the sister's daughter, to be held in trust for her as a moral tale:

> Te mando un cuaderno con mis recuerdos, los del hombre amado y los del país amado. El amor por los dos fue lo mismo, uno solo. Enséñaselo a mi sobrina, a mi ahijada. Dile que su tía Beatriz se lo dejó para que sepa que existe el amor y que existen los sueños. Dile que se puede amar mucho. Dile que hasta es posible amar demasiado, con demasiado amor. (185)

> [I am sending you a notebook with my memoirs, those of the beloved man and those of the beloved country. The love for each was the same, a single love. Show it to my niece, my goddaughter. Tell her that her Aunt Beatriz left it for her so that she knows that love exists and that dreams exist. Tell her that one can love greatly. Tell her that it is even possible to love too much, with too much love.]

This notebook and these letters comprise the novel we have finished reading, placing the reader in the role of voyeuse to the niece's inheritance and overtly marking that reading as feminine. With the novel's final chapter, thus, the hypothetical male reader, who has been hearing echoes of a discourse addressed to him in the notebook chapters that speak to a lover in the second person, must now reevaluate his misgendered reading of the novel and rethink the implications once again from a necessarily feminized role. José Joaquín Blanco comments in *Función de medianoche* [Midnight show] that "el arte ha tratado el amor de las mujeres como un episodio de la vida de los hombres" [art has treated women's love as an episode in men's lives], and he asks, "¿Qué ocurre con una mujer amorosa y totalmente solitaria en el escenario, en la solitaria amplitud de su historia?" [What happens with a loving woman totally alone on the stage, in the lonely amplitude of her history?] (Blanco 1981, 127). The answer might well be a novel like this one.

The reader of the book is necessarily more sophisticated than Beatriz who, in her letters to her sister as in her notebook to her beloved, tends toward a wide-eyed innocence that even her sister apparently views with impatience and incredulity. A few months after her sister's departure for Italy, Beatriz writes a cheerful note to accompany one of her checks for their hotel fund. The extra money she is sending toward their dream hotel, she says, came from a friend. She just happened to go to the Vips restaurant near her apartment and happened to meet this nice guy, and he came up to her apartment, and bingo!, "[C]ada vez que viene me regala dinero" [Each time he comes he gives me money] (35; the sexual double-meaning is the same in English as Spanish). When this guitar-playing friend leaves her, Beatriz feels lonely, so she goes back to the Vips (41), and in a later letter, she more straightforwardly says of another encounter, "[L]o invité a la casa porque necesitaba dinero" [I invited him home because I needed money] (45). Eight months after her sister's departure she quits her office job to work full-time at her new, still unnamed, profession (54–56). Finally, exactly one year after her sister's departure, Beatriz writes an angry letter: "¡Qué carta terrible la tuya! Me enojó y me lastimó muchísimo.... Tres veces dices que mi trabajo 'tiene un nombre muy claro' y las tres veces pusiste ese nombre con mayúsculas" [What a terrible letter yours was! It angered and hurt me a great deal.... Three times you say that my job "has a very clear name," and three times you wrote that name in capital letters] (70). In Sefchovich's book, as in Gamboa's earlier novel, the name of Beatriz's profession never sullies the printed page. Because of the epistolary style, however, the ellipsis reflects the letter writer's improbable linguistic *pudor* rather than Sefchovich's coyness; the result is a kind of textual ironic wink of mutual recognition between the author and her female reader. Beatriz's naïveté protects her from grossness; it also prevents the novel from falling into heavy-handed eroticism or tedious social commentary.

This pervasive irony takes on a specific postmodern cast as the novel progresses. In her later letters to her sister, Beatriz clarifies that "[e]l dinero es lo de menos. Me gusta el teatrito de seducir y de cambiar de personalidad" [money is the least of it. I like the theatrical aspect of seducing and changing personality] (166). If, on the one hand, Beatriz's confession reflects the very real pleasure in their work that many prostitutes admit to — the enjoyment of dressing up, the feeling of power in attracting many men (see transcripts in appendix) — on the other hand, she echoes an ongoing literary and philosophical discussion about performative constructions of identity through the iteration of discursive practices as ritualized productions (Butler). In the world of *Demasiado amor*, these ritualized discursive productions gradually create a shift in the protagonist's subjectivity and her sense of both self and place. The shift in her understanding of affectional relationships changes her understanding of other standards of behavior as well. By re-creating herself constantly for her clients in the circuit of Vips and her apartment, she achieves a kind of aesthetic completion as the mysterious woman who cannot be had or can be had only fleetingly, only in passing: the epitome of the woman as *flâneuse*.

In the second narrative line, with the monologue addressed to the unique lover, Beatriz traces a somewhat different trajectory. Her description of the fateful night in which she meets her lover begins with reference to a nonfungible self: "[V]eintiséis años y setenta y dos kilos tenía yo aquella noche de viernes cuando crucé la puerta de cristal del Vips" [I was twenty-six years old and weighed seventy-two kilos that Friday night when I crossed the glass door into Vips] (11). She is overweight, and so is he — both are fat and mostly silent: "Nunca te oí pronunciar palabra ni vi nada de ti más que aquel tu cuerpo enorme que se me acercaba otra y otra y otra vez para dejarme alucinada y adolorida" [I never heard you say a word, nor did I see anything of you except for your enormous body that drew near to mine again and again and again to leave me hallucinatory and in pain] (12). This man teaches her both to love and to suffer, to remember and to forget, always in excess: "No he vivido sino para ti, como viven las enamoradas, como viven las locas, como viven las mujeres. . . . Yo me convertí en eso que tú querías, una apasionada, una loca, una enferma, llena de ímpetus y languideces, pasiones y ternuras, alegrías y calmas. Fui dos mujeres, diez mujeres para tí" [I have not lived except for you, like women in love live, like insane women live, like women live . . . I turned myself into whatever you wanted: passionate, crazy, ill, full of impetuosities and languid behaviors, of passion and tenderness, happiness and calm. I was two women, ten women for you] (137). It is too much happiness, she writes at one point (123), and for this reason, in contrast with her behavior with her clients, in her relationship with her lover she has lost control of her emotions and her self. Rather than putting on different seductive faces for each different client, with her lover she falls into the language of the woman as a submissive inferior to the man, her ineluctable large body staked out as an object or commodity to be consumed by him.

Since he remains silent, she speaks for him in the notebook. "¿Te acuerdas?" [Do you remember?], she asks him. "Yo no me acuerdo de nada, todo lo he olvidado" [I don't remember anything; I have forgotten it all] (20), and later, contradictorily, she asserts, "De todo me acuerdo, de todo" [I remember everything, everything] (28). If in the theatricality of the prostitute Beatriz discovers a performative identity confirmed through repetition, in her lover's arms and in her travels with him she learns of the repetition that denies identity. Importantly, this narrative of her too-deep love is intertwined with a travelogue account of the couple's

incessant trips through the Mexican countryside, so that the timelessness
of her love stands in tension with a travel guide's superficial, but nevertheless awesomely detailed, account of Mexican history and culture. As
long as the affair is going well, this version of Mexico remains distinctly
utopian; when the love becomes too much, and doubts creep in, Beatriz's
travels take on a nightmarish, distopic quality. There is no middle ground;
her memory — or forgetfulness — of her travels is of necessity inauthen-
tic since it is colored by her desire and by her anticipatory mourning in
her rejection of a perfection that is too static.

*Demasiado amor* is about too much of everything: too many commodities as well as too much sex and too much love. In this book literary values
are linked to consumer values and to a fulfilled sexuality, implicitly in
Beatriz's carelessness about remuneration for her sexual services and more
explicitly in the alternating chapters with their lists of consumable items.
It is a curious feature of this novel, thus, that literary and consumer cultures are twinned, especially in the sections dealing with Beatriz's travels
with her lover. Over and over again in these chapters, the language of
consumption confuses itself with the language of love, as if the only way
Beatriz and her lover find to express their love for each other is through
a checklist of tourist sites and the accrual of tourist objects. As Beatriz
writes, "[A]llí iba yo comprando todas las artesanías que veía, no para
adornar mi casa como tú creías sino para traerme pedacitos de los lugares
donde tanto te amé" [There I went around buying all the handicrafts in
sight, not to decorate my house as you believed, but to bring back pieces
of the places where I loved you so much] (23). Beatriz's lists begin as a
poetic and loving reconstruction of her country; eventually they become
boring in their very excess, and despite the proliferation of objects and
places, they ultimately seem empty, forgettable, skippable.[4]

The first notebook entries offer an overview of the trips and delin-
eate the meticulous process of preparing her body for her lover with a
series of intimately described objects and products that he purchases for
her beautification. Later entries elaborate, seemingly interminably. Beatriz dedicates pages and pages to enumerative lists of cities, landscapes,
museums, churches, markets, restaurants, shops, monuments, historical
sites, haciendas, fortresses, jails, sporting events, musical events, fies-
tas; she includes lists of mountains, deserts, volcanoes, beaches, flowers,
rivers, trees, agricultural products, natural resources; of plazas, foun-
tains, stairways, arches; of diverse native peoples and of authors, painters,
composers. A typical entry begins:

> Las cosas que comimos. ¿Te acuerdas de todo lo que comimos?
> Probé contigo platillos hervidos, asados, cocidos al fuego, al vapor

y bajo la tierra, envueltos y sin envolver. Sábanas de carne delgada en Sonora, armadillo en Guerrero, mono en Catemaco, barbacoa en Tepozotlán y en Actopan, chivo en Putla, venado en Yucatán, chilorio en Sinaloa, chorizo en Toluca y en Pátzcuaro, huachinango en Veracruz, langostinos en Catemaco y langostas en Huejutla, menudo, machaca, tasajo, mixiotes de carnero, pollo y res, tacos de cabeza, buche, nana, maciza, moronga, bistec, chuleta y al pastor. (80–81)

[The things we ate. Do you remember all we ate? With you I tried boiled, baked, grilled, and steamed dishes, ones cooked underground, ones that were wrapped and ones that were not. Thin slices of meat in Sonora, armadillo in Guerrero, monkey in Catemaco, barbecue in Tepozotlán and in Actopan, goat in Putla, deer in Yucatán, chilorio in Sinaloa, sausage in Toluca and in Pátzcuaro, snapper in Veracruz, crawfish in Catemaco, and lobster in Huejutla, menudo, machaca, tasajo, mixiotes made of lamb, chicken, and beef, tacos made of headmeat, lips, nana, loin, blood sausage, beef, rib, and sheepherder style.]

And the list of food continues for two more pages. Another entry, on handicrafts, opens with the statement: "Quisiste que yo tuviera todas las artesanías que hacen en este país y desde entonces te detuviste en cada poblado y en cada rincón para explicarme, enseñarme, comprarme y regalarme" [You wanted me to have all the handicrafts made in this country, and from that time on you stopped in each town and each corner to explain to me, to show me, to buy me and give me things] (108). This statement is followed by several pages with a paragraph each dedicated to blouses, skirts, sweaters and serapes, jewelry, precious stones, shoes and other leather goods, furniture, dishes, clay pots, toys, paintings, and strangely carved natural objects, until finally, Beatriz comments:

Cada vez te invadió más la locura. Cada vez me regalabas más ollas y jarras, cazos, charolas, cazuelas, vasijas y platos, útiles, ceremoniales y de ornato. Me regalabas mantas y cambayas, telas de lana y de algodón, lisas y pintadas, con rayas, con dibujos, con colores; cestos y canastas, piezas de latón de hojalata y de cobre, de fierro y de aluminio, de oro y de plata, de barro y de cerámica, de madera y de piedra, de espejo y de vidrio, de cuero, liso y pirograbado, de hilo, ixtle, mecate, cáñamo, y macramé, de obsidiana y de óniz, de palma y de carrizo, de estambre y de papel, de hueso y de pelo, de cera y de plumas, de conchas y de varas, de azúcar y de pan. (112)

[You kept getting crazier. You kept giving me more bowls and pitchers, kettles, trays, pots, glasses and ordinary, company, and decorative china. You gave me blankets and rugs, wool and cotton cloth both plain and figured, with stripes, with patterns, with different colors; baskets and hampers, metal plate work made of tin and copper, handicrafts made of iron and aluminum, of gold and silver, of clay and ceramics, of wood and stone, of glass and mirrors, of both smooth and figured leather, of string, ixtle, maguey cord, hemp, and macramé, of obsidian and onyx, of palm and reeds, of worsted yarn and paper, of bone and hair, of wax and feathers, of shells and twigs, of sugar and of bread.]

Beatriz, it seems, is as entranced by the consumer objects her lover provides as by the intangible love he offers her. Indeed, these lists intimate a kind of poetic necessity to their elaboration, shaping themselves into the images of Beatriz's desire — for love, for consumption. Mexico comes to exist as a supertourist's checklist of things to purchase, and Beatriz and her lover are the sole active agents in this endeavor. Beatriz's notebook reminds me strongly of an observation by Rachel Bowlby, made in reference to Nabokov's *Lolita* but, I think, equally applicable to the consumer/lover ethics described in Sefchovich's novel. Bowlby writes: "[T]he poetic speed of consumption also mutates into its opposite, a state of tranquil suspension, underwater slow motion . . . , a silently timeless still life." In Sefchovich's novel too, the frenetic pace of travel and purchase slows on the written page into the timeless still life of the list. Bowlby describes this atmosphere as "the literal fulfillment of the fantasy that the appeals to consumption constantly promote; that this is just for you, you are the only shopper in the world, and far from you having to do anything to obtain them, the goods will simply float effortlessly into your hands" (Bowlby 1993, 66). Furthermore, because Beatriz's lover purchases absolutely everything, the effortlessness and the solitude are intensified; she does not even have to desire an object, does not even have to engage in that quintessential consumerly decision of making a choice between two or more attractive products. And even further: the shopping is as effortless as it is meaningless in that the items purchased are all flattened out into an enumerative sequence that gives no more importance to an expensive gold necklace than to a piece of amate paper. If the material objects represent her love, nevertheless they cannot satisfy her desires despite their proliferation, and so she needs to accumulate more and more of them, more of what she calls the souvenirs of her love, more touristic sites, more of her lover's tour-guide versions of Mexican history and culture.

Finally, when it seems there is nothing left to accumulate, deterioration of the relationship is signaled by what the lover does not want to buy
her or take her to see. Whole entries are then composed of places she did
not see, foods she did not try, handicrafts he did not buy her. Furthermore, in this progressive disillusionment with her lover, Beatriz no longer
sees only the beauties of the country but also its faults and its ugliness;
she lists the broken statues, the ruined temples, the pieces missing from
museums, the unromanticized bodies of the poor and homeless; she talks
about the earthquakes and other natural disasters; she describes the factories and the sewage systems, lists the effects of air and land and water
pollution, until, finally, she is tired of seeing things and buying things or
not buying things and of seeing him buying her things and refusing to
buy her things, or of sleeping at night rather than making love during
their weekends together. So she writes a final parallel entry to the one
describing her first meeting with her lover: "Treinta y dos años y setenta
y nueve kilos tenía yo cuando decidí no verte más" [I was thirty-two
years old and weighed seventy-nine kilos when I decided not to see you
anymore] (180). How does she break off the relationship? She simply
takes her lover to her apartment and lets him see her weekday life as a
prostitute, at which point he leaves the narrative as silently as he arrived.

In this notebook narration detailing the progress of desire, with its
imbrication in the ethics of consumption and its deterioration into dis-
interest and the dispersal of material and consumer objects, Sefchovich
reminds her middle-class female readers that such banalities as a Oaxa-
can weaving picked up on a tourist weekend are regulatory mechanisms
and that these mechanisms are capable of generating in a large number
of women a perplexing degree of satisfaction with their traditional roles.
As José Joaquín Blanco says, "El ama de casa no es esclava de su marido,
sino que los objetos que ella y él acumulan para creer en el fantasma del
hogar" [The housewife is not enslaved to her husband but to the objects
that she and he accumulate in order to create the fantasy of a home]
(Blanco 1981, 140). It is precisely this middle-class enslavement to objects that Sefchovich parodies in the excesses of her lovers' purchases,
and it is the attempt to escape from such enslavement that she imagines
in her protagonist's utopic final gesture of liberation when she brings her
lover's world together with her apartment/brothel and opens both to the
cleansing light and air: "No hay un solo mueble, todo lo tiré, ni un sólo
adorno, todo lo regalé. . . . Y por toda la casa los clientes están echados, fumando, bebiendo, durmiendo. Ya nadie se preocupa por vestirse" [There is
no longer any furniture; I threw it all away; nor a single ornament, I gave
them all away. . . . And clients are lying all over the house, smoking, drinking, sleeping. No one any longer worries about getting dressed] (179–80).

The narrator leaves off the doubled story with this image of an urban Eden before the fall, a timeless paradise of purity and light that could not contrast more strongly with the stereotypical image of the beautiful, evil woman in the ersatz opulence of an upper-class brothel. Chubby, uninteresting Beatriz has, in a sense, achieved her former dream of the "casa de huéspedes" right at home, in her own denaturalized domestic space.

For Sefchovich's reader, then, the novel enacts two fantasies of bourgeois liberation: that of the strong woman who begins and ends a relationship with a man on her own terms and that of the domestic housewife who chooses to accumulate consumer items or to free herself from the tyranny of objects, again, as a matter of personal aesthetic preference. While Beatriz has a good series-romance name and is as appropriately naive as a romance heroine, insofar as she is both overweight and closing in on romance-novel old age, she stands as an implicit counterpoint to her series-novel counterpart. Her grossness and ordinariness as well as her frequent and unrepentant sexual activities offer an implicit commentary on the misogynistic underpinnings of novels written for women. Yet, because her narrative is elaborated within a firmly established set of cultural and discursive landmarks involving a clear signposting of their fantastic and excessive nature, the project can never propose itself as anything other than utopic fancy, a conclusion borne out in the hyperbolic and very literary final letter with its ambiguous overtones of transcendence and self-destruction: "Hoy he terminado mi historia de amor y con ella todo el sentido de mi vida. En adelante voy a desaparecer, a perderme en las sombras, a dejarme llevar por los amores fáciles, gozosos" [Today I have finished my love story and with it all sense in my life. From this moment on I am going to disappear, to lose myself in shadows, to allow myself to be drawn into easy, pleasurable loves] (185). For the woman who loves easily and without object, without history, there is no narrative tension, no consumer goodies, no novel. She has become a smooth and impermeable surface with nothing to grasp, no things to hold her desiring body to a state of narrative being.

This discourse is about gender and about how a woman might in fantasy rewrite the social code for sexual relationships and other gendered constructions of male-female interaction. As I have been at pains to point out, *Demasiado amor* offers a critique of the middle-class structure of gender roles; it does not, however, touch upon the question of class itself, nor much less does it theorize about the function of fantasy for a working-class woman. While Sefchovich offers a specific angle of vision on the social organization of sexuality, this angle of vision is marked by its production within and for the middle-class "common" female reader. What is undertheorized and underdetermined in this novel is any consid-

eration of how the class status of the implied author and her presumed
audience plays itself out in the nuances of narrative representation. Certainly, if we remind ourselves once again of Mariño Soto's distinction
between soft- and hard-core porn comic novels based on representation
of characters from a certain class, we can begin to see how Sefchovich's
narrative context, with its preponderance of professional-class men (even
the homosexual character is an architect) and middle-class women (Beatriz and her sister can realistically aspire to a house in Italy), inflects
the novel's structure. These men and women dress well, eat frequently
in moderately expensive restaurants like Vips, live in comfortable houses
or apartments, and have sufficient discretionary income to furnish these
homes and to choose among a variety of available styles so as to reflect
their personality in the manner of decoration and type of ornaments.
Despite the detailed lists of Mexico's urgent social and political problems, the overall aesthetic of the novel suggests that Sefchovich's Mexico,
despite its excesses, is a clean, well-lighted, mostly polite, middle-class
place. Thus her very use of consumerism as a narrative metaphor serves as
one clue to a class-conscious reading, as does the author's representation
of leisure time and leisure activities.

In *La Señora de los sueños* Sefchovich more nearly approaches a textual
representation of an awareness of class-based cultural differences. Her
protagonist is a housewife whose husband complains about money but
who clearly provides her with sufficient funds to indulge her fantasies,
and in one of these fantasies she imagines herself into the role of a poor,
drug-addicted prostitute on the streets of New York. Even more than in
her first novel, in *La Señora de los sueños,* also a best-seller, Sefchovich
deals with themes and images from popular women's fiction, thematically
treating the topic of mass-market fiction for women. The protagonist of
this novel is a Walter Mitty-ish (or Emma Bovary-like) character. She is
the perfect housewife in her humdrum middle-class residence, perfectly
boring and perfectly bored. In fact, the first line of the novel defines
her by this eminently middle-class affliction: "Yo, Ana Fernández, pobre
de mi, soy una mujer que se aburre" [I, Ana Fernández, poor me, am
a woman who is bored] (Sefchovich 1979, 7).[5] She has been married for
twenty years, has watched her children grow and her husband gain weight
and lose interest in sex. She defines herself with respect to her family and
by relationship to the objects she cares for: "Esta soy yo, la reina de la
casa, la patrona de la liquadora, de la ropa sucia, de los sartenes y la plan-
cha, la mujer libre para elegir si gasto mi tiempo en ordenar o en limpiar"
[This is me, the queen of the house, the boss of the blender, the dirty
clothes, the pans, and the iron, the free woman who can choose whether
to spend her time organizing or cleaning] (8). The ironic intent is clear in

the narrator's juxtaposition of her so-called authority and freedom with a choice between equivalent and equally repugnant trivializing activities.

Ana Fernández, the self-described perfect housewife, distracts herself by reading popular fiction, and the novels she reads permit her to project herself into a series of other women. In addition to the New York prostitute, she imagines herself as a noblewoman in the court of King Alexander I of Russia, a biologist and friend of Darwin, a resident of an Israeli kibbutz, Fidel Castro's companion, Gandhi's disciple, and so on. In almost every case, she is the unwritten power behind great historical change, inspiring Castro and Gandhi, for example, or telling Darwin her theory of the origin of the species, which he will later steal and publish under his name. Margit Frenk writes in her review of the novel, "Este personaje femenino es una versión extrema y paradigmática de la mujer-objeto, de la mujer-sombra cuya presencia muda e inerme recorre la historia de la humanidad...con la diferencia, enorme, de que es lúcidamente conciente de serlo y de que su descripción de la vida que lleva tiene ya en sí los gérmenes de la rebeldía que luego va a fructificar en sucesivas liberaciones" [This female character is an extreme and paradigmatic version of the woman-object, of the shadow woman whose mute and inert presence runs through human history...with the enormous difference that she is lucidly conscious of her role and that her description of her life carries within it the germs of a rebellion that will bear fruit in successive liberations] (Frenk 1994, 14). I would differ from Frenk's analysis in that I find the housewife's rebellion more troubling, less liberating, than it might seem on the surface. Ana Fernández's middle-class existence is a blank space played out in the never-ending cycle of housework and cooking. Her real life is no life at all; lost among the objects she cares for and reduced to an insignificant cog in her well-functioning household, she desires liberation and finds temporary escape through reading popular fictions. The successive rebellions are always truncated, and each chapter returns her to the family home, the angry husband, the bemused children.

Despite her initial identity-grounding statement, "I, Ana Fernández,..." the narrative makes it clear that for this protagonist, identity is only provisional and situational. The housewife cannot be said to *be* anything; this is precisely why her continual metamorphosing into other lives can be so overwhelmingly complete. Margaret Morse, in her theorizing about the ontology of everyday distraction, calls such forms "attenuated fiction effects," which she defines as "a partial loss of touch with the here and now" (Morse 1990, 193). Following upon Michel de Certeau and Mikhail Bakhtin, Morse finds that "older concepts of liberation in everyday life based on 'escape attempts' and figurative practices are no longer viable....Indeed older notions of the public realm and of paramount reality have been largely undermined" (213). She further notes that "recognizing the extent and scope of an attenuated fiction effect in everyday life — an effect now largely unappreciated or considered trivial and hence subject to little vigilance — might already be a step toward bringing distraction within a controlled psychic economy of disavowal" (213) that would provide a more consistent and accurate account of the exchanges among economic, social, and symbolic systems in modern everyday life.

For Ana Fernández, her own house serves as the space in which the housewife plays out her fantasies, much like the freeways, malls, and televisions described by Morse. If she is a nonperson, or a screen upon which different fictional personalities can be projected, so too her house becomes a fluid nonspace. In this nonspace reigns the geometry of distraction, a disengagement from the realities of here and now in favor of a shifting elsewhere. Thus, the housewife's tale no longer emphasizes the passive activity of reading but rather the shifting from one fiction effect to another. She becomes a mobile subject in a continuously reframed alternation of discursive segments. The housewife, then, opens up her existence to alternative worlds, while at the same time she retains control over them by compressing the fictional processes into the familiar space of her own home, interiorizing and enclosing public men (Darwin, Gandhi, Castro) as well as the public woman (the New York street prostitute).

For purposes of this discussion, I would like to concentrate on the chapter describing the prostitute, chapter 3, "Atrapar el espíritu" [Trapping the spirit]. Like the other chapters in this novel, chapter 3 opens with three brief passages written, sequentially, from the point of view of the husband, the nearly adult daughter, and the younger son, each commenting on the changes in the household as a consequence of the wife's previous flight of fancy (detailed from her point of view in chapter 2) in which she imagined herself into a romantic, upper-class Russian existence. The pretext is a discussion with a psychiatrist; the diagnosis seems to be that the mother has gone mad from too much reading. The husband complains, "[C]reo que la culpa de todo la tienen los libros" [I believe books have the blame for everything] (103), and he grouses about her sudden drain upon the household economy, her affected mannerisms, her new servant, her constant dressing up, her strange European dishes, her piano lessons, her sudden taste for opera. The daughter finds the elegant dinners appealing for their potential in getting her boyfriend to finally propose matrimony. The son objects to wearing a suit and finds the dinners boring, but in general he takes his mother's part: "[Y]a sé que venimos acá para hablar de mi mamá, dicen que está enferma, pero el que anda mal es mi papá" [I know that we came here to talk about my mother; they say she's sick, but the person that's really ill is my father] (107). In this manner, the tripartite prologue to the chapter also serves as an epilogue to and commentary on the previous chapter, reminding the reader that however spacious (and specious) the fictional projection may have seemed, its concrete representations were limited to the interior of the housewife's domain, and its truncated repercussions to the boundaries of abnormal psychiatry or family therapy.

A similar conversation at the beginning of chapter 4 serves as the family's critical commentary upon the fantasy of prostitution that dominates chapter 3, and in parallel terms; the obsessions of each particular member of the family are already well established. If in the beginning of chapter 3 the husband's complaints concerned elaborate meals with strange sauces and cabbage on the side, in the beginning of chapter 4 his long-suffering palate is forced to deal with junk food and hot dogs. The daughter, as always, worries about the repercussions on her matrimonial prospects, and the son takes a live-and-let-live approach. Thus, the housewife's fantasies are sandwiched between family therapy sessions, and her reading becomes the subject of psychoanalytic interpretation. Importantly for Sefchovich's overall method, in each family member's counter "reading" of the housewife's activities, her fancies are shown to have concrete correlatives in the domestic space — that is, the distraction is not simply a daydream but an elaborate construction that involves real exchanges between the private imaginings and the social/domestic space.

The housewife's own narrative in "Atrapar el espíritu" begins with the line, "[M]i esposo me prohibió leer" [My husband forbade me to read] (109). She consequently goes out for a walk and immediately becomes distracted from her surroundings by an imagined freedom that she, strangely, stereotypically, projects onto the life of a prostitute: "¿Por qué no puedo tener yo libertad? ¿Por qué no puedo hacer lo que me gusta? Me imagino lo que sería mi vida si estuviera sola, dueña y señora de mi persona y de mi tiempo, en alguna gran ciudad donde pase de todo, donde la prostitución sea total, la luz eléctrica también" [Why can't I be free? Why can't I do what I want? I imagine what my life would be like if I were alone, completely in charge of my body and my time, in some great city where everything happens, where prostitution is total, and so is electric lighting]. In this already forming scene of the New York underworld, the housewife/prostitute stops at a stand selling pornographic magazines, which in her Mexican neighborhood would be the newspaper kiosk that also sells cheap comic-book romances and *fotonovelas*. With this mere hint of a hard-core reading/viewing experience, the transition completes itself (110–11). The dream of freedom propels her inevitably into the forbidden realm of reading.

In this particular "hard-core" fiction, the housewife symbolically attaches her domestic invisibility to the invisibility of the criminal underworld, and she projects her dream of total freedom (and electric lights) onto the body of a marginalized, drug-addicted street whore. Literary and social impropriety blend as this improper, marginalized subject takes over the housewife's text, and the narrative of her life merges with the language of cheap mass-market fiction. Performance of this script distracts the housewife from the forbidden impulse to seek her own personal liberation, and thus by giving in to the forbidden desire to read, she masks the even more dangerous longing to escape permanently from her deadening middle-class life. And yet she plays out the fiction once again in the context of her own neighborhood streets, her own defamiliarized home. The deeply pornographic elements of hard-core *fotonovelas* attach themselves to the deeply conventional referents in a staged identification that Sefchovich will, nonetheless, defer until the next chapter.

The prostitute uses a flat narrative tone for the most perverse and scandalous revelations. Here, for example, is how she describes her loss of her virginity and simultaneous inauguration into pornographic films and the life of a prostitute: "A Pete lo conozco desde que mi padrastro me llevó al estudio de filmación. Yo tenía 14 años y él quiso que me tomaran película mientras me estrenaba, para aprovechar a ganarse una lana" [I've known Pete since my stepfather took me to the film studio. I was fourteen years old and he wanted them to film me while he did it to me for the first time so he could earn a little dough] (120). The prostitute's world is garishly lighted, defined by filthy walk-up apartments, overflowing trash cans, nude dancers, unwashed street people, perverse employers, violent punks, and pathetic drug users. She lives on greasy hamburgers, hot dogs, Spaghetti-Os, and Coke, and matter-of-factly trades sex for any of these foodstuffs or gives away her dirty underwear in exchange for drugs. Her language is peppered with English obscenities, and her life involves a round of parties where, for example, she disinterestedly watches a woman cut her veins and, after tranquilly watching the woman's efforts for a while, decides to leave her to her death (137). In this respect, the accumulation of specific objects and near-lists of cultural artifacts brings *Señora de los sueños* into close proximity with the more obvious consumerist lists of *Demasiado amor*, only with an emphasis on the noncommercially attractive objects of modern life.

Yet, despite this superficial wallowing in the disgusting aspects of an imagined underclass life, the geography this fiction effects is clearly defined. Her wanderings take her on a standard tourist itinerary from the Village to Times Square to Riverside Drive, from Soho to Madison Square Garden to Macy's. Her references to sites off the tourist

beat are vague (Brooklyn) or artificially precise. For example, of the architect who employs her as a nude secretary, she says: "Dos veces por
semana toma un tratamiento antistress de quince minutos (Lenox Hospital Health and Education Center, 1080 Lexington Ave, NY 10021) y
dos veces por semana se broncea bajo la lámpara en una clínica especiali-
zada (Famous CEOS Sunshine, 19976 Avenue of the Americas)" [Twice
a week he takes a fifteen minute antistress treatment (Lenox Hospital
Health and Education Center, 1080 Lexington Ave, NY 10021), and
twice a week he tans himself under a lamp in a specialized clinic (Famous CEOS Sunshine, 19976 Avenue of the Americas] (135–36). The
housewife's liberation in New York City can only be a garish pose based
on an incomplete reading of insufficient texts.

   This stumbling reading of the pornographic text confirms by antinomy
the basic qualities of the housewife's existence. Like Ana Fernández, who
defines herself by the objects that define her role (blender, iron, pots and
pans, dirty clothes) and that stifle her (lamps, carpets, curtains, tables
and chairs), the prostitute too defines herself with respect to housework
(her male roommate does all of it; she cannot be bothered [115]) and in
relation to household objects (her day begins when thieves break into the
apartment and carry off everything [114]). In contrast to the housewife's
oppressive dressing up and her religious trips to the beauty parlor to fix
her hair, the prostitute says cuttingly, "[N]unca uso bragas. Tampoco uso
pelo. Hace mucho tiempo que me rapé" [I never wear underthings. Or
hair. I shaved my head a long time ago] (115). The housewife's fiction
effects, then, are propped upon a process of citation (of the prohibited
other) that both transgresses the prohibition against such fantasies while
at the same time relying upon a narrow band of analogous loci and objects
to buttress the illusion. Despite what she imagines as their social and
political promise, the very nature of the choices she makes underlines
their resemblance to the reality they reject; her insubordination confirms
her lack of freedom.

   It is, then, unsurprising that the primary emotional characteristic of
the prostitute, like the housewife, is her unremitting boredom. The prostitute walks dangerous streets, meets strange and unusual people, goes to
parties, and works at exotic jobs, and despite all this activity, she is list-
less. "Pasamos tres días en ese lugar" [We spent three days in that place],
she says of one long-lived party. With nothing to do but drink and have
sex with men she doesn't know, "[E]s suficientemente aburrido" [It was
boring enough] (126). Later in the tale of her adventures, she can think
of nothing better to do than to go home to her television: "[H]ace horas
que veo la televisión. Me encantan los anuncios" [I've been watching television for hours. I love the commercials] (133). When she is out on the

street, she is equally lonely and alone: "Ando mucho rato hanging around
pero no aparece nadie...y no tengo ánimo de levantar a uno nuevo" [I
walk for a long time hanging around but no one shows up,...and I don't
feel like picking up a new guy] (134). New York, she says finally, "es una
ciudad que lo promete todo y todo lo aniquila" [is a city that promises
everything and annihilates everything] (144). Thus, despite her imaginative creation of the prostitute's social context — albeit an imaginative
effort based on a middle-class perception of significant categories of objects — the housewife's fantasy of the prostitute's emotional state differs
very little from the predominant deadening boredom of the housewife
herself.

Ana Fernández's transgressive miming of a prostitutional liberation
hints that all such fiction effects, whether radical or superficial in style,
come back to the same thing. Her character's fluid polyphony, when
broken down into its basic structural elements, limits itself to the middle-
class housewife's implicit values and theoretical range of experience. As
Judith Butler says of the masquerade of femininity in the transvestite film
*Paris Is Burning*, the "'contesting of realness' involves the phantasmatic
attempt to approximate realness, but it also exposes the norms that regulate realness as *themselves* phantasmatically instituted and sustained. The
rules that regulate and legitimate realness (shall we call them symbolic?)
constitute the mechanism by which certain sanctioned fantasies, sanctioned imaginaries, are insidiously elevated as the parameters of realness"
(Butler 1993, 130). In this manner, importantly, while Ana Fernández
will inevitably fall back into the housewife role and into the cycle created by temporary escapes, the reader of Sefchovich's novel will be asked
to meditate upon the structures of realness as elaborated in the fluid
exchanges of words and images that explore the incommensurable differences between class- and culture-determined concepts of reality, while
at the same time the author reminds us that our illusions and our realities
are premised upon a relatively narrow understanding of realness.

Sefchovich's work recognizes the power of fiction effects such as those
described by Morse and of citational practices such as those defined by
Butler, and she suggests how difficult and how necessary it has become
for her readers to understand their functioning. In *La señora de los sueños*
the melodramatic events that motor the plot will pull the reader into the
fiction. At the same time, its obvious soap opera qualities, along with the
emphatic repetition of images signaling the banalization of culture, offer a permanent dissonance — not an escape from fiction, or even from
semifictional effects, but rather a controlled disavowal of distraction from
within. Intertextually, Sefchovich suggests that only truthfulness to the
diversity of the experience of women from different classes, different

races, and different nationalities can break the impasse, repositioning the question of female identities as part of a dynamic map of social and political power relationships according to which such identities are constituted or erased. As the repeated truncation of the fiction-within-a-fiction reminds us, Ana Fernández's seductive and disturbing dream of freedom avoids confrontation with the real issues facing the reading woman and, even more crucially, the woman who reads different texts, who reads them differently, or who does not read at all. It is the project of the next chapter of this book to look specifically at a reading and writing practice that occurs across class lines.

# Chapter 6

# Signifyin', Testifyin'

## Mora, Bandida, Serrano

In his book *Women for Hire,* Alain Corbin writes that the nineteenth-century ethnographic study of Parisian prostitutes by Alexandre Parent-Duchatelet was so influential it not only affected later studies of prostitution in France and in other countries but also — albeit indirectly — became a force shaping women's lives: "Parent-Duchatelet's portrait of the prostitute was repeated so often in the literature on prostitution and inspired so many novelists that, in addition to distorting the vision of later researchers, . . . it determined to some extent the behavior of the prostitutes themselves" (Corbin 1990, 7). What I find fascinating about this quote is Corbin's contention that a specific kind of academic exercise had a major effect on fictional practice and that fictional versions of this produced and shaped version of knowledge in turn influenced certain kinds of social practices (the lives and practices of real prostitutes), which were then reencoded in another version (Corbin's) of the anthropological construction of knowledge about such practices.

A similar process of life influencing fiction influencing life underlies Xorge del Campo's "sociological" study of prostitution in Mexico, when he points directly to the effect of prostitutes' reading practices on their lives: "Fenómeno curioso en las prostitutas: son numerosas las que aman la lectura. ¿Pero qué leen? Fotonovelas, revistillas románticas, por supuesto, en las cuales espigan ideas y lugares comunes que luego expanden a su contorno" [There is a curious phenomenon among prostitutes; many of them love reading. But what do they read? Comic books, romance magazines, of course, in which they spot the ideas and common-places that they later expand to their surroundings] (del Campo 1974, 124). In both del Campo and Corbin, the construction of an informative, even scientific, study of sexually transgressive women is hinged upon and tightly implicated in the relation between lives and fictions. In each of the studies, the prostitutes are seen both as fictional subjects and as fictional objects as well as fictionalizers. The women tell fictions that writers turn into novels; the women read the novels and turn the fictions back into their daily lives and their work as part of a storied experience tailored to the tastes of the client. Consequently, the sociologist can never be sure if the stories he hears are lived or read or imagined since the essence of the life is already a storied artifice. Even basic details about identity are infinitely negotiable: "Con el nombre que quieras, tú pagas" [Whatever name you like, you're paying] begins an interview with a Mexico City prostitute with twenty-two years of experience (Bellinghausen, ed., 1990, 101). And, furthermore, as Corbin recognizes, the knowledge structures that guide the researcher are also artificial in nature; they too are stories that shape the researcher's vision.

A parallel, and equally convoluted, process occurs on another level with *Santa*. Like the nineteenth-century French and English narratives it superficially resembles, Gamboa's novel turns contemporary sociological/ anthropological truisms about fallen women into an aesthetic product, self-identified as artifice and served up to an eager reading public as such. Despite its contrived and aestheticizing frame, however, the novel, taken on one level as a faithful biography, spawns a veritable cult of fans who organize trips to visit the heroine's "birthplace" and "tomb." Santa, like the Velveteen Rabbit, like the characters in *fotonovelas* and *revistillas románticas*, becomes real and, theoretically, would have real effects on a real society. While I would not attempt to follow Corbin's or del Campo's lead and extend conclusions about the influence of Santa and her fictional and cinematic heirs on the *behavior* of other women or on the social formations instantiated by such fictions — an effort that would take me far beyond the scope of this study — I would argue that, to some extent, Gamboa's novel establishes the perimeters for later Mexican intellectual discussions of transgressive women by critics, chroniclers, and novelists like the writers studied thus far in this book as well as other Mexican intellectuals such as José Joaquín Blanco, Xorge del Campo, Margo Glantz, Sergio González Rodríguez, Carlos Monsiváis, Cristina Pacheco, and Luis Zapata. The trouble with all these books, however, is that their ostensible subjects don't usually have the opportunity to read them, much less to respond to the depiction of their lives with their own versions.

Yet *Santa* and its heirs established the tradition within which or against which later memoirs/testimonials by women of a different social or cultural background have been published and read, including the works that I will be studying in this chapter: Antonia Mora's *Del oficio* [The life], Irma Serrano's three volumes of memoirs (*A calzón amarrado* [Knotted panties], *Sin pelos en la lengua* [Telling it straight], and *Una loca en la polaca* [A spoke in the wheel]),[1] and Eduardo Muñuzuri's *Memorias de*

*"La Bandida"* [Memoirs of La Bandida]. These books and others like them — a veritable subgenre in Mexican narrative[2] — point to a situation very different from that described by recent theoretical discussions of loose/fallen/prostituted women in Europe, such as those of Charles Bernheimer, Amanda Anderson, and Jann Matlock. Matlock states the limitations of her study clearly; the prostitute, she says, "has left us few traces, little writing, certainly no novels of her own" (Matlock 1994, 21), and later, Matlock adds: "she never speaks for herself" (25); "she cannot be a speaking subject in the discourse that surrounds her" (28); and "the prostitute's story remains, here and elsewhere, to be told" (59).

In Mexico, the case is so different as to constitute the missing story evoked by the repeated signaling of the prostitute's silence in Europeanist discourse. And yet the two stories (that of the loose woman and that about her) fit together like jigsaw puzzle pieces — perhaps too neatly. Mariano Azuela's chronicles and the memoirs of Antonia Mora, "La Bandida," and "La Tigresa" suggest further the degree to which the middle- to upper-class bias of the narrative voice in traditional works needs to be rethought and reconfigured in the context of an urban, increasingly industrialized society, one disaffected by and disillusioned with the Mexican Revolution.

Mora's story of her life as a ghetto-bred, second-generation prostitute and thief, as framed by novelist María Luisa Mendoza's foreword, becomes a moral tale of sin and redemption. Serrano's books construct an image of a dangerously — at least for the rich and powerful men who become her lovers! — empowered sexuality. Muñuzuri's book mostly outlines his failed efforts to convince the infamous Mexico City madam to dictate her memoirs to him. In each case, the work enters the marketplace as an artifact: like the fictions studied in the earlier chapters of this book, each offers a construction both moral and artificial, a tissue of pregnant and titillating silences that should/should not be broken, an allegory for an unrecognized or ignored national identity. These memoirs are books that at the same time present themselves as, or are framed as, terribly serious, highly entertaining, and slightly naughty. They are familiar and exotic: embodying the Cinderella story of the poor girl redeemed by the love of an honest man or, alternatively, the Mexican archetype of the *mujer bravía* [fierce woman] who combines a masculine arrogance with sexual aggressivity and feminine allure. The women behind the stories are simultaneously untrustworthy liars, able storytellers, deficient fiction writers, and honest chroniclers. María Luisa Mendoza, for example, reminds her readers and herself of the many options in her description of Antonia Mora's relationship to the text, but she carefully does not adjudicate among any of these possibilities. At the same time, Mendoza tacitly acknowledges the reader's expectations and the tradition within which Mora's story will be read when she writes:

> Antonia me trae su novela, su cuento, su escrito, su vida pues, con-
> victa y confesa, sin clasificación literaria porque no es un estudio
> sociológico ni la exaltación del erotismo ni menos de la pornografía
> ni tampoco de la moraleja que sirva de escarmiento, ni nada de
> nada. Es simplemente decir lo que vio, lo que supo, lo que es
> cierto....¿Es necesario, me dije, que esto se sepa? No lo sé, no
> lo sabré nunca porque temo que las letras vencidas de su pasado
> puedan ser ajadas, rayadas, envilecidas por lectores gambusinos de
> lo caliente sólo y no de lo ardiente que es este libro terrible. (10–11)

> [Antonia brings me her novel, her story, her writing, her life, her
> convict's confession, without any literary pigeonhole because it is
> not a sociological study nor an eulogy of eroticism; even less is it
> pornography or a moral tale that serves to teach a lesson, nor any-
> thing else. It is a simple telling of what she saw, what she knew,
> what is true.... Is it necessary, I asked myself, for this to become
> known? I don't know, I will never know, because I fear that the tale
> of her defeated past could be crumbled, torn up, and dirtied by low-
> minded readers only interested in what is hot and not what burns
> in this terrible book.]

Mendoza, of course, has promoted this book and written the foreword for it. Her foreword also offers official recognition of the real existence of the woman, Antonia Mora, and the manuscript that purports to tell of her early life. Thus, like the prologue to *Santa*, it provides an aesthetic frame to appreciate the following text. Furthermore, Mendoza acknowledges the tradition within which this work is likely to be read — sociological study, erotic literature, pornography, moral tale — and the readers that the work is likely to find: aficionados of those genres. Thus, she tries to have it both ways: this book will sell, she hints, because it is full of hot women and titillating erotic details; but it should also sell because it endorses good moral values and teaches the middle-class reader about the painful, terrible reality of poverty in the lower classes. Will the read-ers who buy it for the "wrong" reasons change their mind upon reading the work itself? Mendoza does not want to hazard a guess, leaving the question as open as possible, while at the same time offering a ratio-nalization for those of us who do not want to be identified with *lectores gambusinos* [low-minded readers]. In this respect, her gambit is identi-cal to, though less obvious than, that of the blurb writer for Xorge del

Campo's *La prostitución en México:* "Todas esas mujeres que se enlodan
en la disipación y satisfacen la sensualidad tarifada: ¿qué son?, ¿de dónde
vienen?, ¿a dónde van?... El presente 'dossier' sobre la prostitución en
México hará reflexionar a muchos y, desde luego, divertirá y entretendrá
a todos" [All those women who muddy themselves with dissipation and
satisfy a purchased sensuality: Who are they? Where do they come from?
Where do they go?... This "dossier" about prostitution in Mexico will
make many people think and, of course, will provide enjoyment and entertainment for all]. Curiously, however, in all these formulations, both
the right reasons (higher knowledge) and the wrong reasons (vile entertainment) belong to the same system, the same theoretical structure. It is
a structure that these memoirs retain, but only in a tense, double-voiced
relation.

*Del oficio* (1972) contrasts strikingly with María Luisa Mendoza's
novelistic version of a similarly adventurous life. *De Ausencia* [About
Ausencia (1974)] is not a "terrible" story of sin and redemption. Instead, this is a story of vice rewarded, much more akin to Sefchovich's
best-selling novels. Mendoza's work is a lushly erotic novel about a
nineteenth-century woman who crosses boundaries of sexual taboo and
loves men with a freedom and frequency traditionally accorded only to
the male gender. Ausencia Bautista Lumbre is a woman of two worlds
and neither. Like Antonia Mora, Ausencia Bautista is born in extreme
poverty, and like the author/narrator of *Del oficio,* she fights her way into
the privileged circles of the upper class. Mendoza's novel, however, skips
the tale of the protagonist's early life and focuses on later adventures
as part of a privileged class. Once privy to upper-class circles, Ausencia travels and takes in the Belle Époque splendors of Europe, before
returning home to a comfortable intimacy with her Mexican servants and
nanny. And then she takes off again, on her air or sea adventures. Her
language is sprinkled with Spanish anachronisms, Mexican regionalisms,
and English, French, and Italian phrases. Unlike the sad, waiflike woman
Mendoza describes in her foreword to *Del oficio* in terms of a fading
rose, a woman weighted down with "silencios de ausencia" [absent si-
lences] (9), the character Ausencia calls herself — or the narrator of the
novel calls her — "la bella acostante" [the sleeping-around beauty] and
notes: "En la vejez, descubre que nació para la cama, el libro, el piti-
llo y la dormida.... fuera de la alcoba no había nada que hacer" [In her
old age, she discovers that she was born for bed, books, cigarettes, and
sleeping... Outside of her bedroom there was nothing to do] (174).

The holes in Ausencia's narrative have to do with boredom, not moral
scruples. She too tells the story of her life, and her literary style is inflected by her dominant activity: "Las mujeres cronistas de sus coitos el

cincuenta por ciento los inventan, y las reservadas son las de a de veras cámaras. Yo mi vida se la novelo a mis amantes nada más, y a su manera y estilo, haciéndole en el 'cuéntame Ausencia', saben lo que quieren saber" [Women who tell about their affairs invent 50 percent, and the quiet women are the ones who really get around. I tell stories about my life for my lovers and no one else, and I do it to fit their style and manner, making it up so that from the "tell me, Ausencia" they find out what they want to know] (105). Unlike other women, who elaborate stories to fit their own self-image, Ausencia's stories, like her body, are her gifts to her lover, and she personalizes that gift.

Absent/present Ausencia, then, offers her reputation as a "woman with a past" to her lovers, and she bluntly withholds herself at whim. At one point in the novel, Ausencia tells a travel companion on the *Gigantic*, "A ti yo no tengo por qué darte mi historia: no eres mi amante, ni siquiera mi conocido..., pasa, como la cara del hombre de la aduana que lee tus generales, los sella y se te olvida. Además, alégrate, me aburrirías....Y por ende, ni siquiera te pareces, no eres mi tipo" [I have no reason to have to tell you my story; you're not my lover, not even my acquaintance...; move along, like the face of the customs officer who reads your papers, stamps them, and forgets about you. Besides, cheer up, you would bore me....And to top it all off, you don't look right, you're not my type] (105–6). Implicitly, each reader of Ausencia's tale is drawn into a love affair with her; we are relieved not to be cast out with the man on the ship. In the end, nevertheless, Ausencia's tale bores even her. "Ojalá me muriera," she says prophetically on boarding the *Gigantic* for its first and final voyage. "Esta historia me aburre" [I hope I die. This story is getting boring] (190).

María Luisa Mendoza's Ausencia is generous with herself but can be recalcitrant. She begins her life as a motherless child; her father carries the significant and unlikely name of Gerundio Bautista. From her father, Ausencia inherits a certain "plus cuán perfecto el pasado" [plu- and how-perfect past] (98), and it is she who lives up to his name: "Irlanda. De ir, de un lugar a otro ir, ir a la deriva, ir caminando, ir tirando, del imperativo ¡ve!, del gerundio yendo...la hizo volver" (192–93).[3] *De Ausencia* begins in midair, in a notably phallic dirigible, and ends with the midsea orgasmic encounter between the cruise ship *Gigantic* and an iceberg. While Ausencia Bautista feels intermittent twinges of remorse over the death of her first lover, a U.S.-Arab businessman sadistically murdered by her second lover and herself, such remorse only adds piquancy to a life delivered up to the amply rewarded pleasures of the body and of the text. "¿Puta yo?" asks Ausencia rhetorically. "Si mi padre me viera...se volvería loco de amor por mí...Si yo fuera hombre, me gustaría hacerme el amor a mí misma" [Whore? I? If my father saw me . . . he would go crazy with love for me. . . . If I were a man, I'd like to make love to myself] (22–23).

Ausencia is "a prodigal daughter," in Jerry Aline Flieger's words. For Flieger, the prodigal daughter "goes beyond the fold of restrictive paternal law, only to return. But unlike the prodigal son of legend, who returns repentant, she returns enriched — for she is 'prodigal' in the second sense of the term as well: she is lush, exceptional, extravagant, and affirmative" (Flieger 1990, 59–60). Flieger's discussion may itself sound a bit extravagant and utopic; it does, however, suggest a critical practice that resists dominant voices and challenges readers to rethink the category of the woman as discursive subject/object outside the essentialist frame into which she has so traditionally been cast. It counterposes a practice of heterogeneity to false assumptions of universality and forces us to return to a question relative to the field at large, that of the struggle with and against the power of words — either as they are used to liberate women or to hold women back — or as they are deployed structurally in the canonical texts that provide our common resources and common language. Thus, Ausencia lives up to her father's name in living up to her own — in leaving her father's house, in absenting herself from Mexico, and in crossing traditional ethical and actual political borders. Her land is also an island, when seen on the global scale, and she is the absent (un)inhabitant of that "irlanda," the land of departure. Like the prodigal son, she always returns, and she returns prodigal with stories and with herself. Mendoza's novel, then, in some ways can be seen as a second part and an idealized response to the more conventional prodigal-daughter tale in Mora's *testimonio*.

If the novels, sociological studies, and chronicles referred to in earlier chapters of this book are one antecedent for these memoirs, another is the kind of literary journals that collect erotic adventures in order to preserve them like objects in a display case. One excellent example is Mariano Azuela's 1889–97 "Registro" [catalogue] detailing his encounters with young prostitutes in Guadalajara. "En mi registro," he writes, "las curiosidades se archivan" [My catalogue is an archive of curiosities] (Azuela 1960, 1205). He writes brief narrative descriptions of the women from whom he purchases sexual favors and frequently retells abbreviated versions of their life stories. In this manner, Azuela not only purchases a short-term sexual relation but also turns the women into collectible erotic objects, who serve him at least doubly: first, in the sexual relationship and, second and subsequently, as narratives that he, the master collector, can return to and enjoy again and again. In fact, he tells his journal, collecting prostitutes has become his only serious hobby: "Yo no bailo, no tengo novia, ni juego al billar, necesariamente he de buscar distracciones, y como el juego no me conviene, me dedico a las mujeres fáciles" [I don't dance, I don't have a girlfriend, I don't even play billiards, so I obviously need to look for hobbies, and since gambling is not right for me, I dedicate my time to easy women] (1197). Over and over, Azuela repeats in the "registro" the stories women tell him. He clearly finds these stories, often gained under pressure, to be infinitely seductive, highly collectible: "Anoche estuve con ella a falta de otra cosa. . . . La hice hablar como a todas" [Last night I slept with her because I had nothing better to do. . . . I made her talk, just like all the others] (1210); "Me traje su libreta . . . pues creí encontrar en ella, si no un 'diario,' si cosa por el estilo; esperaba ver consignados allí pensamientos suyos sobre lo que llamaba su atención" [I took her appointment book . . . because I believed I would find in it, if not a "diary," then at least something of the sort; I thought I would see her thoughts about whatever captured her attention written down there] (1231–32).

He frequently records in the "registro" his reactions to these tales, especially his disappointment at their incompleteness or their inferior literary quality. Of the woman whose appointment book he borrows, Azuela comments, "Señora mía, voy a decirla, tan pronto como vuelva a verla, 'esto no es suficiente, decididamente debe haber algo más'" [My dear lady, I am going to tell her, as soon as I see her again, "This is not enough, there definitely has to be something more"] (1232); of another he complains: "F. y yo estuvimos preguntando a Flora . . . desde cuándo y cómo se había dedicado a su noble profesión, y nos contó una historia muy inverosímil" [F. and I were asking Flora . . . about how and when she came to dedicate herself to her noble profession, and she told us a very unbelievable story] (1199; the story follows); of still another he writes, "[S]u caída aparece a mis ojos vulgar, su estado no puede ilusionarme, y ya torturará su cabeza con las historias por contar, escogiendo la más verosímil" [Her fall from grace looked so vulgar to my eyes that I couldn't summon any illusions about her state even though she tortured herself trying to come up with stories to tell, trying to choose the most believable one] (1201). Sometimes he delights in his own role in creating future tales: "[L]a maltraté tan despiadadamente" [I mistreated her pitilessly] (1213); "[T]uve la sensación, gozosa por momentos, de creer que pervertía su espíritu" [I had the momentarily delicious feeling of believing that I perverted her spirit] (1221); "[M]e llevaron . . . una indita insignificante, apenas salida de la pubertad. ¡Qué sensaciones podríamos experimentar . . . y yo indiferente y haciéndolo casi por puro compromiso!" [They brought me an insignificant little Indian girl, barely pubescent. What kind of sensations could we feel? . . . And I was indifferent and doing it with her almost because I had to] (1216). His own role, as he records it in the "registro," is as artificial and storied as the women's, whether he is behaving as a knowledgeable seducer or an abusive client.

Sometimes he complains not only about lack of verisimilitude but also about the lack of imagination in the women's tales of woe: "La mujer pública debe poner su inteligencia lo mismo que su cuerpo a disposición de los clientes" [The public woman ought to put her intelligence as well as her body at the disposition of her clients] (1205). Essentially, Azuela is concerned with locating interesting characters for his "registro"; the result is that his own powers of imagination are not taxed in creating an attractive and realistic erotic collection, and he achieves instead a collection composed of admittedly fictionalized, unbelievable life stories. What Azuela critiques in the public women of Guadalajara is basically their lack of an acceptable storytelling style. He is completely uninterested in the political or social problems that cause women to become prostitutes and even less concerned with the specific plight of any of the women whose stories he repeats with such delight. He does not want their testimony; he wants to be suitably entertained.

Indeed, the very concept of a *testimonio* by such a woman is theoretically fraught with contradiction. The linchpin of testimonial narrative for Western readers is its absolute reliability; the narrator must be a real witness, who gives evidence about true happenings. By definition, the transgressive woman, and particularly the prostitute, cannot testify. Azuela's "registro," del Campo's "dossier," and Mendoza's and Gamboa's novels all highlight the invented quality of a loose woman's storytelling, its mutable nature. On the one hand, the prostitute is relegated to silence as a victim with no personal agency, only a body that she sells as a commodity on the market. Alternatively, she is silenced as an inherently untruthful storyteller, reprimanded for an excess of agency and for irresponsibly trafficking in fantasies (and trite, secondhand fantasies at that). Xorge del Campo says it bluntly:

Las posibilidades de mixtificación de una prostituta suelen ser extraordinarias. Son capaces de contarse tres veces (o más) la misma historia — la suya, por ejemplo — reinventándola cada vez de cabo a rabo. ... Esta imaginación desordenada, esta ausencia de discernimiento entre lo verdadero y lo falso, este sentimentalismo novelesco crea en las prostitutas una verdadera sed de aventuras. (del Campo 1974, 116–17)

[The prostitute tends to have extraordinary possibilities for confusion. (Prostitutes) are capable of telling someone the same story — their own story for example — three or more times, reinventing it from beginning to end each time.... This disordered imagination, this absence of discrimination between truth and falsehood, this novelistic sentimentalism, creates in prostitutes a true thirst for adventure.]

Curiously, in the case of these women, del Campo sees the excessively active and creative imagination as a sign of mental deficiency, subject to early detection in young girls: "[D]e la incapacidad pragmática inicial deriva sistemáticamente un despego intelectual (que se manifiesta, por ejemplo, en una afición desmesurada por la lectura de novelistas sentimentales) y esto origina un descenso cotidiano del coeficiente de inteligencia" [A detachment from intellectual activities derives from an initial practical inability (which is manifested, for example, in an exceptional love for reading sentimental novelists) and from this point originates as daily decrease in the intelligence quotient] (116). I assume that implicitly del Campo is telling his readers that only young men can safely read such dangerous books about the contagious qualities of reading on weak minds — books like *Don Quixote* or *Madame Bovary* — since such books adversely affect only female IQs and are symptomatic of purely female mental deficiencies. Males may safely become "lectores gambusinos" — to use Mendoza's phrase — for they retain both their intellectual agency and their sanity. In Matlock's terms, "Unless the male reader is a worker or a young heir, his indulgence in books will simply keep him away from other kinds of mischief (gaming tables, brothels, adulterous affairs). It may feminize him, but its effects... seem to wear off. The girl who reads a novel is... irredeemably lost.... The married woman who reads submits her fragile nervous system to potentially permanent shocks" (Matlock 1994, 215). Claims such as del Campo's about the power of the written word are so clearly overstated as to sound humorous to our ears. Nevertheless, as Matlock perceptively comments, "these complaints asserted the hopes that had been pinned to books in general and mass literacy in particular" (205). It is, in this context, no coincidence that del Campo's book appeared at about the same time as the first postrevolutionary successes in rural literacy efforts were beginning to make their effects felt.

The loose woman who writes is in the same double bind as the prostitute who speaks of her past. She points toward her life but without license to discuss it, without the reader having to openly acknowledge her or accept her testimony as part of the socially real. She is, by convention, an unacceptable witness to her own reality, since she cannot be counted upon to see the difference between truth and falsehood. In more abstract terms, she is, by definition, always already speechless and unreadable —

Emmanuel Lévinas speaks, for example, of the "non-signifyingness of the wanton" (Lévinas 1969, 261) that excludes the (public) woman from the public sphere. Feminist philosophers echo Lévinas from a very different ideological point of view. As Luce Irigaray notes in a highly influential formulation, cited earlier, on the relation of women's sexuality to patriarchal discourse:

> Commodities, as we all know, do not take themselves to market on their own; and if they could talk... So women have to remain an "infrastructure" unrecognized as such by our society and our culture. The use, consumption, and circulation of their sexualized bodies underwrite the organization and the reproduction of the social order, in which they have never taken part as "subjects." (Irigaray 1985, 84)

There is no place for "woman" as such in the social contract that Irigaray defines here, except as a shifter defining men's relationship to each other and as the alien otherness that establishes male self hood. Sex, and specifically the woman's sexuality, is the unspoken, silenced term that shapes the social contract, and from within that contract, within those terms of discursive possibility, there is no place for a woman's subjectivity. Since there is no subjectivity, no possibility of saying "I" except as an othered being, there can be no speech. As Judith Butler succinctly frames the paradox: "To speak within the system is to be deprived of the possibility of speech; hence, to speak at all in that context is a performative contradiction, the linguistic assertion of a self that cannot 'be' within the language that asserts it" (Butler 1990, 116). In the specific context I am addressing here, for an admittedly sexually active woman to speak within the Mexican social system, she must silence both her femaleness and her sexuality. Within the system, "woman" ventriloquizes or performs "man," and there are no women except as a convenience of discourse when referring to female persons. Such, at least, is the typical state of affairs in a traditionally conceived social formulation of a male-dominant society.

It all comes down to the fundamental question exercising me in trying to read these women's personal writings, these memoirs, these *testimonios*, these texts — that is, What kind of theoretical frame can I give this discussion without recourse to insupportable "truth" claims or to trite pronouncements about domination and silencing of women? In his much-acclaimed book *The Signifying Monkey*, Henry Louis Gates Jr. describes the African-American practice of "signifyin'," which is both a linguistic style of expression and a cultural ritual that always involve a double-voicedness, repetition with formal revision, and a play of ambiguity. Signifyin' is aggressive and ambiguous. It is performance talk that both calls attention to its performativity and is only completely successful if it convinces the target. As Gates reminds us, signifyin' on us theoretically in his own critical text, the standard English word "signification" "is a homonym of the Afro-American vernacular word. And . . . these two homonyms have everything to do with each other and, then again, absolutely nothing. . . . This confrontation is both political and metaphysical" (Gates 1988, 45). Gates extends the concept from a definition borrowed from literary critic and anthropologist Roger D. Abrahams, who describes signifyin' as "the language of trickery, that set of words or gestures which arrives at 'direction through indirection'" (Abrahams 1962, 125), and elsewhere Abrahams gives specific examples:

> It can mean . . . the propensity to talk around a subject, never quite coming to the point. . . . Also it can denote speaking with the hands and eyes, and in this respect encompasses a whole complex of expressions and gestures. Thus it is signifying to stir up a fight between neighbors by telling stories; it is signifying to make fun of a policeman by parodying his motions behind his back; it is signifying to ask for a piece of cake by saying, "my brother needs a piece of cake." (Abrahams 1970, 51–52)

The effects of signifyin', however, extend far beyond the kind of one-up-manship described here. In his lucid discussion of the complexities of signifyin', Gates — taking as his key word the concept of arriving at direction through indirection — demonstrates how this vernacular style both participates in and subtly undermines dominant discourse. It is, as he says, both a form of troping and a style of political action. It is, in terms of the Mexican social context, a kind of *transa* that requires not only a victim but also an appreciative audience. The signifier needs to have his/her style recognized, optimally, by the person signified upon. It is precisely in the interstices of this kind of double-voiced style that the transgressive woman inserts herself as a subject, or as a third term.

While the commodification of women as objects of consumption or of exchange undergirds and helps organize the social order, some female persons find a way to reconstruct that order in their favor. In an unpublished paper entitled "The Whore/Madonna Complex," Janet Feindel, a Canadian playwright and sex-worker activist, suggests that in some ways the prostitute reinscribes the social order to her own benefit: "By bartering and naming her price she is breaking the 'silent' exchange of women. By naming it and defining it and consciously bringing into light what has traditionally been repressed she is no longer a passive participant in the exchange" (quoted in Bell 1994). To this statement, Shannon Bell adds, "The prostitute negotiates sexuality only as a commercial exchange inside the male exchange economy; but she does at least negotiate it.... [She is] an active participant who exchanges her own use-value" (91). The women in the books discussed above have certainly discovered another method of trading their own use-value, in producing and selling a written work that corresponds neither to the genre of autobiography as conventionally described nor to the genre of *testimonio* but to a third kind of self-writing. On an analogy with Gates's study on signifyin', we can say that these women are testifyin'.

Often, as del Campo complains, the prostitute sells her body through selling her story or through creating an imagined narrative for the client's pleasure; it is only another step to decouple the body from the text, and it is one that Gamboa and Sefchovich among others have already made part of a common currency linking writing and (metaphorical) prostitution. When the loose woman/writer brings her textual goods to market, she is only literalizing the established metaphor and eliminating the middleman. There is, then, at the level of publication and book sales, an overlapping of projects at the same time as the mechanism of exchange is exploited and reversed to allow a formerly silent nonsubject to speak.

The two terms of this negotiation — this *transa* — remain the loose woman/storyteller and the client/reader. On the one hand, the reader expects the life story to give the impression at least of authenticity. In this respect it should speak to and within the growing body of life stories by people marginal to the collective experience of the reading public, those books collected by anthropologists, journalists, and historians and marketed as *testimonios*. The text's charm and its charge come partly from its status as an authentic document referring back to a specific female body in which its veracity can be tested. Thus, for example, we can recognize the significance of photographs of the narrator/subject to *Memorias de "La Bandida"* and to Serrano's books. Likewise we can appreciate the value of a foreword by an officially recognized truth-bearer like Elizabeth Burgos (who edited *Me llamo Rigoberta Menchú* [I, Rigoberta Menchú]) or María Luisa Mendoza, who describes the physical characteristics of the narrator and at some level attests to her concrete physical existence in the case of *Del oficio*. Furthermore, the book's use-value for the reader is intimately connected to its presumed truth value; the currency that the sexually transgressive woman exchanges within the textual economy is both her particularity as an unusual or unique human being and her representability as an extension of a collective — if marginal and generally silenced — experience.

At the same time, on the other hand, unlike canonical *testimonios*, where the very root of the word defining the genre involves a presumption of juridical truth-telling, the loose woman's *testimonio* is presumed to be less trustworthy. Since the narrator is, again by definition, an inherently unreliable storyteller — we readers may uneasily suspect that we are victims of a *transa* on her part — and the life described in the text continually involves *transas* of one sort or another (in bodies and stories and goods), then what is finally authenticable is only the staged performance of the *transa* in the referential frame of the narrator/author/testifier. More than other *testimonios,* then, the works that I will be looking at here operate within the borderlands of the genre, in a *transa*-inflected, transitional culture. Roland Barthes, in a statement used as an epigraph for this book, says: "A writer...must have the persistence of the watcher who stands at the crossroads of all other discourses, in a position that is *trivial* in respect to the purity of doctrine (*trivialis* is the etymological attribute of the prostitute who waits at the intersection of three roads)" (quoted in Felman 1983, 117). In telling us about the trivia of their lives, invented for us or in conjunction with us, these women are testifyin' to their own storied *transa*/ctions, both physical and literary.

# I

Open the book *Del oficio* by Antonia Mora, and flip past the title page to the foreword. Here is the first paragraph:

> Antonia es una niña grande con los ojos inusitados de verde y de vida, de estupor. Es menudo y debió de ser frágil. De piel muy blanca, el único maquillaje que luce, el de sus redondos ojos, la adelgaza más aún. Antonia tiene una hija inmensa, triste y adolescente, preocupada como la madre en todos los problemas sociales que urge desentuertar. Antonia tiene un marido joven, elegante. Abogado. Es campeón de las viejas causas difíciles, un loco enamorado de la justicia. Antonia tiene una casa con ventanas a las horas del día que la miran escribir, coser bellos trajes Chanel, hermosísimas capas coloradas de Stendhal, abrigos de Colette, pijamas para ir a bailes o trajes de soiré para dormir; cocinar ricos platillos japoneses o convertir en cristales higos y piñas, naranjas y membrillos. (9)

> [Antonia is an overgrown child with unusual, speaking green eyes, full of life and amazement. She is tiny and must be fragile. Her skin is very white, and the only makeup she wears — on her round eyes — makes her look even slimmer. Antonia has an immense, sad,

adolescent daughter, as concerned as her mother with social problems that need to be straightened out. Antonia has an elegant young
husband. A lawyer. He is a champion of the old, difficult causes, a
madman in love with justice. Antonia has a house with windows full
of daylight that watch her write; watch her sew beautiful Chanel
suits, lovely red Stendhal capes, Colette overcoats, pajamas to go to
balls or evening dresses to go to sleep; watch her cook delicious Japanese meals or turn figs and pineapples, oranges and quinces into
sweetmeats.]

With these opening sentences, Mendoza serves up to the reader a richly
seductive banquet of innocence and sensuality, of an unusual and beautiful woman (slim, elegant, with pale skin and green eyes) surrounded by
all the markers of an upper-middle-class life. This vision of chaste but
sensual matronly good taste is essential to the book that Mendoza introduces, providing the reader with all the codes s/he needs to understand
the Cinderella story that follows, to recognize the narrator as a jewel shining in the mud of her surroundings, a pearl among swine, a diamond in
the rough.

By beginning the foreword in this manner, Mendoza reminds us of
the fluidity of the identity of the protagonist while masking the unpleasant past she elsewhere evokes. Surrounded by all the material props of
an upper-middle-class life, Mora becomes the quintessential Madonna,
indistinguishable from other similarly privileged women. Strikingly, the
outward markers of a bourgeois life serve a curious function as references
for both the story's and the subject's truth and purity, while cannily avoid-
ing truth-claims on the part of the author of the foreword. At the same
time, the story Mora shares with Mendoza, and with us, is of another,
and altogether different, life, dealing in what she might call "naked truth"
rather than glittering costumes and succulent fruits. Mora is, in Mendoza's foreword, both the same as and different from other women in her
access to the double and disturbing truths of degradation and purity — in
that order. Furthermore, her story, in both the extremes of poverty and
privilege, offers a glimpse into two lifestyles that are each on their own
terms exotic. Mendoza's catalogue of exoticisms ends on a pious note:
"Todo esto no volverá a pasar nunca más. Cuando el lector como usted
y como yo entendamos a la mujer de otra manera, a manera de imagen de Dios. Y cuando México sea un país de hombres mejores...de
hombres, simplemente" [This will never happen again. When readers like
you and I understand women in another way, as God's image. And when
Mexico is a country of better men...of men, simply] (12). Thus, simply,
facilely, mechanically, Mendoza offers Mora's *testimonio* as an exotic fruit

and as a morality play to solve Mexico's gender-related problems, at the same time as she hints that it will provide the sticky/slippery substance of the truth, and she does it without making any particular claims about the irreducible essence of anything except Mexican manhood.

Even the rather vague, if evocative, title of the book, *Del oficio*, hints at a multiply voiced play of significations, since *oficio* could as easily refer to a religious rite (e.g., Rosario Castellanos's novel *Oficio de Tinieblas*, which takes its title from a Roman Catholic service) or to a deeply seated vocation (*oficio de escribir*) as to the particular story told through these memoirs. Even further: the play of association that charmingly suggests an author's metaphorical identification with the prostitute s/he portrays or the literary pimp s/he represents becomes scandalously literal in this work's presentation of a prostitute turned author.

Antonia Mora's own narrative begins, stripped of rhetorical flourish and exoticizing garnishes, as follows:

Mi madre estaba en la puerta de la accesoria. La oía:
— Ven guapo. Mira que vas a disfrutar.
Y a mí me decía:
— Estoy jugando. Vete para adentro a jugar con los demás niños.
Mis amigos y amigas jugaban a lo mismo. (17)

[My mother was standing in the outbuilding doorway. I heard her, "Come on, handsome. Let me show you a good time." And she told me, "I'm playing. Go inside and play with the other children."
My boy- and girlfriends played the same game.]

Mora is the daughter of a prostitute and, almost inevitably, from her barely pubescent childhood until her jailing for theft and assault with a deadly weapon, she also sells her body. She is born in abject poverty, and when told to "go play," she and her friends play at the adult games familiar to them from their mothers' profession, dressing up in their mothers' clothes and playing at prostitutes and clients, or entertaining themselves by inflating and deflating used condoms discovered lying around the area. Unsurprisingly, but still hurtfully, "decent" women do not allow her to play with their children (49). She tells us of unintentionally shocking one of her teachers when she answers the stereotypical question: What are you going to be when you grow up? with a matter-of-fact, "Voy a coger, señorita" [I'm going to fuck, miss] (23). When she is fourteen years old, she is kidnapped and raped — her first sexual experience. Her mother's reaction is to beat her up for being so stupid as to be tricked into giving her virginity away for free. The lesson is pounded into the young girl with her mother's fists: "Tengo que coger, y cobrar para que todo esté bien" [I have to fuck, and to charge for it, so that everything is OK] (64). It is not the only time she is raped, but as she becomes more and more integrated into the sites of prostitution, more and more visible on the streets and in the rent-by-time hotels, rape becomes something like an occupational hazard, a constant threat that adds to her fear and her hatred but does not prevent her from accepting more clients, from going back out onto the streets.

Mora's trajectory is familiar to her audience from our reading of nineteenth-century novels and viewing of twentieth-century movies. The young woman runs off with an equally young man. She suffers abandonment and abortion. She learns to drink and to steal. She commits and she suffers assaults. She pays off corrupt police with kickbacks from her robberies and with sexual favors. She details her dealings with pimps (not so good) and with matrons of houses of prostitution (excellent relationships). She tells of working in strip joints ("[E]ra una sensación rarísima sentirme utilizada y sin coger a nadie" [It was a really strange sensation to feel I was being used but without having to fuck anybody] [90]). In each detail, at each stage of her life, Mora's simple, straightforward prose strips away the veil of exoticism from the ugly, sordid details of an abject life. Here, for instance, Mora's friend Alicia passes along tips for taking care of herself in dealing with potentially diseased clients, the tips being interspersed with gossip about Alicia's pimp:

Antes de irse, mi viejo me hizo recomendaciones. "Vieja, ponte verga: antes de meterte con el buey le vas apretando el canal en medio de los huevos; así le sigues hasta llegar a lo grueso. Si le sale agua clarita, ya sabes: está sano. Pero si le sale como pus le das su dinero y no te metes con él. Acuérdate, toda la tarde te enseñé. No se te olvide. Ya me voy, vieja. Cobra adelantado, no sea que te vean maje."

Y muy celoso. Siempre se para enfrente, cuidando de que no me tarde mucho con el cliente. Se encabrona. Me reclama y después en el cuarto me madrea. Dice que no debo de gozar con otras vergas. (82)

[Before he left, my old man gave me advice, "Woman, smarten up. Before you let a john do it, you press on the channel between his balls, and keep doing it until stuff comes out. If it's clear liquid, then you know he's healthy. But if some pus-like stuff comes out, then give him his money back and don't mess with him. Remember

what I taught you this afternoon. Never forget it. Now I'm off.
Charge in advance and don't let them take advantage of you."

And he was really jealous. He stands outside to make sure I don't
take too long with any client. He goes crazy. He grabs me and then
beats me up in our room. He says that I shouldn't enjoy any dicks
but his.]

As Mora becomes more and more deeply involved in serious criminal
activity, she also portrays herself more and more as the victim of circumstance, trapped by acquaintances into acts that horrify her. At the same
time, the protagonist of the *testimonio* has a vitality, a force, a strength
that is no longer present in the pale, sad, beautiful lawyer's wife. She
asks pointed questions and stands her ground when challenged. Where
the lawyer's wife has dedicated herself to alleviating problems related to
unspecified worthy social causes, the young prostitute takes a more direct
approach to women's concerns, and her critique of male-defined social
customs and sexual practices is entirely transparent:

— Bueno — le dije — , ¿tú nunca le das el mameyoso a tu mujer?
— No, nunca.
— ¿Por qué? Si es igual que todas.
— Pues porque se prostituye, se volvería morbosa. Además que
no es igual. Es una dama decente.
— Entonces, ¿cómo haces con ella?
— Normalmente, como debe ser.
— ¿Qué tal si le da tentación por saber? (92)

["So," I asked him, "don't you ever turn your wife on?"
"No, never."
"Why not? She's the same as any other woman."
"Because it would turn her into a prostitute; she'd turn morbid.
Besides, it's not the same thing. She's a decent woman."
"So, how do you do it with her?"
"Normally, the way it ought to be."
"What if she gets tempted to find out?"]

Good question.

Finally, when Mora is required to give legal testimony after her arrest,
things become even more theoretically interesting. It seems that everyone involved in the courtroom proceedings has a *transa* to complete,
that everyone concerned is testifyin': "Tanto los agentes como nosotros

mentíamos" [Both we and the police lied] (142). To the police psychia-
trists, Mora lies again, and she assumes that they are equally dishonest
with her. Although she is uncertain of what story will best serve her purposes, Mora cannily avoids anything that might resemble a confession,
assuming that a fairy-tale story of an exotic, artistic family (or alternatively, a poor but honest mother) would serve her better. On the first day
she tries out one story; on the next day, she tries again: "Al día siguiente
decidí no contarle nada verdadero. Le narré una infancia que no era mía"
[The next day I decided not to tell anything that was true. I narrated
a childhood that was not mine], and on the following day she comes up
with a different, equally elaborate, narration for the nosy shrink (148–49).

Similarly, Mora learns about tailoring a story to the wider public when
her case becomes of interest to the news services. "¿Puedo decir lo que
pienso?" [Can I say what I think?], Mora asks a reporter who is advising
her on a statement to the press. On hearing his assent, she begins with
a summary of the police abuse and torture she has suffered in the prison
system, a story already told to the reader of this text in far greater and
more horrific detail: "El médico legista no me hizo examen a conciencia
y por lo tanto no me reconocieron los golpes ni el aborto que me oca-
sionaron los agentes de la jefatura y..." [The state-appointed doctor did
not give me a complete examination and so did not notice the bruises
or the miscarriage that the police officers caused and...]. The reporter
interrupts her: "No, no. Eso no causa simpatías en el público. Mejor di
otra cosa" [No, no. That won't gain the audience's sympathy. Better say
something else] (163). What he advises her to do, essentially, is to say
something innocuous and to look as repentant and as pretty as possible
for the cameras. The book ends with Mora's transcription of her brief
statement to the press — a very different statement from the exposé she
planned, and one that was written for her by personnel at the television
station: "Estoy arrepentida de haber faltado a las leyes y de haber delin-
quido, insultado de esta manera a la sociedad, así como a la seguridad
y moral de todo ciudadano honesto" [I am sorry for having broken laws
and committed crimes, for insulting society and the security and morality of all honest citizens]. This television appearance, with its saccharine
performance of a rehabilitated criminality, leads directly to the puzzling
final sentence of the work. That sentence hints at a complicity between
the former prostitute and the television producer (should we extend the
analogy to the book publisher?), a completed *transa* of which the television audience (the readers of the book?) are the willing victims, the third
term in this slippery game of signifyin', of testifyin': "El hombre me dio
las gracias junto con cien pesos" [The man gave me his thanks along with
a hundred pesos] (163). Would it not be totally naive at this point to

ask about the truth-status of this *testimonio*, this confession we have just finished reading?

## II

An entirely different form of testifyin' informs the maladroit "memoirs" of one of Mexico's most famous madams: Marina Adeo (or Acevedo), alias Graciela Olmos, alias Loreto González Velázquez, alias La Bandida. Xorge del Campo mentions that she has a special claim to our attention because "su gran simpatía le való amistad y protección de presidentes y alcaldes" [her great attractiveness earned her the friendship and protection of presidents and mayors] (del Campo 1974, 80). Sergio González Rodríguez reminds readers of his book that La Bandida was a legendary figure during her lifetime, renowned not only as the madam of one of the most famous — and famously untouchable by legal authorities — houses of prostitution in Mexico but also as an ex-*soldadera* in the Mexican Revolution, a friend of Pancho Villa, and a composer of well-known popular ballads like "El Siete Leguas." For González Rodríguez, Muñuzuri's recopilation of La Bandida's memoirs is "el testimonio del un mito" [the testimonial of a myth] involving a complicated mixture of politics, sexuality, gossip, and prurient voyeurism (González Rodríguez 1989, 74). Muñuzuri is even more hyperbolic, and more discreet, in his own opening statement. La Bandida's most infamous contribution to Mexican society is mentioned in the enumeration of her sterling qualities, but somewhat euphemistically described:

> Esta mujer, famosa como compositora de canciones y corridos revolucionarios; famosa como confidente de grandes personajes de la política; famosa por su bondad humanitaria; famosa como crítica crudelísma de líderes siniestros o falsos para ella; famosa como soldadera de la época heroica en las filas del villismo; famosa siempre como mujer bella y valiente, vendedora de alegrías y de placer, elevada a la pureza de un profesionalismo temperamental... (Muñuzuri 1967, 7)

> [This woman, who is famous as a composer of revolutionary songs and ballads, famous as the confidant of great political figures, famous for her humanitarian goodness, famous as straightforward critic of leaders who seemed to her sinister or false, famous as a soldier in Villa's army during the heroic period, always famous as a

beautiful and brave woman who sells happiness and pleasure, lifted
to the purity of a professional temperament...]

This insistence on La Bandida's "purity," always associated with her "professionalism," is the most important leitmotiv in the book and one of the
more carefully elaborated ruses/*transas* that Muñuzuri deploys to assure
himself of both La Bandida's attention and our approval.

In his foreword to the volume, Muñuzuri says that on first contemplating this project, "no me imaginaba de 'La Bandida', su gran importancia
en la vida pública de México y privada vida también, de los hombres
públicos" [I didn't realize the great importance of "La Bandida" to Mexican public life and to the private lives of public men] (13). Muñuzuri's
opening gambit is rather surprising. For while the revelation of the connection between erotics and politics is certainly not new, Muñuzuri seems
to be suggesting that La Bandida's influential role behind the scenes in
the lives of politicians justifies, even demands, that this "public woman"
be offered a voice in the public forum alongside the more traditional
voices of "public men." Thus, La Bandida's "historia" — with its double charge of signification in Spanish — rightfully takes its place in "la
historia de la nación"; that is, her story becomes part of History; her history makes this unusual woman into an appropriate historical subject. At
the same time, of course, women in general are excluded from the public sphere of political action, and the "public woman" like La Bandida
is relegated even more firmly to the margins of public discourse. While
the hero who gives his body to the nation (the public man, the historical
hero) seems the proper subject for history, the heroine who quite literally does the same (the public woman, the whore) is scandalous and out
of place.

We shouldn't give too much credit to Muñuzuri, however, and for
several reasons. His project is firmly planted within the decorum of a
male-centered practice of information gathering, and he is peculiarly in-
ept at extracting memoirs from his recalcitrant subject. Once he realizes
La Bandida's unique status in the Mexican underworld, Muñuzuri decides
to take on the project, wooing the reader with his best pseudoscientific
language: "[R]esultaba interesante el personaje de por sí, y todo dependía
de lo que pudiera decir, el modo de decirlo, la capacidad de recordar, y
desde luego, la definición misma en que se fuera implicando el sujeto
relator" [The character is interesting in and of herself, and everything
depended upon what she might say, her style of delivery, her ability to
remember, and, of course, the definition through which the relating subject defines herself] (15). Frankly, time is of essence in this project, since,
as the author reminds us, La Bandida is old and ill, and "quién sabe

si no sobreviviera mucho, luego de una vida tan agitada y activa" [who knows if she would survive for long, after such an active and agitated life] (14). Nothing is more likely to stymie a potential ghostwriter than the death of his chosen memorialist. And since this is essentially what happens, Muñuzuri stretches his thin stock of anecdotes by and about La Bandida with a surrounding text detailing not La Bandida's memoirs but Muñuzuri's memoirs of his efforts to extract memoirs from the famous madam.

In *Función de medianoche,* José Joaquín Blanco describes what he calls the semiotics — or the phenomenology — of the *transa* as composed of two overt elements (*el transa,* or the con man; and *el lento,* or the person conned) that, like signifyin', often count upon the implicit interaction of a third, covert element: "el Intratransa o, en términos más populacheros, el viejo truco de que en realidad el transa es un previamente transado" [the *intratransa,* or, in more pop-culture terms, the old trick of conning the con man] (Blanco 1981, 67). It seems to me that something of the sort is happening in this book. Muñuzuri is in the position of the con man with a transaction to make, and he is trying to operate his *transa* in two directions simultaneously: first, on La Bandida, the veteran of many *transas,* and herself an artist in the genre; and second, on the prospective audience for the book, whom Muñuzuri hopes to attract with his potent combination of scientific detachment and transgressive excitement. Muñuzuri, however, is at each stage a victim of another elaborate and subtle *transa,* for La Bandida, despite her relative immobility, is no *lenta* to be fooled by his transparent tactics. To some degree, her *intratransa* functions as a result of her resistance to his blandishments; to some degree, as in the best of such signifyin' practices, she allows Muñuzuri to fool himself.

If scientific detachment is the method Muñuzuri uses to remind the reader that this book is a valid historical and cultural contribution to the Mexican self-concept, his plan to convince La Bandida to loosen her tongue uses slightly different tactics:

El propósito de entrevistarla surgió entre el amigo Carmona y yo, con motivo de una plática sobre la función social que representa el ejercicio de la honorable prostitución, elevada a dignidad profesional precisamente en las "casas de citas," donde aparecen sacerdotisas de Venus, rodeadas de un ambiente exquisito y delicado, pulcro y limpio.... Con este ánimo íbamos, esperanzados en obtener de ella — "La Bandida" — confidencias o anécdotas o juicios al borde de su peculiar actividad. (14)

[The idea of interviewing her came out of a conversation between my friend Carmona and I, (when we) were discussing the social function represented by the exercise of honorable prostitution, as elevated to professional dignity precisely in the houses of assignation where the priestesses of Venus appear surrounded by an atmosphere that is delicate and exquisite, neat and clean.... Off we went with this idea in mind, hoping to obtain from her — from La Bandida — confidential information or anecdotes or judgments about her peculiar activities.]

It is an interesting rhetorical sleight of hand that the two reporters plan here: to describe the prostitute as pure because (1) she honestly exchanges sex for money, and (2) she preserves the purity of wives and virgins of good family. The conspirators assume that the highlighting of such rhetorical "purity" not only will assuage any readerly discomfort with the subject of the interviews but will also serve as an equally convincing argument with La Bandida, whom they assume will be swayed by this culturally biased compliment. Accordingly, Muñuzuri reproduces in the text Carmona's first effort to approach La Bandida on these terms: "Mi querida señora, nosotros pensamos que 'casas' como ésta hacen un incalculable servicio, son verdaderos dispensarios de higiene mental, y... salvan muchas vírgenes y protegen la pureza de las novias" [My dear lady, we think that "houses" like this one provide a priceless service; they are true dispensaries of mental hygiene, and... they save many virgins and protect the purity of girlfriends] (25). Thus, directly and indirectly, the reporter rehearses his appeal in terms of the time-worn, time-honored masculinist justification that prostitution is a moral good in that it saves decent women from men who would otherwise become uncontrollable. By draining excess aggressivity and erotic impulses, the pure-hearted and (implicitly — the author is never so crass as to make the outright statement) disease-free whore provides an important public service.

But since La Bandida's role in Mexican society has not just been that of indirectly saving the purity of young women of good family by having sex with their fathers and brothers, but also more directly influencing the course of Mexican political movements through her active role as a soldier in the revolution, Muñuzuri also reproduces in the opening pages of his book the predictable strains of flattery, combined with a patriotic appeal, that he hopes will convince the old woman to open up to him. Since he is clearly concerned about losing the journalistic scoop, either to another reporter or to death, Muñuzuri rehearses his hyperbolic line at some length and with several variations, all of which involve the most conventional interpretations of the imbrication of erotics and politics, but which, in context, could be read as far more radical in scope.

One frustrating feature for the journalist in this effort is that he never manages to convince the wily old woman to give him private or exclusive interviews, although she does allow him to visit her, along with her musicians, favored friends, and an assortment of whores, pimps, hit men, petty criminals, and hangers-on of various sorts whom she finds amusing. The implication, which Muñuzuri never picks up on, is that she finds him intermittently amusing as well. Certainly, she shows no particular eagerness for his company, no burning desire to commit anything at all to paper for posterity, except — and only perhaps — her songs. From her throne/bed, La Bandida dispenses advice, drugs, and elaborate dinners to Muñuzuri and the other men and women who surround her; she sings her own compositions, offers insights into the characters of famous men she has known, and tells her own version of historical events that changed the shape of the Mexican political system during the early part of the century. In transcribing this eroto-political material — the stated purpose of his efforts — Muñuzuri, curiously, becomes reticent and selective. He records in this book neither impure acts nor impure political statements that might offend the eyes of his audience. In his prologue, Muñuzuri describes a strange double bind: "[E]s impublicable casi todo lo que concierne la auténtica 'Bandida'" [Almost everything concerning the authentic Bandida is unpublishable]; nevertheless, he commits himself to publishing an authentic, if fragmentary and selective, set of memoirs, confessions, or testimonials based on material that can be shared with the general public (10). For instance, Muñuzuri censors the very first thing he hears upon entering La Bandida's presence for the first time. Instead, he makes reference to a conversation, which he does not reproduce in the pages of this text, that touches upon "un tema impropio, inadecuado, comprometedor, impolítico e inoportuno, incompatible con aquel sitio" [an improper, inadequate, compromising, impolitic, and inopportune topic of conversation, one incompatible with that location] (25). What kind of discourse is he policing here? Clearly, the professional purity he ascribes to La Bandida does not extend to the substance of her discussions with her acquaintances, whose "impolitic" rejoinders to her "improper" comments might offend some very important persons indeed. Furthermore, given such censorship, what kind of memoirs does he hope to produce? Despite his stated intention of providing a complete and unvarnished account of La Bandida's life and times, he recognizes that the uncensored revelations of the aging prostitute must be kept under tight control. Given such practices of control and censorship, his account can never be anything but partial, anything but partisan.

Moreover, the theatricality of Muñuzuri's and his colleague's own performances of sympathetic interest upon their first meeting with the intended subject of their work underscores and emphasizes the artificiality and constructedness of these proceedings.

From one point of view, Muñuzuri's blandishments are intended to turn La Bandida into another sort of object for consumption, one that, in Philippe Lejeune's terms, offers "a kind of *underside* of the autobiographical text . . . : what would come to light is truly lived memory, the spontaneous word, everything that writing uses but transforms, and finally hides" (Lejeune 1989, 207). Unfortunately, in Muñuzuri's case the transition between orality (often, apparently, obscene or politically dangerous) and writing (pure) forces the unhappy reporter into less spontaneity, more transformation. In his footnotes, Muñuzuri gives some indications of the concrete political grounds that shape his writing practice. Official history and conventional nationalist ideology determine which aspects of her life are deemed interesting and worthy of reproduction. Documentation of La Bandida's own, often divergent, ideological stance is accompanied by jovially paternalistic footnotes that betray Muñuzuri's bias. Like most Mexican reporters, Muñuzuri espouses a firmly leftist rhetorical position: "El tema de Cuba y de Castro parecían tener obsedida a 'La Bandida' y venían a relucir con frecuencia; mas, queremos dejar sentado definitivamente . . . que la interpretación de su criterio debe relacionarse con su postura ideológica, claramente reaccionaria. Nosotros, naturalmente, tendríamos que chocar con muchas de sus opiniones" [La Bandida seemed obsessed with Cuba and Castro, and the topic came up frequently; however, we need to make it absolutely clear . . . that the interpretation of her criteria should be related to her clearly reactionary ideological position. Naturally, we disagree strongly with many of her opinions] (83). Here, the author's unquestioning support for the ruling political party is so obvious as to verge on satire: "[C]onviene aclarar aquí, que es una fantasía popular — casi un vicio — , achacar a los Presidentes de México fortunas fabulosas hechas a la sombra del poder. . . . [S]on hablillas y exageraciones que el pueblo difunde gustoso como revancha a su miseria crónica" [It is important to clarify here that it is a popular fantasy — almost a vice — to accuse Mexican presidents of making fabulous fortunes in the shadow of power. . . . This is petty gossip and exaggerations that the people cheerfully spread as revenge for their chronic misery] (114).

Thus, Muñuzuri performs a pretense of alliance with La Bandida in the main text to try to elicit her memoirs, while at the same time he emphasizes his enthusiastic support for the ruling party's interests in the running commentary in the footnotes: a double betrayal. In this manner, despite Muñuzuri's initial statement about the importance of La Bandida's perspective in revising and rethinking recent Mexican political history, her views on Mexican history and politics are never allowed to take a protagonic role even in this text, supposedly her memoirs. Her ideological statements are either censored or interrupted by the reporter's corrective voice; in no case is her production of meaning allowed to stand unchallenged. The initial strangeness of seeing a book entitled "Memoirs" of one person, but authored by another, turns out to point toward the accurate and appropriate resolution of the question, Whose book is this? La Bandida is the subject of the book, not its author; she is not a memorialist of any kind but rather an anti–folk heroine whose *historia* has been captured and purified by another.

It should come as no surprise that the epilogue to this volume would be very easy to critique, even on its own terms. In the final two pages of the volume, the author recapitulates the theme of textual purity as applied to his loosely constructed series of anecdotes around the infamous madam and casts his rationalization for this rather disjointed style into a comically masculinist metaphorical discourse. This formal apology at the same time offers what is almost certainly an unintentional trophic commentary on the foregoing text and its interestingly unconventional protagonist:

> Me sería fácil...engrosar y rellenar huecos y ampliar recuerdos y agregar anécdotas....Pero todo eso...estaría en serio y casi seguro peligro de falsearla y adulterarla y hasta enviciarla con mentiras intencionadas y perversas o mutilaciones interesadamente silenciadas.
>
> Por lo cual, preferimos rescatar y preservar estos recuerdos sueltos y dejarlos tal como están, en su pureza inocente y trivial, sin alijos ni adiciones, sin remilgos ni aderezos, sin cortes y composturas. (158–59)

> [It would be easy for me...to enlarge this volume, to fill holes and amplify memories and add anecdotes....But all that...would be in serious and almost certain danger of falsifying it and adulterating it and corrupting it with intentional and perverse lies or interestingly silenced mutilations.
>
> For that reason, we prefer to rescue and preserve these scattered memories and to leave them as they are, in their trivial and innocent purity, without smuggled goods or additions, without prudishness or embellishments, without cuts or neatening.]

Muñuzuri's commentary is thick with metaphors of adultery, corruption, perversion, silencing, mutilation, and illegal transactions, against which his overstated claims to textual purity read very strangely and awkwardly indeed. Furthermore, I find it very curious in this context of an insistence upon incorruptible purity that this book came to me in its third edition, "revisada y aumentada" [revised and expanded], as the title page tells us. To some extent and necessarily, Muñuzuri's prose feeds upon and grows around La Bandida's, even after her death. In fact, with the madam's death and the consequent loss of whatever meager anecdotes La Bandida was willing to share with him, and which Muñuzuri felt were politic to repeat, the reporter hints at his longing to be unfaithful to his subject in favor of a seductive new love. As he tells us, "la maravillosa y admirada Estrella" [the marvelous and admired Estrella] (152) burns on the literary horizon, and she suggests to him an equally intriguing opportunity for his memorializing art — a transparent narrative fishing expedition about the potential audience for "La Bandida, the sequel": "La vida de Estrella, por lo demás, es tan preciosa y valedera e interesante y movida en altibajos, que muerta 'La Bandida', no hay en México otra mujer de mayor seducción biográfica" [Estrella's life, by the way, is so beautiful and valuable and interesting and shaped by highs and lows that, with the death of La Bandida, there is no woman in Mexico offering a greater biographical seduction] (87). Once again, the reporter's hegemonic perspective works to appropriate the woman and to repress her voice while at the same time affirming that it was her female seductiveness that induced the production of this piece of writing. Her own account of her life, or her refusal to speak, is read into the specific ideological frame of the already existing biography created through the reporter's garrulousness.

The reporter's insistence upon the purity of his motive and of his antiheroine's essential character is particularly striking in view of the Rabelaisan content of the scenes he describes. Before he meets her, Muñuzuri repeatedly portrays the famous madam as a beautiful woman inhabiting an elegant setting, a valiant public heroine, and a hardworking professional whose dedication to her job has endowed her with incontestable purity and a higher morality. Whenever he attempts to describe the actual woman and her context after meeting her, however, he falls back into the depiction of an aging, bloated, foul-mouthed drug addict who never leaves her bed because she is incontinent, a diabetic whose unwillingness or inability to exercise the most minimal control over her diet is bringing her to the verge of death. She tells the reporter that she used to be beautiful but that "cuarenta años de apuraciones, sustos y borracheras, acabaron conmigo" [forty years of pressures, frights, and drunken binges finished me off] (20). Muñuzuri surrounds his description of her health problems with eulogies to her character. Among her more grotesque symptoms, "[P]adecía La Bandida de hidropesía crónica y sufría la horrible punción del vientre cada tres meses" [La Bandida suffered from chronic dropsy and suffered the horrible puncture of her womb every three months] (11). In other descriptions, incongruous juxtapositions abound: "[H]abía perdido control de la orina pero no el buen humor" [She had lost control of her urine but not her good humor] (11). La Bandida is a woman who, while retaining her financial control over her underworld cohorts, is herself out of control, a fleshly compendium of organs that do not obey her commands.

This lack of control is particularly evident in Muñuzuri's repeated references to La Bandida's orgies of eating and drug taking. The first meeting with La Bandida occurs while she is having a late supper: "Ella estaba cenando cuando llegamos (las dos de la madrugada), y a pesar de estar hidrópica (la punzan cada tres meses) y enferma del hígado y los riñones y el páncreas y con azúcar en la sangre; . . . pese a su regimen de dieta, comió con bastante apetito (con bolillo y tortillas), una serie de cinco platillos abundantes, fruta de granada y chocolates" [She was eating when we arrived (at two o'clock in the morning), and despite her dropsy (they puncture her every three months), and her illnesses of the liver, the kidneys, and the pancreas, and with sugar in her blood; . . . despite a strict diet, she was eating with a healthy appetite (with bread and tortillas), a series of five abundant main dishes, along with pomegranates and chocolates] (23). At the end of another meeting, the writer reports: "Luego de haber cenado como a las once de la noche, volvió a comer con igual apetito, cinco o seis horas después" [After having dined at about eleven o'clock at night, she ate again with equal enthusiasm, five or six hours later] (55). In fact, the reporter's last meeting with La Bandida takes place at one of her Rabelaisian second suppers of the evening (120). La Bandida's voracious appetite is marked and discussed again and again, as are the consequences of such excesses on her already grotesquely distorted body — often in multiple parenthetical asides that enforce an editorializing viewpoint over the scene. Thus, the surface admiration for the famous madam gives way at every point to a horror of the prostitute's aging body, as well as a horror of the woman's appetites, which at this time in her life suffer a displacement from sexuality onto food. In this respect, Muñuzuri's imagery is totally conventional, following a widespread metaphorical association of appetites that links sexuality and food in a conjoined pornography.[4] What is striking — and distasteful — about La Bandida in Muñuzuri's description is her frank enjoyment of food and her indulgence in such a heavily eroticized/demonized pastime with obscene frequency and at unusual times of the night. Her refusal to restrain herself from consuming pomegranates and chocolates and her favorite, forbidden frijoles ("[N]o los cambiaba por caviar" [She wouldn't change them for caviar] [23]), points to La Bandida's violation of taboo and her willingness to feed forbidden desires of all sorts.

Her addiction to illegal drugs is also fully, and overly fully, documented. La Bandida always has a supply of cocaine at hand, and one of her assistants has the job of weighing out the drug in one-gram packets as an important part of her position (80). In an early exchange, La Bandida expresses her disappointment with the Mexican president, who has revoked her pension over what she clearly sees as a banality: "[É]l me protegió en una racha muy mala, me pasaba cinco mil pesos mensuales, y yo ¿qué más quería?... Pero los chismes del periódico me hicieron un escándalo, diciendo que yo traficaba en drogas, y desde entonces me retiró la pensión" [He protected me during a very bad time and gave me five thousand pesos a month. What else did I want?... But the newspaper gossip created a scandal about me, saying that I sold drugs, and since then he took away my pension]. When Muñuzuri asks if there is anything to the charge of drug dealing, she responds tranquilly, "Claro que yo compro de vez en cuando un gramo y medio, para uso doméstico, pero no comercio con eso; no me lo pagan, lo doy, lo uso, lo fío y eso es todo" [Of course I buy a gram and a half now and then, just for personal use, but I don't do business with it. No one pays me for it; I give it away, I use it, give credit for it and that's all] (61). While La Bandida's protestations of relative innocence are inconsistent with the quantities of cocaine Muñuzuri observes as well as with frequent references to clients who stop in to purchase a snort or two, her impunity to prosecution upholds La Bandida's own perception that such infractions of the law are trivial and that the president's supposed indignation is a pretense aimed at hypocritical newspapers. And it goes practically without saying that this particular newspaper reporter transcribes La Bandida's complaint about newspaper hypocrisy without making a connection between his profession and his goals with respect to the infamous woman and his frustration at not getting her story. There is no hint in the volume that he has ever realized the most probable interpretation of La Bandida's reluctance to speak to him.

Sharing drugs is an important aspect of her social interactions, and besides her favored cocaine, Muñuzuri documents her use of marijuana, which she smokes and shares with her companions (45); opium (her gradual withdrawal from this drug has caused another series of minutely described repellent symptoms [71]); and alcohol, from which she now abstains due to liver problems. As with her lavish dinners, she invites her guests to share her supply of whatever she is using: "[L]e invitó al recién llegado 'un toquecito,' y extendió la invitación por igual a todos" [She invited the new arrival to a snort of cocaine, and extended the invitation to everyone else as well] (98), including in her general invitation, on another occasion, a government official working in the Mexican prison system (112). During yet another of her late-night social events, La Bandida makes fun of her habit, with a cleverly self-denigrating comparison of her claim to fame with that of the heroine of the independence movement, Josefa Ortiz de Domínquez:

> Allí en Belisario Domínguez, tiene su monumento doña Josefa
> Ortiz de Domínquez, con esta leyenda, me parece:
>   ...A la Heroína doña Pepa...
> Cuando lo vi, yo me dije, pues que en el mío pongan:
>   ...A la Cocaína Chepa... (109)

[Doña Josefa Ortiz de Domínquez has a monument there in Belisario Domínguez, and it says something like: "To the Heroine doña Pepa." When I saw it, I said to myself, well, on mine put: "To the Cocaine Chepa."]

Here, as at other points in the narrative in which we are finally allowed to hear La Bandida's voice directly, without mediation, her commentary surprises us with its derisive literalness. The famous prostitute shifts between indifference to conventional values and amusement at the antics of her contemporaries. If, as González Rodríguez claims, Muñuzuri's intentions in seeking out La Bandida are to create a "testimonial of a myth," La Bandida herself — by her physical presence and her acerbic commentaries — continually disrupts the reporter's efforts by demythifying her own perversely monumentalized status in the popular imagination.

Muñuzuri's *transa*, as I mentioned earlier, is double: to sell this book to the Mexican public as La Bandida's memoirs, as her testimonial, and to convince La Bandida to cooperate in this mythmaking venture. He is frustrated in the first instance because he is unconvincing in the second. What we readers expect to find when we come to this book is largely missing — the book is the tale of the absent memoirs, of the recalcitrance of the woman to dictate her testimonial to the importunate reporter, although she tolerates his presence on occasion. Likewise, the intermittent comments of La Bandida about her life and her role in Mexican society and politics disturb us in another sense, for they appear to be skewed, as the woman insistently derides the sense that these memoirs, from our point of view, ought to have. Thus *Memorias de "La Bandida"* details the process of an *intratransa*, in which La Bandida tells her *historia*, but does so on her own terms, and mostly in the refusals to speak, in her resistances to the reporter, in the practical jokes she plays. Unlike Antonia Mora, who ostensibly tells the reader everything and then undermines that telling with a piquant anecdote, La Bandida tells almost nothing. Margo Su, herself a well-known member of Mexico's nighttime artistic community, describes something very similar to La Bandida's modulated interventions as a learned technique, one that served the community of elite prostitutes well in their striving for recognition and power:

> La prostitución se tomaba muy en serio y cualquier muchacha lista podría utilizarla como su primer paso firme camino al lugar soñado bajo el sol. Las pupilas eran oyentes de largas pláticas de negocios entre industriales y impresarios con políticos; de ellos aprendían el arte del lenguaje que promete sin conceder, despierta sospechas sin confirmar, aporta pistas y claves para engañar y envuelve misterios con más velos que Salomé. (Su 1989, 148)[5]

> [Prostitution was taken very seriously, and any smart girl could use it as her first real step toward the dreamed-of place under the sun. The whores were the audience to long business discussions between industrialists and impresarios with politicians; from them, they learned the linguistic art of promising without conceding, of awakening suspicions without confirming them, of offering clues and keys in order to deceive, of wrapping mysteries in more veils than Salome's.]

It is only partially due to the reporter's ineptness that the text of *Memorias* seems clumsy even to him, that it refuses to flow or form itself into a conventional oral testimony. Su's commentary suggests that the powerful men who visited the more exclusive houses of prostitution like Estrella's or La Bandida's inadvertently taught the women valuable lessons, which they then appropriated for their own uses. Additionally, Su reminds us that the attentive reader of La Bandida's words will look closely not only at the voice revealed in the quoted comments but also at their context; that is, we need to look at the language she uses, at how, when, and where she speaks, at what mysteries she tantalizingly veils and what she duplicitously reveals.

If, in the first instance, Muñuzuri is hampered by prudent journalistic instincts that prohibit him from revealing too much about the authentic woman, since the woman tends to be most authentically defined by material that it would be impolitic to publish, he is, more importantly still, frustrated by the cat-and-mouse game she plays with him. Muñuzuri's prose, thus, is peppered with expressions of exasperation at the famous woman's unwillingness to be more forthcoming about herself: "No tuvimos la oportunidad de interrogar a 'La Bandida' sobre su familia" [We didn't have the opportunity to question La Bandida about her family] (21); or, "[N]o pude ir a copiar los corridos" [I wasn't allowed to copy the *corridos*] (75); or, "'La Bandida' se ha negado y todavía no accede 'de hecho' a relatar sus *memorias*. . . . Nuestra impresión . . . es que ella no ha tomado en serio nuestro empeño" [La Bandida has refused to see us and still has not agreed "in fact" to dictate her *memoirs*. . . . Our impression . . . is that she hasn't taken our proposal seriously] (41); or, earlier: "[E]ntre la fecha anterior y ésta, han corrido diez meses, y en ese lapso, la hemos buscado dos o tres veces cada mes, para el objeto dicho, con una persistencia incansable" [Between the previous date and this one, ten months have gone by, during which time we attempted to speak to her two or three times a month with the aforestated object, with a tireless persistence] (27). Or yet again, the hapless reporter is left to document her resistance to providing any information, since she suspects that Muñuzuri, like other reporters in the past, is mainly interested in what he describes as the kind of prurient and pornographic speculations about her life that appeared in the more sensationalist yellow press accounts: ". . . negado toda especie de documento relativo, y desautorizando cualesquier tipo de obra anterior, como no hecha con su conocimiento, consentimiento ni participación. Dijo que a nadie había dado permiso ni dato alguno para ese fin . . . ; se ha negado a considerar la cuestión" [ . . . refusing any kind of document of the sort and deauthorizing whatever kind of previous work as done without her knowledge, permission, or participation. She said that she had given no one permission nor any information toward that end . . . ; she had refused to consider the question] (43). Furthermore, despite repeated requests for private interviews, it turns out to be impossible to see La Bandida alone; it is Muñuzuri's most insistent request, but it is never granted. When Muñuzuri is allowed to join La Bandida's evening revels, it is always as part of a large and mutable group of hangers-on (see 37, 46–47, 49–50, 77, 79, 97, 105, 107, 117, 119).

Ultimately, Muñuzuri's interests and those of La Bandida do not coincide, despite his efforts to construct an ingenious rationale about the purity of the professional prostitute. In an article entitled "Resisting the Heat," Doris Sommer asks, apropos of Edward Said, but in terms equally applicable to Muñuzuri and readers/writers like him: "Did we imagine that the desire was mutual or that we were irresistible? Could we consider . . . the possibility that our interest was not returned?" (Sommer 1993, 412–13). Muñuzuri, then, cannot write about La Bandida's private life or her past, since she won't tell him about them; he cannot write

about the most well-known features of her present and public life since
he has officially condemned yellow journalism; he has to censor almost
certainly true and deeply revelatory stories about powerful political figures
for his own continued personal and professional health; he is deeply suspicious of the tales she tells in constructing her public persona as he has
grounds to suspect that she is playing to her audience; and she refuses to
help him in his dilemma because she repeatedly ignores his requests for
in-depth, private interviews. The only potentially libelous commentary
Muñuzuri permits himself to record has to do with a beloved, influential
figure — another loose woman:

> Un periodista quiso saber si la película que ya se anunció con el
> título de "La Bandida" y protagonizada por María Félix, está basada
> en su vida.
> Ella respondió:
> — Me han invitado a verla, pero nada tiene que ver conmigo.
> — Entonces, ¿por qué se aprovechan de su nombre?
> — Hijo, es que no lo tengo patentado.
> — ¿Y hará buen papel María Félix?
> — Si la hace de lo que ella sabe, lo hará bien, porque es co-
> lega. (52)

> [A newspaper reporter wanted to know if the movie that had been
> announced with the title La Bandida and starring María Félix is
> based on her life. She answered, "I've been invited to see it, but it
> has nothing to do with me."
> "So then why are they taking advantage of your name?"
> "Son, I don't have a patent on it."
> "And will María Félix do well in the role?"
> "If she bases it on what she knows, she will, because she's my
> colleague."]

The celebrity status of the famous movie actress makes her vulnerable
to the press and to insinuations about her personal life. It is exactly the
kind of marginally pertinent detail about an exotic world that temporarily
deflects Muñuzuri from his purpose.

    In the face of this reiterated refusal to testify, Muñuzuri contradicto-
rily finds a potential opening: "[L]a realidad es que, parece en principio
como aceptando la idea, y sólo aplaza su realización. Pero como todo lo
que allí se ve y se oye es de primera mano, eso nos sirve, y no tenemos más
remedio que fijar al máximo la atención y observación: para ir perfilando
la figura" [The fact is that it seems that in principle she is coming around

to the idea, and only delaying its realization. But since whatever one sees and hears there is firsthand information, it is useful, and we have no recourse but to focus the maximum possible attention and observation on it in order to begin profiling her] (44). Since he cannot write a traditional memoir, he can at least provide a profile study of her social circle. The profile thus ingeniously constructed is, however, even by Muñuzuri's own account, both unfaithful and unreliable because the woman he meets is always on stage in his presence, always performing, even when — or perhaps especially when — she is self-consciously performing some *historia* related to herself or her past:

> [L]a costumbre de estar acompañada y de necesitar un público ligero, estorbó doblemente la confidencia y la confianza, anulando la posibilidad misma de hablar en privado, o de cosas más serias que las motivadas por la espontaneidad de una tertulia...a la que restringió su actuación en mucho teatral...Al condicionar de este modo su conducta, está visto que "La Bandida" no hablaría nunca en forma abierta. (117)

> [Her practice of always being accompanied and of needing a light-minded public doubly hindered both confession and confidence in her, annulling the very possibility of private speech or conversation about anything more serious than the topics motivated by the spontaneity of an informal gathering,...a spontaneity restricted by her highly theatrical performance....By setting such conditions, it is clearly seen that La Bandida would never speak openly.]

We have here an instance of testifyin' in its most elaborate and, to use Muñuzuri's own term, "purest" form: testifyin' as the only record of her life, as the most authentic testimonial to that life. La Bandida effectively erases Marina Adeo (or Acevedo) or Graciela Olmos or Loreto González Velázquez, leaving only the empty/full signifier of her professional alias — her stolen name. With her refusal to speak, La Bandida resists the monumentalizing impulse into which Muñuzuri or any other representative of nationalist ideological interests would pigeonhole her. With her equivocal and performative speech, she parodies the sharing of privileged, confidential information that Muñuzuri hopes to gain from his relentless (and entertaining) assault on her social evenings. In allowing the newspaper reporter limited access to her, she inaugurates her own *intratransa* in which the writer, perpetually tantalized by the potential of the big scoop, is never allowed anything that he can grasp as real or true. *Memorias de "La Bandida"* is nothing of the sort, is neither real nor true;

it does, however, reveal a clever woman's testifyin' at the expense of a venial reporter.

## III

At one point in her "interviews" with Muñuzuri, La Bandida appropriates an old joke as a personal anecdote about an affair with a revolutionary general:

> Cuando yo empezaba mi vida mundana, y había que tumbarles la "lana," yo era mimosa con mis amigos, y un general se prendó de mí, y luego de vernos, me escribía carta de enamorado.... Una vez, acababa yo de despertar, a las diez de la mañana, y recibí una carta suya, que contesté como entonces se usaba: mandándole un retrato y un ricito y mis labios pintados en el papel; y le decía: "...Al recibir tu cartita, mi adorado general, acababa de estar en los brazos de Morfeo...." Eso, entre otras lindezas. Y mientras yo esperaba los "centenarios" [monedas de oro de 50 pesos] a vuelta de correo, recibí mis pelos y mis besos y su respuesta indignada:
> "...Hemos terminado, vieja, porque está bien que seas puta, pero no que me digas con quién te acuestas." (73–74)

[When I was getting started in my worldly life, and had to extract cash from the men, I was very affectionate with my friends, and a general got stuck on me, and after I had seen him, he wrote me a love letter.... Once, when I had just woken up, around ten in the morning, and I had received one of his letters, I answered in the way we used to: by sending him a picture, a lock of hair, and lipstick impressions on the paper, and I told him: "...When I received your note, my beloved general, I had just been in the arms of Morpheus...." That, along with other sweet talk. And while I was waiting for the gold coins by return mail, what I got was my hair, my kisses, and an indignant response: "...It's over, lady, because while it's fine that you're a whore, it is not OK to tell me who you're sleeping with."]

Irma Serrano, in one of her books, tells almost exactly the same story with reference to one of her lovers (Serrano and Robledo 1979, 274–75), which just goes to show, I suppose, that a good story bears repeating and that the public — lovers, *lentos*, clients, or readers — is assumed to have an infinite capacity for gullibility if the woman's story is sufficiently entertaining.

Equally important is the implicit moral lesson of the story: the intelligent woman must keep her head at all times, especially in supposed affairs of the heart. Irma Serrano specifically extends the analogy of the slow-witted lover to her autobiographical books, where the relation between the sexually transgressive woman and the angry client is played out to her benefit. Thus, at the end of *Calzón*, the first volume of her memoirs, she addresses the members of the press in terms that would have been familiar to La Bandida and to Antonia Mora and should have been heeded by Muñuzuri in his efforts to get La Bandida to give him exclusive rights to her story/body: "[Q]ue traten este libro como trataron a *Naná*, como trataron a Irma al principio de su carrera. . . . Por favor, por piedad, síganme llenando de lodo, de estiércol, vuelquen a mí sus frustraciones y amarguras, que aquí, Santa Irma, con veladora en la mano, los espera tranquilamente, ya que cada descarga suya es un bonche de oro para mí" [May they treat this book as they treated *Naná*, as they treated Irma at the beginning of her career. . . . Please, I beg you, keep throwing dirt and manure on me, vent your bitterness and frustrations, because here I am, Saint Irma, with candle in hand, calmly waiting for you, for each of your attacks is a pile of gold for me] (296).[6] In addition to satirizing the press for its inefficient efforts to make money out of her scandalous career as nightclub singer, actress, and mistress of famous men (a talent that, she hints, she possesses in abundance), Serrano reminds the reader of her own literary heritage — Zola's *Nana*, Gamboa's *Santa*, works familiar to her not only in printed form but also in popular Mexican movies, including those movie and theatrical roles for which she is best known (she starred as Naná on both stage and screen).

Serrano, like La Bandida, is always on stage in her work in whatever genre: in the theater, films, courtroom, shopping centers, or in these books. She is always performing, and her expansive memoirs offer a long theatrical monologue on the theme of her real or invented life. As Carlos Monsiváis reminds us, the truth about La Tigresa Irma Serrano is completely irrelevant; Irma Serrano "es lo que se dice de ella, lo que uno imagina que se dice de ella, lo que ella supone que uno dice cuando comenta su existencia. . . . Es — seamos jerárquicos — un *fenómeno comercial* y luego un *escándalo social* y un desconcierto (artificiosamente) moral y una provocación (ciertamente) sexual" [is what is said about her, what one imagines that is said about her, what she supposes about what one says when commenting on her existence. . . . She is — let us be hierarchical — a *commercial phenomenon* and then a *social scandal* and an (artificially) moral

disruption and a (certainly) sexual provocation] (Monsiváis 1977, 298).
Like La Bandida, Serrano also self-consciously fits herself into a specific
literary/cultural heritage, which she then appropriates and rewrites to her
own purposes. As Monsiváis writes of another famous nightclub actress,
"Una vedette es, por donde se le vea, una *mujer pública*, y para detener las
connotaciones degradantes de la expresión, hay que asumirla al extremo,
vivir fotográfica y escénicamente las fantasías del público" [A nightclub
performer is, no matter how you look at it, a *public woman*, and in order
to arrest the degrading aspects of that expression, she must assume the
role to the fullest, to live out the public's fantasies photographically and
scenically] (Monsiváis 1981, 39). Following Monsiváis, then, the best tactic for a woman like Serrano is to assume the outward signs of the woman
everyone takes her to be: to out-Naná Naná, to play to the thrill-seeking,
titillation-seeking audience. This is exactly what Serrano does, while at
the same time pointing out to the readers both her strategy and our
predictable response. In other words, she "reads" her audience perfectly,
coming up with a *transa* that works, even when she announces openly
that she is *transando* with them: with us.

In the epilogue to her second book of memoirs, Serrano further speci-
fies the intent of her work, again in terms that point to a specific literary
heritage, as she mocks the intellectual pretensions of high art: "[N]o pre-
tende ser de mensaje. Tampoco tiene como fin, la comunicación con las
masas, al estilo político. Mucho menos lograr un *tête-à-tête* con la in-
telectualidad de este país.... [L]o hice con gusto porque aquí entre nos,
pretendo ganar el premio Pulitzer o el Nóbel de literatura" [It's not a
book with a message. Nor does it have as its goal communicating with the
masses in the political sense. Even less achieving a tête-à-tête with this
country's intellectuals.... I did it with pleasure because just between you
and me, I hope to win the Pulitzer Prize or the Nobel Prize for literature]
(Serrano and Robledo 1979, 325). As with the first book, where Serrano
satirizes the press for their hypocritical posturing, here she specifically rejects as readers the overeducated intellectuals who critiqued her first book
and dedicates this volume of her memoirs to provincial women "que,
como yo, fueron educadas en una malentendida religiosidad y una idea
retorcida del sexo" [who, like myself, were educated according to a mis-
understood religiosity and a twisted idea about sex] (15). She includes,
presumably, in her reeducation campaign the women who wrote to compare Serrano to Mary Magdalene—an unwanted beatification effort that
she dismisses on three grounds: she is neither close to Jesus Christ, nor a
prostitute, nor a weeping woman (4).

In the third and, at this writing, final book in her inconclusive series
of memoirs, Serrano once again ups the ante; while in the second she

proclaims her indifference to politics and sarcastically asks us to judge her work on its literary merits, in *Una loca en la polaca* she revives the furor that surrounded her 1991 bid for a senatorial seat for her home state of Chiapas as a representative of the Partido Frente Cardenista de Reconstrucción Nacional [Cardenist Front for National Reconstruction (PFCRN)]. With what we must assume is wholly intentional delight, Serrano describes her qualifications for political office by reminding us that she considers herself a better actress than other politicians and recalling that from early adolescence she has been the mistress of important political figures in national government. The book ends, equally gleefully, with the reproduction of political cartoons from the national press. One shows a supporter carrying a "Serrano for senator" placard and commenting to a bystander, "¡Nosotros también tendremos nuestra Cicciolina!" [We too will have our Cicciolina!] (300), underlining her similarity to the infamous Italian political figure and former porn movie star. Another cartoon, with the title "Circo, maroma, teatro" [Circus, flips, theater], shows Serrano with a tiger body in a circus ring, holding the whip as the PFCRN performs tricks (304; the last page in the book). Serrano's third book, a combined sensual-political memoir of this 1991 senatorial campaign, was received with the same appalled fascination as her earlier two. After all, Serrano, in her own outrageous way as the ex-mistress of at least one ex-president, is a political insider, although she was never expected to have the supreme bad taste to bank on her background as a politician's trophy woman and toy.

What is striking in these books is Serrano's playing with the extremes of high seriousness and complete irresponsibility, her successful use of a parodically frivolous persona. Her rhetorical strategy is to keep this parodic character constantly in motion, to amuse and to ironize, taking nothing seriously: not her sometimes disturbing revelations, not even her own ironic and amused commentaries on severe social problems. From her first exposure to the Mexican film industry, Serrano learned the lesson of accommodation: "[Y]o quería llevar una carrera limpia, digna, honesta, pero era inútil" [I wanted to have a clean, dignified, honest career, but it was useless] (Serrano and Robledo 1978, 21). Of the three writers studied here, Serrano is the most consistently and consciously aware of the value of a hardheaded exploitation of apparent frivolity for extremely businesslike ends.

She is also, in her own way, highly responsive to her public, giving them what they want, while at the same time reminding them that they are the *lentos* in this *transa*. At the end of *Calzón*, Serrano informs the potentially concerned politicians and industrial magnates in her audience that she swears not to write a second part of her memoirs — a promise

no sooner made than broken. The second volume was released one year
after the first as a kind of encore performance: "[E]n el epílogo de mi
primer libro, prometí no hacer una segunda parte de mis memorias.... El
público...me ha pedido un segundo tomo. Yo no me hago mucho de
rogar" [In the epilogue to my first book I promised not to write a second
part of my memoirs.... The public...has asked for a second volume. I
don't need to be begged] (1979, 1). She is perfectly amenable to extending
her scam on those readers willing to come back for more and mockingly
aware that her detailed descriptions of her affairs are making powerful
men squirm. One of the attractions of her books, then, is that she offers
social scandal with an unusual — if mockingly understated — political
thrust, one that ties in as well with a flagrantly transgressive and theatrical
sexuality.

A number of childhood incidents ranging from disagreeable to horrifying serve to define the essential qualities of her mature feminine
persona and also help establish the conditions for her ability to manage that public self-image as parody and as a moneymaking asset. Here
again, the necessary *transa* with her own femininity and her physical
attributes underlies these books' provocations and seductions. Her first
book, *A calzón amarrado*, takes its title from the specially constructed underpants the narrator is forced to wear in her childhood to preserve her
chastity. These underpants, she explains, have several complicated knots
that the young Irma Serrano is unable to release without assistance. The
result, says the author of these memoirs, is a permanent trauma: "Muy
segura, muy segura con mi calzoncillo de la virginidad, pero el conde-
nado me provocó una cistitis crónica que hasta la fecha me trae asoleada.
Necesito una mucama a mi lado para que a la hora de *las ganas* me traiga
una bacinica o me acompañe al baño. Manías que se quedan bien pren-
dadas" [My virginity underwear was very, very safe, but the damn thing
provoked a chronic cystitis that bothers me to this day. I need a servant
at my side at all times so that when I have "to go," she can bring me a
pot or accompany me to the bathroom. Habits that stick with you] (81).
The underpants are intended, of course, to protect her from her own untrustworthy instincts as well as from the potential brutality of the young
children of hacienda workers who are her playmates. And so, thus ar-
mored, she is allowed outside to play. However, her mother's horror of
sex further prompts her refusal to allow this rural child to go near the
barns and corrals, just in case her daughter should happen to perceive
the behavior of animals in heat: a mental chastity belt to accompany the
knotted underpants. Predictably, this prohibition whets Serrano's natural
curiosity at the same time as it reinforces a connection between sexuality
and bestiality.

Serrano's childhood association of sex with animality is more than confirmed with her first glimpse into human sexual relations. She is the horrified witness of a brutal rape and tries to defend the girl against the man attacking her by hitting him with a cane. When the rape inevitably comes to the attention of Serrano's grandfather, the head of the family and the owner of the hacienda, the grandfather pays it scant attention. He officially deplores the rape, but because the man who committed the offense is a good worker, he makes the decision to keep him on the job. The young girl, in contrast, is no longer "una hija digna" [a worthy daughter] (1979, 36) in her family's eyes, so she is not allowed to return to her family home. The lesson of male solidarity is reinforced in other later anecdotes. When Serrano herself suffers an attempted rape after accepting a ride in the car of a male acquaintance and turns to her father for support, her father's reaction is calm: "No ha pasado nada. Esto le enseñará a no andarse trepando en los carros de los muchachos" [Nothing happened. This will teach you not to go jumping into boys' cars] (78). Later, Serrano's first efforts to break into the world of Mexican cinema are marked and marred by seduction and rape attempts on the part of agents, producers, directors, cameramen, and assorted hangers-on who all demand sex in exchange for roles in movies, decent camera angles, and so on (see, e.g., 1979, 149–50). From such early experiences, Serrano retains — or so she tells us — a distinct distaste for the sexual act, which she learns to disguise in the company of her wealthy lovers but which provides her with a weapon and a crucial distancing edge in her relationships with men.

In the theatrical life, where sex and politics are often closely linked, this thinking approach to emotional ties serves her well. Monsiváis comments that on-stage performers like Serrano "aparece[n] una especie diferente, ya no la Madre, ni la Virgen, ni la Prostituta, sino la mujer inaccesible para quienes carecen de poder y dinero, a quien le encomiendan interpretar a la Mujer Accesible y Deslumbrante" [seem like a different species, no longer the Mother, nor the Virgin, nor the Prostitute, but rather the woman who is inaccessible to those who lack power and money, who is charged by them with interpreting the Dazzling, Accessible Woman] (Monsiváis 1981, 42). It takes skill to juggle the contradictory desires of her audience: to be at one moment and for one set of appreciative viewers Naná, the distant and dazzlingly unrepentant whore, and at another moment, and for a more exclusive clientele, the (not quite) unachievable prize who puts her seductiveness into play and convinces the next rich and powerful man she has identified as a potential lover of her universal desirability and of her personal desire to be dominated precisely by *him*.

While the rapes she witnesses and to which she nearly falls a victim herself confirm the lesson of the knotted underwear and teach her to maintain an independent aloofness in her sexual relationships, attractive and abusive men bring her to a premature exploration of her sexuality. The first of these attractive men is her uncle, César Domínguez, whom she describes as the nearest landowner to her family's hacienda and the local representation of evil: "Las mujeres palidecían al oír hablar de don César....A los niños les enseñaba a santiguarse cuando pasaba cerca de ellos" [Women went pale to hear of Don César....Children were taught to cross themselves when he came near] (1979, 42). Most prominently figuring in local gossip about this character were the two young girls who lived with the aging landowner, all three sharing the same bedroom and engaging in activities the narrator was never allowed to discover, but which were spoken about in hushed voices and which resulted in the birth of several children. Young Serrano finds in her uncle the seductiveness of all forbidden things and enjoys following him around until finally he captures her, sits her on his knees, and plays pleasurable tickling games with her while telling her of the enchantments of sin (43).

The second, and more important, of the childhood figures who initiate Serrano into the potential of her sexuality is a prominent politician whom Serrano calls simply "Fernando," identified by Elena Poniatowska as Fernando Casas Alemán (Poniatowska 1993, 115). Fernando plays a centrally important role in her late childhood and, indeed, in the direction her entire life takes. Serrano describes her affair with this man in all three volumes of her memoirs, and in the second volume she refers the reader back to the first to remind us of the implications of the affair's denouement — "para detalles anteriores a esta pinche situación en que me encontraba, favor de leer el primer libro" [for previous details about this shitty situation in which I found myself, please read the first book] (109). The third book begins with a brief reference to her lover's presidential hopes, described in relation to her adolescent coming to consciousness of the *transas* and hypocrisies of the political system. The first two books, however, provide the most sustained discussion of this relationship, each contributing different details about this long affair that lasted from the time she was thirteen years old until she was seventeen, and hence too old to hold his interest much longer.

Fernando is an older, married man, a powerful politician and precandidate to the presidency of Mexico when Serrano first meets him as a beautiful, blonde, thirteen-year-old child. Fernando flatters the little girl, sits her on his lap, gives her presents, and, when he leaves town, kidnaps her on his private plane (though volumes 1 and 2 insist upon her delight at being so surprisingly abducted [1978, 101; 1979, 84]). During the first eight months of their association, Fernando arouses her sexually but does not have relations with her since, as Serrano says, she is still too young; nevertheless, Serrano describes both this early stage of the affair, as well as their subsequent sexual relations, as the most satisfying of her life (1978, 103). During almost the entire period of their affair Fernando keeps her cloistered: "[P]refirió que conservara toda la inocencia posible, que estuviera forjada solamente a su imagen y semejanza" [He preferred to preserve as much of my innocence as possible, to have me forged entirely in his image and likeness] (1978, 108). The most disagreeable feature of their long affair, says Serrano, is Fernando's unwillingness to use any method of birth control; every couple of months he sends this child-mistress of his to get an abortion, with the result, says Serrano, that she retains "un enorme temor al embarazo, por eso tomo todos los anticonceptivos habidos y por haber para no salir preñada" [an enormous fear of pregnancy, which is why I take all the contraceptives ever invented so as not to get pregnant] (1978, 111). It is easy enough to read between the lines in the story of this affair, with its protestations of affection marching alongside descriptions of child abuse. Serrano, however, cannily displaces the overt revelation of her disillusionment onto a third person, allowing her to retain her pose of semi-innocent seductiveness and disinterested affection.

It is at a party with other politicians that Irma Serrano is finally forced to see what is happening with her life. The lovely Italian mistress of another political figure feels sorry for the little girl and advises her to get as much money out of Fernando as she can, while she still can: "Por Dios, pequeña, ¿qué no lo sabes? En cuanto cumplas 16 años ya estarás demasiado vieja para él. ¿En qué mundo vives? El seguirá cambiando de amantes y nunca dejará a sus esposa y a sus hijos" [My God, child, don't you know what's going on? As soon as you turn sixteen you'll be too old for him. What world are you living in? He'll keep changing mistresses and will never leave his wife and children] (1979, 100, 102). Although Serrano initially resists such blunt and unwelcome advice, she soon learns that the Italian woman is quite correct. By that time, however, the young woman has absorbed the primary lesson Fernando had to teach her, one that set the tenor of their relationship beginning with his version of the tickling games that brought the child to orgasm. In the real world, sex and politics and money and pleasure all run together, and innocent courtship is a nostalgic dream. As Serrano says at the end of *Pelos*, "[M]uchas veces soñé con un noviecito que me tomara de la mano y me llevara al cine, que me comprara palomitas...y que me diera kikitos al arrullo de la película o acurrucados bajo un arbolito. No se me concedió" [Often I dreamed of a nice little boyfriend who would take me by the hand and bring me to the movies, who would buy me popcorn . . . and would give me little nuzzles to the movie's lullaby, or curled up under a nice little tree. But it never happened] (1979, 259). Instead, Serrano learns the harder lesson of the tortuous relationships of politics and beautiful women, of the potent and dangerous sexual lure of rich men. And she learns about the pleasures to be found in things.

There is a certain brutal in-your-faceness about Serrano's consistent connection of politics and money, money and love. Despite occasional references to the sentimental dream of romantic love, Serrano never entertains such illusions for long. She is determinedly unromantic and equally insistent on not seeing herself as a victim. There is in Mexican society as in the United States a frequently evoked truism that love is an episode in a man's life but is everything to a woman. Serrano plays with this truism at the level of a trick, a *transa*, a style of testifyin'. Her life is all about "love," but it is love expressed at the level of satire or a theatrical performance. Thus, for instance, her performance of naïveté allows her to describe even the repulsive Fernando as a lovable man, to imagine the exploitative Don César as an attractive human being.

Like La Bandida, Serrano comes to expect gold coins, or their equivalent, in exchange for her affection. As she tells us frankly in the first volume of her memoirs: "Mentiría si dijera que toda la fortuna la he acumulado con mi trabajo profesional. También he juntado muchos millones como mujer" [I would be lying if I said I accumulated my entire fortune through my professional work. I also piled up many millions as a woman] (1978, 133). It is no wonder, given her interest in money and her lack of interest in sex, that, as she says later, she becomes somewhat mercenary, even cannibalistic: "[M]is platos predilectos son los políticos y los industriales" [My favorite dishes are politicians and industrialists] (249). Again and again, Serrano uses a rich man to pull her out of a difficult situation: "[M]e dejé seducir por interés" [I allowed myself to be seduced for what I could get out of it] (1979, 121); or "[E]l primer hombre que conquisté con mi inteligencia fue Selem" [The first man I conquered with my intelligence was Selem] (1979, 123); or "Necesitaba su protección, así que traté de volverme dócil y complaciente" [I needed his protection, so I tried to become docile and complacent] (1978, 155).

Even when her fortune is secure, Serrano is careful always to have a rich lover to provide her with the extra material luxuries she adores. Upon being introduced to a rich businessman by a mutual acquaintance, Serrano moves quickly to establish herself in a position of some importance in his life: "[A]l rato ya lo estaba seduciendo. El se portaba medio arisco; antes de llegar a relaciones íntimas quería que nos regaláramos primero amor. Pero en lugar de oír sus sugerencias lo llevé derechito a la cama" [In a little while I was already seducing him. He acted skittish; before becoming intimate he wanted us to gift each other first with our love. But instead of listening to him I took him straight to bed] (1979, 250). Of another lover, she writes: "[E]l único hombre que resumió el amor a mi belleza y a mi talento, el que me conquistó por los dos flancos en el terreno material y sentimental, fue un ex-gobernador" [The only man who combined love for my beauty with love for my talent, the one who conquered me from both flanks in the material and the sentimental territory, was an ex-governor] (1978, 270). Of yet another, "[Y]o quería llegar a conquistar el hombre más poderoso y él era ya un alto funcionario: ministro. Como anillo al dedo" [I wanted to conquer the most powerful man there, and he was already an important figure, a minister. A perfect fit] (1979, 138). The verbs *conquistar* and *seducir* are used interchangeably in these accounts and always with an ironic undertone. Serrano conquers the man or allows him to conquer her; she seduces or is seduced. In each case, despite the apparent power of the man in controlling the shape and intensity of the relationship, Serrano wants her readers to recognize that the ultimate power is hers. She identifies the prey, sets the tone, marks the boundaries. She initiates the connection and determines when it will come to an end. By playing with male expectations of female sentimentality, Serrano is able to *transar* with these powerful men: to let them pretend they are the hunters, to flatter them into providing her with the material rewards and the intellectual satisfactions she craves.

Serrano tells us of having attended many, many parties held in the homes of mistresses of politicians and industrialists; no legitimate wives are invited to these events; instead the company of rich men is rounded out by women that Serrano describes as "elastic": "[E]l adjetivo es por la elasticidad en el amor, o sea, casi casi del oficio más antiguo" [The adjective comes from elasticity with respect to love, that is, almost — but not quite — the oldest profession in the world] (1978, 220). In these parties, there is no crass or overt payment for sex; however, it is customary for the host to give out party favors to the women. One industrialist "nos regalaba a todas (jalaran o no jalaran) un centenario de oro" [gave each of us (whether we slept with anyone or not) a gold coin]; another gave out gold bracelets and bangles (1978, 227–28). The women collect the souvenir coins and bracelets; the men collect women. In this highly traditional economy of exchange, the rich man establishes a secret erotic collection, a mental harem of sexual objects. It is an economy in which the objects that the female collects, as well as the woman herself, tend to be erased after the sexual exchange is completed.

The lesson learned from these experiences is not complicated. Serrano understands herself as a commodity, more valuable because she is more

highly desired by more powerful men than other women in the same circles. While she describes herself as not having a very sexual nature, she
has become very astute at presenting herself in such a way that important
men compete against each other to seduce her. Her sense of women's
roles in general in these men's lives is very clear, as is her evaluation of
the reasons for her success when compared to other women: "[S]omos
un objeto, una bacinica, nada más que yo era una *bacinica pensante*. Me
imagino que las demás mujeres que incursionan en estos menesteres...no
pasan de ser bacinicas puras" [We are an object, a chamberpot, except
that I was a *thinking chamberpot*. I imagine that the other women who
get involved in these tasks...never go beyond being plain chamberpots]
(139). Serrano enjoys — or tells us that she enjoys — the subtleties of the
hunt, the reality of conquest masked under the discreet game of seduction. She remembers her commodity nature at all times and gets a rush of
satisfaction when she dictates the terms of the exchange of commodities.

Serrano sells this access to her body on many different levels. When
one of her lovers turns out to be an important drug trafficker and Serrano is ordered to appear in court to testify, she knows that the tabloids
will turn out in force for the occasion. She obligingly dresses for court in
an outfit calculated to earn her the attention of the press on terms that
mock their firmly established impression of her: a dress cut to the waist
and accessorized with an enormous ruby hanging between her breasts (a
photograph is thoughtfully reproduced in the text as well; see Serrano
1978, 235, 239). In this outfit, she not only confirms their conclusions
about her immorality and her frivolity but also reassures her prospective
audience with a willing and willful demonstration of her difference from
the powerful man under investigation — How can anyone take her seriously when she is so clearly a rich man's toy? Similarly, she attributes
her success as a singer less to the qualities of her voice than to her willingness to appear on stage, television, and album covers in a blouse that
is tantalizingly transparent and low-cut and a skirt that shows all of her
legs right up to the panty-line (1979, 167–68, 178, 181). Likewise, as an
actress, she feels she is merely good rather than great (despite her high
name-recognition) mostly because she is too lazy to work hard; she has
the advantage, however, that she has absolutely no reluctance to appear
nude (C. Pacheco 1990, 112–13). She is aware that she is turned into
a sex object ("[Y]o, diosa de la carne, la belleza, el sexo, os digo..." [I,
goddess of love, of beauty, of sex, tell you...] begins an autobiographical
play written and directed by, as well as starring, Irma Serrano [C. Pacheco
1990, 109]); she collaborates in and promotes this fetishization and would
clearly be disappointed if all her effort in this respect didn't pay off as
handsomely as it has.

Like Sefchovich in *Demasiado amor,* one of the twists that Serrano gives to this drama of erotic collecting is precisely that of seeing herself both as commodity and as collector. In so doing, she specifically disrupts the traditional boundary between male collector and female collectible. Furthermore, her collections are richer than those of the men, since they are both abstract and concrete. She reminds us that the gold coins and jewels, as well as the more mundane gifts like a *molcajete* from a Mexican president during their love affair (Serrano 1979, 233), are also collectible items and things that serve her in a triple function as treasure trove, memory props, and character references. Likewise, those men who make the mistake of seeing women as mere objects (chamberpots) discount the independent actions of women like Serrano (the thinking chamberpots) who are as capable as men of forming mental catalogues or collections of their lovers and of turning them into ornaments in their mental seraglio. If the women are chamberpots, then men, as Serrano tells us repeatedly, are consumable objects ("platillos fuertes") that provide basic sustenance: "Me han dicho los allegados que trato a los hombres como si fueran obje-tos, y creo que en el fondo lo son" [The accused have said that I treat men as if they were objects, and I think that basically they are] (1978, 261). "Loving" men is consuming them; conspicuous consumption is both a sign and the consequence of love. Irma Serrano would not be an attrac-tive woman unless she also possessed the pigeon-egg-sized rubies, the expensive gowns, and the other toys that define loveliness and pleasure in the world of Mexican high society.

Serrano, accordingly, fetishizes such objects. Ever since early child-hood, she tells us, she has been obsessed with shopping and has been dominated by the irrepressible desire to own things. To some degree, it is the shop-till-you-drop mentality that both normalizes Serrano (she's just like any other middle-class housewife) and sets her apart (both by the quantity and cost of the things she purchases as well as by the fact that she seems to include a series of rich men on her shopping list). Serrano describes unapologetically her need to always be surrounded by objects, a need that results in both her home and her dressing rooms prominently featuring heaped-up mountains of purchases for visual feasting. In set-ting the scene for her interview with Serrano, reporter Cristina Pacheco describes one such hoard: "Aunque el camerino es inmenso no basta para contener la infinita variedad de objetos que hay en él: un retrato de Irma Serrano pintado al óleo, libros, espejos, colecciones de sombreros, bo-tas, zapatos; un abrigo de piel, blusas, juguetes, maquillajes" [Although the dressing room is immense it is not big enough for all the infinite variety of objects within it: an oil painting of Irma Serrano, books, mir-rors, collections of hats, boots, shoes; a fur coat, blouses, toys, makeup]

(C. Pacheco 1990, 111). This visual feast parallels and reminds us of the gluttonous consumption of men, and the heaped-up disorder of these objects suggests Serrano's own famously exaggerated lust. The perverse excess hinted at in the obsession with material goods spills over into staged hysteria in one of Serrano's more striking descriptions of her love of things:

> El año pasado me sentí muy sola en Nochebuena, así que saqué todos mis brillantes, centenarios, esmeraldas, rubíes, collares de perlas, cadenas de oro, anillotes, pulserotas, aretotas, etcétera. Los eché a la tina de mármol negro que tengo al fondo de mi recámara, rodeada de espejos, que ayudaron para que la cantidad se viera multiplicada.
>
> Entonces me eché un clavado imitando a Rico Mac Pato. Regocijé mi cuerpo desnudo entre las olas brillantes. Metía y sacaba brazos y piernas de mi pequeña alberquita. Luego me senté y empecé a echar las joyas para arriba, como los bebés que chapotean en el agua. (*Calzón* 269–70)

> [Last year I felt very alone on Christmas Eve, so I took out all my diamonds, gold coins, emeralds, rubies, pearl necklaces, gold chains, all my enormous rings, bracelets, earrings, etc. I threw them into the black marble bathtub I have in the back of my bedroom, that was surrounded with mirrors so that the quantity looked multiplied.
>
> Then I dove in, in imitation of Scrooge McDuck. I enjoyed my naked body among the shining waves. I moved my arms in and out of my little swimming pool. Then I sat up and began to throw the jewels into the air, like a baby splashing in the water.]

With such descriptions, Serrano mocks middle-class aspirations as she also mocks the middle-class emphasis on respectability as defined by a tasteful restraint in clothing and material possessions. Since excess in dress and adornment is associated with perverse lusts of all sorts, Serrano's marked love of things points directly to her gleeful association with *maldad* (evil [see Serrano 1979, 61]) and with her early association of evil and pleasure.

In such statements, the character that dominates the storytelling in these books is Serrano's professional alter ego, "La Tigresa" [The Tigress]. Unlike "Irma," the repressed personality of the innocent girl who is forever sweet and feminine, La Tigresa is aggressive and vengeful, a strong and solitary cat-woman. In both books she tells the reader that she, that is, La Tigresa, has an old soul and has lived many lives, that she was born a witch, though she hasn't developed her natural talents. Always at risk in her adoption of this strong personality is the potential for a loss of male attention and of female approval. La Tigresa doesn't care. Often men accuse her of frigidity, of being too "butch" in her actions; most of all, she says, they fear her aggressivity (1979, 297–98). In her 1982 interview with Cristina Pacheco, La Tigresa is fully present as Serrano responds with equal indifference to the reporter's questions about her relationships with men and with women: "[A] los hombres no les temo, no los necesito, no los respeto.... Creo que por eso un hombre me dijo una vez: 'Eres una mujer castrante'" [I neither fear, need, nor respect men.... I believe that is why a man once told me, "You are a castrating woman"] (C. Pacheco 1990, 115). If the man she is referring to in this quote is Jorge Ayala Blanco, there is as much admiration as criticism in his comments. Ayala Blanco once wrote that Serrano "ejerce la castración como una de las bellas artes de la comedia ranchera" [exercises castration as one of the fine arts of the ranchera comedy] (quoted in Poniatowska 1993, 117).

When queried about women's attitudes toward her and her work, she replies, "[L]a verdad es que no me importa lo que piensan.... Le he dicho de muchas maneras que no tiene por qué ser la estúpida que dependa de un hombre.... Una puede ser libre, pero la libertad se paga" [The truth is I don't care what they think.... I've said in many ways that (a woman) doesn't have to be the idiot who depends on a man.... A woman can be free, but freedom has to be paid for] (115–16). Among the freedoms that La Tigresa arrogates to herself is that of crossing and recrossing lines of taboo and middle-class morality. She is unapologetic for her notorious affairs with rich men and calmly triumphant about her extreme affluence in a poor country. In the interview with Elena Poniatowska, she repeatedly emphasizes her beauty and her intelligence, at one point commenting, "Me gusta comprarme todo lo que mi cuerpo desea. Hay que darle un poco de gusto al cuerpo, ¿no cree?" [I like to buy everything that my body desires. One has to give the body a little pleasure, don't you think?]. And she answers her own question with a typical put down: "No, usted no tiene cara de las que le dan gusto al cuerpo" [No, you don't have the face of a woman who gives her body pleasure] (91). Her mannered indifference to people and things is, after all, part of her image, an important prop to her act.

Along the same lines, La Tigresa plays with her readers' expectations by cheerfully describing other scandals as well. For the literary readers, she reminds us repeatedly in both books that Rosario Castellanos was her first cousin and an early supporter in her bid for freedom against parental and teacherly oppression. In *Calzón*, for example, she cites Castellanos as crucially important in giving her an insight into her own character: "Tú,

Cielo, nunca vas a ser como las demás, nunca vas a ser *normal*. . . . El ser
diferente es un premio que te ha dado la vida, aunque quizás el precio
sea la soledad" [You, my dear, are never going to be like other girls, you
will never be *normal*. . . . Being different is a prize that life has given you,
but the price might be loneliness] (27). Both difference and loneliness are
permanent features in Serrano's life, as they were in her famous cousin's,
and in reminding us of their familial relationship, Serrano also implicitly
suggests a literary connection. She and Castellanos, Serrano hints, reflect
two different versions of an inherently Mexican feminist practice, two
alternatives for a literary (and artistic) feminist expression.

Even as a political candidate, Serrano chooses the flamboyant gesture rather than a toned-down performance of dowdy professionalism she
pointedly associates with the very few influential female literary and political figures in her country, people like Elena Poniatowska and Rosario
Castellanos. Thus, for example, she describes her first real political action, her public acceptance of the PFCRN candidacy for senate, in terms
of the grand gesture she makes with her body and her clothes: "[P]ara
esta ocasión me atavié entre la folclórica escandalosa que va a un coctel y
la cancionera de palenque" [For that event I decked myself out in an outfit halfway between a scandalous version of a folkloric cocktail gown and
that of a chorus line singer], describing a costume that included exag-
geratedly long blonde eyelashes and diamonds at the corners of her eyes
(1979, 191). Here she reproduces the gesture she has learned at all those
unsavory parties of her adolescence; politics resides in the grand gesture,
in the physical impact of the body's control of space, since the message
of political addresses tends toward the insipid and unmemorable. Unsurprisingly, she reports that later, when she goes out campaigning to give
her political addresses, the crowd is uncertain how to react: "[E]speraba
el momento de cerciorarme si la gente se iba a soltar pidiéndome que
cantara *La Martina* o actuara una escena de *Naná*" [I was waiting for the
moment of confirmation as to whether the people were going to burst out
asking me to sing "La Martina" (one of her best-selling musical compositions) or to act a scene from *Naná*] (208). Here again, by the very fact of
insistingly reinforcing the shock of her scandalous presence in the political arena, Serrano literally represents the role of the public woman in its
double valence, bringing to the fore the transgressive potential that other
women operating in the public realm would prefer to downplay.

In *Sin pelos en la lengua,* La Tigresa takes particular delight in opening
up one of the most insistently silenced topics in this very machista country: the problem of homosexuality, both male and female. She describes
her entrance into the world of film as dating from the time when "los in-
telectuales eran los únicos que se daban el lujo de declararse abiertamente

homosexuales. Y no se veía mal; al contrario, era costumbre de mucho *cachét*" [intellectuals were the only ones who had the luxury of openly declaring themselves homosexuals. And it wasn't badly seen; quite the contrary, it was very fashionable]. Nowadays, by contrast, she says, homosexuality no longer has the same glitter — everyone is doing it (147). Furthermore, La Tigresa constantly flirts with scandalous transgression herself, describing her own attraction to ambiguous sexualities. She and male transvestites together bemoan the lack of real men in the twentieth century (291); she is profoundly attracted to a female transvestite whom she calls "Coquito," after the male role for which s/he is hired in Serrano's play *Naná,* and describes in detail the process of her interrupted mutual seduction of the person she thinks is a young boy (294–96). On another occasion she describes meeting "un ser enigmático" [an enigmatic person] dressed in a caftan and turban. La Tigresa expresses her interest in meeting this sensual being and is introduced by a mutual friend. Their first exchange goes like this:

— Soy Mario y la admiro mucho. . . .
— ¡Eureka! ¡Un padre para mi hijo! . . .
— Será *madre,* porque a mí *no* me gustan las mujeres. . . .
— Oye, estás muy guapo, ¿no podrías hacerle la lucha?
— Mira, directamente no puedo. (287–88)

["I'm Mario, and I admire you a lot. . . ."
"Eureka! A father for my child! . . ."
"Maybe a mother, because I don't like women. . . ."
"Listen, you're very handsome. Couldn't you give it a try?"
"Well, not directly I can't."]

These remarks, combined with her reiterated reference to her aggressivity and to the accusations that she is "machorra, hombruna" [butch], suggest that La Tigresa is at least flirting with the scandalous possibilities of same-sex and transgendered relationships. In each case, the process of seduction is described in detail, followed by a shocked disillusionment or the evolution of a comfortable companionship. Thus, the homosexual or the transvestite offers the possibility of a disinterested relationship on both sides, one that is quite different from the more common pattern in La Tigresa's life where "giving herself" to another is the first step in an implicit quid pro quo requiring adequate "gifts" from the lucky man. Among the scandals of La Tigresa's life, there is, then, a repeated and persistent divergence from her pursuit of men toward another woman, one who is also described in terms that evoke masculine qualities ("hombruna") and one who, like her, is free, independent, and strong. This doubling of herself in the figure of the transvestite hints at another option for seductive masking in modern Mexican society. For while La Tigresa has chosen the mocking face of hyperfemininity, there are other women who choose different versions of rejecting normality (to come back to Castellanos's term) and alternative means for discovering a freedom that is equally valid, if potentially less lucrative.

With her third book, Serrano takes her mocking *transa* into another realm, in which her long training by and association with powerful politicians, her propensity for saying the outrageous, and her theatrical flair all come together in a powerfully literal way. Here is strong confirmation of Margo Su's commentary that elite courtesans learned much of their craft from the politicians and businessmen that frequented them; Serrano turns the tables on the politicians by marking the literalness of the exchange and the moral equality of the actors involved. In the opening pages of *Una loca en la polaca,* Serrano describes a conversation between Rosario Castellanos and Fernando when Miguel (de la Madrid) was unexpectedly chosen over Fernando as the next presidential candidate of the ruling party. From this conversation, Serrano draws her own cynical conclusions about the operations of the political system:

> Entonces entendí bien el verdadero significado del *dedazo:*
> "Palabra castellana que en México se utiliza para señalar, por medio del dedo índice, al títere que la mente presidencial de turno considera el más pendejo, porque así cree que a través de la fidelidad y servilismo del escogido seguirá gobernando con poder eterno."
> (1992, 30)

> [Then I fully understood the true meaning of the Fingering: "Castilian word which in Mexico is utilized to signal, by means of the index finger, the puppet which the presidential mind of that moment considers the most idiotic, because thus he believes that through the faithfulness and servility of the chosen one he will continue to govern with eternal power."]

When Serrano makes her own staged appearance in the government offices, her self-presentation could not be more carefully calculated, both on political and gender grounds, to play off this assumption of female inferiority and political ingenuousness and servility: "¿Qué postura tendría que ser la mía? La de una idiota. Una pobre tartamunda, insegura de su lenguaje y de pensamientos confusos. Esta pose me ha sido provechosa cuantas veces he tenido que enfrentarme a este tipo de personajes"

[What pose would I have to assume? That of an idiot. A poor stutterer, unsure of her language and with confused thoughts. This pose had worked well for me whenever I needed to confront this type of character] (195). Serrano is aware that one result of this superbly managed act is that her candidacy is understood as a joke, but it is a joke read back against the Mexican people's awareness that politics in general in that country is a joke of another sort. As one of the political cartoons she cites in her book puts it: "Julio Alemán, Silvia Pinal e Irma Serrano sin saber de política van pa' candidatos.... Bueno, por fin habrá actores profesionales en las cámaras y no payasos de tercera" [Julio Alemán, Silvia Pinal, and Irma Serrano without knowing anything about politics are running for candidacy.... Well, at last there will be professional actors in the house of representatives and not only third-rate clowns] (34). Here Serrano reminds her reader that her own flamboyant candidacy takes place in an atmosphere of increasingly vocal dissatisfaction with Mexico's political system, such that a protest vote could well take the form of electing Mexico's home-grown version of La Cicciolina to high political office.

And yet, though Serrano in the first half of *Loca* seems cannily and consistently aware of the performative qualities of her candidacy as an attention-getting protest, by the second half of the book she projects a more embittered, more embattled version of herself and what she represents. In the first part of the book, Serrano includes a seminude photograph of herself in one of her most recent and notorious roles (73); in the last photographic sequence she reproduces images of women selling their products in the San Cristóbal de las Casas market with the caption, "[T]ienen carencias y tienen hambre" [They have needs and go hungry] (156). The transition occurs at the point at which Serrano no longer controls the conditions of the joke she has set in motion: "Tantas cosas soy para el público, que me pregunto: ¿Qué haría México sin este chiste llamado Irma Serrano?" [I am so many things for the public that I ask myself, What would Mexico do without that joke named Irma Serrano?] (96). She calls herself too decent for politics (185), reproduces an impassioned political plea for the rights of the downtrodden (224–32), describes her purported kidnapping at the hands of political enemies (251–58), and complains how the election she had clearly won with the overwhelming support of the common people had been stolen from her by the forces of the ruling party (272–95).

In the 1994 elections, she seemed to have recovered her sense of humor and her flamboyance, successfully running for the Mexican house of representatives as a member of Cuauhtémoc Cárdenas's Partido de Revolución Democrática [Revolutionary Democratic Party (PRD)].

Throughout the campaign, the press focused with fascination on her unlikely candidacy, reviving the scandal provoked by the 1991 campaign she
describes in *Loca*. In 1994, at one point, she rejected the ruling party's
presidential candidate as too boring for words, but indicated her interest in debating the presidential hopeful from the conservative Partido
de Acción Nacional [National Action Party (PAN)]. Of PAN's Diego
Fernández she commented: "Sería para mí un placer absoluto debatir con
uno tan majadero, tan grosero, con tan buena voz como la mía, como
Diego: estaríamos muy parejos. Una vez dijo que yo era una serpiente
dinosáurica de la farándula. Con alguien tan bocón como yo, sí debato"
[It would be for me a pure pleasure to debate someone like Diego, who
is as peevish, as insulting, and has as good a voice as mine; we'd be
even. Once he said that I was a dinosauric serpent from vaudeville. With
someone who has as big a mouth as mine I would debate] (*La Jornada*,
July 7, 1994, 16). Unsurprisingly, major political figures ignored Serrano's
campaign, although tabloid interest remained high. Then too, her candidacy again highlighted, as it satirized, the nature of long-traditional,
polite *transas* that have marked Mexican politics since the 1910 revolution. The year 1994 — which began with the insurrection in Chiapas
and the enshrinement of guerrilla leader "Subcomandante Marcos" as
the latest popular hero and first postmodern revolutionary — ended with
the election of La Tigresa Irma Serrano to the national congress as a
representative for that same state.

Finally, in all three of Serrano's books, credit for authorship is divided.
The title page for the first book highlights Irma Serrano's name and puts
the name of her coauthor/ghostwriter in smaller caps at the bottom of
the page. In the second book, the authorial credits look like this:

Irma Serrano
LA TIGRESA
Elisa Robledo

Here, and fittingly, it is La Tigresa whose voice is given pride of place.
In its outspokenness this book is more clearly La Tigresa's than Irma
Serrano's. In the third, the title, *Una loca en la polaca*, is superimposed
over a stylized graphic image of La Tigresa, complete with diamonds
glittering in the corners of her eyes, again with the double authorship
recognized.

Nevertheless, after reading Mendoza's foreword to Mora's text, with
its patronizing frame, and after reviewing Muñuzuri's antics in trying to
extract memoirs from La Bandida, the question naturally arises as to Elisa
Robledo's role in shaping Serrano's work.

Surprisingly (or not, as the case may be) Robledo is as shifty and theatrical as her subject. There is no scholarly foreword to these books, no
hint at all of Robledo's presence in *Pelos* or in *Loca* beyond the coau-
thorship credit on the title pages. In *Calzón*, however, the ghostwriter
appears in the final chapter with her own voice to summarize and comment upon the preceding book. She reminds us of the salient episodes
in Serrano's life, praises her strength of character, and informs the reader
parenthetically that the book was constructed around a series of taped and
transcribed interviews. The impersonal summary of the book that opens
this chapter, written in the third person, gives way to a more direct address that serves as a transition to a final interview/dialogue with Serrano
in which both women speak in the first person and which is transcribed
directly, without erasing the questions. Elisa Robledo, too, like her collaborator, is aware of her performative, even metafictional, role in this text
from the moment at which she makes her presence directly felt: "Y ya que
la redactora de este libro metió las narices en el escenario cuando nadie
la había llamado, quiere dar su punto de vista" [And since the transcriber
of this book has stuck her nose onto the scene when no one asked for
her, she wants to give her point of view] (283). For Robledo, one of the
defining moments of this collaboration is recalled with an anecdote that
demonstrates Serrano's professional willfulness and highlights a paradigmatic interaction with her public: "Esta reportera recuerda a Irma en una
de las funciones de *Lucrecia Borgia,* cuando a la mitad de la escena del
desnudo, un espectador de primera fila se atrevió a echar relajo con un
acompañante. Entonces Irma bajó del escenario y le dio una cachetada"
[This reporter remembers seeing Irma in one of the performances of *Lucrecia Borgia,* when, right in the middle of her nude scene, one of the
spectators in the first row dared to begin goofing around with his companion. Then Irma got down from the stage and slapped him across the
face] (284). Serrano's book audience is similarly divided into the inatten-
tive or unappreciative readers, to whom she deals out mental slaps, and
polite readers like us, who sit back and enjoy the show. With her audience
back to attentive appreciation and her readers toeing the line, Serrano
and Robledo are able to get back to business as well. What follows this
anecdote is a comfortable series of questions and answers about Serrano's
daily life and her beliefs. The book, as I already noted, concludes with
Serrano's first-person epilogue.

Of the three professional writers — Mendoza, Muñuzuri, and Robledo — it is only Serrano's collaborator who grasps the ludic potential in
her role. She is the only one of the group who acts upon the performative possibilities of her interaction with the scandalously well-known
actress. Mendoza's foreword to Mora's book is too concerned with cre-

ating a piously conventional coda to the prostitute's tale, one in which the protagonist's core goodness is recognized and everything falls into place for a perfect happy ending of upper-middle-class prosperity. But, of course, readers did buy the book, so Mendoza's (and Mora's) testifyin' *transa* was successful. Muñuzuri is unable to recognize the *intratransa* perpetrated by his subject, since he is too taken with his own cleverness to recognize hers. But, again, at least at a certain level, his *transa* was effective; the misnamed book was published, and at least a few of us *lentos* purchased it, read it, and even took the time to write about it. Serrano's and Robledo's collaboration, with its cheerfully insouciant alignment of the performers in cahoots with the well-behaved and appreciative audience to Serrano's stunts, at the same time offers readers a glimpse into the lifestyles-of-the-rich-and-famous, while it subtly or not-so-subtly provides testimony to the level of corruption in the Mexican power structure. For the purchase price of the book, we *lectores gambusinos* get to hear the inside gossip about the privileged classes and glimpse their lives; we can laugh at the powerful; we can even slaver over nude and seminude photographs of the author. In Serrano's books, more than in the other two works, the *testimonio* reveals its constructed quality, its latent storytelling power. Serrano and Robledo join forces to signify on us; the signifyin', testifyin' voice reminds us of the power of story to affect the real and also of the slippery boundaries of the real when it comes into contact with an able *transa*.

# Chapter 7

# No Conclusions

Jonathan Culler has usefully summarized the functions of the literary image of the prostitute in nineteenth-century France as "a structure through which a number of elements of modernity can be situated," and his comments resonate with the modern Mexican literary scene as well. Literary prostitutes (1) make visible the effects of modern capitalism, especially threats of social disorder accompanying the emergence of a proletariat on the edge of misery; (2) fascinate writers as a source of plots; (3) are scandalous both for their display of artifice and for their ability to pass as decent women; (4) represent the commodification of feminine erotic power; and (5) illuminate the role of the modern writer, who, like a prostitute, offers himself for sale (Culler 1995, 2–4). Culler is quite correct in his use of "himself" as a referent for the modern European writer, not only in the context of his paper about Baudelaire but also with reference to the dominant aesthetic of modernity in general. Not the least of the conflicts involved in the Mexican debates has to do precisely with the passing from popularity of the great male writers of the 1960s boom, as indexed by the sales figures and publication runs of best-selling novels and their replacement by what is often referred to as the *boom femenino* [female boom] of the 1980s. Likewise, reviewers and critics have noted (or lamented) that a (presumably) male audience has given way to a presumably female audience. Taking the two phenomena together marks a significant shift; the figure of the sexually transgressive woman in a novel no longer is the implied target/object of discussion but rather becomes a figure for that text's implied reader.

Like the texts studied in this book, which turn on the figure of a sexually transgressive woman as a narrative fulcrum, so too contemporary literary debates turn on a historical and cultural conjuncture caught between two literary practices, in which the variant of *literatura fácil* associated with popular women writers like Angeles Mastretta and Laura Esquivel, and featuring sexually active female protagonists, serves as the focal point of discussion, often to the disparagement of the writers and their works. Aralia López González has commented perceptively on this

215

phenomenon: "En general, existe un recelo al juzgar la narrativa escrita por mujeres en la década del ochenta, pues su gran cantidad ha constituido lo que ya se conoce desdeñosamente como *boom* femenino. Esta producción hace pensar más en un fenómeno comercial y no tanto en una creación de buena ley" [In general there is a reluctance to value the narrative written by women in the decade of the 1980s, as its great quantity has constituted what is now disdainfully called the female boom. This production makes one think more in terms of a commercial phenomenon and not creative quality] (López González 1993, 659–60). López González reminds us of the sexism inherent in such responses; what I would like to highlight is the way in which such misogyny implicitly recalls anxieties associated with the submerged metaphors of the transgressive woman.

All of the points made by Jonathan Culler in his summary of nineteenth-century fiction are valid here; the female writer tempts and terrifies to the degree that she can be accused of all the worst excesses male writers have metaphorically assigned to their own provenance and because she, by her popularity, succeeds in putting pressure upon these slippery terms. If the *literatura difícil* espoused by Octavio Paz et al. in the journal *Vuelta* no longer dominates the literary cultural scene as it did thirty years ago, the *literatura fácil* — particularly problematic when authored by women writers — rather than the technically difficult male-authored boom text, becomes the style of choice that addresses the effects of modern capitalism. David Martín del Campo notes that in his own fictional practice, "busco hacer una narrativa del país real que vivimos" [I try to write a narrative about the real country in which we live], and Hernán Lara Zavala adds, "Lo que ocurrió...fue que los escritores se empezaron a alejar cada vez más de los lectores....Sí creo que una de las responsabilidades actuales del escritor es replantearse cómo dirigirse a su público" [What happened was that the writers began to distance themselves ever further from the readers....I do believe that one of the real responsibilities of the writer is to reevaluate how to reach the audience] (*Macropolis*, March 26, 1992, 37, 36).

Even more distressingly for the proponents of *literatura difícil*, there seems to be a promiscuity of styles in the more recent narrative; Sefchovich, for example, notes that "el código de masas ha penetrado a la 'alta' cultura" [pop art has penetrated "high" culture] (Sefchovich 1987, 203). While Sefchovich celebrates such interminglings as a positive sign of vitality in modern art, "A. A." (Aurelio Asiain), among others, finds in such promiscuous blendings the danger of a noxious "democratization" in literature. For Asiain, curiously, this new literature finds its most powerful allies in the educational institution (I find this curious since intuitively most critics would guess that it is difficult, rather than easy, literature that the educational establishment supports — and, in fact, publishers confirm that institutions of higher education are almost the sole sales outlets for difficult literature). Asiain, however, comments in his introduction to the *Vuelta* special issue on *literatura difícil*:

> [L]as obras "democráticas" defienden como su mayor virtud su ligereza y propagan por el gusto por lo pintoresco y lo anecdótico.... No es extraño que estas bodas de la ideología y el mercado reciban el padrinazgo de nuestros educadores, cuya visión instrumental no percibe en la literatura sino un instrumento didáctico.... De la literatura *light* al libro de texto hay un solo paso. (See Paz, ed., 1992, 11)

> ["Democratic" works defend lightness as their greatest virtue and they advertise a taste for the picturesque and the anecdotal.... It is not surprising that these marriages of ideology and the market receive the patronage of our teachers, whose instrumental vision does not perceive in literature anything but a didactic instrument. ... From light lit to textbook is only a single step.]

Octavio Paz's critique is, if anything, even more stringent: through the market forces and the increasing attention given to contemporary bestsellers, "una literatura se muere y una sociedad se degrada...," he says. "Es imposible olvidar que la historia de la literatura del Occidente, especialmente de la edad moderna, ha sido y es la de minorías:... artistas considerados herméticos y difíciles" [a literature dies and society degenerates.... It is impossible to forget that the history of Western literature, especially of the modern age, has been and is that of minorities:... of artists considered hermetic and difficult] (Paz, ed., 1992, 14). Such disparagements of popular narrative in favor of a presumably purer, more virile, and certainly more aristocratic style — which Paz dissimulates by speaking of a "minority" literature — do indeed, in Culler's terms, "bring into visible, accessible experience the effects of modern capitalism" (2), but in much more ambiguous terms. In her seminal article, "On the Superficiality of Women," Susan Noakes points out that "it is Christianity that stresses that superficial reading (for 'adventure,' plot, to find out 'what happens') is not, as one might suppose today, merely stupid but, more importantly, morally wrong" (Noakes 1988, 347). Bad reading and moral turpitude come to be associated with each other and with a typical feature of femininity. From this point, says Noakes, it is only a small step to the conclusion that reading for enjoyment is reading as a woman, is reading in a morally deficient manner: "[W]oman as seducer behaves like woman as reader; thus, woman reads in the same way she seduces" (344). Behind Paz and Asiain's antidemocratic concerns, one can easily intuit a fear of literal and figurative feminization of literature; worse: it is a feminization that operates through the agency of the easy woman (writer).

While images of sexually transgressive women continue to fascinate writers as a source of plots, the unsettling shift in authorial and readerly perspectives forces a reevaluation of all parties involved in the production and reception of works of art. This is particularly true when the loose woman is no longer a token of a readerly exchange between male narrator and male reader but rather a projection of the female reader within the text of a female writer. In order to effectively study the Occidental literature praised by Paz, women readers have been traditionally taught to imagine themselves into this discourse as pseudomen, a process Judith Fetterley identified several years ago and called "immasculation" in her book on American fiction, *The Resisting Reader*. In order to read the text appropriately, the immasculated woman allows it to draw her in, agrees to identify with the masculinist point of view, to accept its authority, and to become complicitous in this denigration of female difference. Along parallel lines, one can imagine the consternation of a male reader who is asked to "feminize" himself for the purposes of an appropriate reading of a female-identified text.

Third, not only are the fictionalized easy women able to pass as decent women in these narratives of unpunished female sexuality, but, more importantly, the easy woman writer — like Sefchovich, Mora, and Serrano — tends to celebrate this slippage between two artificial social constructs of a moralizing discourse and of open expressions of sexuality. Likewise, if traditional representations of easy women help metamorphose the commodification of feminine erotic power, they also reveal the consolidation of male privilege, a tradition that, if not undermined in whole in recent women's texts such as those studied in this book, at least serves as the basis for a contemporary feminine transgressive literary practice.

Finally, if traditional novels like Gamboa's *Santa* illuminate the role of the modern (male) writer who, like a prostitute, offers himself for sale or, like a pimp, sells his product, then more recent works by women remind us insistently of the femaleness of the bodies in such exchanges. They remind us as well that in referring "disdainfully" to the commercial quality of the female boom, the male proponents of *literatura difícil* necessarily also call to mind a suppressed recognition of the commerciality of their own earlier literary boom — although in their time their works were best-sellers, they reject both the Gamboas and the Sefchoviches of the past and present Mexican literary scene for their commercial success.

The debates about literary authority as they relate to the topic of this book are, then, to a large extent, also debates about gender roles and about how the play of commercial power and narrative authority affects discussion of consolidated images of femininity. The trajectory traced in these literary shifts of attention points up the role of gender bias in the construction of knowledge, and the contributions of the female boom portend a more nuanced understanding of human relationships (involving women as well as men). At the same time, the loose woman in these texts by men and women of the Mexican literary establishment remains largely configured in terms of an adherence to or transgression of norms such as those summarized by Culler. In the contemporary climate, celebrations of the sexually active woman can only occur as transgression, thus producing an effect opposite to the one ostensibly promoted; the loose woman's image in such works becomes a response to that earlier, and highly marketable, figure: in some sense a caricature reinforcing the norm by the very fact of her exceptionality.

When we turn from literary to social debates, things become even less clear cut than they may appear when looking at a purely literary depiction of society, pointing to ongoing struggles in popular culture about gender-right. The 1990 Mexican census turned up an interesting anomaly: approximately two million more women than men say they are married (16,081,451 married women versus 14,715,040 married men). Investigators suggest several possible explanations, ranging from the simple conclusion that someone is lying, to blaming the social phenomenon of absentee husbands due to periodic migrant work in the United States, to marking the persistence of the male tradition of keeping a second established household (*la casa chica*) (*Nexos* 90). The validity of the statistics is only partly the issue here; more to the point are the explanations themselves, which range from a sober consideration of male migration patterns and the problems they cause in Mexican households to a somewhat jocular marking of the "folkloric" tradition of multiple households.

In a different vein, the newspaper *Unomasuno* reports on a recent prosecution of a white slavery ring in Guadalajara, which sent at least three thousand young Mexican women to Japan over a period of ten years. According to the article, the attorney general "señaló que el delito por el cual fueron detenidos los dos extranjeros no es considerado como grave" [noted that the crime for which the two foreigners were arrested is not considered major] (Zenteno 1996, 1). These two reports seem to me to belong to a similar order of reporting, in which materials touching upon women who transgress traditional social boundaries are publicized more

as entertaining trivia than as hard news stories requiring sustained investigation or serious contemplation of the social structures that license such
gender bias.

In still another realm of popular culture, Víctor Manuel titled a song
about AIDS ("el SIDA," in Spanish, with a male gender-marker) "La
dama del alba" [Lady of the morning]. More than merely making the
gender shift from masculine to feminine, from *el sindrome* to *la dama*,
when referring to this deadly, sexually transmitted disease, Víctor Manuel's song evokes and participates in a long tradition in middle-class
culture of associating sex workers with the femme fatale stereotype and
of stigmatizing female sexuality as contaminated. Leo Bersani reminds us
that such cultural phenomena "'legitimate' a fantasy of female sexuality
as intrinsically diseased; and promiscuity in this fantasy, far from merely
increasing the risk of infection, is the *sign of infection*" (Bersani 1988,
211). According to this model of promiscuity as the linguistic/literary
*sign* of infection, a model indexed implicitly in the song, sexually transmitted diseases like AIDS are marked as and associated with the female
and transmitted via the promiscuous woman's unrestrained and unnatural
sexual activity to innocent male victims.

At the same time, Claudia Colimoro, president of an organization of
sex workers[1] called Mujeres por la Salud en Acción contra las Enfermedades de Transmisión Sexual y el SIDA [Women for Health in Action
against Sexually Transmitted Diseases and AIDS (MUSA), formed in
1985], presents a very different story. In contrast with the glamorous and
terrible fatal woman image of "La dama del alba," Colimoro points out
that 80 percent of Mexican female sex workers are mothers, a reality that
"hace que las mujeres tengan que llevar una vida doble para satisfacer las
necesidades de sus hijos y ocultar su ocupación y diciendo en su casa que
trabajan de meseras o enfermeras" [forces women to live a double life
in order to meet the needs of their children and hide their profession,
by saying at home that they work as waitresses or nurses] (Ojeda 1994,
78). Colimoro's observation hints at a tense and often bitter renegotia-
tion of accepted roles within the community, in which the prostitute and
the saintly mother occupy the same social space, revisiting the home and
the brothel environments and rendering each more complicated. And yet
even Colimoro does not go far enough in her observation, since reference
to a "double life" and "hiding their profession" suggests that the women
in prostitution tend uniformly to accept the strictures of the dominant
culture's moral rhetoric, which condemns them as immoral within the
home space while covertly demanding their sexual availability within the
various recognized zones of tolerance.

Unfortunately, existing scholarship does not well reflect the complexities of social practice, nor does it explore these women's complex sense of self, in which personal identity is reconstructed according to an awareness of the multiple spaces they inhabit. In their study of Mexican border cities, Daniel Arreola and James R. Curtis report that of the thirteen thousand citations in leading bibliographies on the borderlands, only four dealt with prostitution or with red zones (Arreola and Curtis 1993, 79). Furthermore, "the few published scholarly studies on contemporary aspects of prostitution in the border cities have been anthropological or sociological treatments based on research conducted during the 1960s and 1970s in either Tijuana or Ciudad Juárez.... In all cases, they were not comparative, lacked a spatial component, and were devoid of concern for the character of the place" (106). From the other side of the border, María Gudelia Rangel Gómez concurs: "Todas estas investigaciones han sido tan generales y en ocasiones tan particulares que los resultados de los mismos no pueden ser usados de manera apropiada. Sin embargo, algunos de los resultados de estas investigaciones reflejan un gran vacío de conocimiento respecto al comportamiento de la prostitución en México" [All this research has been so general, and in some cases so particularized, that the results cannot be used in an appropriate way. Nevertheless, some of the results of these investigations reflect the great vacuum of knowledge with respect to the behavior of prostitution in Mexico] (Rangel Gómez, n.d., 1). Her point is well taken. Studies that reach sweeping conclusions based on a minuscule sample of opinions are necessarily suspect; studies that are too narrowly focused have no generalizing force, and these two typical variations of existing scholarly argument on the topic most accurately reflect the lack of systematic research in the field.

To take a single example from among many: an article by Marta Lamas, informed by international feminism and published in her prestigious journal, *Debate feminista*, frames a discussion of street prostitution in two areas of Mexico City — Cuauhtémoc and Miguel Hidalgo — through a debate on symbolic violence and stigmatized behaviors (Lamas 1993). For a number of researchers involved directly in the field, this study has been particularly unfortunate with respect to its potential and actual consequences, because of its author's privileged location in Mexican society and Mexican government circles, and because the journal's international reception guarantees the article a certain influence. In a trenchant critique of Lamas's work, Armando Rosas Solís of the Universidad Autónoma de Baja California writes:

> El artículo tiene una estructura poco clara ya que salta de una presentación de tipo moralista, sin especificar si ésta se refiere al contexto mexicano o internacional, para ligarla inmediatamente al

contexto laboral y de ahí al político, para enlazarlo al movimiento de organización internacional de las prostitutas, para terminar con una serie de aseveraciones, que según se interpreten...son muy aventuradas....En todo el texto se ayuda de citas para hacer propuestas y un análisis de sus sentimientos hacia Claudia [una trabajadora sexual] no hacia la prostitución. (Rosas Solís 1995, 2)

[The article has a very unclear structure, since it leaps from a moralistic presentation, without specifying whether it refers to the Mexican or the international context, connecting it immediately to the context of labor and from there to politics, in order to tie in the international prostitutes' movement, concluding with a series of statements that, depending on how they are interpreted, . . . are very risky. . . . The whole of the text depends on quotes to make propos- als, and on the analysis of her feelings toward Claudia (a sex worker who assisted in the project) and not about prostitution.]

Lamas's article, then, purports to offer a new perspective on female pros- titution based upon the author's experience with government-sponsored research groups and confirmed by her own participant observer status in the prostitutes' community. Most significantly, however, as Rosas Solís comments, her work remains structured by the moral codes it decries, unconsciously speaking to the stereotypes that derive from a particular class location.

Lamas recognizes her own preexisting prejudices and discusses in the article how these biases were dissipated through her work with women in prostitution. She concludes the article with a call for more equitable treatment: "Una lucha por establecer mejores condiciones sociales tiene que incluir la tarea de desconstruir esta simbolización de las prostitutas como el mal o el pecado, tan ligada al pensamiento religioso y tan lejana de aspiraciones democráticas y libertarias" [A struggle to establish better social conditions has to include the task of deconstructing this symboliza- tion of prostitutes as evil or sin, so linked to religious thought and so far from libertarian and democratic aspirations] (132). In his commentary on this work, Rosas Solís marks precisely how this conclusion demonstrates that Lamas does not in fact deconstruct the model describing women as either decent or whores but rather reinstates the stereotypes her rheto- ric apparently rejects, in that her work asks not for a more nuanced understanding of the multiple roles and spaces occupied by sex work- ers in Mexico but rather for a revision of the dominant class's symbolic structure for appropriating the image of women in prostitution. In other words, the discussion that Lamas promotes remains within a single moral horizon and does not recognize alternative structures in which the figure of the prostitute interpolates herself — or is interpolated — on terms other than evil/not evil. This negative typing of the prostitute suggests to Rosas Solís that Lamas has a theoretical/structural stake in maintaining a discussion of prostitution in terms of marginality and stigma; her perspective, despite her six months of fieldwork on the Mexico City streets, remains that of her upper-class background rather than taking into account in a more than anecdotal way the perspective of the women who work within the very different class structures of prostitution.

The difference of opinion between Lamas and Rosas Solís has important material effects on how the studies of prostitution in the Mexican context are conducted and by whom. In Mexico, where competition for scarce resources is often fierce and where the different regions of the country vary widely, current research has tended to be so narrowly focused that the results are not useful in reaching generalizations of wider import, nor have they been able to influence public policy at a national level. Furthermore, prostitution has seldom been studied as a social phenomenon in itself at any level, creating a knowledge vacuum about a population that, with the appearance of AIDS, has recently come under greater scrutiny. In terms of my book, too, Rosas Solís's critique is equally valid since similar class-bound limitations of the theoretical frame define this study. Unlike Lamas's work, however, this book makes no pretense of speaking in the voice of those women engaged in sex work. Instead, the contribution of this book is, I hope, to point out the workings and the reversals of the stereotype of the sexually transgressive woman within that privileged sector of Mexican society that has access to books and means of publication, including the ambiguously testifyin' voices of loose women consciously speaking within and to the communities of those of us who make a practice of reading books.

Despite its wholly literary content, however, this book would remain incomplete without some effort to remind us of the reality in which it is grounded. What, then, finally, is the perspective of the easy woman who does not write and is not particularly concerned with framing her narrative for consumption by the privileged classes? With respect to the familiar stereotypes, Rosas Solís — whose conclusions are drawn from personal experience and from professional interviews with hundreds of sex workers in more than two dozen Mexican cities in seventeen states over a period of thirty years — suggests that

> [e]l simbolizar a las prostitutas como el mal, el pecado o la escoria social, no es algo que esté dirigido a las mujeres que tienen este oficio. . . . Se da para las mujeres que no siendo prostitutas se dedican

al goce sexual. . . . Por otro lado, este simbolismo, que tanto preocupa a los investigadores sociales, tiene sin cuidado a la mayoría de las mujeres que se dedican a la prostitución.

El otro simbolismo . . . de que la prostitución es un trabajo como cualquier otro, es por mucho algo que tampoco les preocupa. . . .

El problema de la prostitución no se debe de enfocar desde el punto de vista de demanda por parte de los hombres. . . . El problema se debe de abordar desde el punto de vista de la educación, familiar, escolar, de influencia del medio social, los cuales determinan las conductas y estereotipos a seguir, en estos radica la creación de necesidades y por lo tanto se da forma para que ésta se convierta en negocio. (6)

[Symbolizing prostitutes as evil, sin, or social trash is not something directed toward women who hold this job. . . . It is used for women who are not prostitutes and who are interested in sexual pleasure. . . . On the other hand, this symbolism, which so worries social scientists, does not bother the majority of the women who work in prostitution.

The other symbolism . . . of prostitution, as a job like any other, is something that most of the time doesn't worry them either.

The problem of prostitution should not be focused from the point of view of male demand. . . . The problem should be addressed from the point of view of education in families and in schools, of the influence of the social setting; these things determine conduct and the stereotypes people follow; from these derive the creation of necessity, and this opens the space for it to become a business.]

Rosas Solís points to the curious fact that it is within so-called decent society that women are excoriated for showing evidence of sexual desires. Thus, a woman who comes from a class background and upbringing that would seem to locate her within the category of "decent women" may be stigmatized with the hurtful epitaph of "whore" if she behaves in a manner understood within her social context as overly sensual/sexual. At the same time, within the social space of the prostitute's community, such accusations would be irrelevant; it is only with relation to the stigmatized and abjected female other that the insults acquire their force. In a similar manner, the debate over prostitution in terms of labor practice and laws is equally unrelated to the actualities of these women's lives. Typical discussions of labor organizing tend to base themselves upon a series of premises about the choice of a particular job and about the expectations of continuance in the labor force that do not hold true for prostitutes. As

Rosas Solís explains, sex workers can not be assimilated to other workers' movements because most women see prostitution as a purely temporary measure and one forced upon them by circumstances when all other labor options are closed (4).

We need also recall that for the women in prostitution, their work often occurs in a space that is not unambiguously illicit. Within the red zone, certain behaviors are accepted; outside of that particular space, both clients and prostitutes enter into another set of social, familial, and sexual relationships that may or may not reflect very different expectations for male and female behavior. It is, says Angie Hart, speaking of a Spanish red zone, precisely the permeability of the boundary between what is allowed and what is prohibited that makes the space of prostitution so titillating for clients: "Many clients...describe their presence in the barrio as 'vice.' However, they were able to enjoy this 'vice' in an atmosphere in which this was accepted as a leisure pursuit" (Hart 1995, 219). For both the men and the women, then, the relationships they establish within the red-light district are ambiguously coded. For the men, it is a leisure activity, often imagined not as strictly evil, but in terms of playing at transgression, of practicing a "vice" imagined within ironic quotation marks; for the women, it is a temporary and generally unpleasant job. If the clients sometimes express interest in crossing these limits between differently coded spaces — wanting home addresses or even begging to marry sex workers — it is the women themselves who make an effort to retain some separation in the two parts of their lives: rejecting overtures, only infrequently allowing men they have known as clients to become permanent members of their lives outside of their work.

In a large sample study of over sixteen hundred female sex workers in six cities taken in 1987–88, researchers with the Secretaría de Salud [Ministry of Health] in one series of interview questions asked women working in prostitution about attitudes toward a variety of sexual practices. The women responded to a number of statements and were asked to discriminate between what they found acceptable for themselves and acceptable for others. Clearly, these women know the codes of dominant-culture moral rhetoric; however, their own sense of appropriate behaviors does not always coincide with those norms. Evidence of this lack of fit between cultural mores can be observed in the results of the May 1988 interviews with 783 of these women, reproduced in part in table 1 (Secretaría de Salud 4:6–7).

Reading these responses in sequence elicits a picture of the loose woman's social context that is not strictly bound by dominant-culture moral strictures but looks a good deal more fluid. For instance, compare the high degree of agreement with the statement that faithfulness

## Table 1

| Behavior or attitude | OK for me | | OK for others | |
|---|---|---|---|---|
| | # | % | # | % |
| Sexual relations with someone of the same sex | 35 | [4] | 110 | 14 |
| Sexual relations with someone of the opposite sex | 737 | 94 | 690 | 88 |
| Sex before marriage | 289 | 37 | 315 | 40 |
| Extramarital relations | 224 | 29 | 255 | 33 |
| Sexual abstinence | 308 | 39 | 308 | 39 |
| Be faithful | 627 | 80 | 548 | 70 |
| Have sexual relations with unknown people | 342 | 44 | 327 | 42 |
| Pay for having sexual relations | 43 | [5] | 383 | 49 |
| Receive money for sexual relations | 641 | 82 | 539 | 69 |
| Use condom | 681 | 87 | 705 | 90 |
| Oral sex | 101 | 13 | 144 | 18 |
| Have homosexual friends | 318 | 41 | 372 | [48] |
| Have lesbian friends | 211 | 27 | 265 | [34] |
| Have prostitute friends | 625 | 80 | 536 | [68] |

to one's partner is an approved behavior (80 percent/70 percent; though about one-third of the women interviewed also find nothing particularly reprehensible in extramarital relationships) with the almost equally high agreement with the acceptability of the practice of receiving money in exchange for sexual favors (82 percent/69 percent). Likewise, the almost eight hundred women interviewed also evince a surprisingly high approval rate with respect to society in general (42 percent) for having sexual relations with strangers.

The findings of this large-scale questionnaire add to the picture I have been drawing in these pages of ambiguous attitudes on the part of women working in prostitution — partly determined by the women's background, partly coded with respect to the interlocutor (reader, client) and presumptions about his desires and expectations, and partly dependent upon the space of utterance (whether published in a book or interviewed in the workplace, in their homes, in a clinic, or at another location). Thus, for example, in an interview with Javier Aranda Luna, a street sex worker frames her comments with the reminder that telling her story to him is an alternative service for which the interviewer-client is paying, occurring within the space of paid sex and, thus, subject to the narrative ambiguities of the genre. "Con el nombre que quieras, tú pagas" [With whatever name you want; you're paying for it] (Aranda Luna 1990, 101) is the opening line of the recorded interview. Likewise, the narrative is structured temporally by the same considerations; the last anecdote she tells her interlocutor begins with the hint that it is offered as a kind of narrative bonus, like the extra pastry or piece of fruit a vendor will throw into the bag for the good customer: "ya para acabar, porque ya se acabó tu tiempo" [to finish up, because your time is up] (105).

Recently, María Gudelia Rangel Gómez has been working on a series of projects aimed at improving health services for sex workers in Tijuana and creating opportunities for them to learn more about sexually transmitted diseases and other health risks. In order to refine her research instruments, Rangel Gómez conducted a series of in-depth interviews with sex workers in that city. These recorded interviews complement the more general findings of the large statistical study made by the Ministry of Health by highlighting the complexities and ambiguities of the loose women's lives and by underscoring the range of their responses to circumstances that have shaped them. The final pages of this book summarize what I have learned from these tapes, speaking, finally, to the major ellipsis left open throughout this entire text.

These women range in age from their twenties to their fifties, have been involved in prostitution for a period ranging from a few weeks to many years, and work in a variety of establishments ranging from the least exclusive to the more expensive venues. While family circumstances vary, most of the women indicate that they come from the countryside, often from situations of extreme poverty. Family violence (father beating the mother, parents beating the children) is common, and the women frequently seek to escape from the abusive home either by forming partnerships with young men at a very early age (often as young as thirteen or fourteen) or by seeking work. They tend to fall into prostitution, which they may or may not drop in and out of over the years, from economic necessity, propelled either by the failure of a relationship or by intolerable working conditions in other jobs. Some of the women are wholly independent; others have partners; most have children. Some of their children and partners know about their jobs; others do not. Their attitudes toward the sex industry vary widely, but most women indicate that they create certain boundaries within their work and insist upon specific practices that allow them to establish a comfort zone within the profession, while at the same time they point to the failure of other women in the same community of sex workers to do so — a commonly seen contributing factor to drug addiction and venereal disease.

A number of the women indicate that their first sexual experience was rape. One describes being kidnapped in a car by a young man she knew only by sight and being so injured by the rape that her attacker took fright and dropped her off at a hospital. Another describes being coerced into having sex when she was thirteen. A third describes an acquaintance rape by her employer:

Pues como fue tan frío, tan cruel. No me la vas a creer, pero ese
señor después de violarme me pagó. Sí, me botó el dinero. Y yo
lo necesitaba. Yo estaba estudiando en ese entonces en Hermosillo
y trabajando y este señor era el gerente de la empresa, me ofreció
raite y de ahí en lugar de ofrecerme un raite, y yo le acepté raite
porque estaba lloviendo mucho, entonces, de ahí me llevó a un hotel. Así con todo lujo de violencia y prepotencia me metió a un
cuarto a empujones hizo lo que quiso, todavía me amenazó, y pues.
Nosotros habíamos sido de una condición no precisamente humilde,
sino clase medio pero muy retraídas por mi mamá. Entonces, la
educación que nos habían dado, ¿no? No fui capaz de reclamar ni
nada de eso ¿no? Me sentía avergonzada, me sentía humillada, im-
potente. Y lo tomé con tranquilidad, no me podía quejar con nadie.
Y ya después, pues seguí, seguí más o menos la misma ruta nomás
que seguí cobrando.

[How it was so cold, so cruel. You are not going to believe me,
but that man after raping me he paid me. Yes, he threw money at
me. And I needed it. I was studying in Hermosillo at that time
and I was working and that man was the manager of the business.
He offered me a ride and there instead of giving me a ride, well,
I accepted the ride because it was raining hard, and then he took
me to a hotel. There, with a lot of violence and superior strength
he forced and shoved me into a room, did what he wanted to do,
and even threatened me afterwards and then . . . We had come from
a background that was not precisely poor, more like middle-class,
but very repressed by my mother. So the education that she had
given us, well, I wasn't able to file a complaint about any of this,
right? I felt ashamed; I felt humiliated, impotent. And I took it
calmly; I couldn't complain to anyone. And afterwards, then I continued; I continued more or less down the same path only now I
began charging.]

This woman's story of rape by her employer is but a more violent form
of the many stories of sexual harassment in the job place, confirming a
widespread machista stereotype that unattached women are fair prey for
sexual advances. As one of the interviewees says simply, she became a
prostitute "porque no tengo estudio y cualquier parte que vaya el caso es
lo mismo" [because I don't have any schooling, and wherever I go it's the
same story]. Another woman describes moving from job to job in order to
avoid overfamiliarity on the part of male bosses and expresses her frustration when it is assumed that a young widow with a child will be sexually

available as one of the normal perks of the boss's job. Eventually, she concludes that there is no way to avoid being forced into sexual relations, so she decides to prostitute herself voluntarily and for pay: "[Y] resulta que al final de cuenta tienes que hacerlo . . . y ya no tienes hasta donde libertad de hacer" [And it turns out that you have to do it after all, . . . and you don't even have the freedom to do it]. Over and over again in these stories the women describe a societal structure based on male dominance in the workplace and male gender-right over women who are perceived as stepping out of their traditional roles, first by remaining unattached to a male protector and second by attempting to enter the realm of paid labor. The alternatives — to have sex with male co-workers or to constantly change jobs — are seen as increasingly unviable and unstable options.

The women freely admit that prostitution provides a better living than other unskilled labor, since a minimum-wage job is not enough for them even to buy sufficient food to support themselves and their family, much less pay the rent. Furthermore, besides paying for the food and rent, the relatively high wages earned in sex work allows for a certain discretionary income and consequently a certain freedom. Thus, while many of the women indicate that circumstances forced them into sex work, because voluntarily or involuntarily it would become part of any job, the narrowing of employment options paradoxically offers certain advantages to the woman who is able to use the system to her benefit. The women can choose the number of days and number of hours in a day they work; they can choose the number of clients they attend and pick specific clients from among the men soliciting their services; they can save their money and leave prostitution entirely or drop out for a period of time. Because sex work, while tension-wrought and exhausting, allows for this flexibility, several of the women describe holding other jobs in the informal economy as well as selling sexual favors; they talk about buying and selling items from the other side of the border, about working in shops, or about selling foodstuffs.

A number of women see in prostitution the opportunity to live an independent life, in which they are no longer dependent upon an abusive, unreliable, or unfaithful partner. As one woman says, "[N]o me gusta depender de nadie, ni que se posesionen de mi mente, de mi tiempo, de mi persona. No me gusta que me manejen por el hecho de estarme dando un cantidad a la semana o al mes" [I don't like to depend on anyone, nor to have anyone own my mind, my time, my body. I don't like them to control me by the fact of giving me so much per week or per month]. One woman tells Rangel Gómez that she has come to Tijuana from her home in the countryside for a few months only, so as to earn the money to pay off a debt. Another has come out of retirement to pay for ex-

penses inconsiderately incurred by her immediate former partner. Others
are saving money to establish a small business or to buy a truck. Still
another is working for a time because she wants to be able to give her
children the kinds of presents she missed as a child. Several women indicate that they are the sole support of extended families, including their
own children, their parents, and the families of siblings, and that they
work longer hours, or quit working for a time, depending on family necessity. As one woman among many notes, "[N]o me gustaba al principio
pero me hice la idea de que me tenía que gustar porque tenía que atender
a mi mamá, a mi hermana y dos niños que tengo" [I didn't like it at first
but I told myself that I had to like it because I had to take care of my
mother, my sister, and my two children].

This attitude of looking for the positive side of an experience that
otherwise would be very unpleasant is common to all the women Rangel
Gómez interviews. Importantly, the women in these interviews almost
invariably describe themselves as exceptions to the general rule within
the communities of sex workers and indicate that their difference resides
precisely in the attitude they bring to their work. Women who are egotis-
tical or uncertain of their motives and goals, say the women interviewed,
are the ones most likely to destroy themselves through substance abuse.
Women like themselves, who are able to step outside their immediate
environment and focus on the positive side of their jobs, are the ones
who survive, remain healthy, and have the intelligence to use the system
against itself. Most important among the positive aspects are the rewards
that accrue from seeing the family better itself; many of the women point
with pride to how well their own children and their nieces and nephews
have done, precisely because of the assistance that they have been able to
provide: these are children with enough to eat and decent clothes to wear,
children who have finished high school, technical school, or even college.
One woman even sees human development prospects within prostitution
itself, when it is approached with the right attitude: "[R]ealmente es una
escuela... si se toma de una manera positiva.... A mí me ha servido mucho en que he aprendido a valorar a la gente, a valorarme yo misma, a
comprender, a entender, a investigar también" [It really is a school,... if
taken in a positive way... It's helped me a lot in that I have learned
to value people, to value myself, to comprehend, to understand, and to
investigate as well].

At the same time, the women interviewed do not lose sight of the ugly
aspects of their lives. They freely recognize the potentiality for women
to get lost if they are not strong enough to overcome the environment,
which by its very nature is ugly and depressing. One woman describes
how difficult it is to work on a daily basis, "hagas o no hagas el acto

sexual" [whether or not you do the sex act]. She explains: "[E]s la tensión, es la desvelada, es el alcohol, es, aunque no fumes, ya estás fumando" [It's the tension; it's the lack of sleep; it's the alcohol; it's, even if you don't smoke, you're smoking anyway]. Another adds the stress of pretending to be happy and having to laugh when she least wants to laugh. Still another comments on the high degree of alcohol and drug use among the women: "A veces yo comprendo a las muchachas cuando yo las veo que se dan su pase de coca o de cristal y sus acá todos lo que traen. Yo las considero porque yo sé que tienen que aguantar a cualquiera, a cualquiera. Y para aguantar a cualquiera hay que, no hay que andar en sus cinco sentidos. Apenas tomándose unos tragos o la droga para que así pueda uno soportar a cualquier" [Sometimes I understand the girls when I see them and they shoot up their coke or their rock or their whatever it is that they bring. I feel sorry for them because I know that they have to put up with everyone, with everyone. And to put up with everyone, you can't go around sober. Only by drinking a few glasses or with drugs can one survive it]. Indirectly, in this manner, the women talk about their own drug or alcohol problems, while they directly and specifically describe themselves as the exception to this general rule of exhaustion, violence, and substance abuse.

In order to exert some control over their circumstances, these women describe techniques they employ to carve out a comfort zone for themselves in the midst of the tense, uncertain environment. One of the ways in which the women mark out boundaries within prostitution is by definition of specific practices that they use to create reserved spaces, often spaces on their bodies. Thus, all of the women interviewed insist that they require condom use of their clients, and, uniformly, any of the women who admit to having caught a venereal disease at some time in their lives insist that it occurred outside of work, with a partner who was not a client and with whom, hence, they were more careless about insisting upon safe-sex practices. One of the women says that her only experience of sexually transmitted disease dates from her youth, before beginning as a sex worker, when a boyfriend gave one to her, and she did not even realize why she was sick. Another woman comments that she was infected because she wanted a social life outside of work, one involving going out for dinner and to movies and showing affection to a man. However, "los hombres andan sueltos como las mujeres de las maquiladoras" [men run around loose like the women from the maquiladoras], and these contacts outside of the professional setting of prostitution to her mind cause all the problems because, unlike responsible sex workers, women and men who act promiscuously in an unprofessional manner tend to spread disease. Still another describes her disgust upon finding out that her partner has gonorrhea. She immediately had herself tested for the disease as well and was able to prove exactly where the guilt lay when her test turned out negative. In response, she not only threw her erstwhile boyfriend out of her life on the spot but refused to give him a ride home from the clinic in her car ("[N]o, no, no, le dije, no vayas a dejar aquí microbios" [No, no, no, I told him, you aren't going to leave your microbes in here]). Once again, I take these stories not so much as an accurate account of the relative safety from contagion within prostitution but rather as modern mythologies, cautionary tales that reverse the dominant culture's myth of prostitution as a site of infection. In these stories, unlike the more familiar middle-class tales of the evil women who make men sick by passing on their vile female-associated diseases, it is the hypocritical dominant culture that victimizes sex workers, who are constantly alert to these persistent threats that derive from a contaminated space outside formal sex work.

In an analogous manner, the women describe the specific sexual practices in which they engage with reference to a code that also sets boundaries indicating physical and mental reserve or even a kind of patriotic *pudor* [modesty]. When Rangel Gómez asks the women about sexual practices, the responses are surprisingly uniform: the women consistently indicate that they prefer "normal" vaginal sex. Some of them express ignorance about other sexual practices; some indicate that under special circumstances they will perform oral sex, albeit reluctantly; all vehemently deny that they ever agree to anal sex with a client. When the inquiry is made, one woman says she typically responds: "[S]oy mujer, no maricón" [I'm a woman, not a fag]. Another hints that such unnatural perversions could come only from foreigners or contagion by foreign practices: "Todavía soy muy mexicana, ¿verdad? Yo sexo anal no lo realizo por ningún concepto" [I am still very Mexican, right? I don't perform anal sex under any circumstances]. Another indignantly responds to the inquiry about sexual practices other than vaginal sex: "¡Jamás! Te estoy diciendo que yo soy limpia en todo aspecto sexual....Nunca jamás en la vida permití que me hicieron cochinadas ni que me dijeran que yo tenía que hacerlo" [Never! I am telling you that I am clean in every sexual aspect....I never ever in my life permitted anyone to do dirty things to me nor to tell me that I had to do it]. Still another describes her technique with insistent clients; she tells them, "[M]ira, la verdad es que quiero llegar virgen de un lado de mi cuerpo para el día que yo me case" [Look, the truth is that I want to arrive virgin at least on one side of my body on the day I get married]. Again, what the women are marking with these comments is a certain comfortable social space, perhaps real, perhaps constructed in the imaginary exchanges of interview expectations. Clearly, demands for oral and anal sex are extremely common — as one woman notes, "[M]e imagino que como la novia o su mujer no pueden vienen con una a ver si pega" [I imagine that since the girlfriend or the wife can't, they come to one of us to see if they can talk us into it] (Aranda Luna 1990, 99); what the interviewed women are signaling is a particular personal reserve, a chastity within prostitution that implicitly figures as one of the differentiating qualities separating these women interviewed from the mass of sex workers who are, perhaps, less stable, less moral, more prey to the destructive side of their jobs.

Another way the women ameliorate the insecurities of their work is through their choice of clients. Many of the women in this very international sex market indicate that they prefer Mexican clients, since the common cultural grounding gives them a certain comfort zone both in knowing what to expect of the sex act and in establishing a relation beyond sex that involves some conversation. As one woman says, "[A]mericanos poco, porque estoy estudiando inglés entre otras cosas, no lo domino bien. Además me dan un poquito de desconfianza porque hay señores muy tranquilos y como no son mexicanos no conoce uno muy bien la reacción. Es otra cultura pues. Otra todo" [Few Americans, because while I am studying English among other things, I don't speak it well. Besides, they make me a little uncomfortable because there are very calm men, but because they are not Mexicans, you don't know how they will react. It's another culture. Another everything]. For many of the women, talking to clients not only alleviates their natural anxieties about exposing themselves to unknown men but also helps reduce the tedium and disgust of their jobs: "Yo platico, cuento, o sea me doy amistad primero y luego. Para que no me tomen como lo que, ta, rápido y lo que viene.... Y ya pues se va formando la cosa más bonita para que no sea tan, vaya, tan fastidioso" [I talk, tell stories, that is, I give friendship first and then. So that they don't just grab me like, quick and then do it.... And that way, well, something nicer develops so that it is not, so, so boring]. Several of the women indicate that this dialogue is equally important to the men, overriding their ostensible purpose for seeking out a sex worker: "[M]uchas veces ya a la hora de hacer la relación ya no es tan importante para mí el sexo o sea porque yo les introduzco una cierta terapía mental del cual muchas mujeres ni en su casa.... [E]l cliente mentalmente cambia lo que es el sexo por una convivencia" [Often when the time comes to have the relation sex is not so important for me because I offer them a certain mental therapy that many women don't even in their homes.... The client mentally changes from what is sex to conviviality]. For another woman, conversation with clients has become her specialty, to the degree that many of them seek her out primarily for her sympathetic ear. In these cases, she suggests that she and her client go to a more congenial setting — a restaurant or café — and talk for a while, with sex as an open option, paying her a modest rate for her time.

For the women who prefer foreign clients, other factors create the comfort zone. One woman who says she prefers to work with Iranians, Arabs, and other foreigners over either Mexicans or U.S. visitors indicates that she prefers such clients because they are clean, pay well, and are careful to use safe-sex practices — sometimes even doubled condoms. One of the women offers a kind of hierarchy of preferences, reinscribing cultural biases and racisms into the very different space of professional sex work: "[D]e preferencia japonés. Y de allí pues simplemente oriental porque la tienen chiquita, chiquita. . . . De allí . . . un mexicano guapo y pues casi no me cae el gabacho porque se creen muy inteligentes. . . . Entonces, ya y de allí . . . como no hay más, pos el árabe" [Preferably Japanese. After that any Oriental because they have tiny, tiny ones. . . . After that a handsome Mexican, and then I really don't like Americans because they think they're so smart. . . . And after that, if there is nothing else, then an Arab].

Most of the women give an impression that the sorting process is relatively easy; men tend to like to return to the same woman over and over, and many of the women find it less tension-producing to go with repeat clients. Some of the women specialize in tourists and foreign clients; others indicate a definite preference for Mexicans. In any case, they feel that experience allows them to size up a client relatively quickly according to criteria like cleanliness, courtesy, and degree of drunkenness. One of the problems that frequently arises, however, involves the intersection between the client's choice of women and the women's freedom to choose her clients. While understated in the interviews, these considerations are clearly a common source of conflicts between women, sometimes escalating to violence. Thus, for instance, one woman's "regular" client may approach another woman for sex, or, alternatively, another sex worker may inadvertently approach as a potential client a man that one of the other women considers hers. These contacts are fraught with dangerous possibilities for misunderstandings and hard feelings.

Condom use is one of the most contested problems in establishing the ground rules for a sexual relationship between a woman and her client. While Marta Lamas's study of street prostitution in Mexico City arrives at the conclusion that "ninguna *chica* se niega a hacerlo sin condón, pues eso representa perder al cliente" [no girl would refuse to do it without a condom, since that would mean losing the client] (Lamas 1993, 123),[2] Rangel Gómez's interviewees are far more united and adamant about condom use, to the degree that one of the more common topics of conversation involved an exchange of stories and suggestions of methods to convince reluctant clients. As one of the women notes, it is important to have an unbreakable agreement among the women that they will only accept clients with condoms since, as she says, 99 percent of the men try to get out of using one: "[V]amos a suponer que yo aceptara irme con un cliente sin condón, al ratito ya le gustó otra y también sin condón. Y es donde va el contagie" [Let's suppose that I agreed to go with a client without a condom, and then after a while he likes another woman and also without a condom. And that is where epidemics start]. One of the more common arguments is to say that the sex worker knows she is disease-free because of her regular checkups but that the client can give no such assurances; this argument has the benefit of reinforcing the message that the professional sex worker offers advantages to a man careful of his health and that the red zone is a safer environment for nonmonogamous men than the larger community. The alternative argument is also common: that the client may believe he is disease-free, but since he cannot have the same confidence about his partner, condom use is in his best interests.

The national *Informe técnico* indicates that 95 percent of the sex workers surveyed feel that prostitutes should use condoms (Secretaría de Salud 1989, 6:4), that 57 percent of them used condoms in the nine months previous to the study (6:8), and that approximately 15 percent use them at all times (6:11). Obviously, the responses of the women interviewed in depth in Tijuana, in their uniform insistence on their unwavering commitment to consistent condom use with their clients, do not accord with the national statistics. I would not attempt to resolve the question of whether the women are lying or not, though anecdotal information from clients who use the Internet suggests that condom use in Tijuana is a universal requirement for the women with whom they have paid sex,[3] but I would like to point out in evaluating these responses merely that these women's awareness of the importance of condom use indicates a consciousness of the issues involved in safe-sex practices and serves implicitly to define two important ideological spaces: (1) of the woman interviewed as wholesome and intelligent and (2) of prostitution as an infection-free site where knowledge is put into practice, in contrast to the less professional, less careful practices of the general population. Once again, comments about consistent condom use help to create certain limits and boundaries within the sex worker's environment and to confirm her self-worth.

At another, closer level of analysis, still another boundary can be established, in this case linguistically. Frequently the women shift from first person to second or third person at crucial points in their narration, thus distancing themselves from a disagreeable personal experience. For example, in the quote that follows, the woman describes her experiences in the bar where she works in the second person, displacing and generalizing her experiences, while her comments on her home life are expressed in the first person:

> Y va de todo, y tanto pues tienes que soportar un viejo borracho que anda hasta las mangas y te diga cosas y tienes que aguantarte porque estás ahí. No vas a darle una cachetada, pues no, ¿cómo te verías? todo el mundo te corre. Te aguantas y te quitas nada más del lugar.... Sales ya aquí, piensas, a respirar aire fresco. Es lo que te digo. Yo llego a la casa y quisiera... pero como llego tan cansada, tan malhumorada, a veces fastidiada. Duermo, descanso y al día de mi descanso lo primero que hago, me levanto, me doy un regaderazo, y me voy a caminar al parque.

> [All kinds go there, and so many that you have to put up with an old drunk who's falling all over himself and tells you things and you have to put up with it because you're there. You aren't going to slap his face, oh no, how would that look? Everyone would throw you out. You put up with it, and you just move from that spot.... You are getting out of here, you think, to breathe fresh air. That is what I am telling you. I arrive home and I wish... but I arrive so tired, in such a bad mood, sometimes disgusted. I sleep, I rest, and on my day off the first thing I do is I get up; I take a shower, and I go for a walk in the park.]

There is a certain poetry to this passage, which falls so neatly into two parts. The second-person narration of the first few sentences evokes a restricted space, where movement is limited, as are options for verbal responses to provocative remarks. In the bar, the woman feels dirtied and yearns for fresh air. The second half of the passage provides the counterpart to the first; here is the cleansing of body and soul; the shower, the walk in the park, the recuperation of the "I."

This division of the self in language — of the first-person voice shifting to second or third person and back again — duplicates a common division in the essential spaces of the woman's life. Many of the women hide their real jobs from their families, telling them that they are waitresses in a restaurant, cashiers in a store, assembly plant workers, salespeople, or street vendors or that they clean houses, in some cases using a secondary source of income as a disguise for their primary one. Many sex workers, especially those with children, avoid the topic of their jobs with their families; as one woman says, "[Y]o no les voy a dejar

el trauma a mis hijos" [I am not going to leave my children with that
trauma]. More realistically, perhaps, as one woman says, it would be very
difficult for their children not to guess what is going on at some point:
"[P]osiblemente cuando era niño pues lo podía engañar. Yo sé que hoy
siendo él un adulto no lo voy a poder engañar porque en primer lugar
una persona que no tiene un empleo, que es una mujer, que se ve más or
menos físicamente y que trae mucho dinero en la bolsa y compra carro y
hace esto y hace lo otro, pues es muy difícil de que alguien se la trague"
[Maybe when he was a child I could fool him. I know that now that he is
an adult I will not be able to fool him because in the first place a person
who doesn't have a job, who is a woman, who is more or less good looking
and who carries around a lot of money in her purse and buys a car and
does this and that, well, it's difficult for someone to swallow]. Similarly,
while extended families may receive a distanced and buffered version of
the women's employment history, most of the women's long-term, live-in
partners know about their girlfriend's profession, though considerations
of "respect" make that profession an open secret that is not discussed. In
response to the question, Would you tell your son about your job? one
woman says specifically: "No, porque yo sé que él lo tiene sobrentendido.
Y si él guarda silencio es por respeto. Entonces, si yo hablo, ¿qué caso
tiene?" [No, because I know that he implicitly understands. And if he
maintains silence, it is out of respect. Thus, if I speak, what purpose
would it serve?]. Here, the delicate dance of silenced mutual understanding creates a closer and more respectful relationship with her child, in
which each of them respects implicit distances established by love and
custom.

In any case, for most of these women the topic of their work is
more or less taboo outside their working environment; whether out of
shame, or concern about showing the children a bad example, or simply
a kind of unspoken respect for privacy on their partner's and their children's part, the woman's profession remains unacknowledged. "A veces
digo yo, no tiene por qué saber de mi vida cualquier persona. . . . Tengo
muchas . . . amistades pero no, muchas no saben ni la mitad de mi vida
porque soy muy reservada" [Sometimes I say, not just anyone has the
right to know about my life. . . . I have many . . . friends but, no, many
don't know even half of my life because I am very reserved]. Once again,
virtues valued by the dominant society — reserve, respect, caretaking —
are reinscribed with a difference in the double life of the sex worker,
where what is spoken and what remains unsaid, both at work and in the
home, constitute the very warp and woof of her life.

This double-voiced silence around an open secret is not always the
rule. One of the women interviewed indicates that in her family the re-

lationship she has built with her children has allowed them to go beyond the tacit recognition of her profession to a point at which the mother's job becomes an unspoken matter of concern. The woman indicates that all her children know exactly what she does for a living and that their support is extremely important to her in maintaining an integrated life. She argues reasonably that since her children know exactly what their mother is doing and why, they will never feel the betrayal or shame that afflict some families whose mothers try to maintain the secret of their real jobs. She also uses her life as an object lesson for her children on the values of education and points proudly to the success her children have achieved in school. Likewise, another woman tells Rangel Gómez that her children have always known about her profession; however, now that her daughters are reaching the age of having boyfriends, they have decided as a family that they do not want the boyfriends to know, for fear that it would lead to misinterpretations of explanations that could only be awkward.

While most of the women indicate that they prefer to keep the two halves of their lives completely separate, a common theme running through the interviews is the economic necessity of working in prostitution in order to support a family and, in a parallel commentary, the importance of maintaining a focus on the family when working so as to preserve their health and self-respect. Thus, paradoxically, the same forces that propelled them into prostitution are the ones that give them the strength to survive its destructive aspects. Maternity, then, is both a precondition for many of these women as well as the single most important factor in defining their sense of self. "Yo me dediqué por entero a mi hijo" [I dedicated myself entirely to my child], says one woman. Another adds, "Sea yo una prostituta,... siempre las tuve bien cuidadas" [I may be a prostitute, but my daughters were always well taken care of], implicitly recognizing the dominant-society prejudice that sees women working in prostitution as irresponsible and evil: the sinner or femme fatale stereotype. Another woman, whose children know that she works in prostitution, uses her own life as an object lesson in motivating her children to work hard at their studies. In reproducing one such conversation for the interviewer, she cites what she would tell her child: "[Y]o no quiero que Ud. sea lo que yo soy. Si Ud. sabe que está mal lo que yo estoy haciendo por esto y esto otro, yo quiero que estudie y que Ud. sea muy diferente a mí" [I don't want you to become what I am. If you know that what I am doing is wrong because of this or that, I want you to study so that you can be different from me]. In this instance, the woman marks out for the interviewer a clear distance between what she is (a responsible mother) and what she does (sells her body to pay for her children's education). Likewise, the language she uses in describing the conversation with her child projects a household in which open communication between the parents and the children is accompanied by distinct signs of respect — the use of the formal *Usted* rather than the informal *tú*, pointing to an old-fashioned courtesy between interlocutors, a courtesy and formality that exist as well on the level of the dialogue between the interviewer and the woman interviewed, also in this case couched in the *Ud.* form rather than the *tú* used in many of the other interviews.

The responsible mother is not only valued as an absolute social good; she is perceived as a survival mechanism in the otherwise destructive world of the red zone. One example stands for many:

> Pero he visto muchas mujeres que nada más se prostituyen para drogarse y ni siquiera se dan cuenta de como están sus hijos. Nos les importa su alimentación, ni estudio, ni nada. Nada más ellas se prostituyen para el beneficio de ellas, para satisfacer los deseos que ellas traen. Y eso es lo que a mí en la prostitución no me admira de nada. Simplemente uno se metió a esa clase de vida pues hay que sacarle provecho y cuidarse uno.

> [But I have seen a lot of women who just prostitute themselves for drugs and don't even notice their children. They don't worry about their food, their schools, or anything. They just prostitute themselves for their own benefit, to satisfy the desires that they carry around. And that is something about prostitution that I don't care for at all. Simply put, if one has gotten into that kind of life, one has to get the best out of it and take care of oneself.]

The pathos evoked in these comments is too strong to be ignored. This woman eloquently defines the constraining qualities of a sex worker's life; in order to work in the dehumanizing world of the red zone, self-respect and respect for others are the keys to survival. At the same time, to be able to function at all, the women must separate within themselves the roles of mother/caretaker and sex worker. However, if the separation is too absolute, the woman falls prey to the dangers of the prostitute's world: the drugs, the egoism.

And yet, of course, the very process of interviewing brings together the two parts of the women's lives, and whether or not it is a consequence of the questionnaire, the resulting picture is strikingly consistent with stories of professional women in other, more traditionally accepted venues. Overwhelmingly, stories about professional women — whether a Tijuana street prostitute or a prominent lawyer like Hillary Rodham Clinton —

at some point place emphasis on the woman's concept of herself with respect to her home and her children: a feature generally elided in stories of professional men. It is assumed that a woman's identity is most clearly elucidated with respect to her home life, whereas a man's identity is consumed in his profession. This factor, with respect to the in-depth interviews of Tijuana women involved in sex work, and perhaps with respect to their real lives as well, allows them that most important distancing quality: for whatever good they see in their profession has to do with service to others, and it is the weak or the unwary who are consumed by the profession and hence destroyed.

What is most powerful for me in these interviews is the glimpse they permit into the lives of these women, as women, neither symbols of evil, metaphors of disease, nor displaced representatives of a narrative style. Their stories speak to the elliptical silence around the image of the sexualized woman in modern Mexico and open up an entirely new space for continued study, one that does not merely repeat dominant-culture understandings — even though the women themselves clearly articulate a selective appropriation of these mores, at least in dialogue with non-prostitute interviewers. By focusing on the sex worker as a deviant or marginal member of society, commentators in the past have tended to greatly undercomplicate a very complex issue that cuts directly to the heart of how men perceive women and how women perceive themselves in variously different adumbrated social and narrative interactions. Even with respect to the degree that the sex worker's livelihood "depends on the maintenance of the very ideology which degrades her and makes her into a social outcast" (Davidson 1995, 9), her liminal status in society casts a strong light on questions of the social construction of gender and on issues of control and consent in human relationships. Over and over again, in these interviews with Tijuana prostitutes we are brought up short by the need to understand the dynamics of the interview process itself, in which, inevitably, a narrative about the self is constructed in dialogue and situationally. Barbara O. de Zalduondo, Mauricio Hernández Avila, and Patricia Uribe Zúñiga remind us that an understanding of the social context of paid sex requires the perspectives of clients, pimps and bar owners, rooming house owners, and police and other authorities (Zalduondo, Hernández Avila, and Uribe Zúñiga 1991, 173). Likewise, a fuller social characterization of the sex worker would include, minimally, the perspective of her family — and this perspective, except in extremely unusual situations, is impossible to access.

James Clifford describes the predicament of postcolonial ethnography as an unnerving process of negotiating across resistances while at the same time dealing with the moral tensions, inherent violence, and tactical dissimulations of modern fieldwork. His comments seem apposite to the way we undertake a study of marginalized persons in society as well:

> Some "authentic encounter," in Geertz's phrase, seems a prerequisite for intensive research; but initiatory claims to speak as a knowledgeable insider revealing essential cultural truths are no longer credible. Fieldwork... must be seen as a historically contingent, unruly dialogic encounter involving to some degree both conflict and collaboration in the production of texts. Ethnographers seem to be condemned to strive for true encounter while simultaneously recognizing the political, ethical, and personal cross-purposes that undermine any transmission of intercultural knowledge. (Clifford 1988, 90)

Existing scholarship on sex workers in Mexico does not well reflect the complexities of social practice, nor does it explore the relationship to these women's complex sense of self, in which personal identity is reconstructed according to an awareness of the multiple spaces they inhabit. In this chapter too, in commenting upon the prostitutes' stories — created in dialogue with a non–sex worker interviewer — we find ourselves striving for some version of "true encounter" in the realization that the stories we hear, or eavesdrop upon, are narratives shaped for a particular audience and with a particular political, ethical, and personal stake. Wendy Chapkis suggests "we need new tools that allow us to listen to the different stories told without simply asking 'is this True?' We need tools that help us listen for meaning rather than fact — to ask what it means that a story is told in this way" (Chapkis 1991, 2). The question is still open.

# Appendix

# Transcripts

What follows are selected passages chosen from thirty in-depth 1995 interviews between María Gudelia Rangel Gómez and sex workers in Tijuana, originally solicited for background information in creating a public health questionnaire to address specific health-related issues of concern to CONASIDA (Consejo Nacional para la Prevención y Control del SIDA [National Commission for the Prevention and Control of AIDS]). The participants are identified by pseudonyms.

## Lola

**G:** Can you tell me why you decided to work?

**L:** Well, because economically I need money. But I almost always worked in Los Angeles. And I didn't know where to go, but I had to work.

**G:** What kind of work did you do in Los Angeles?

**L:** I worked in a restaurant.

**G:** In a restaurant. Did you have a passport, or...?

**L:** I used to, but they took it away, and that's why I am here. That's why I haven't left.

**G:** And why did you decide to work in [prostitution]?

**L:** The truth is because I can earn more money. Economically I can't do anything with a single salary. It doesn't stretch even to cover food. Because with a minimum wage no one can eat, that's for sure. Not even beans; even they're expensive.

**G:** Can you tell me about your experience working there?

**L:** My experience? Living something that one has not lived before but that is not very pleasant. To stay up all night, to drink and do things, that is, to be pleasant when one doesn't feel like it. To have to be there laughing when it's not really so, right? It's not a good experience; they are experiences...that happen.

**G:** What do you do to pull together the family budget? Do you have money problems now?

**L:** Yes, a lot of them. Economically, yes, because I'm a little behind, and my children are in school and need quite a bit of money.

**G:** Do you feel that although you work, for example, in a place like a nightclub, that it poses any problems for your family life, for your children, for you?

**L:** It's not a problem in and of itself; what happens is that society has always been like this. This type of work is the worst, and it is what is rejected, right? But in and of itself, it's a job like any other. Because any person in any job could be behaving exactly the same, but they just cover up.

**G:** And the man that you married, what did you think of the way he looked, the way he acted with you?

**L:** Yes, I liked him, only that he was a mommy's boy.

**G:** Did you love him?

**L:** Well, at the time I thought I loved him, but sometimes one gets confused. One thing is to be in love, and another thing is to love, and one has to get used to that.

**G:** Do you think he loved you?

**L:** Maybe he was just like me.

**G:** How would you have liked him to be with you? If you could have asked him to change something so you could be happier, what would it be?

**L:** Of course, not living right with his family.

**G:** Can you tell me more about that? What was the...?

**L:** Well, you know, his family had a lot of influence over him. What his family said, had to go, in fact...A man will never reach his potential if he is doing what the family tells him. It has to come from him.

**G:** How did the separation happen? Tell me a little.

**L:** It came about because his mother wanted him to have another woman, and they chose one for him even though we were married. They wanted him to have a different women and kept after him until he went along.... They changed him totally.

**G:** I don't know if you can tell me, what is it like in this environment? What do you think about this? What feelings do you have?

**L:** I think that, well, it's a job like any other job, but, well, for me it is not pleasant. They think that one is destined for that one's whole life. Of course there are people like us who just can't make it economically, and there is nothing else we can do but to be there. We don't have any other opportunity. We have to be here.

**Aurora**

**A:** My father was a salesman. When he died, my mother took us to Acapulco. In fact, I might have been born in Michoacán. My birth certificate and all that is from Acapulco, so I can't consider myself from Michoacán.

**G:** When did you go to work for the first time in any job?

**A:** The very first time, I was about fifteen years old and I worked... What did I work at? The first time I worked in a shoe store in Acapulco. Then in a furniture store, then I went and worked in a tobacco shop, then in the Hyatt Hotel in Acapulco. That was where I began this. Well, I had already been widowed for several years and I had a lot of problems in my jobs because I always collaborated sexually and, well, because I never wanted to get myself into a... The thing is, in my mind I told myself that if I am going to do it I am going to do it as it ought to be and not to go around doing it with one guy and with another and messing myself up with married men who are only here to mess one up. And because they see you a widow and because they see you divorced, and they see you young and with a child. But it always comes out. So then I left Acapulco and went to Guadalajara to work. There I began at twenty-six; I was about twenty-six years old. I worked about four years straight. I left; then I bought myself a house in Cancún. I lived there in Cancún for about seven years, inactive. And then I went back to it for about a year and a half and just now spent another five years in Cancún. And here I am again for two or three months. So in fact the longest period I worked was when I was twenty-six, because at that time my son was very small and in school. I have been alone mostly. Just the kid and I.

**G:** And can you tell me what made you decide to take a job as a sex worker?

**A:** It was precisely the same thing as my whole life: the economic situation more than anything else. Because it is not for nothing, but often influences you that men do not respect you at work. When one is working, one wants to have a calm life, but you have to be constantly changing jobs every little while because otherwise you have to sleep with the boss, not to mention that they only pay you the going rate for a salary. All sorts of things. And you find yourself becoming his mistress and his personal prostitute. The thing is, I always analyzed that and how it was possible that I fought it so much. And the long and short of it is that I was offended. And then I met a girl, an Uruguayan woman, and it was she who invited me to Mexico City the first time to a dinner with some workers and it was there. That was the very first time, in Mexico City. I was there for about a weekend, and after that I already had friends in Guadalajara, and there I went with her. The fact is that . . . in those days when one was alone with a small child, and a widow, the guys were harassing you sexually all the time. And you say to yourself, Why?, you're offending me. And it turns out that you have to do it after all because besides the fact that you need the money, in any case you are doing it after all. And you don't even have the freedom to do it. Because they turn it into another situation. And it is really hard, in fact, when one is young, and single, and has a child. It was a tough situation.

**G:** And during those five years when you stopped working, what did you do?

**A:** I was a housewife. I was with my partner. And I worked sometimes in other things, since I speak other languages; I even have some skills. But sometimes, like right now for example, in my case there is a big amount of money that I owe that I can't pull together with a salary, so then I have to do it. I think that I can try to sell my house. If they tell me that it's taken care of tomorrow or even right now, I won't wait a minute, I'll go back right away because I don't have the slightest wish to have to work here.

**G:** Are you living with someone right now?

**A:** No, and it was precisely because of living with someone that time went by and my debts piled up. A person that wouldn't let me work — I'm not saying work in this, but in any type of job. He wanted me there at his disposition twenty-four hours a day. That type of man that wants you so that you are just there cooking and being there for him, nothing else, and these absurd jealousies and the whole thing is selfishness. So that now that I have so many debts, it's better that I came far away. I didn't even say good-bye.

**G:** And more or less what type of client did you usually deal with? What kind of people were they? What you saw.

**A:** What I looked for in a client was someone with whom I wouldn't feel too bad. More or less like this: that he didn't look drugged, that he didn't look extremely drunk, that his body looked clean. A certain clean personality, right? That more than anything. The age is not important; what is more important for me is the personality. His mouth, his behavior, self-assurance, a kind of education. Because besides, I don't have such a good character myself. I sometimes get in the mood of "Enough already! Why are you grabbing me? Hicks!" I defend myself.

**G:** When you are working, can you give yourself the luxury of choosing your clients?

**A:** At any particular time, yes, of course yes, because there are always two or three or four clients and you rank them in all the aspects you wish if you want to have a relationship with anyone at any particular moment. It's even important to have a conversation.

**G:** At any time did any client that you recall ever hurt you physically?

**A:** Of my clients, never. Although there was once a problem and I was involved in it, and for that reason also I left, because I didn't like it that they treated me that way. . . . What happened was one night we went out with a man and his brother, a young guy who had another woman, and another girl. And it all went well. And the next day the man shows up behaving very aggressively toward me and almost trying to beat me because he accused me of having taken his gold watch. So then I said, " . . . [Y]ou and I have never been together. I never left the other guy." After about forty minutes of this, the girl arrives and tells him, "Hey, remember that you gave me your watch? I came to give it back to you because you were so drunk that you had forgotten you gave it to me to take care of." But by that time I was so terrified that the next day I packed my suitcases and left. Because I am not used to putting up with these things. For one reason, because I don't provoke them. And second, it hurts me a lot that people confuse me with someone else. And then of course he begged my pardon. And he even wanted to give me something for making me upset. The guy didn't know what to do. He offers me a bottle of cognac: "Here, have a little glass of cognac for your nerves. Forgive me, really, you see it was that I was so drunk." And I said to myself, no, better that I leave because ... And then afterward I began to cry, on account of the depression that grabbed me. I suffered from a tremendous moral and spiritual depression.

**G:** How long does a sexual relation last? What is it like?

**A:** A half-hour, at most. Because there is afterward, and I like to get together with the person a little. I have the idea in my head that although they are paying for a service, it's not just a service but also a companionship. A moral and spiritual companionship, and that they too need to share things sometimes. Often when it is time for the relationship the sex is no longer so important perhaps because I provide a certain mental therapy that many women do not, whether at home or in the street. They grab on to me as their friend afterward.

**G:** And now that you are speaking of it, as a sex worker, how do you think that you ought to treat a client, and how should he treat you?

**A:** Well, that's exactly what I am telling you about. With a lot of subtlety, a lot of intelligence, and along the way trying to have a certain conversation. So that the client mentally changes what is sex for being together.

**G:** Do you remember ever having sexual pleasure in a relation with a client?

**A:** Well, yes. If the client also is able to make me feel comfortable and has treated me well, and there are people who also look for — just because they pay a woman doesn't make her a wastepaper basket. They also try to show that even though they've paid something they are capable of transmitting desire to a woman. The truth is, it's very nice to meet this type of person. Because in any case you have to make them feel that way. It's a "I give you, you give me," but if we can do it together then it's "what can I do, what can you do." So it's better, right? To get something out of it.

**G:** When you married for the first time, you say your husband died?

**A:** Yes. The marriage lasted ... I got married when I was almost nineteen until I was twenty-six.

**G:** And how was your intimate relationship with your husband?

**A:** Well, it was a little bit different from many marriages because since he was a reporter for a newspaper he had to travel a lot, so we traveled a lot too. And we had problems, because with the baby it was hauling everything. But the fact is that he was a good person with me. Except that sexually, he was only interested in his own satisfaction. And there I was, a hot Acapulcan woman with her hormones all turned on. And the truth is, I stuck with it only because I respected him a lot, because sexually there was nothing. Besides the fact that he was one of those who falls asleep on top of you, snoring in your ear and everything. Even that. No way, it was horrible.

**G:** And after that you had another partner?

**A:** Yes.

**G:** And how were your sexual relations with him? How did he treat you?

**A:** Definitely a lot better. That was where I was sexually awakened. Because right away you fall in love, and that's another story, right? It's a different thing. There isn't so much money between you, but there are many other things to compensate. Of course, when you say, "Well, enough of me being here all happy," and that was the time that I went to work because my son was there suffering the consequences of my happiness. At that time I didn't have even enough money to pay his school; I didn't even have enough to feed him. So I picked up and left. In my marriage there was a lot of money, a lot of everything, but no stability as a couple in the home. It was a cold relation but there was no...we didn't have a home.

**G:** How many partners have you had?

**A:** You mean that lived with me? Two or three. Three at the most.

**G:** And what was your experience with your last partner?

**A:** That's exactly what I'm telling you about, that I got divorced. A very selfish person that does not want...Do you mean in the moral or the sexual sense?

**G:** Moral and sexual.

**A:** Morally and emotionally and all that he is very selfish since he just wanted to have me at his disposition. With respect to the sexual question, the truth is that many times you don't even say that you are in love. A sexual passion is all there is and nothing else. Because it turns out that the man is very good at doing the sexual act, and so then you fall in love and there you are, passionate, right? And for that reason too I had to break off the relation. It was hurting me from all sides.

**G:** And did any of your partners ever beat you?

**A:** No. It was more that I hit them.... Look, for example on that occasion I was telling you about, I couldn't get rid of that person because there was this thing where he wanted to grab my car keys with the suitcases. I was already leaving with my suitcase. And then my purse; he grabbed my purse so that I wouldn't leave. So then I grabbed his T-shirt and gave him a good bite so that he would let go of my purse. And I did get it back.

**G:** How old were you when you had your first sexual relation?

**A:** I was...It was before I was fifteen years old, but it wasn't a sexual relation. It was a rape.

**G:** And what happened, how...?

**A:** It was an aggressive rape. He didn't beat me, but there was force; the guy overpowered me, pulling off my clothes and...

**G:** Did you know this person?

**A:** I only knew him by sight, and I didn't have any kind of friendship or other relation with him. He stopped me, well, like the dogs, just checking out his prey and looking for an opportunity. He practically kidnapped me, in his car.

**G:** And what did you do after he raped you?

**A:** Well, I didn't do anything, because he ripped me totally apart and I lost consciousness. Then he took me to a hospital, and isn't it just like life, that there in the hospital was my sister's mother-in-law.... So she came to help me, and there I was pouring streams of blood.... It turns out that the doctor in that clinic was a good friend of his. So he told him, "Do you know what? This happened. Help me out. Fix her up, sew her up, do what you want. But make her well because she's been bleeding badly for quite a while." So then my sister's mother-in-law went and talked to the doctor. She asked what had happened to me, if I had been run over by a car, because I was the sister of her son's wife. And the guy went to Cuernavaca, but they brought him back; they arrested him.... So he offered me a lot of money and jewels and whatever. And my brothers didn't want the money; they wanted him to go to jail. So that's why I say it wasn't a sexual act; it was a sexual violation.

**G:** And five years ago when you were working here, did you work every day?

**A:** No, you can't work every day. Just yesterday I went. I almost can't work every day; it's impossible because you lose so much energy, so much energy whether or not you do the sexual act. It's the tension; it's the lack of sleep; it's the alcohol; it's, even if you don't smoke, you're smoking anyway, so that the time comes when the body just gives up. Four or five days a week at the most.

**G:** Yes. Ah, OK. Can you tell me a little about your sexual practices? What type of sex do you practice: anal, vaginal, or...?

**A:** No, anal sex never. No, no, no. I tell them, "Look, the truth is that I want to arrive virgin at least on one side of my body on the day I get married. Otherwise I would be very happy to, but right now I can't. But keep in mind that what if you were the one who marries me and I wanted to give something virgin to you."

**G:** And, for example, when you have a sexual relation, do the majority use condoms or not?

**A:** The majority. No, what majority: all of them. At least with us, all of them have to use them.

**G:** With you they have to use them?

**A:** Yes, yes, because before they pay me, before we arrive at any agreement on price, before I waste my time, for his sake and for mine: a condom.

**G:** Do you have the condoms or does the client have to bring them?

**A:** Well, I always have them in my purse because I am the one who is most concerned and the most interested in taking care of myself. I am not going to start discussing about a condom with some ignorant guy who is going to say, "I don't have any." Can you imagine?

**G:** Have you ever taken the AIDS test?

**A:** Yes, many times. Even with my partner because we stopped seeing each other for four or five months and when we got back together we went and had an AIDS test. Yes, many times. And he turned out to have gonorrhea. Because we did that test too. And I didn't. And we had been having sex for a month. The AIDS test had already come out negative. But he had a strange feeling in his penis; he felt odd and so we went. And they did the exam on him and not me because I didn't know what he had. And he had gonorrhea. No man, I felt I was going to die. Because I told myself, look, so many years working and I never had gonorrhea, never had any problem like this. And you give it to me, my partner infects me. No, no, I said. Of course, we broke up. And I went and took the test and I came out negative. And then the doctor said, the one who did the test on him: "The fact is it is very odd that you did not infect her." Because he had been casting the blame on me, that it was probably my fault. And it turned out that he had it and I paid for the mistake. We were fighting like little kids in front of the doctor. So we got out of that mess. I didn't even want to let him get into my car. "No, no, no, I told him, you aren't going to leave your microbes in here." I treated him badly because the fact is that I hated him.

# Notes

## 1 / Ellipses and Intersections

1. Analogous contemporary statements from other parts of the country reaffirm the insistence of the stereotype of fixed gender roles. For instance, in her article on the innovative Mayan theater group Sna Jtz'ibajom, Cynthia Steele discusses the persistence of traditional gender roles even in members of this group, devoted to social consciousness-raising. On visiting the small museum set up by three members of Sna, she notes: "When my students toured the museum immediately after it opened in April 1993 the brothers' introductory speech stressed the need to preserve appropriate gender roles in contemporary Mayan society, with men taking their place in the fields and women remaining at the cooking fire and the loom. This speech seemed ironic, since the men in this family have deviated from these traditional roles" (Steele 1994, 243). Likewise, one of the two women members of the troupe commented on the stigmatized nature of their work: "[I]t is very daring for a woman to become an actress.... In Highland Chiapas no more than five indigenous women, including us, have acted.... [I]t is an activity that can only be engaged in by widows or single mothers, like us" (255).

2. The persistence of the myth of the *soldadera* is well recognized. More controversial is the evaluation of her impact on modern Mexican society. Anna Macías recognizes her popularity but finds in this very popularity an index of her essentially traditional function within the Mexican Revolution and in the reinscription of her figure into popular culture:

> In general, Mexican men view women as "others," not as equals. To be female is to be reticent, subordinate, and self-sacrificing. To be male is to be decisive, dominant, and courageous. The *soldadera* of the Mexican Revolution fits perfectly the traditional view of womanhood, which may help to account for her popularity in novels, films, and folk music. But what of the woman who takes on heroic qualities...? As Asunción Lavrín says of La Coronela, "She does not represent womanhood; she is an imitation of manhood." As a result, the heroines' exploits during the revolution did not bring immediate changes in the status of women.... The heroine was the exception; the uncomplaining, stoical *soldadera* was the norm. The experience of women in the revolution shows how rigid sexual stereotyping was but one more obstacle Mexican feminists faced in their struggle for equality. (Macías 1982, 158)

In their book *Virginidad y machismo en México* [Virginity and machismo in Mexico], Roberto Martínez Baños, Patricia Trejo de Zepeda, and Edilberto Soto Angli state

almost exactly the opposite opinion, suggesting that the *soldadera* was the first true
equal of men in modern American society and that her example permanently shifted
the relation between the sexes in Mexico:

> [E]l caso de la revolución mexicana es bien diferente por cuanto pudo inte-
> grar y de hecho integró a las cantineras, las enfermeras, laicas or religiosas, y
> sólo en un porcentaje muy mínimo a las alegres muchachas, esto último en
> virtud de, precisamente, la indiscriminada presencia de la mujer al lado de su
> hombre: la revolución unifica al hombre y la mujer en un mismo nivel de com-
> batientes que no hace factible que la mitad femenina de la pareja sea relegada a
> posiciones inferiores.... Por eso México es el único país que tiene en este con-
> tinente, en la etapa que estamos refiriéndonos, guerrilleras que al convertirse
> según la definición oficial de las fuerzas armadas del ejército regular, habrán
> de volverse soldaderas.... En suma, la revolución hace posible que la sufrida y
> abnegada hembra mexicana que es la madre, la hija, la hermana o la esposa, se
> convierta en la compañera con todo lo que esto significa de igualdad y con todo
> los que la igualdad tiene de verdadero, genuino respeto a la dignidad humana.
> (58–59)

> [The case of the Mexican Revolution is very different because of how much
> it was able to integrate into it the barmaids, the lay and religious nurses, and
> a very small percentage of the good-time girls, the latter by virtue of precisely
> that indiscriminate presence of the woman at her man's side: the revolution
> unifies man and woman at the same level as combatants and makes it unreason-
> able to relegate the feminine half of the couple to an inferior position.... For
> this reason, Mexico is the only country on this continent, at the historical junc-
> ture to which we are referring, that has women fighters who, upon conversion
> according to the official definition of the regular army's armed forces, would
> become *soldaderas*.... To sum up: the revolution makes it possible for the long-
> suffering and self-sacrificing Mexican female — the mother, the daughter, the
> sister, or the wife — to become the man's companion, with all that it signifies
> of equality, and with all that equality allows of true, genuine respect for human
> dignity.]

3. There are scattered literary analyses of the figure of the prostitute in Mexican
culture and literature as well, including a book that came to my attention just as I
was making the final revisions on this manuscript: María González's *Imagen de la
prostituta en la novela mexicana contemporánea*. While there is a slight overlap in the
texts we choose to study — both of us read Gamboa and Mora — our approaches are
quite different.

4. Barrón Salido is referring to a specific report on the situation in Tijuana. She
quotes Martín de la Rosa's extensive list of marginal persons: "Vamos a ocuparnos
en este apartado de los peones, los albañiles, meseros, lavacoches, periodiqueros, las
'marías,' los que 'ya volvieron del otro lado' (metedólares), los que 'quieren ir al otro
lado,' las empleadas domésticas, las 'que lavan ajeno,' los yonkeros, los 'cholos,' los
barrenderos, los artesanos, los vendedores ambulantes,...los desocupados" (9) [We
are going to concern ourselves in this report with the peons, the construction workers,

the waiters, the car washers, the newspaper sellers, the indigenous women workers, those who came back from the other side, those who want to go to the other side, the servants, the washerwomen, the junkies, the gang members, the street sweepers, the handicraft makers, the street salespeople, the unemployed].

5. As Miguel Matrajt and Mirta Arbetman write in an article on women and work in Mexico, "La 'liberación femenina'... no pasa de ciertos hábitos de consumo y una mayor permisividad frente a la ingesta de alcohol.... Pero esta liberación no ha llegado aún a su cuerpo. En realidad, a su esquema corporal. Las mujeres de este sector [Ciudad Nezahualcóyotl in Mexico City] siguen concibiendo a su cuerpo como algo para otros." Later, they continue, "De allí la expresión 'darle un hijo,' que trasciende largamente el giro semántico para representar lo que literalmente dice, o la actitud de deshabitar el propio cuerpo" [Women's liberation... does not affect more than certain habits of consumption and a greater permissiveness about ingestion of alcohol.... But this liberation has not reached their bodies. In fact, the women of this sector still conceive of their bodies as something for others.... From this derives the expression "give him a son," which transcends greatly the semantic turn of phrase to represent what it literally states, or, the attitude of uninhabiting her own body] (Matrajt and Arbetman 1990, 21, 23).

6. See Matlock 1994, 60–86, for a fascinating discussion of *Marion de Lorme* and the reading of the prostitute as an image of revolution.

7. The character's observation is consistent with at least some prostitutes' reflections on their clients' peculiarities. A French prostitute interviewed in Høigård and Finstad says, "When it comes down to it, men need to feel that sex is dirty, forbidden, in order to enjoy it.... They can't help wanting it, but at the same time they don't want to accept it. So they arrange things so that they can despise the women instead of themselves. When a guy asks for 'specialties,' he never blames himself for asking, he blames the woman for agreeing to it" (Høigård and Finstad, eds., 1992, 56–57). See also Perlongher 1990, 128.

8. The term is hard to translate. Roughly, it means the "con novel." *Transa* is a Mexicanism for a con artist; the word probably derives from *transacción* [transaction] and referred originally to the transactions between hip middle-class urban youth and lower-class drug dealers in the late 1960s. See Blanco's suggestive "Elogio de la transa" in Blanco 1981, 65–68, from which the material in this paragraph is paraphrased. Elaboration of the concept of the *transa* in the context of Mexican memoirs/*testimonios* by loose women will be the specific charge of chapter 6 of this book.

## 2 / Meat Shop Memories: Gamboa

1. Blanco's observation can be corroborated by a brief glance at the works by Monsiváis, González Rodríguez, and Torres, along with their respective bibliographies.

2. Gamboa here follows what is the common contemporary understanding of the contributing factors in prostitution. For a fascinating insight into this attitude, see Xorge del Campo. In his book, *La prostitución en México*, del Campo writes: "Médicos, psicólogos y sociólogos coinciden en admitir que existe una categoría de 'jóvenes predispuestas a la prostitución.' Esta tendencia se observa generalmente desde la infancia" [Physicians, psychologists, and sociologists coincide in the conclusion

that there exists a category of "young women predisposed to prostitution." This tendency can generally be observed from infancy] (de Campo 1974, 97). Del Campo demonstrates through citing statistics that this predisposition rather strangely and coincidentally aligns itself along class boundaries: prostitutes tend to come from a poor background. He does not underline, but it remains implicit in his unmotivated association of class affiliation and a lack of moral sense, that this predisposition is heavily racialized, since poorer women tend to be also less white. He further comments that in interviews prostitutes will always claim that "ellas han adoptado este oficio empujadas por el hambre, por el desempleo, por la insuficiencia de salarios, etcétera" [they had been pushed into this job by hunger, unemployment, low salaries, etcetera]. He warns against accepting the prostitutes' testimony in the face of expert analysis, however: "Nada puede estar más sujeto a dudas que este género de testimonios" [Nothing could be more subject to doubt than this type of testimony], presumably because the women hope to play on the sympathies of prospective customers with such farfetched stories (100). Thus the "expert" testimony of scientists on a genetic (racial?) predisposition to prostitution overrides the personal testimonies of lower-class women who say they are forced into it.

3. See p. 38, above, for the text of the Porfirian legal code.

4. The force of this rhythmic pull is evident in attempts to disrupt it. In 1959, Mexico City mayor Ernesto P. Uruchurtu proclaimed that "deben de cerrarse los establecimientos a la una de la mañana para garantizar que la familia del obrero reciba su salario, que no se dilapide en centros de vicio el patrimonio familiar" [establishments should close at 1:00 A.M. in order to guarantee that the worker's family receives his salary, that the family patrimony is not frittered away in centers of vice] (Monsiváis 1977, 38).

5. Besides the butcher shop, one of the other important industries in the brothel's neighborhood is the production of tombstones, and the reference to stones, especially tombstones, is one of the minor leitmotivs of the novel. The Tivoli, for example, is described as having tables "que á modo de lápidas de un cementerio fatídico de almas enfermas y cuerpos pecadores parecen aguardar á que en su superficie graben fugaces epitafios" [that like tombstones in a prophetic cemetery of diseased souls and sinful bodies seem to await someone to inscribe fleeting epitaphs on their surfaces] (Gamboa [1903] 1989, 111). Later in the text, the narrator informs us that Santa's only recourse is to bury her illusions so as to survive in the inhospitable world of the brothel. The young woman complains to Hipolito: "Si parece que me empujan y me obligan á hacer todo lo que hago, como si yo fuese una piedra. . . . Luego, también me comparo á una piedra, porque de piedra nos quisiera el público, sin sentimientos ni nada, y de piedra se necesita ser para el oficio" [It seems like they're pushing me and forcing me to do what I do, as if I were a stone. . . . Then again, sometimes I compare myself to a stone, because our clients would like us to be stone, without feelings or anything, and one has to be of stone to take this job] (143). Santa's self-recognition as stone becomes her epitaph, her figurative burial stone.

6. See J. E. Pacheco 1977, 34.

## 3 / Desire in the Streets: Rulfo, Garro

1. I borrow the term from Stephen Heath, who defines "scriptural" as "the saturation of a series of propositions and relations in the practice of writing" (Heath 1972, 69). And later he adds, "The alignment of these elements horizontally, in the play of repetition and variation, produces a kind of 'declension' of the elements of fiction, giving what was called at the beginning of this chapter a *scriptural* of narrative (as Leibniz talked of the *geometral* of an object) that invites the reader to read the writing of the text" (136).

2. See, for example, Søren Kierkegaard: "A woman comprehends finiteness... therefore she is beauteous.... Woman explains finiteness, man is in chase of infinitude. So it should be, and each has one's own pain; for woman bears children with pain, but man conceives ideas with pain, and woman does not have to know the anguish of doubt or the torment of despair" (quoted in Flax 1989, 135).

## 4 / Deterritorializing Women's Bodies: Castillo, Campbell

1. The author's compositional method offers an interesting insight into how he arranged his thoughts about the fluid border-reality he conveys in the novella. *Everything about Seals* began as a story sequence, which the author then cannibalized, putting bits of paragraphs and phrases in folders with names like "Everything about Beaches," "Everything about Airplanes," "Everything about My Father," or "Everything about Seals." The final title of the book, he says, is purely accidental (personal communication).

2. I am borrowing loosely from Sánchez-Tranquilino and Tagg's argument on pages 562–63 of their essay (1992). I thank them for the thought-provoking study and apologize for the violence I have done their elegant analysis.

## 5 / Reading Women: Sefchovich

1. At least I haven't found any literary-sociological studies analogous to Janice Radway's pathbreaking study (1988) of women romance readers in the United States. Reputable Mexican scholars confirm that, as far as they are aware, such studies do not yet exist.

2. See the introduction to my *Talking Back* (D. Castillo 1992) for a discussion of this issue in relation to modern Latin American fiction by women.

3. Romance writer Laura Kinsale makes an analogous commentary about mass-market romances in the United States. She notes that a common reader complaint is to object to what she calls the "clinch covers, ... with particular complaints voiced about the over-endowment of the illustrated females." She attributes the success of her novels partly to her insistence on a hero-only cover illustration and suggests that, while romances are ostensibly aimed at women, the bodice-ripper clinch covers are tailored to male buyers: "The persistence of the clinch cover goes beyond market identification" and has a great deal to do with "the subconscious appeal of pornographic illustrations of females to male wholesale book buyers (a penchant rather amusingly hinted at in the very real and very serious apprehension of two male buy-

ers with whom I spoke about *The Prince of Midnight*'s hero-only cut-back cover: 'But where's the girl?')" (Kinsale 1992, 41).

4. My experience in teaching this novel is that students and I tend to skim over these chapters when reading the novel and skip them almost entirely in class discussion. In this manner and because of the alternating chapter structure, the epistolary novel becomes even more fragmented and punctuated by extensive, opulently imagined ellipses.

5. There is in this self-consciously literary opening sentence more than the hint of an allusion to Sefchovich's own illustrious foremothers: for example, Teresa de la Parra's classic 1922 novel, *Ifigenia: Diario de una señorita que escribía porque se fastidiaba* [Ifigenia: The journal of a young woman who wrote because she was bored].

## 6 / Signifyin', Testifyin': Mora, Bandida, Serrano

1. Serrano has also announced a fourth book, *Mujeres en la política* (see Serrano 1992, 289). As of this writing, the announced book has not yet appeared.

2. The interest in fictional loose women has spilled over into a parallel publishing boomlet in the *testimonios* of actual loose women. See, for example, Marta Lamas's work in collaboration with "Claudia" and other prostitutes. I also have in my possession a copy of Richard Browning's *testimonio* of a woman he calls "Rosa González Gómez," who worked as a prostitute in various cities in Mexico for over twenty years. While this publishing phenomenon has been noted with increasing frequency in current critical discussions of contemporary Mexican literature, the implications have remained largely unexplored.

3. Untranslatable play on words.

4. See Claude Lévi-Strauss, *The Raw and the Cooked* (1969), for the classical exposition of the link between food and sexuality. For more recent, woman-oriented discussions, see Rosalind Coward, *Female Desires* (1985), and Tania Modleski, *Feminism without Women* (1991).

5. Su is here talking specifically about "Estrella," a famous elite prostitute also mentioned in glowing terms in Muñuzuri's book and described as a friend of La Bandida.

6. Serrano's books have a disturbingly scandalous resonance for the elite power brokers, though Serrano herself laughs at reprisal attempts. As Elena Poniatowska points out, the editor of her first book, a Swedish national named Gerd Fleischer, was deported for participating in this project (Poniatowska 1993, 118).

## 7 / No Conclusions

1. Some of the women working in prostitution prefer the term "sex worker" (*trabajadora sexual*); others insistently reject it as an academic affectation. I use it in the pages that follow in the awareness of its conflictive acceptance.

2. Lamas's conclusion is also consistent with other local studies, though not with the statements made by the women interviewed in depth for the Tijuana study. For example, the CONASIDA report on sex workers in the area of Tuxtla Gutiérrez, in the south of Mexico, indicates that women in that area "no realizan en su práctica

diaria negociaciones para utilizar el condón, la experiencia parece ser poca. Reiteran un rechazo hacia el uso del condón en casi todo tipo de cliente, con excepción de 'los hijos de riquillos'" [do not include negotiations about condom use as part of their daily practice, and their experience is slight. They reiterate a rejection of condom use in almost all types of clients, except "rich boys"] (CONASIDA 1995b, 13). Similarly, clients interviewed in Ciudad Hidalgo, also in the south of Mexico, tell interviewers that in that city the reported condom use by sex workers is much higher than actual condom use by clients (CONASIDA 1995a, 19).

3. This information was found especially through the relatively large body of client reports available on two main sites: the Usenet site <alt.sex.prostitution.tijuana> and the Tijuana listings on the World Wide Web's extremely complete "World Sex Guide" (http://www.paranoia.com). By and large the reports are remarkably consistent; all Tijuana sex workers always require condoms. Brockton O'Toole's "World Sex Guide" FAQ (Frequently Asked Questions) is adamant: "Condoms are an absolute must for both oral sex and anything else," and his admonition is repeated in report after report. Of course, these "reports" are very partial — discussing relations with women from only a very limited range of high-end sex clubs — and also self-selective: the clients all use the World Wide Web and various Usenet sites, and almost all write in English.

# Works Cited

Abrahams, Roger D. 1962. "The Changing Concept of the Negro Hero." In *The Golden Log*, edited by Mody C. Boatright et al., 119–34. Dallas: Southern Methodist University Press.

———. 1970. *Deep Down in the Jungle: Negro Narrative Folklore from the Streets of Philadelphia*. Chicago: Aldine.

Anderson, Amanda. 1991. "Prostitution's Artful Guise." *Diacritics* 21, nos. 2–3:102–22.

———. 1993. *Tainted Souls and Painted Faces: The Rhetoric of Fallenness in Victorian Culture*. Ithaca, N.Y.: Cornell University Press.

Anderson, Benedict. 1991. *Imagined Communities: Reflections on the Origin and Spread of Nationalism*. Revised edition. New York: Verso.

Anderson, Danny J. 1995. "Difficult Relations, Compromising Positions: Telling Involvement in Recent Mexican Narrative." *Chasqui* 24, no. 1:16–29.

———. 1996. "Creating Cultural Prestige: Editorial Joaquín Mortiz." *Latin American Research Review* 31:3–41.

Anderson, Robert. 1980–81. "La realidad temporal en *Los recuerdos del porvenir.*" *Explicación de textos literarios* 9:25–29.

Apter, Emily. 1989. "Cabinet Secrets: Fetishism, Prostitution, and the Fin de Siècle Interior." *Assemblage* 9 (June): 7–19.

Aranda, Clara Eugenia. 1976. *La mujer: Explotación, lucha, liberación*. Mexico City: Editorial Nuestro Tiempo.

Aranda Luna, Javier. 1990. "Una también es gente." In *El nuevo arte de amar: Usos y costumbres sexuales en México*, edited by Hermann Bellinghausen, 99–106. Mexico City: Cal y Arena.

Arreola, Daniel D., and James R. Curtis. 1993. *The Mexican Border Cities: Landscape Anatomy and Place Personality*. Tucson: University of Arizona Press.

Azuela, Mariano. 1960. "Registro." In *Obras completas*. Vol. 3, pp. 1197–1236. Mexico City: Fondo de Cultura Económica.

Barlow, Linda. 1992. "The Androgynous Writer: Another View of Point of View." In *Dangerous Men and Adventurous Women: Romance Writers on the Appeal of the Romance*, edited by Jayne Anne Krentz, 45–52. Philadelphia: University of Pennsylvania Press.

Barrón Salido, Patricia. 1995. *Las "Marías Magdalenas": El oficio de la prostitución y su estrategía colectiva de vida*. Draft of Bachelor's thesis. Tijuana: Colegio de la Frontera Norte.

Barthes, Roland. 1975. *The Pleasure of the Text*. Translated by Richard Miller. New York: Hill and Wang.

261

Bartra, Eli, et al. 1983. *La revuelta: Reflexiones, testimonios y reportajes de mujeres en México, 1975–1983.* Mexico City: Martín Casillas Editores.

Bataille, Georges. 1986. *Eroticism: Death and Sensuality.* San Francisco: City Lights Books.

Bell, Shannon. 1994. *Reading, Writing, and Rewriting the Prostitute Body.* Bloomington: Indiana University Press.

Bellinghausen, Hermann, ed., 1990. *El nuevo arte de amar: Usos y costumbres sexuales en México.* Mexico City: Cal y Arena.

Bernheimer, Charles. 1989. *Figures of Ill Repute: Representing Prostitution in Nineteenth-Century France.* Cambridge, Mass.: Harvard University Press.

Bersani, Leo. 1988. "Is the Rectum a Grave?" In *AIDS: Cultural Analysis, Cultural Activism,* edited by Douglas Crimp, 197–222. Cambridge, Mass.: MIT Press.

Bhabha, Homi K. 1990. "DissemiNation: Time, Narrative, and the Margins of the Modern Nation." In *Nation and Narration,* edited by Homi K. Bhabha, 291–322. New York: Routledge.

———, ed. 1990. *Nation and Narration.* New York: Routledge.

Blanchot, Maurice. 1982. *The Space of Literature.* Translated by Ann Smock. Lincoln: University of Nebraska Press.

Blanco, José Joaquín. 1981. *Función de medianoche: Ensayos de literatura cotidiana.* Mexico City: Ediciones Era.

———. 1988. *Cuando todas las chamacas se pusieron medias nylon (y otras crónicas).* Mexico City: Joan Boldó i Climent.

———. 1990. *Las intensidades corrosivas.* Villahermosa: Instituto de Cultura de Tabasco.

Bowlby, Rachel. 1993. *Shopping with Freud.* London: Routledge.

Brooks, Peter. 1984. *Reading for the Plot: Design and Intention in Narrative.* New York: Vintage.

Browning, Richard L. N.d. "Rosa González Gómez: A Ranchera's Odyssey." Manuscript.

Bullough, Vern, and Bonnie Bullough. 1987. *Women and Prostitution: A Social History.* Buffalo, N.Y.: Prometheus Books.

Butler, Judith. 1990. *Gender Trouble: Feminism and the Subversion of Identity.* New York: Routledge.

———. 1993. *Bodies That Matter: On the Discursive Limits of Sex.* New York: Routledge.

Cabrera Infante, Guillermo. 1975. "Una inocente pornógrafa: Manes y desmanes de Corín Tellado." In *O,* 39–60. Barcelona: Seix Barral.

Campbell, Federico. 1989a. "Tijuana como la madre, la tierra, la ubre, la matriz y el troquel." *Textual* (October): 39–41.

———. 1989b. *Tijuanenses.* Mexico City: Joaquín Mortiz.

———. 1995. *Tijuana: Stories on the Border.* Translation of *Tijuanenses.* Translated and introduced by Debra A. Castillo. Berkeley: University of California Press.

Careaga, Gabriel. 1990. *Mitos y fantasías de la clase media en México.* Mexico City: Cal y Arena.

———. 1992. *La ciudad enmascarada.* Mexico City: Cal y Arena.

Carrera Damas, Felipe. 1978. *El comportamiento sexual del venezolano.* Caracas: Monte Avila.

———. 1980. *¿Es usted un macho?* Caracas: Publicaciones Seleven.

Castellanos, Rosario. [1973] 1984. *Mujer que sabe latín…* Mexico City: Fondo de Cultura Económica.

———. [1975] 1992. *El eterno femenino.* Mexico City: Fondo de Cultura Económica.

Castillo, Ana. 1986. *The Mixquiahuala Letters.* Binghamton, N.Y.: Bilingual Press.

———. 1990. *Sapogonia.* Tempe, Ariz.: Bilingual Press.

Castillo, Debra A. 1992. *Talking Back: Toward a Latin American Feminist Literary Criticism.* Ithaca, N.Y.: Cornell University Press.

Chapkis, Wendy. 1991. "Suggestive Language: On Sex Workers and (Other) Feminists." *Sub/versions* (winter). Working paper series. University of California, Santa Cruz.

Christian-Smith, Linda K. 1990. *Becoming a Woman through Romance.* New York: Routledge.

Cixous, Hélène. 1980. "The Laugh of the Medusa." In *New French Feminisms: An Anthology,* edited and introduced by Elaine Marks and Isabelle de Courtivron, 245–64. Amherst: University of Massachusetts Press.

Clifford, James. 1988. *The Predicament of Culture: Twentieth-Century Ethnography, Literature, and Art.* Cambridge, Mass.: Harvard University Press.

*Códigos penales y de procedimientos penales para el D. y T. F. y federal de procedimientos penales.* 1964. Puebla: Editorial Cajica.

CONASIDA (Consejo Nacional para la Prevención y Control del SIDA). 1995a. *Análisis de la situación de Ciudad Hidalgo, Chiapas.* Internal technical report.

———. 1995b. *Resultados del análisis de la situación y propuesta para desarrollar una intervención para aumentar la seguridad del sexo comercial, en Chiapas, area de Tuxtla Gutiérrez.* Internal technical report.

Conde, Rosina. 1982. *De infancia y adolescencia.* Mexico City: Pantomima.

———. 1984. *En la tarima.* Mexico City: Colección Laberinto.

Corbin, Alain. 1990. *Women for Hire.* Translated by Alan Sheridan. Cambridge, Mass.: Harvard University Press.

Coria, Clara. 1986. *El sexo oculto del dinero: Formas de dependencia femenina.* Buenos Aires: Grupo Editor Latinoamericano.

Coward, Rosalind. 1985. *Female Desires.* New York: Grove.

Culler, Jonathan. 1995. "Lyric and History: Prostitution and *Les Fleurs du Mal.*" Manuscript.

Cypess, Sandra Messinger. 1990. "The Figure of *La Malinche* in the Texts of Elena Garro." In *A Different Reality: Studies on the Work of Elena Garro,* edited by Anita K. Stoll, 117–35. Lewisburg, Pa.: Bucknell University Press.

———. 1991. *La Malinche in Mexican Literature: From History to Myth.* Austin: University of Texas Press.

Davidson, Julia O'Connell. 1995. "The Anatomy of 'Free Choice' Prostitution." *Gender, Work and Organization* 2, no. 1 (1995): 1–10.

De la Rosa, Martín. 1985. *Marginalidad en Tijuana.* Tijuana: Cuadernos CEFNO-MEX.

Del Campo, Xorge. 1974. *La prostitución en México.* Mexico City: Editores Asociados.

Epple, Juan Armando. N.d. "De Santa a Mariana: La ciudad de México como utopía traicionada." Manuscript.

Espinosa Damián, Gisela. 1987. "Feminism and Social Struggle in Mexico." In *Third World — Second Sex*, edited by Miranda Davies, 31–41. London: Zed.

*Familia y sexualidad en Nueva España*. 1982. Mexico City, n.p.

Felman, Shoshana. 1983. *The Literary Speech Act: Don Juan with J. L. Austin, or Seduction in Two Languages*. Translated by Catherine Porter. Ithaca, N.Y.: Cornell University Press.

Felski, Rita. 1991. "The Counterdiscourse of the Feminine in Three Texts by Wilde, Huysmans, and Sacher-Masoch." *PMLA* 106:1094–1105.

Fernández de Lizardi, José Joaquín. 1985. *"Don Catrín de la Fachenda" y "Noches Tristes y Día Alegre."* Edited by Jefferson Rea Spell. Mexico City: Porrúa.

Fernández Robaina, Tomás, ed. 1984. *Recuerdos secretos de dos mujeres públicas*. Havana: Editorial Letras Cubanas.

Flax, Jane. 1989. *Thinking Fragments: Psychoanalysis, Feminism, and Postmodernism in the Contemporary West*. Berkeley: University of California Press.

Flieger, Jerry Anne. 1990. "The Female Subject: (What) Does Woman Want?" In *Psychoanalysis and...*, edited by Richard Feldstein and Henry Sussman, 54–63. New York: Routledge, Chapman and Hall.

Flores, Juan, and George Yúdice. 1990. "Living Borders/Buscando America: Languages of Latino Self-Formation." *Social Text* 8, no. 2:57–84.

Foucault, Michel. 1977. *Discipline and Punish: The Birth of the Prison*. Translated by Alan Sheridan. New York: Random House.

———. 1986. "Of Other Spaces." Translated by Jay Miskowiec. *Diacritics* 16, no. 1: 22–27.

Franco, Jean. 1988. "Beyond Ethnocentrism: Gender, Power, and the Third World Intelligentsia." In *Marxism and the Interpretation of Culture*, edited by Cary Nelson and Lawrence Grossberg, 503–15. Urbana: University of Illinois Press.

———. 1989a. "The Nation as Imagined Community." In *The New Historicism*, edited by H. Aram Veeser, 204–12. New York: Routledge.

———. 1989b. *Plotting Women: Gender and Representation in Mexico*. New York: Columbia University Press.

Frase, Brigitte. 1993. "Woman on the Page." *Hungry Mind Review* 25 (spring): 5, 10.

French, William E. 1992. "Prostitutes and Guardian Angels: Women, Work, and the Family in Porfirian Mexico." *Hispanic American Historical Review* 72:529–53.

Frenk, Margit. 1994. "Los sueños de la señora." Review of *La señora de los sueños*, by Sara Sefchovich. *Semanal* (weekly magazine of *La Jornada*) 264 (July 3): 13–14.

Fuentes, Carlos. 1981a. "Mugido, muerte y misterio: El mito de Rulfo." *Revista Iberoamericana* 47, nos. 116–17:11–21.

———. 1981b. *Myself with Others*. New York: Farrar, Straus, Giroux.

Gallagher, Catherine. 1986. "George Eliot and *Daniel Deronda:* The Prostitute and The Jewish Question." In *Sex, Politics, and Science in the Nineteenth-Century Novel: Selected Papers from the English Institute, 1983–84*, edited by Ruth Bernard Yeazell, 39–62. Baltimore: Johns Hopkins University Press.

Galván, Delia. 1990. "Elena Garro and the Narrative of Cruelty." In *A Different Reality: Studies on the Work of Elena Garro*, edited by Anita K. Stoll, 136–58. Lewisburg, Pa.: Bucknell University Press.

Gamboa, Federico. [1903] 1989. *Santa*. Mexico City: Fontamara.

Garber, Marjorie. 1992. *Vested Interests: Cross-Dressing and Cultural Anxiety.* New York: Routledge.

García García, María de Lourdes, et al. 1995. *Enfermedades de transmisión sexual y SIDA.* Mexico City: Secretaría de Salud, Instituto Nacional de Diagnóstico.

García Jiménez, Marcelino. 1987. *Breve estudio sobre la prostitución en México.* Law thesis. Tijuana: Universidad Autónoma de Baja California.

Garrido, Felipe. 1982. "*Pedro Páramo y El llano en llamas* de Juan Rulfo." In *Para cuando yo me ausente,* edited by Juan Rulfo, 13–34. Mexico City: Grijalbo.

Garro, Elena. [1963] 1977. *Los recuerdos del porvenir.* Mexico City: Joaquín Mortiz.

———. 1969. *Recollections of Things to Come.* Translation of *Los recuerdos del porvenir.* Translated by Ruth L. C. Simms. Austin: University of Texas Press.

Gates, Henry Louis, Jr. 1988. *The Signifying Monkey: A Theory of Afro-American Literary Criticism.* Oxford: Oxford University Press.

Gibson, Pamela Church, and Roman Gibson, eds. 1993. *Dirty Looks: Women, Pornography, Power.* Worcester, England: British Film Institute.

Glantz, Margo. 1983. *La lengua en la mano.* Mexico City: Premiá.

———. 1984. *De la amorosa inclinación a enredadarse en cabellos.* Mexico City: Océano.

Gomezjara, F., et al. 1978. *Sociología de la prostitución.* Mexico City: Ediciones Nueva Sociología.

González, María R. 1996. *Imagen de la prostituta en la novela mexicana contemporánea.* Madrid: Pliegos.

González de la Vega, Francisco. 1968. *Derecho penal en México: Los delitos.* Mexico City: Porrúa.

González Rodríguez, Sergio, ed. 1989. *Los bajos fondos: El antro, la bohemia y el café.* Mexico City: Cal y Arena.

———. 1993. *Los amorosos: Relatos eróticos mexicanos.* Mexico City: Cal y Arena.

Good, Carl. 1995. "Testimonio especular, testimonio sublime en *El eterno femenino* de Rosario Castellanos." *Gestos* 20:55–72.

Gordon, Donald K. 1976. *Los cuentos de Juan Rulfo.* Madrid: Playor.

Grewal, Inderpal, and Caren Kaplan, eds. 1994. *Scattered Hegemonies: Postmodernity and Transnational Feminist Practices.* Minneapolis: University of Minnesota Press.

Guy, Donna. 1991. *Sex and Danger in Buenos Aires: Prostitution, Family, and Nation in Argentina.* Lincoln: University of Nebraska Press.

Hart, Angie. 1995. "(Re)constructing a Spanish Red-light District: Prostitution, Space, and Power." In *Mapping Desire: Geographies of Sexualities,* edited by David Bell and Gill Valentine, 214–28. New York: Routledge.

Heath, Stephen. 1972. *The Nouveau Roman: A Study in the Practice of Writing.* Philadelphia: Temple University Press.

Hélie-Lucas, Marie-Aimee. 1994. "The Preferential Symbol for Islamic Identity: Women in Muslim Personal Laws." In *Identity Politics and Women: Cultural Reassertions and Feminisms in International Perspective,* edited by Val Moghadam. Boulder, Colo.: Westview Press.

Hicks, D. Emily. 1988. Untitled manuscript. Unpublished review of *The Eye of the Prey,* by Herbert Blau.

————. 1991. *Border Writing: The Multidimensional Text.* Minneapolis: University of Minnesota Press.

Høigård, Cecile, and Liv Finstad, eds. 1992. *Backstreets: Prostitution, Money, and Love.* Translated by Katherine Hanson, Nancy Sipe, and Barbara Wilson. University Park: Pennsylvania State University Press.

Ibargüengoitia, Jorge. 1985. *Las muertas.* Mexico City: Joaquín Mortiz.

*La industria sexual mexicana.* 1994. Special section of *Nexos* 17, no. 203 (November).

Irigaray, Luce. 1985. *This Sex Which Is Not One.* Translated by Catherine Porter. Ithaca, N.Y.: Cornell University Press.

Kaminsky, Amy Katz. 1984. "Women Writing about Prostitutes: Amalia Jamilis and Luisa Valenzuela." In *The Image of the Prostitute in Modern Literature,* edited by Pierre L. Horn and Mary Beth Pringle, 119–31. New York: Frederick Ungar.

Khatibi, Abdelkebir. 1990. *Love in Two Languages.* Translated by Richard Howard. Minneapolis: University of Minnesota Press.

Kinsale, Laura. 1992. "The Androgynous Reader: Point of View in the Romance." In *Dangerous Men and Adventurous Women: Romance Writers on the Appeal of the Romance,* edited by Jayne Anne Krentz, 31–44. Philadelphia: University of Pennsylvania Press.

Krentz, Jayne Anne, ed. 1992. *Dangerous Men and Adventurous Women: Romance Writers on the Appeal of the Romance.* Philadelphia: University of Pennsylvania Press.

Lamas, Marta. 1993. "El fulgor de noche: Algunos aspectos de la prostitución callejera en la ciudad de Mexico." *Debate Feminista* 8:103–33.

Lara y Pardo, Luis. 1908. *La prostitución en México.* Mexico City: Librería de la Vda. de Charles Bouret.

Lejeune, Philippe. 1989. *On Autobiography.* Edited and with a foreword by Paul John Eakin. Translated by Katherine Leary. Minneapolis: University of Minnesota Press.

Lévi-Strauss, Claude. 1969. *The Raw and the Cooked.* Vol. 1. Translated by John and Doreen Weightman. Chicago: University of Chicago Press.

Lévinas, Emmanuel. 1969. *Totality and Infinity: An Essay on Exteriority.* Translated by Alphonso Lingis. Pittsburgh: Duquesne University Press.

Lewis, Oscar. 1964. *Pedro Martínez: A Mexican Peasant and His Family.* New York: Random House.

Lihn, Enrique. 1979. *El arte de la palabra.* Barcelona: Pomaire.

Lionni, Leo. 1959. *Little Blue and Little Yellow.* New York: Ivan Obolensky.

López González, Aralia. 1993. "Quebrantos, búsquedas y azares de una pasión nacional (dos décadas de narrativa mexicana: 1970–1980)." *Revista Iberoamericana* 164–5:659–85.

Lyotard, Jean-François. 1992. *The Inhuman.* Translated by Geoffrey Bennington and Rachel Bowlby. Stanford, Calif.: Stanford University Press.

Macías, Anna. 1982. *Against All Odds: The Feminist Movement in Mexico to 1940.* Westport, Conn.: Greenwood.

MacKinnon, Catherine. 1987. *Feminism Unmodified: Discourses on Life and Law.* Cambridge, Mass.: Harvard University Press.

Mariño Soto, Germán. 1990. *Análisis y elaboración de fotonovelas: Una aproximación desde los cuentos de hadas y el melodrama.* Bogotá: Enda.

Martín del Campo, David. 1990. *Dama de noche.* Mexico City: Joaquín Mortiz.

Martínez Baños, Roberto, Patricia Trejo de Zepeda, and Edilberto Soto Angli. 1973. *Virginidad y machismo en México.* Mexico City: Posada.

Matlock, Jann. 1994. *Scenes of Seduction: Prostitution, Hysteria, and Reading Difference in Nineteenth-Century France.* New York: Columbia University Press.

Maytrajt, Miguel, and Mirta Arbetman. 1990. "La condición de la mujer, el proceso de trabajo y la salud mental." *Fem* 14 (February): 15–24.

McClintock, Anne. 1993. "Sex Workers and Sex Work: Introduction." *Social Text* 37:1–10.

Mendoza, María Luisa. 1974. *De Ausencia.* Mexico City: Joaquín Mortiz.

Modleski, Tania. 1991. *Feminism without Women: Culture and Criticism in a "Postfeminist" Age.* New York: Routledge.

Molloy, Sylvia. 1992. "Too Wilde for Comfort: Desire and Ideology in Fin-de-Siècle Spanish America." *Social Text* 31–32:187–201.

Monsiváis, Carlos. 1977. *Amor perdido.* Mexico City: Era.

———. 1980. "La mujer en la cultura mexicana." In *Mujer y sociedad en América latina,* edited by Lucía Guerra-Cunningham, 101–17. Irvine, Calif.: Editorial del Pacífico.

———. 1981. *Escenas de pudor y liviandad.* Mexico City: Grijalbo.

Mora, Antonia. 1972. *Del oficio.* Prologue by María Luisa Mendoza. Mexico City: Editorial Samo.

Mora, Carl J. 1989. *Mexican Cinema: Reflections of a Society 1896–1988.* Berkeley: University of California Press.

Moreno, Antonio de P. 1968. *Curso de derecho penal mexicano.* Mexico City: Porrúa.

Morse, Margaret. 1990. "An Ontology of Everyday Distraction: The Freeway, the Mall, and Television." In *Logics of Television: Essays in Cultural Criticism,* edited by Patricia Mellencamp, 193–221. Bloomington: Indiana University Press.

Muñuzuri, Eduardo. 1967. *Memorias de "La Bandida."* Mexico City: Costa-Amic.

Noakes, Susan. 1988. "On the Superficiality of Women." In *The Comparative Perspective on Literature: Approaches to Theory and Practice,* edited by Clayton Koelb and Susan Noakes, 339–55. Ithaca, N.Y.: Cornell University Press.

Ojeda, Néstor L. 1994. "Prostitución en los noventa." *Nexos* 17, no. 203 (November): 76–80.

Pacheco, Cristina. 1990. *Los dueños de la noche.* Mexico City: Planeta.

Pacheco, José Emilio. 1977. Foreword to *Diario de Federico Gamboa 1892–1939,* edited by José Emilio Pacheco. Mexico City: Siglo Veintiuno.

Pacheco Ladrón de Guevara, Lourdes C. 1988. "Haz conmigo lo que quieras: La prostitución urbana en Nayarit." In *Mujeres y sociedad: Salario, hogar y acción social en el occidente de México,* edited by Luisa Gabayet et al., 125–40. Mexico City: Colegio de Mexico.

Paz, Octavio. [1959] 1980. *El laberinto de la soledad.* Mexico City: Fondo de Cultura Económica.

———. 1961. *The Labyrinth of Solitude.* Translation of *El laberinto de la soledad.* Translated by Lysander Kemp. New York: Grove.

———. 1992. "Cuantía y valía." In *Defensa de la literatura difícil,* edited by Octavio Paz. Special issue of *Vuelta* 188 (July): 11–15.

———, ed. 1992. *Defensa de la literatura difícil.* Special issue of *Vuelta* 188 (July).

Peri Rossi, Cristina. 1991. *Fantasías eróticas.* Madrid: Temas de Hoy.

Perkins, Roberta, and Garry Bennett. 1985. *Being a Prostitute: Prostitute Women and Prostitute Men.* Sydney: George Allen and Unwin.

Perlongher, Néstor. 1990. "Avatares de los muchachos de la noche." *Nueva sociedad* 109 (September-October): 124–34.

Pheterson, Gail, ed. 1989. *A Vindication of the Rights of Whores.* Seattle: Seal Press.

Poniatowska, Elena. 1988. "Xaviera Hollander o las glorias de la prostitución." In *Fem: Diez años de periodismo feminista,* 74–78. Mexico City: Planeta.

———. 1993. *Todo México.* Vol. 2. Mexico City: Diana.

Posada García, Miriam. 1995. "Prostitución: Del engaño al abuso cotidiano." *La Jornada* (July 25).

Quijada, Osvaldo A. 1977. *Comportamiento Sexual en México: El hombre.* Mexico City: Tinta Libre.

Radway, Janice. 1988. "The Book-of-the-Month Club and the General Reader: On the Uses of 'Serious' Fiction." *Critical Inquiry* 14:516–38.

Ramírez, Armando. 1989. *Crónica de los chorrocientos mil días del barrio de Tepito, o en donde se ve cómo obrero, ratero, prostituta, boxeador y comerciante juegan a las pipis y gañas o sea, en donde todos juntos comeremos chi-cha-rón.* Mexico City: Grijalbo.

Rangel Gómez, María Gudelia. N.d. Manuscript on prostitution in Tijuana.

Remy, Anseleme. 1974. "The Unholy Trinity." *Caribbean Review* 6, no. 2:14–18.

Río de la Torre, Guadalupe. 1996. "La Revolución mexicana y la prostitución." *Casa del tiempo* 14, no. 55 (September): 58–61.

Rosas Solís, Armando. 1995. "Comentarios al artículo 'El fulgor de la noche' de Marta Lamas." Manuscript received by fax transmission (July 19). Eight pages.

Rulfo, Juan. 1976. "Juan Rulfo examina su narrativa." *Escritura* 2:305–15.

———. 1977. *Antología personal.* Mexico City: Editorial Nueva Imagen.

Russo, Miguel. 1994. "Un fenómeno de ventas: La literatura romántica." *Primer plano* (cultural supplement of *Página/12*) (October 2): 1–3.

Salazar González, José Guadalupe. 1986. *Reglamentación del trabajo de las mujeres en los centros nocturnos.* Law thesis. Tijuana: Universidad Autónoma de Baja California.

Sánchez-Tranquilino, Marcos, and John Tagg. 1992. "The Pachuco's Flayed Hide: Mobility, Identity, and *Buenas Garras.*" In *Cultural Studies,* edited by Lawrence Grossberg, Cary Nelson, and Paula Treichler, 556–70. New York: Routledge.

Schaefer, Claudia. 1992. *Textured Lives: Women, Art, and Representation in Modern Mexico.* Tucson: University of Arizona Press.

Secretaría de Salud. 1989. *Informe técnico: Evaluación del impacto de la estrategía educativa para la prevención del SIDA en México 1987–88.* 5 volumes: *Mujeres dedicadas a la prostitución*; *Hombres homo-bisexuales*; *Estudiantes universitarios*; *Personal de salud*; and *Público general.* Mexico City.

Sefchovich, Sara. 1987. *México: País de ideas, país de novelas (Una sociología de la literatura mexicana).* Mexico City: Grijalbo.

———. 1990. *Demasiado amor.* Mexico City: Planeta.

———. 1993. *La señora de los sueños.* Mexico City: Planeta.

Serrano, Irma, and Elisa Robledo. 1978. *A calzón amarrado.* Mexico City: Fleischer.

———. 1979. *Sin pelos en la lengua.* Mexico City: Cia. general de ediciones.

———. 1992. *Una loca en la polaca.* Mexico City: Selector.

Showalter, Elaine, ed., 1989. *Speaking of Gender.* New York: Routledge, Chapman and Hall.

Shrage, Laurie. 1994. *Moral Dilemmas of Feminism: Prostitution, Adultery, and Abortion.* New York: Routledge.

Simpson, David. 1994. "Feminisms and Feminizations in the Postmodern." In *Feminism and Postmodernism,* edited by Margaret Ferguson and Jennifer Wicke, 53–68. Durham, N.C.: Duke University Press.

Sommer, Doris. 1990. "Irresistible Romance: The Foundational Fictions of Latin America." In *Nation and Narration,* edited by Homi K. Bhabha, 71–98. New York: Routledge.

———. 1993. "Resisting the Heat: Menchú, Morrison, and Incompetent Readers." In *Cultures of United States Imperialism,* edited by Amy Kaplan and Donald Pease, 407–32. Chapel Hill, N.C.: Duke University Press.

Steele, Cynthia. 1992. *Politics, Gender, and the Mexican Novel, 1968–1988: Beyond the Pyramid.* Austin: University of Texas Press.

———. 1994. "'A Woman Fell into the River': Negotiating Female Subjects in Contemporary Mayan Theater." In *Negotiating Performance: Gender, Sexuality, and Theatricality in Latin/o America,* edited by Diana Taylor and Juan Villegas, 239–56. Durham, N.C.: Duke University Press.

Stern, Steve J. 1995. *The Secret History of Gender: Women, Men, and Power in Late Colonial Mexico.* Chapel Hill: University of North Carolina Press.

Stoekl, Allan. 1985. *Politics, Writing, Mutilation: The Cases of Bataille, Blanchot, Roussel, Leiris, and Ponge.* Minneapolis: University of Minnesota Press.

Stoll, Anita K., ed., 1990. *A Different Reality: Studies on the Work of Elena Garro.* Lewisburg, Pa.: Bucknell University Press.

Su, Margo. 1989. *Alta frivolidad.* Mexico City: Cal y Arena.

Suárez Escobar, Marcela. 1996. "El fenómeno de la prostitución en México." *Casa del tiempo* 14, no. 55 (September): 64–76.

Suleiman, Susan Rubin. 1990. *Subversive Intent: Gender, Politics, and the Avant-garde.* Cambridge, Mass.: Harvard University Press.

Toledo, Martín. 1981. *El drama de la prostitución: Las que nacieron para perder.* Mexico City: Editores Mexicanos Unidos.

Torres, Vicente Francisco. *Esta narrativa mexicana: Ensayos y entrevistas.* Mexico City: Universidad Autónoma Mexicana, 1991.

Trilling, Lionel. 1971. *Sincerity and Authenticity.* Cambridge, Mass.: Harvard University Press.

Uribe, Patricia, et al. 1996. "Prostitución en México." In *Mujer: Sexualidad y salud reproductiva en México,* edited by Ana Langer and Kathryn Tolbert, 179–206. New York: World Health Organization, the Population Council, and EDAMEX.

Usigli, Rodolfo. [1952] 1966. *Jano es una muchacha.* In *Teatro completo.* Vol. 2, pp. 388–459. Mexico City: Fondo de Cultura Económica.

Valdés, Gina. 1986. *Comiendo lumbre: Eating Fire.* Colorado Springs: Maize Press.

Vargas, Ana, compiler. 1986. *La casa de cita: Mexican Photographs from the Belle Epoque.* London: Quartet Books.

Vidal, Hernán, ed. 1989. *Cultural and Historical Grounding for Hispanic and Luso-Brazilian Feminist Literary Criticism.* Minneapolis: Institute for the Study of Ideologies and Literature.

Wicke, Jennifer. 1988. *Advertising Fictions: Literature, Advertisement, and Social Reading.* New York: Columbia University Press.

Wilden, Anthony. 1968. "Notes and Commentary" to *The Language of the Self,* by Jacques Lacan. New York: Dell.

Wittig, Monique. 1985. "The Mark of Gender." *Feminist Issues* 5:3–12.

Ximena, María, and Alejandro Toledo. 1992. "Por una literatura fácil." *Macropolis* (March 26): 332–37.

Yánez Cossío, Alicia. 1989. *La casa del sano placer.* Quito: Planeta.

Zalduondo, Barbara O. de, Mauricio Hernández Avila, and Patricia Uribe Zúñiga. 1991. "Intervention Research Needs for AIDS Prevention among Commercial Sex Workers and Their Clients." In *AIDS and Women's Reproductive Health,* 165–77. New York: Plenum.

Zenteno, Alejandro. 1996. "3,000 mexicanas vendidas en Japón." *Unomasuno* (May 3): 1, 16.

# Index

Abrahams, Roger D., 171
*De la amorosa inclinación a enredadarse en cabellos* (Of the loving inclination to be tangled up in hair) (Glantz), 143
Anderson, Amanda, 46, 162
Anderson, Benedict, 94
Anderson, Robert, 65
Aranda Luna, Javier, 226
Arbetman, Mirta, 255
Arreola, Daniel D., 221
Asiain, Aurelio, 216–18
"Aurora" (interviewee), 3, 245–52
*De Ausencia* (About Ausencia) (Mendoza), 164–66
authenticity and inauthenticity: Clifford's "authentic encounter" and, 241; in Gamboa, 48–49; in Muñuzuri, 183, 190–91, 193–94; in Sefchovich, 147
autobiography. See *testimonio*
Ayala Blanco, Jorge, 207
Azteca. See Tepoztlán
Azuela, Mariano, 162, 166–68

"Bandida." See *Memorias de "La Bandida"* (Memoirs of La Bandida) (Muñuzuri)
Barlow, Linda, 140
Barrón Salido, Patricia, 4, 15–16, 254
Barthes, Roland, 125
Bartra, Eli, 19–20
Bartra, Roger, 5
Bataille, Georges, 21–22, 78–79
Bell, Shannon, 172
*Belle du jour* (Buñuel), 138
Bellinghausen, Hermann, 161
Bernheimer, Charles, 162
Bersani, Leo, 220

bestsellers, 38, 136–39
Bhabha, Homi K., 102, 132
Blanchot, Maurice, 73
Blanco, José Joaquín: on consumer culture, 150–51; on the erotics of misery, 39–41, 42–43, 54–55; *transa* narrative and, 31–32, 181, 255; on women and love, 144–45
boom literature, 215
Bowlby, Rachel, 149
Brooks, Peter, 69
Browning, Richard L., 258
Buñuel, Luis, 138
Butler, Judith, 64, 80, 90–92, 97–98, 158, 170

Cabrera Infante, Guillermo, 140
Calderón de la Barca, Pedro, 63
*A calzón amarrado* (Knotted panties) (Serrano), 161–62, 194–214
Campbell, Federico: *Tijuanenses* (Tijuana: Stories on the border), 106, 113–14; *Todo lo de las focas* (Everything about seals), 33, 100–101, 104–9, 111–27, 132–34
Campobello, Nellie, 5
Cárdenas, Cuauhtémoc, 211
Cárdenas, Lázaro, 118
Careaga, Gabriel, 9
Carreño, Antonio Manuel, 135–36
Castellanos, Rosario, 138, 207–8, 210; *El eterno femenino* (The eternal feminine), 21, 27–31
Castillo, Ana: *The Mixquiahuala Letters*, 33, 101–11, 127–34; *Sapogonia*, 101
Castro, Fidel, 184
Chapkis, Wendy, 241

271

Chaplin, Charlie, 111
"Chingadalupe," 5
Christian-Smith, Linda K., 139
Cicciolina, 197, 211
Cixous, Hélène, 47
Clifford, James, 240
comic book romances, 142–43, 155–
    56, 161
commodification: in Gamboa, 44, 48,
    56; in Rulfo, 72; in Sefchovich, 137,
    147–51; in Serrano, 195, 202–3,
    205–6
*Como agua para chocolate* (Like water
    for chocolate) (Esquivel), 135–36,
    215
CONASIDA (Consejo Nacional para
    la Prevención y Control del SIDA),
    259
Corbin, Alain, 160–61
Coria, Clara, 13–14, 20–22
*corridos* (ballads), 5
Culler, Jonathan, 215, 216, 217
Curtis, James R., 221
Cypess, Sandra Messinger, 84, 93

Davidson, Julia O'Connell, 240
Decency League, 21
De la Madrid, Miguel, 210
De la Rosa, Martín, 254–55
Del Campo, Xorge, 10–11, 13,
    160–61, 163–64, 168–69, 172
*Demasiado amor* (Too much love)
    (Sefchovich), 143–52
Derrida, Jacques, 126
*Diario* (Gamboa), 60
Díaz, Porfirio, 37, 41, 56
difficult literature, 35, 216–19

Elizondo, Salvador, 38
equivoice: in Gamboa, 47–48
erotics of misery, 40–41, 42
Esquivel, Laura: *Como agua para
    chocolate* (Like water for chocolate),
    135–36, 215
*El eterno femenino* (The eternal
    feminine) (Castellanos), 21, 27–31

Feindel, Janet, 171–22
Felix, María, 192
Felski, Rita, 48
Fernández, Diego, 212
Fetterley, Judith, 218
film industry, 17–18, 38, 195, 199
Finstad, Liv, 255
*flâneuse*, 138, 145–46
Flaubert, Gustave, 41, 152, 169
Flax, Jane, 257
Flieger, Jerry Anne, 166
Flores, Juan, 122
Foucault, Michel, 52, 60, 68, 98
Franco, Jean, 16, 135–37
Frase, Brigitte, 137–39
Frenk, Margit, 153
Fuentes, Carlos: *Myself with others*, 9;
    *Región más transparente* (Where the
    air is clear), 9; on Rulfo, 76–77

Gallagher, Catherine, 60
Galván, Delia, 85–86
Gamboa, Federico: *Diario*, 60; *Santa*,
    7, 32, 37–63, 137, 161, 163, 195,
    218, 256–57
García Ponce, Juan, 143
García Riera, Emilio, 38
Garci-Ordóñez de Montalvo, 121
Garrido, Felipe, 69
Garro, Elena: *Los recuerdos del porvenir*
    (Recollections of things to come),
    32–33, 63, 65–67, 77–99
Gates, Henry Louis, Jr., 170–71
gestural economy, 39–40, 44
Glantz, Margo: *De la amorosa incli-
    nación a enredarse en cabellos* (Of
    the loving inclination to be tangled
    up in hair), 143; on Gamboa, 47,
    53
Gomezjara, F., 8
González, María R., 9, 254
González de la Vega, Francisco, 15
González Gómez, Rosa, 258
González Rodríguez, Sergio, 179, 189,
    255
Good, Carl, 27

Gordon, Donald K., 69
Goya, Francisco José de, 104
Guy, Donna, 99

Hart, Angie, 225
Hayworth, Rita, 111
Heath, Stephen, 65, 257
Hegel, G. W. F., 126
Helie-Lucas, Marie-Aimee, 27
Hernández Avila, Mauricio, 240
heterotopia (Foucault): in Gamboa, 60;
    in Garro 77, 97–99; in Rulfo and
    Garro, 68–69. *See also* temporality
Hicks, D. Emily, 106
Høigård, Cecile, 255
Hugo, Victor, 22

Ibargüengoitia, Jorge, 9
Irigaray, Luce, 74, 137, 170
Isaacs, Jorge, 63

*Jano es una muchacha* (Janus is a girl)
    (Usigli), 21–27, 138

Kaminsky, Amy Katz, 30
Khatibi, Abdelkebir, 118, 122
Kinsale, Laura, 257–58

*El laberinto de la soledad* (The labyrinth
    of solitude) (Paz), 5, 40
Lamas, Marta, 221–23, 234, 258, 259
Lara, Agustín, 17–18
Lara y Pardo, Luis, 10–11, 13
Lara Zavala, Hernán, 216
Lejeune, Philippe, 184
Lévinas, Emmanuel, 170
Lewis, Oscar, 1–2, 35–36
Liga de Decencia, 21
Lihn, Enrique, 121
limit behavior, 65, 74, 95–97
Lionni, Leo, 100–101
*literatura* lite, 35, 215–19
"Lola" (interviewee), 243–45
Lombroso, Cesare, 10
López González, Aralia, 215
Lyotard, Jean-François, 67–68

Macías, Anna, 4, 253
MacKinnon, Catherine, 140
*Madame Bovary* (Flaubert), 41, 152,
    169
*Maja desnuda* (Goya), 104
Malinche, 5, 20, 22, 28, 135
Mariño Soto, Germán, 142–43
Martín del Campo, David, 216
Martínez Baños, Roberto, 6, 253–54
Mastretta, Angeles, 136, 215
Matlock, Jann, 22–23, 61–62, 162, 169
Maytrajt, Miguel, 255
memoir. See *testimonio*
*Memorias de "La Bandida"* (Memoirs
    of La Bandida) (Muñuzuri), 34,
    161–62, 179–94, 212–14
Mendoza, María Luisa: *De Ausencia*
    (About Ausencia), 164–66; pro-
    logue to Mora's *Del oficio*, 162–63,
    169, 172, 173–75, 212–14
*The Mixquiahuala Letters* (Castillo), 33,
    101–11, 127–34
Modleski, Tania, 258
Molloy, Sylvia, 140
Monsiváis, Carlos: on Carreño's
    etiquette book, 135–36; on erotic
    systems, 37, 39–40, 64; on Lara's
    *boleros,* 17
Mora, Antonia: *Del oficio* (The life),
    34, 161, 173–79
Moreno, Antonio de P., 15
Morse, Margaret, 153–54, 158
Muñuzuri, Eduardo: *Memorias de "La
    Bandida"* (Memoirs of La Bandida),
    34, 161–62, 179–94, 212–14; as
    *transa,* 180, 189–90, 193–94
*Myself with Others* (Fuentes), 9

Nabokov, Vladimir, 149
*Nana* (Zola), 41, 195, 199, 208–9
Noakes, Susan, 217

*Del oficio* (The life) (Mora), 34, 161,
    173–79
Ojeda, Néstor L., 220
O'Toole, Brockton, 259

Pacheco, Cristina, 204, 205, 207
Pacheco Ladrón de Guevara, Lourdes C., 8
Parent-Duchatelet, Alexandre, 160
Paz, Octavio, 5; on "la chingada," 19–20, 135; on difficult literature, 216–17, 218; on femininity, 74, 89–90; Garro's response to, 91–92; *El laberinto de la soledad* (The labyrinth of solitude), 5, 40; on nostalgia for death, 73
"Un pedazo de noche" (A piece of night) (Rulfo), 63–65, 69–77, 99
*Pedro Páramo* (Rulfo), 69, 73, 76
penal code, 15, 37–38
Peri Rossi, Cristina, 124
Poniatowska, Elena, 5, 200, 207–8, 258
public woman, 13–14, 196, 211–12

Quijada, Osvaldo A., 11–13

Radway, Janice, 141, 257
Rangel Gómez, María Gudelia, 2–3, 8, 221, 227–39
*Los recuerdos del porvenir* (Recollections of things to come) (Garro), 32–33, 63, 65–67, 77–99
red light districts. See *zonas de tolerancia*
*Región más transparente* (Where the air is clear) (Fuentes), 9
Revolution of 1910: in Garro, 80–81, 98; in Usigli, 23–26; women in, 4–5, 253–54
Robledo, Elisa, 212–14
romance novels, 139, 143, 155–59
Rosas Solís, Armando, 221–25
Rulfo, Juan, 32–33, 100; "Un pedazo de noche" (A piece of night), 63–65, 69–77, 99; *Pedro Páramo*, 69, 73, 76
Russo, Miguel, 139

Salazar González, José Guadalupe, 15
Salinas de Gortari, Carlos, 80

Sánchez-Tranquilino, Marcos, 133–34
*Santa* (Gamboa), 7, 32, 37–63, 137, 161, 163, 195, 218, 256–57
*Sapogonia* (Castillo), 101
Secretaría de Salud: technical reports of, 225–26, 235
Sefchovich, Sara, 34, 135–59, 205, 216; *Demasiado amor* (Too much love), 143–52; *La señora de los sueños* (The lady who dreamed), 152–59
*La señora de los sueños* (The lady who dreamed) (Sefchovich), 152–59
*Sergas de Esplandián*, 120
Serrano, Irma, 34, 36, 204; as *transa*, 196–97, 202; various works discussed (*A calzón amarrado* [Knotted panties]; *Una loca en la polaca* [A spoke in the wheel]; *Sin pelos en la lengua* [Telling it straight]), 161–62, 194–214
Simpson, David, 141–42
*soldaderas*, 4–6, 253–54
Sommer, Doris, 16, 135–37, 191
Soto Angli, Edilberto, 6, 253–54
Steele, Cynthia, 253
Stern, Steve J., 5
Stoekl, Allan, 78–79
Su, Margo, 190, 210, 258

taboos, 56, 77, 237
Tagg, John, 133–34
Tellado, Corín, 139–40
temporality, 23–24, 78–79. See also heterotopia
Tepoztlán, 1, 35
testifyin', 36, 170–73. See also *testimonio; transa*
*testimonio*, 34, 166, 168–73; in Gamboa, 57; in Mora, 177–79; as *transa*, 171–73. See also testifyin'; *transa*
*Tijuanenses* (Tijuana: Stories on the border) (Campbell), 106, 113–14
*Todo lo de las focas* (Everything about seals) (Campbell), 33, 100–101, 104–9, 111–27, 132–34

Torres, Vicente Fransciso, 255
*transa,* 31–32, 61, 173–214 passim,
  255. *See also* testifyin'; *testimonio*
Trejo de Zepeda, Patricia, 5, 253–54
Trilling, Lionel, 48–49

Uribe Zúñiga, Patricia, 240
Usigli, Rodolfo: *Jano es una muchacha*
  (Janus is a girl), 21–27, 138

Valdés, Gina, 103–4
Vidal, Gore, 46

Wicke, Jennifer, 142
Wilden, Anthony, 70
Wittig, Monique, 68, 81, 90
women readers, 139–43, 151–52

Yúdice, George, 122

Zalduondo, Barbara O. de, 240
Zenteno, Alejandro, 219
Zola, Émile, 41, 195, 199, 208–9
*zonas de tolerancia,* 4, 29–30, 37–38,
  256

**Debra A. Castillo** is professor of romance studies and comparative literature at Cornell University, where she specializes in contemporary Hispanic literature, women's studies, and postcolonial theory. Among her many publications are *The Translated World: A Postmodern Tour of Libraries in Literature* (1984) and *Talking Back: Strategies for a Latin American Feminist Literary Criticism* (1992). Castillo is a board member of *Diacritics* and a book review editor for *Letras femeninas*.